The Economic Geography of Air Transportation

T0341153

Like the railroad and the automobile, the airliner has changed the very geography of the societies it serves. Fundamentally, air transportation has helped redefine the scale of human geography by dramatically reducing the cost of distance, both in terms of time and money. The result is what the author terms the "airborne world," meaning all those places dependent upon and transformed by relatively inexpensive air transportation.

The Economic Geography of Air Transportation answers three key questions: how did air transportation develop in the century after the Wright Brothers, what does it mean to live in an airborne world, and what is the future of aviation in this century? Examples are drawn from throughout the world. In particular, ample consideration is given to the situation in developing countries, where air transportation is growing rapidly and where, to a considerable degree, the future of the airborne world will be determined.

The book weaves together the technological development of aviation, the competition among aircraft manufacturers and their stables of airliners, the deregulation and privatization of the airline industry, the articulation of air passenger and air cargo services in everyday life, and the challenges and controversies surrounding airports. It will be of particular interest to students and researchers in air transport history, the geography of the airline industry, air transport technological development, competition in the commercial aircraft industry, airport development, geography, and economics. It will also be useful to professionals working in the airline, airport, and aircraft manufacturing industries.

John Bowen is currently Assistant Professor in the Department of Geography at Central Washington University, USA.

Routledge studies in the modern world economy

The Economic Geography of Air Transportation

Space, time, and the freedom of the sky

John Bowen

Routledge
Taylor & Francis Group

LONDON AND NEW YORK

First published 2010
by Routledge
2 Park Square, Milton Park, Abingdon, Oxon OX14 4RN

Simultaneously published in the USA and Canada
by Routledge
711 Third Avenue, New York, NY 10017

Routledge is an imprint of the Taylor & Francis Group, an informa business

Typeset in Times by Wearset Ltd, Boldon, Tyne and Wear
First issued in paperback in 2013

British Library Cataloguing in Publication Data
A catalogue record for this book is available from the British Library

Library of Congress Cataloging in Publication Data
Bowen, John, 1966–
The economic geography of air transportation: space, time, and the
freedom of the sky/John Bowen.
p. cm.
Includes bibliographical references and index.
1. Aeronautics–Social aspects. 2. Aeronautics–Economic aspects. I. Title.
HE9774.B69 2010

387.7′1–dc22

2009034401

ISBN13: 978-0-415-74991-6 (pbk)
ISBN13: 978-0-415-77805-3 (hbk)
ISBN13: 978-0-203-85735-9 (ebk)

To my mother, Nancy Betit Bowen Clark (1941–2005)

Contents

Figures

Tables

Acknowledgments

This book grew out of a chapter that I co-wrote with Thomas Leinbach for the book *Geography and Technology* (Brunn *et al*. 2004). Until then, my research had emphasized liberalization and other changes within the airline industry, but the chapter I wrote with Tom forced me to think more broadly about the development of aviation and the changes in everyday life fostered by air transportation – and my curiosity has led me further down those avenues of inquiry. Although this book and certainly its shortcomings are my own, I owe a profound debt to Tom who was my advisor many years ago at the University of Kentucky and with whom I have collaborated on a variety of aviation-related projects ever since.

This book could not have been written without the support of several institutions. In particular, the University of Wisconsin-Oshkosh, where I worked for ten years, granted me a sabbatical in 2005 during which several parts of the book were first written. The university also provided funding for several smaller projects whose results have been woven into this book. The National Science Foundation funded a large project about air cargo services that Tom Leinbach and I undertook together several years ago. The results of that project inform Chapter 9. And Central Washington University, where I now work, purchased an airline schedules database, which I have used in many of the analyses in the book. David Cordner, my colleague at Central, prepared Figure 10.6.

I am deeply indebted to four anonymous reviewers, to Thomas Sutton whose kind support was instrumental in getting this book to publication, and to Sue Littleford who carefully copyedited the final manuscript.

Finally, I thank my friends and family for their active interest in this project. My friends Heike, Harold, and Angela provided valuable advice over the years that I have worked on this book. I am especially grateful for the unremitting curiosity of my former neighbor, Brady. His repeated queries about my progress helped to keep me typing away in the Wisconsin basement where most of this book was written. And finally and most of all, I am grateful for the support, faith, and patience of my wife Maureen and our children.

Ellensburg, Washington
February 2010

1 Introduction

Troubled but triumphant

On December 17, 2003, a crowd of 40,000 including then-President George W. Bush, astronauts John Glenn and Buzz Aldrin, and actor-aviator and master of ceremonies John Travolta, watched as a replica of the Wright Brothers' 1903 *Flyer* attempted to repeat the famous first flight exactly 100 years later. The odds were stacked against a successful re-enactment. The underpowered *Flyer* needed sustained winds no lower than 16 kilometers per hour to get airborne but no higher than 35 kilometers per hour to be controllable in flight. At the appointed time on the centenary, 10:35 a.m., the winds were too calm amid intermittent downpours as dignitaries, aviation devotees, and curious onlookers waited. So the re-enactment was postponed for two hours. Still, the weather would not cooperate. The *Flyer* was gamely sent down its launch track; but, instead of climbing into the sky, the replica promptly fell into a mud puddle. Before a thinning crowd, another attempt was made before sunset; but once again, poor weather – still the single most important cause of flight cancellations and delays for airliners many times the size of the *Flyer* – frustrated the effort (Ruane and Gugliotta 2003; Sanger 2003). The day ended with the *Flyer* replica having never left the ground.

The disappointment at Kitty Hawk was emblematic of what would turn out to be a hard decade in the history of air transportation. The attacks of September 11, 2001. The launch of the Second Gulf War. The outbreak of Severe Acute Respiratory Syndrome (SARS) and the corresponding collapse of Asia-Pacific air travel in early 2003. The huge run-up in oil prices in 2007 and 2008. And, finally, the worst financial crisis since the Great Depression (Figure 1.1). Between 2001 and 2008, the global airline industry made just $16 billion in operating profits, on revenues of more than $3.2 trillion;[1] the last two years of the decade could well turn that tiny profit into a loss. Even the long march of technology, which had propelled aviation to such astonishing heights in the century before, seemed to falter in the first years of the twenty-first century. Following the earlier example of Air France, British Airways ended Concorde services in late 2003. For the first time in the history of commercial aviation, the fastest aircraft was withdrawn from service without a faster one ready to take its place. And the Airbus A380 and Boeing 787, upon which their respective manufacturers placed so much hope, both faltered mightily in moving from the drawing board to the sky.

Yet, if air transportation was deeply troubled in the first decade of this century, it was also triumphant. For 12 seconds on December 17, 1903, Orville Wright had been alone in the sky. While the *Flyer*'s replica remained stranded on the ground, the number of people airborne at any one moment somewhere around the globe, averaged more than half a million.[2] In the years since 2003, passenger volumes have risen still higher and by 2014, the centennial of the first scheduled passenger airline service, an average of about one million people will be airborne somewhere overhead at every moment. Of course, many passengers are repeat customers, flying again and again. Their comings and goings show how routine the once elusive dream of human flight has become. Indeed, a century on from the Wright Brothers, air transportation had become overwhelmingly dominant in transcontinental and intercontinental passenger travel. Already in the 1950s, transatlantic flights carried more passengers than the ocean liners; and within the US, more people flew from coast to coast than took transcontinental railroads. In the decades since, air travel has become more competitive for progressively shorter trips in an ever larger part of the world. In the US, for instance, air travel is the most important mode for trips more than 700 miles (1,130 kilometers) in one-way length (BTS 2006a). Low-cost carriers (LCCs), with intercity fares sometimes lower than the cost of an airport taxi, have been instrumental in the encroachment of aviation upon other modes for shorter-haul travel. The pioneer LCC was Southwest Airlines,[3] which prospered in part by trying to make short-haul flying cheaper than driving one's own car – a goal that the carrier reached on many routes.

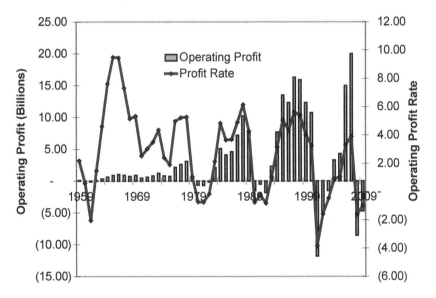

Figure 1.1 Global airline profits, 1959–2009 (sources: ICAO 1998; ICAO 2008; IATA 2009).

The combined operating profits of the world's airlines have swung widely, especially since the spread of liberalization. The profit for 2009 is estimated.

Meanwhile, trucks, freight trains, and containerships have also lost a measure of their business to air transportation, although railroads and shipping lines remain much more important than in passenger travel. By one estimate, air cargo accounts for 40 percent of world trade by value (Kasarda *et al.* 2004) – though less than 1 percent by weight.

Where we vacation, how large and anonymous our employers are, what we eat and wear, how far we live from our relatives and how often we see them, where our cell phones were assembled, where our neighbors were born, which infectious diseases scare us – these and many other dimensions of everyday life on the ground at the beginning aviation's second century are shaped, to varying degrees, by commercial aviation. In fact, by the Wright Brothers' centennial, air transportation had become the most important element of the world's circulatory system, moving millions of people and a rising share of trade in goods at speeds so high, over distances so great, and at costs so low that in the process the way the world works has been changed. This book is about the world that air transportation has made, both on the ground and in the sky above us.

The airborne world

This book is about great hubs like Heathrow and O'Hare and Narita, the spokes to which they are linked, and the countless spaces in between – beaches, ski resorts, export processing zones, world heritage sites, and a kaleidoscope of others – that have been transformed by the advent of air transportation. Together these places comprise what I call the airborne world. Of course, the hubs and hamlets of that world remain firmly at ground level, but life within them has been changed in its speed and its scale, in its delights (think sushi, for instance) and in its dangers – by aviation. In that sense, it is an airborne world.

The central premises of this book are that air transportation has afforded an extraordinary new kind of freedom to move faster over greater distances than would have been imaginable a century earlier and that, like other kinds of freedom, the freedom of the sky has had great consequences. It has helped to redefine the scale of human geography by dramatically reducing the cost of distance, both in terms of time and money. The same jetliner that makes it feasible to cast silicon wafers in one country and cut them into microchips thousands of miles away or to daily deliver fresh cut flowers from Kenya to homes across Western Europe has also afforded unprecedented mobility to tourists and immigrants, backpackers and business executives.

Yet the diminution of the "friction of distance" has had a darker side as well. Aviation has been implicated in the more rapid spread of infectious diseases such as SARS. It has become an attractive target for terrorists drawn by the air transportation system's inherent vulnerabilities and its visibility. And, of course, aviation has featured prominently in discussions about global climate change.

The world shaped by aviation is remarkably uneven, and the diffusion of SARS reflected that unevenness – with the disease arriving faster in Canada, the

United States, and Australia that in several of China's neighbors. Even in the US, there is something like an aviation archipelago, with scattered islands of bustling frenzy like LAX and JFK interspersed by the wide-open spaces of "flyover country."[4] In the least developed parts of the world, whole countries are practically "flyover country."[5] This book examines the development and impact of air transportation both in the giant hubs like Chicago and London and in impoverished areas of the developing world such as Laos.

In exploring the geography of the airborne world, the book also tells the stories of its creation. In particular, I argue that the freedom wrought by aviation has depended upon breaking two kinds of shackles: the technological and the political. In examining the technological development of aviation from Douglas DC-3s that refueled five times en route from New York to San Francisco to today's airliners that can fly nearly halfway around the planet without stopping, the triumphs and travails of aircraft manufacturers and of airlines are woven together. The threads of this fascinating tapestry include the intense rivalry between Boeing and Douglas a half century ago and between Boeing and Airbus today and the pivotal roles played by airlines from Pan Am to Singapore Airlines.

A key point made in these pages, however, is that the freedom of the sky is not just about the technologies that have made the everyday defiance of gravity routine. Particularly in the past three decades, the removal of government constraints on the airline industry has transformed the airborne world and the experience of flight. The liberalization of the airline industry – meaning the removal or relaxation of rules on air fares, routes, service levels and other aspects of competition as well as the privatization of government-owned carriers – has made possible the low-cost carrier phenomenon which began with Southwest Airlines in the US and has now spread across much of the globe. While Blue Air in Hungary, AirAsia in Malaysia, Gol in Brazil and dozens of other new airlines are by no means carbon copies of Southwest, they too have lowered the cost of the sky so that as AirAsia declares in bold print on all of its aircraft, "Now everyone can fly." That is hyperbole, of course, but the idea that there is a new freedom in the air is not so great an exaggeration.

Three questions

This book integrates aspects of airborne world that are not commonly treated together, from the design of the Douglas DC-3 to the role of air transportation in the story of sushi, from the growth of sex tourism to the persistent problems of aircraft noise near hub airports, from the alliances among major carriers to the formation of the Airbus consortium. This book is also integrative in that I draw upon hundreds of different sources, including books and academic journals, newspaper and magazine articles, a wide variety of published data sources, and my own primary research into several dimensions of the air transportation system. I have cast my net wide to make sense of the complex development and pervasive reach of airborne world.

This book is also partly personal: I have been captivated by aviation since I was a child living in rural Maine 10,000 meters beneath the heavily trafficked air corridor linking Western Europe and the eastern United States. My fascination then with the airliners passing overhead led me to make the study of air transportation central to my academic career and even to a job in Singapore, one of the airborne world's hotspots. I worked there for the Cargo Division of Singapore Airlines (SIA), getting a front-row seat on the global economy as part of the bargain. The insights I gained then are among the ingredients in this book.

Years after I left Singapore and SIA, the city and the airline drew the attention of the world when the A380 began its maiden commercial flight at Singapore bedecked in SIA's blue, gold, and white livery. At 8:15 on the morning of Thursday, October 25, 2007, the Airbus A380 ascended from Runway 02C at Changi Airport and headed towards Sydney and into the history books. The maiden commercial flight of the Airbus was not just history, however; it was also geography. The A380 was the first significant Western jetliner to debut on a route not involving Europe or the United States (Figure 1.2). So why Singapore? Why indeed. This book is intended to answer questions like that.

More broadly, this book tackles three big questions. First, *how did civil aviation and its relationship to society beyond airport perimeters develop in air transportation's first century*? The chronicle of aviation is heaped high with colorful personalities, but in describing the development of air transportation I look beyond those personalities and emphasize instead three essential, often-overlooked dimensions – namely, technology, policy, and geography.

Technological change in air transportation, from the development of the first commercial jets after World War II through to the present-day cutthroat competition among aircraft manufacturers, is the primary theme in the first major section of this book (Chapters 2 through 4). I examine the triumphs of early aviation, the advent of the jet age, the big splash made by wide-body jets, and finally the more recent offerings of Boeing and Airbus and the regional jet (RJ) manufacturers. The organization of this section is largely historical and while the focus is on successive generations of airliners, I also discuss the increased societal significance of aviation that accompanied the greater power, speed, capacity, range, and reliability of the commercial airplane.

The liberalization of the airline industry and its effects upon established and new carriers are the subjects of the second major section of this book (Chapters 5 through 7). I examine the wave of deregulation that has swept over the industry since the late 1970s and the emergence of a relative handful of global carriers and hundreds of new airlines – especially the LCCs – since then.

Throughout these two sections, I give particular emphasis to the geography of transportation for I am a geographer rather than a historian. How did Seattle gain its particular significance in the aircraft industry? In what ways did the structure of air transportation networks change with the development of pivotal aircraft such as the DC-3, Boeing 707, and Airbus A300? Where do LCCs fly and why? Why *did* the A380 debut in Singapore? Air transportation is inherently spatial,

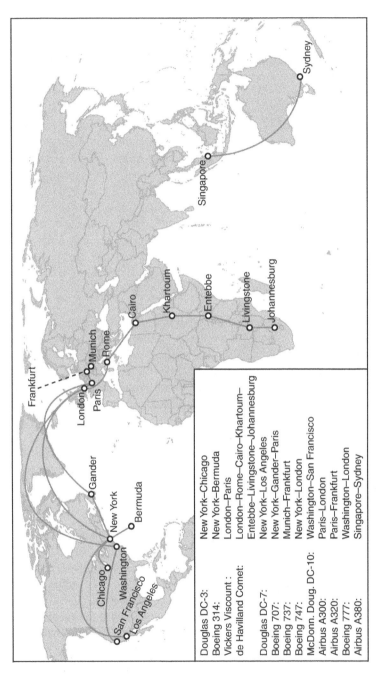

Douglas DC-3:	New York–Chicago
Boeing 314:	New York–Bermuda
Vickers Viscount :	London–Paris
de Havilland Comet:	London–Rome–Cairo–Khartoum–
	Entebbe–Livingstone–Johannesburg
Douglas DC-7:	New York–Los Angeles
Boeing 707:	New York–Gander–Paris
Boeing 737:	Munich–Frankfurt
Boeing 747:	New York–London
McDonn. Doug. DC-10:	Washington–San Francisco
Airbus A300:	Paris–London
Airbus A320:	Paris–Frankfurt
Boeing 777:	Washington–London
Airbus A380:	Singapore–Sydney

Figure 1.2 Geography of first flights for several significant airliners (sources: see Tables 2.1, 2.2, 3.1, and 4.5).

Until the debut of the Airbus A380, almost every commercially significant airliner model had entered service on a route to, from, or within North America or Western Europe.

of course, and I try in these pages to make sense of that geography and the ways in which it has changed.

The second big question I tackle in these pages is: *what does it mean to live in an airborne world?* In answering it, I leave behind aircraft and airlines and consider life on the ground. I am interested in how the speed and increasingly global reach of affordable aviation have reshaped the way the world works. Specifically, in a chapter on passenger travel (Chapter 8), I explore such features of the airborne world as the airborne peregrinations of the transnational capitalist class and the "pleasure periphery," the network of places to which the affluent and the increasingly the not-so-affluent repair for recreation. I follow that with a chapter on the air cargo (Chapter 9). I sketch the kinds of goods that move by air, from electronics to fresh fish to emergency equipment, and ponder the ramifications of the resulting aerial ballet.

Of course, the places on the ground that most exhibit the blessings and burdens of the airborne world are its major airports (Chapter 10). Drawing on examples from across the globe, I describe the difficulties of finding sites for new airports, the spiraling cost of terminal and runway construction, and the persistent issue of aircraft noise; but I also analyze the positive economic impact of airports upon the communities they neighbor and the new importance of airports as gateways to and symbols of the cities and regions they serve. An airport such as Bangkok's new Suvarnabhumi Airport is a multibillion dollar investment, an economic engine but also a potential bottleneck for the metropolis, the core of a future edge city, and a place where first and last impressions of Thailand are made. Thus the care with which the airport, whose site was originally called Nong Ngu Hao ("cobra swamp") but later was assigned the hopeful appellation Suvarnabhumi ("golden land") (Lindsay 2006), embraced a design that synthesizes efficiency with architectural elements meant to reflect the country's Buddhist inheritance.

The increased importance of aviation on the ground and in the air has far-reaching implications, not all of them good. I consider in detail several adverse, broader consequences of the widespread inexpensive air transportation (Chapter 11). These include the new fears engendered by a smaller, faster world, including the global reach of airborne terror and the potentially transonic speed of infectious disease diffusion (evident in the rapidity with which SARS leapt across the Pacific in 2003). An even broader concern is the depredations of aviation upon the environment, particularly the role of air transportation in global climate change. What should be done to limit aviation's contribution to greenhouse gas emissions and what would that mean to the airline industry and the faster, more interconnected world it has helped to forge?

Considering the links between aviation and climate change means looking into the future; yet how the challenge of global warming is managed is only one dimension of aviation's second century. The last of this book's major questions is: *what is the future trajectory of the airborne world?* What is going to happen next is a concern of most of the chapters in this book and is the central focus of Chapter 12. On the one hand, the huge volume of untapped traffic seems to offer the promise of further rapid growth. After all, most people in the world have never flown including huge majorities in most poor countries. Air transportation is growing rapidly in many such markets, propelled in part by the new keenness of liberalized competition. Likewise, the stunning growth of air cargo flows in recent decades still has left most of the world's commerce at ground- and sea-level. The adoption of time-based competition, increased value-to-weight ratios in many products (making the greater expense of air transportation more afford-able), and fiercer competition among cargo carriers promise to increase those fractions, further expanding the scope of the airborne world. And yet, there are a host of threats to air transportation and its future importance. Higher fuel prices, terrorism, and the loss of traffic to reinvigorated surface modes. Furthermore, there is growing interest in more closely regulating commercial aviation to mute its environmental effects.

Aviation began with inventors who decided to fly and then sought the means to do so. By the end of this century the real innovators may be those who find ways to fly less frequently or not as far. In a way, that would be a fitting next chapter to a story that began at Kitty Hawk. The great breakthrough of the Wright Brothers was not getting airborne – that had been done before – but rather discovering how to control an airplane once it was airborne. They found the answer in nature, in the way a bird warped its wings to slow or to turn. As discussed at the end of this book, there is unprecedented interest today in better directing the trajectory of the broader air transportation system, lest its uncontrolled development lead us into harm.

Part I

Getting airborne

The development of the airliner and commercial air transportation

2 Jetting toward a smaller world

Early commercial aviation

Farther, faster, higher, wider, bigger, better

The contrasts between aircraft of the early twentieth century and those of the early twenty-first century are enormous. The Wright Brothers' *Flyer* had a wingspan of 12 meters and weighed just over 270 kilograms (Solberg 1979: 6). By comparison, the initial version of the Boeing 787 – which is partly assembled in Charleston, South Carolina just down the Atlantic coast from Kitty Hawk – has wingspan of 60 meters[1] and a maximum takeoff weight of 220,000 kilograms. The *Flyer* flew no farther than 260 meters and had a design speed of 37 kilometers per hour. The Dreamliner has a maximum range of more than 15,000 kilometers and a cruising speed of just over 900 kilometers per hour. Like many other early aircraft, the *Flyer* was remarkably fragile, making just three flights. In contrast, a typical 787 will make thousands of flights before its retirement after 20 or more years of service. The *Flyer* was an "all-vegetable" airplane, made almost entirely of wood, fabric, and other natural products. The 787, conversely, is revolutionary in its extensive use of carbon fiber-reinforced plastic to produce a lightweight, fuel-efficient, durable airframe. Boeing and its top (or tier one) subcontractors have sunk at least $15 billion into developing the Dreamliner and each 787 will have a selling price of more than $100 million. The Wright Brothers spent $2,000 (about $40,000 in year 2008 dollars[2]) on their airplane. The *Flyer* was a one of a kind while thousands of 787s are likely to lumber into the sky. Orville and Wilbur worked on the *Flyer* with little help. The 787 production network, just for major components, spans nearly a dozen countries and employs tens of thousands of people.

The pace of contemporary technological change makes it easy to take for granted that airplanes today are overwhelmingly superior to those of a century ago in every respect. Yet it is well to recall the stasis that characterized transportation technology for long stretches of the past (Knowles 2006). For centuries, the maximum speed attainable on land and on water barely changed. Then came the Industrial Revolution and a quickening in the pace of technological change. The speed with which air transportation technology, specifically, has improved has no precedent in any other mode.

The jet in particular shrunk the world, or so it seemed. A 1961 *New York Times* article at the time captured the exuberance of the early Jet Age:

In a little more than two years 600-mile-an-hour speeds have become an accepted part of the traveler's world, and anything slower is regarded as distinctly old-fashioned. Six and a half to seven hours is par for the average trans-Atlantic jet crossing. The jet age has arrived so solidly that passengers now shop for the fastest plane and insist on non-stop flight.

(Berkvist 1961)

A figure that accompanied the story was titled "JET TENTACLES COMPRESS THE EARTH" and showed 22 nonstop jet routes from New York extending in every direction. From other major hubs a similar bundle of tentacles stretched out, and it was on these routes that the time-space convergence made possible by jetliners was most apparent. In this regard, the jet airplane was like other space-shrinking innovations: its deployment and effects in terms of time-space convergence were highly uneven (Knowles 2006). The jet drew London and Bombay (now Mumbai), for example, much closer in terms of time in the 1950s (Figure 2.1), but jet travel has only recently been extended to some more peripheral regions of India.

Yet if the airplane did not shrink the world evenly, it nevertheless *did* shrink the world, with enormous and far-reaching implications. Those implications are elaborated in later sections of this book. This first section is primarily about the technological improvements in the world's commercial aircraft since 1903. Were it not for the gigantic changes in the airplane, its engines, and the supporting infrastructure on the ground, the airborne world would not be.

Before the jet

Before examining the birth of the Jet Age, it is useful to consider how far the airborne world had traveled on airliners powered by piston engines and how strongly that earlier period in aviation history influenced what followed.

Flying for a profit: the American airliner

We can begin our brief account with the Douglas DC-3, the first airliner that could fly profitably without government subsidies (Table 2.1). In August 1932, Jack Frye, a vice president with Transcontinental & Western Air (TWA[3]), asked several aircraft manufacturers to develop an airplane with a top speed at sea level of 185 miles per hour (almost 300 kilometers per hour), space for 12 passengers, nonstop range between Chicago and New York in either direction, and the ability to take off with one engine out from any airport in the airline's system (Anderson 2002: 185–6). The highest altitude airport, and therefore the one at which the latter criterion would be most difficult to meet was Winslow, Arizona (Figure 2.2). Remarkably, Douglas met these criteria and won TWA's business with an airplane that had just two engines at a time when three was the usual minimum for an airliner of such size.

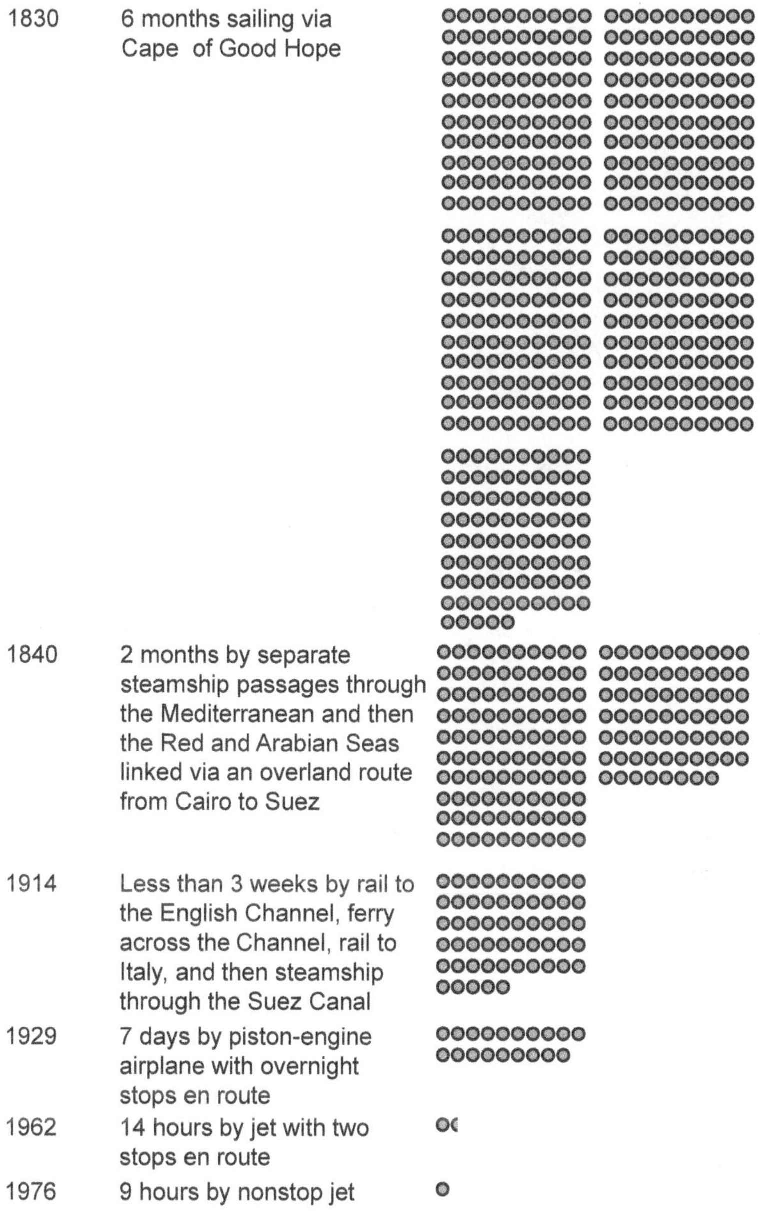

| 1830 | 6 months sailing via Cape of Good Hope | ○○○○○○○○○○ ○○○○○○○○○○
○○○○○○○○○○ ○○○○○○○○○○
○○○○○○○○○○ ○○○○○○○○○○
○○○○○○○○○○ ○○○○○○○○○○
○○○○○○○○○○ ○○○○○○○○○○
○○○○○○○○○○ ○○○○○○○○○○
○○○○○○○○○○ ○○○○○○○○○○
○○○○○○○○○○ ○○○○○○○○○○
○○○○○○○○○○ ○○○○○○○○○○
○○○○○○○○○○ ○○○○○○○○○○ |

Figure 2.1 Travel time between London and Bombay, 1830–1976 (sources: Marshall 1997: 15–19; *New York Times* 1929; BOAC 1962; *Aviation Week & Space Technology* 1976).

The introduction of jet travel furthered a trend begun more than a century earlier towards a radically smaller world, measured in travel time. In the case of the passage from London to Bombay, travel time has fallen by a factor of nearly 500 in 150 years. Each circle represents nine hours of travel time.

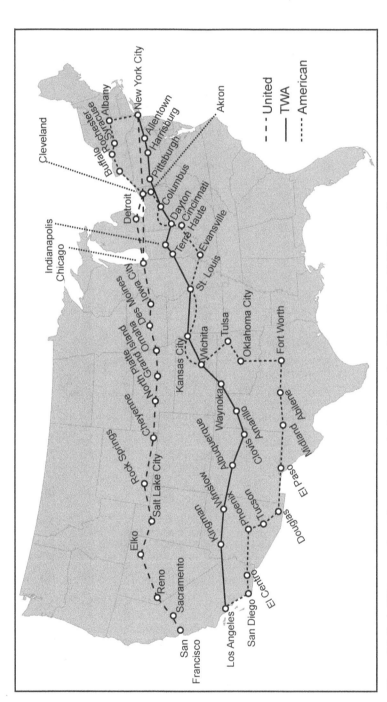

Figure 2.2 Early US transcontinental passenger routes (sources: adapted from Davies 1964: Figure 9).

By 1930, several transcontinental routes spanned the US. The number of intermediate stops en route from New York to the West Coast illustrated both the technological limitation of the era's aircraft as well as the propensity of early airlines to follow railway routes. United's service linked New York and San Francisco in as few as 28 hours, down from the 48 hours a combination of rail and air travel had taken just three years earlier.

Table 2.1 Significant early piston-engine and turboprop airliners

	Douglas DC-3	Boeing 314	Douglas DC-6	Vickers Viscount	Douglas DC-7
Length (m)	20	32	31	25	36
Wingspan (m)	29	46	36	29	33
Engine number and type	2 piston	4 piston	4 piston	4 turboprop	4 piston
Total takeoff power (hp)	2,400	6,400	9,600	6,300	13,000
Typical passenger load	28	74	56	34	60
Cruising speed (kph)	290	295	500	521	590
Normal maximum range (km)	805	5,530	4,425	2,100	7,160
Date of first airline service	June 1936	March 1939	April 1947	July 1950	Nov 1953
First passenger airline	American	Pan Am	United	British European	American
First passenger route[1]	New York–Chicago	New York–Bermuda[2]	New York–San Francisco[3]	London–Paris	New York–Los Angeles[4]

Sources: Davies 1964: Table 51; Boeing Company 2008b; Airliners.net 2008.

Notes
1 First passenger routes identified through author's research of various sources.
2 The Boeing 314 flying boat, a Pan Am Clipper, departed from the Port Washington seaplane base on Long Island.
3 Via Omaha.
4 First sustained nonstop service in both directions.

Douglas was able to make this leap because of the rapid progress then being achieved in aircraft engines and because of the increasingly scientific approach to airplane development (Anderson 2002: 141–51). Wind tunnel testing at California Polytechnic University, for example, was crucial to the success of Douglas in the early 1930s; both Douglas and Cal Tech were located in the suburbs of Los Angeles.

In fact, it is worth noting that aircraft production was the first manufacturing industry strongly associated with the Far West of the US. Although the early development of airplanes had been concentrated in America's Manufacturing Belt, including the Wright Brothers' Dayton, the most enduring US airframe manufacturers, including Boeing (Seattle), Douglas (Long Beach), Northrop (San Diego), and Lockheed (Burbank) emerged as western businesses. Southern California was particularly important because, first, it offered fine weather for flight-testing and, second, it was home to a new class of millionaires with the daring to invest in risky ventures (Biddle 1991: 68). Engine manufacturers, conversely, were and are still found in the old Manufacturing Belt, especially Pratt & Whitney in Hartford and GE near Cincinnati. The disparate geographies of these two closely linked industries reflect different histories. The aircraft engine industry built upon an already established engine industry in the early twentieth century and shared that broader industry's location in the heavily industrialized Northeast and Midwest; but the aircraft business was brand new and was drawn towards a similarly new frontier in the country's industrial geography.[4]

So rapid was the progress of Douglas that only one DC-1 was ever finished. New, more powerful engines permitted the airplane to be enlarged and its capacity boosted to 14 passengers (the DC-2) and then enlarged still further to 21 seats (the DC-3). These aircraft were distinguished by a combination of features that would soon become routine across the industry: better streamlining (including the use of cowlings around engines and retractable landing gear), better use of stressed skin structures,[5] flaps and slotted wings, and high-octane fuels (Solberg 1979: 172).

With unbeatable economics, the DC-3 would become one of the most influential and important airliners ever built. Just before the DC-3 entered service in 1936, airlines in the US operated 460 airplanes. Five years later, the nation's commercial fleet had fallen to 358, but 80 percent of them were DC-3s. And the combination of the airplane's speed, size, and efficiency (meaning lower fares) enabled the total number of air passengers in the US to quadruple in the same five years (Solberg 1979: 172). Indeed, the DC-3's impact was so great that it effectively generated much of the traffic it carried (Heppenheimer 1995: 73). Geographically, the airplane facilitated the emergence of a much more extensive network of air services with many more scheduled routes linking many more airfields. Nor was the DC-3's popularity limited to the US. By 1938, the plane was in use by 30 foreign airlines (Miller and Sawers 1970: 102). It gave KLM, for instance, a significant advantage over other European airlines that were compelled by the governments that owned them to use domestically produced aircraft (Dick and Patterson 2003: 174–5).

Indeed, the DC-3 was a part of the broader eclipse of European aircraft manufacturers by their American rivals. Although national airlines became captive markets for domestic aircraft producers in France, the United Kingdom, and some other European markets, the scale of production for any one company was much smaller than for American manufacturers. Moreover, the fragmentation and politicization of air travel in Europe deterred the development of long-range aviation (Hugill 1993: 271). And the fractured European airline market lacked the competitive drive of its American counterpart which in turn slowed the development of new European airliners. In the US, conversely, airlines locked in relentless competition pressured plane-builders to develop new and better products. Jack Frye's letter to Douglas and the other manufacturers, for instance, was inspired by an airplane called the Boeing 247. That airplane, which debuted a few years before DC-3, was remarkably innovative, too, but its first two years of production had already been committed to United Air Lines.[6] Placed at a competitive disadvantage, TWA asked the plane-builders for a new plane, and the result was an airliner that trumped the 247.

American dominance continued after World War II. In tandem with rising traffic volumes and the expanding limits of airframe and aircraft engine technology, airliners became progressively larger, but they remained overwhelmingly American in origin. For example, the venerable DC-3 was supplanted by the 44-seat DC-4 in 1942, the 56-passenger DC-6 in 1947, the 60-passenger DC-6B in 1951, and the 76-passenger DC-7 in 1956 (Davies 1964: Table 51).

The intense transcontinental competition among America's "Big Four" airlines (American, TWA, United, and to a lesser extent Eastern) had encouraged the development of these new aircraft, but their capacity, range, and speed also made it possible to use landplanes on a regular basis across the Atlantic (Vance 1986). The North Atlantic had long presented the greatest obstacles to the expanding network of international airline services (Davies 1964: 218). More than 3,000 kilometers separated the closest airfields in Newfoundland and Ireland; and the ferocity of prevailing winds and frequent violent storms in the North Atlantic ate into the fuel economy and consequently range of early airliners. Conversely, island-hopping Pan American Airways had spanned the immense distances across the Pacific in 1935. Pan Am's "Clippers" (Sikorsky flying boats) stopped at US possessions Honolulu, Midway Island, Wake Island, and Guam on the six-day voyage from San Francisco to Manila (Allen 1981).[7]

The first regularly scheduled services across the North Atlantic also took the form of a Pan Am flying boat. In 1939, Pan Am introduced the Boeing 314 flying boat service to Southampton, England, via Newfoundland and Ireland (*New York Times* 1939). The appeal of the flying boat was its ability to use long stretches of open water for its takeoff run. In the 1920s and 1930s, long takeoff runs compensated for the weak engines constraining civil aviation and once airborne, flying boats had long nonstop ranges. The double-decked fuselage also offered space for washrooms, a bar, a galley, and a dining room. Yet flying boats were slow and had poor economics. The 314, in particular, cruised at just 295 kilometers per hour. And its costs per available seat-kilometer were more than twice as high as the Boeing 247 and DC-3 (Miller and Sawers 1970: Appendix I).

Pan Am's transatlantic services had barely begun when the outbreak of World War II forced their suspension. By the time the war ended, the era of flying boats was nearly over as new, longer-range landplanes were deployed on routes of increasing directness. In October 1945, American Overseas Airlines was the first to use a landplane on a scheduled commercial flight across the North Atlantic; it flew a DC-4 from New York to Hurn, England, via Gander, Newfoundland and Shannon, Ireland, taking nearly a full 24 hours to do so in October 1945 (Davies 1964: 326). In 1953, KLM became the first to fly nonstop from New York to Europe, introducing the Lockheed Super Constellation 1049 to Amsterdam, though the strength of prevailing winds precluded nonstop service in the opposite direction. And finally, Pan Am introduced the DC-7C Seven Seas in 1957 with the capability to fly nonstop in either direction (Solberg 1979: 355). The DC-7 was the last truly significant piston-engine airliner. The Jet Age had already begun by the mid-1950s and would gain momentum with the debut of the Boeing 707 in 1958 as discussed below.

Jets not only knocked piston-engine airliners off many routes, they also cut short the heyday of the turboprop. A turboprop is powered by engines much like those in a jet except that the engines turn propellers rather than relying directly on the force of the hot gases expelled from the engine (Heppenheimer 1995: 146). One result is that a turboprop is generally more fuel efficient than a comparably sized jet but not as fast. The first commercial turboprop, the UK-built Vickers Viscount, flew in 1950 and in 1957 the Bristol Britannia – also from the UK – debuted. The latter aircraft, like the DC-7C, could also fly nonstop across the Atlantic in both directions but it could do so with a 50 kilometer per hour cruising speed advantage. But both the DC-7 and the Britannia proved no match on long-haul routes for the big jets that were coming.

Growing up: civil aviation on the eve of the jet age

The freedom proffered by technological change in aviation was partly offset by government intervention in the airline industry. In the US, for instance, the Civil Aeronautics Board (CAB), which was created during the vast Depression-era expansion of government, was given the power to award routes, approve fares, and limit mergers. The CAB profoundly affected the geography of the US airline industry in ways that are still evident, even though the CAB has long since ceased to exist (Solberg 1979: 201–2). Delta Air Lines' hub at Atlanta, for instance, sprang from a 1940 agreement between the carrier and the CAB. In exchange for launching services from Atlanta to destitute communities in the rural South, Delta was awarded longer-range routes from the Georgian capital (Peterson and Glab 1994: 120).[8]

On international routes, meanwhile, aviation developed in a highly regulated fashion, especially after World War II. In 1944, delegates from 52 countries met in Chicago to decide the future of international flight (Doganis 1991: 26). The outcome of the conference reflected the balance between naked national interest and the idealism of a war-weary world yearning for peace. Both elements were evident, for instance, in the stance taken by the US Vice President of the time, Henry Wallace. Wallace waxed eloquent in advocating freedom-of-the-air, which he argued would help to prevent a postwar depression and secure the peace. Under Wallace's plan, airlines from any country would be permitted to fly traffic to and from any other country – a vision that fit the vice-president's view that "[a]irplanes and airpower have eliminated the old significance of national borders" (quoted in Veseth 2005: 15). Yet the position that Wallace favored was the same as that of major US airlines who saw in the freedom-of-the-air great potential for expansion; but rather than emphasize the narrow, pecuniary interests of an important industry, the Vice President spoke ardently about a peaceful, prosperous "air-minded" world freed from the shackles of its "earthbound" forebears.

Ultimately, the American government sought an open, multilateral agreement based on "five freedoms" (Figure 2.3):

1 To fly across a foreign state's territory without landing;
2 To land in a foreign state for non-traffic purposes (e.g., to refuel);
3 To put down in a foreign state passengers and cargo taken on in a carrier's home state (e.g., for Air France to carry traffic from France to the US);
4 To take on in a foreign state passengers and cargo destined for a carrier's home state (e.g., for Air France to carry traffic from the US to France);
5 To take on and put down passengers and cargo transported between two foreign states on a route continuing from or to a carrier's home country (e.g., for Air France to carry traffic from the US to Mexico on a Paris–Washington–Mexico City route).

If this set of freedoms had been exchanged freely among the participants in the Chicago Conference, the result would have been extremely advantageous to Pan Am and TWA – and probably disastrous for most foreign airlines. The US airline industry, already the largest before World War II, was in an even more commanding position as the end of the war approached.

Acting out of national self-interest, too, Britain sought a bilateral system of negotiation. At the end of World War II, the British Empire still included colonies in Asia, Africa, and Latin America. In a bilateral system, to get landing rights for its airlines in one of those colonies or in Britain itself, a foreign country would be forced to concede landing rights in return. Somewhat grudgingly France and Commonwealth members Australia and New Zealand – though the latter country had initially argued in favor of a single global airline under United Nations control – sided with Britain. Other countries, including Canada, Sweden, and the Netherlands, were in closer agreement with the US

In the end, a Dutch compromise proposal to accept only the first two freedoms on a multilateral basis was approved. The remaining freedoms, the truly valuable commercial rights, would be negotiated between pairs of countries in what would become hundreds of air service agreements (ASAs). Historically, most ASAs were patterned after the 1946 bilateral agreement between the US and

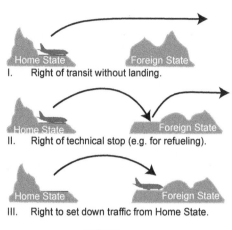

I.   Right of transit without landing.

II.   Right of technical stop (e.g. for refueling).

III.   Right to set down traffic from Home State.

IV.   Right to pick up traffic bound for Home State.

V.   Right to pick up or put down traffic between Foreign States
on a route that continues to or from Home State.

VI.   Unofficial right to pick up and put down traffic between two
Foreign States via Home State combining 3rd and 4th freedoms.

VII.   Right to use aircraft based in a Foreign State to
pick up and put down traffic in another Foreign State.

VIII.   Right to pick up and put down traffic which
originates and terminates in the same Foreign State.

Figure 2.3 The five freedoms and beyond (source: Doganis 2006: 292–3).

The 1944 Chicago Conference on Civil Aviation dealt with the first five "freedoms of the air." Subsequently, several additional freedoms have been identified and have become important in the liberalized airline industry. See Chapter 5.

Britain. Known as "Bermuda I," the agreement stipulated which city-pairs (e.g., London–New York) could be served, designated the airlines that could fly between the two countries, and set the rules to govern capacity, air fares, and freight rates (Kasper 1988).

The system of ASAs has been likened to a vast "cobweb." The metaphor of a "cobweb" (Cheng 1962: 26, quoted in Sampson 1984: 72) is apt because, on the one hand, the ASAs formed the basic architecture of the international airline industry; but, on the other hand, the same ASAs often choked the growth of the industry. ASAs both protected carriers that would have been squashed by mighty foes like Pan Am and kept afloat inefficient, sometimes unsafe carriers that had guaranteed international traffic rights.

Moreover, except in the US, most large airlines, especially international carriers, were fully state-owned in the decades immediately after World War II, reflecting the prevailing ideology in rich and poor countries alike favoring government ownership of the economy's "commanding heights" (Yergin and Stanislaw 1998: 12). And many of those carriers belonged to a cartel, the newly created International Air Transport Association (IATA), which set passenger fares and air freight rates on international routes (Miyagi 1969: 22).

Together, state ownership, domestic regulation, international regulation, and IATA's power in the industry meant that competition among carriers was muted. Given that, it is surprising perhaps that air travel and air cargo flows grew so rapidly during those same decades, but grow they did, borne aloft by rapid technological advances.

The increase in the speed delivered both by piston-driven aircraft and turboprops in the 1950s enabled airlines to lower fares; because while airline revenue is principally related to the distance flown, airline costs are more closely related to flying time (Solberg 1979: 172). The minimum 20 hours required by a DC-4 operating the eastbound route between New York and London had fallen to just 12 hours with the introduction of the stretched Lockheed and Douglas airliners of the mid-1950s. Over the same brief span, the roundtrip fare for New York–London, for instance, fell from $675 for the only class of service in 1946 to $720 for first class and $522[9] for tourist class in 1955 (Miller and Sawers 1970). The introduction of tourist class was itself testament to the new breadth of the traveling public. Indeed, describing air coach, Pan Am's Juan Trippe said, "The importance of that change, which preceded the arrival of jet, was that for the first time the ordinary man began to fly with us." (quoted in Solberg 1979: 345).

Propelled by the combination of lower fares and faster speeds, airlines rapidly ate into the market of older, slower ways of traveling. In the US, the passenger share of rail began to fall precipitously in 1950; and by 1956, airlines were carrying more people than traveled in luxury Pullman and coach class rail services combined (Heppenheimer 1995: 170). Almost simultaneously, the big new airliners overtook the great ocean liners across the Atlantic (Davies 1964: 470). Air travel and sea travel accounted for about the same number of Atlantic crossings in 1957; but thereafter the share of the latter plunged.[10]

Means of ascent: the jet engine and its first commercial use

The jet engine was the first significant innovation in air transportation to have substantial use in military aircraft before its first commercial application (Miller and Sawers 1970: 154). The jet engine was invented independently in Britain and Germany in the 1930s by Hans von Ohain, then working at the University of Göttingen, and Frank Whittle, a Cambridge-educated Royal Air Force officer. Their ideas were developed fairly quickly so that, although they played a small role in World War II, German, British, and American military jets had all flown by 1942. After the war, governments on both sides of the Atlantic poured vast sums into the development of military jets as the Cold War heated up, creating a solid footing for the first civilian jetliners. Indeed, the jet engine has been described as the "most unequivocal gift that governments made to the aircraft industry" (Miller and Sawers 1970: 156).

Although the US would go on to dominate the jetliner business, by the end of World War II the Germans were furthest ahead in the development of the jet. One pair of aviation experts opined that "[o]nly the military defeat of Germany in 1945 prevented the German [aircraft] industry from becoming as dominant as the American industry" (Miller and Sawers 1970: 247). To a greater degree than in the preceding decades of airplane development, success in the Jet Age was dependent upon the advance of basic science; and Germany had a better-developed theoretical base in aerodynamics and a stronger tradition of collaboration between universities and industry (Miller and Sawers 1970: 166; Hugill 1993: 288).

Germany's deeper base of theoretical expertise was most evident in the development of the swept-back wing, a necessary corollary to the jet engine. At transonic speeds, a straight-winged aircraft experiences significantly reduced lift and greater drag than one with swept-back wings (Anderson 2002: 322–7). So among the spoils of war were German drawings of the swept-back wing, which were spirited out of the defeated country to Boeing's Seattle headquarters (Rodgers 1996: 95–9). There, the drawings helped the American plane-builder develop the first jet bomber, the B-47, which was introduced in 1947. Up to that time, the only jet aircraft to have flown were fighters, whose size and range bore little resemblance to the specifications for airliners. The B-47, on the other hand, was a much larger airplane and helped spur interest in jets among airlines (Solberg 1979: 388).

Jet engines offered commercial carriers the prospect of far greater power than could be attained from the traditional piston engine-propeller combination. More power meant greater speeds and payloads, offering the promise of much higher productivity, lower airfares, and a bigger air transportation market. Nevertheless, airlines were reluctant to adopt jet technology. Jet engines had many disadvantages, especially the combination of very high fuel consumption and poor range. The B-47 overcame this limitation with in-flight refueling, but airlines had no interest in such a practice (Heppenheimer 1995: 152).

The application of the jet engine to civilian airliners required greater fuel efficiency. The first engines to offer enough power and efficiency to meet airline requirements, the Rolls-Royce Avon and the Pratt & Whitney JT-3, were available by 1950 and 1953, respectively (Miller and Sawers 1970: 186). Apart from the similarity in their basic designs, the most important factor the two engines shared in common was that the development of each was paid for entirely by government (Miller and Sawers 1970: 156). In the case of the JT-3, the US government spent $150 million[11] on its development before the engine passed its type test and a similar amount on its subsequent improvement (Miller and Sawers 1970: 161–2).

The helping hand of government was certainly visible in the launch of the world's first passenger jet (Table 2.2). The de Havilland Comet that took off on May 2, 1952 not only sported Avon engines whose development had been paid for by the British government. The same government had selected de Havilland to build the first British jetliner and had then heavily subsidized its development. The first Comet was flown by BOAC, a fully government-owned airline; and the route upon which it debuted (London–Rome–Cairo–Khartoum–Entebbe–Livingstone–Johannesburg) was a legacy of Britain's sprawling empire.

For Britain, the Comet represented an attempt to leapfrog the competition – especially the American competition. Powered by four jet engines that were also built by de Havilland, the Comet was 40 percent faster than any other airliner in the early 1950s (Davies 1964: Table 51). The first jetliner was small, however, seating just 40, substantially fewer than the contemporary DC-6 and Lockheed Super Constellation; further, like other early jets, the Comet had a voracious thirst for fuel. As a result, the Comet's operating costs per available seat-kilometer (one seat flown one kilometer) were nearly triple those of the Douglas DC-6 (Miller and Sawers 1970: 180). Airlines could make up the difference through higher load factors – that is selling more of the available seats. And because the Comet was the sole jet operating when it was introduced in 1952, BOAC achieved an astonishing 88 percent load factor in the first year (Miller and Sawers 1970: 180).

By being first in the jetliner business, de Havilland was able to win orders from airlines in France, Canada, Australia, Venezuela, Brazil, and the US. In 1952, fewer than six months after BOAC began flying the Comet, Pan Am ordered three (Davies 1964: 453). The order from the world's most important airline was for a 76-seat, longer-range derivation called the Comet III and was planned for deployment on the crucial transatlantic market – a market well beyond the reach of the Comet I. In the meantime, by 1953, BOAC and two French carriers were already flying the Comet to 30 cities in Europe, Asia, and Africa (Figure 2.4). Passengers raved about the plane's quiet, smooth ride[12] compared to the vibrating, deafening big piston-engine airliners; one passenger, when asked for her assessment, simply remarked, "I fell asleep." (quoted in Serling 1982: 37).

For a time, de Havilland's gamble and Britain's strategy to regain its lost stature in the aircraft industry looked like winning bets. Then, on January 10, 1954 a BOAC Comet crashed near the island of Elba shortly after it took off from Rome. The British airline grounded its fleet of Comets and undertook a

Table 2.2 Significant early jetliners

	De Havilland Comet 1	Tupolev 104	Boeing 707-120	Sud Caravelle 1	Boeing 737
Length (m)	28	39	44	32	29
Wingspan (m)	35	35	40	34	28
Engine number and type	4 turbojet	2 turbojet	4 turbojet	2 turbojet	2 turbofan
Total takeoff power (lb. s.t.)[1]	20,000	30,000	54,000	21,000	28,000
Typical passenger load	36	70	132	70	85
Cruising speed (kph)	710	820	915	730	850
Normal maximum range (km)	2,415	2,650	5,230	2,010	2,850
Date of first airline service	May 1952	Sept 1956	Oct 1958	May 1959	Feb 1968
First passenger airline	BOAC	Aeroflot	Pan Am	Air France	Lufthansa
First passenger route[2]	London–Johannesburg[3]	Moscow–Irkutsk[4]	New York–Paris[5]	Paris–Istanbul	Munich–Frankfurt

Sources: Davies 1964: Table 51; Boeing Company 2008b; Airliners.net 2008.

Notes
1 lb.s.t. = pounds of static thrust.
2 First passenger routes identified through author's research of various sources.
3 Via Rome, Cairo, Khartoum, Entebbe, and Livingstone.
4 Via Omsk.
5 Via Gander.

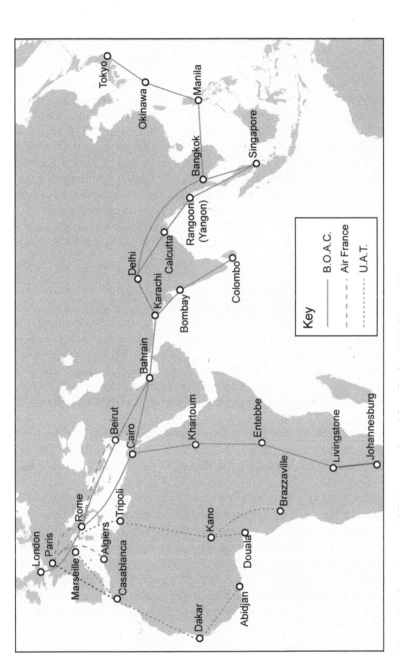

Figure 2.4 Comet routes, 1953 (source: adapted from Davies 1964: Figure 74).

The network of early jetliner services reflected both the technological limitations of the de Havilland Comet (it lacked the range for transatlantic operations) and the geography of the British and French colonial empires.

long study to determine the cause of the disaster. Finding nothing that would suggest the problem lay with the airliner, it reinstated its fleet to service in late March 1954. A little more than two weeks later, a second BOAC Comet went down, killing all on board, also near Rome. A second, even more exhaustive investigation found the problem – metal fatigue, specifically at the corners of the Comet's unusual square windows (Serling 1982: 42).

The Comet was withdrawn from service across the world for four years while the British government and de Havilland worked to establish the safety criteria for high-altitude pressurized airliners (Serling 1982: 42). The redesigned aircraft, the Comet IV, was first flown commercially by BOAC in early October 1958. And later that month BOAC's Comet IV became the first jet in use on the North Atlantic, as a pair of Comet IVs simultaneously flew in either direction between London and New York[13] three days before Pan Am introduced the Boeing 707 on the same route (Davies 1964: 482). But it was the 707 that would triumph. Despite the redesign during its forced hiatus, the Comet remained smaller and slower than its American rival. By the mid-1960s, de Havilland had built fewer than 50 Comet IVs while Boeing would go on to sell more than a 1,000 copies of the 707 in its several versions.

The big jets: the Boeing 707 and the Douglas DC-8

About 40 percent of all the jetliners ever sold have been built by Boeing (Table 2.3). The company's remarkable success began with the Boeing 707. Though it entered commercial service six years after the Comet, the 707 was a much more influential aircraft than its British predecessor. Its success rewarded Boeing's boldness in developing the first large jetliner and ushered in the Jet Age. Douglas, the dominant manufacturer of propeller commercial aircraft before World War II and well into the 1950s found itself playing catch-up with its own four-engine jetliner, the DC-8. The cutthroat competition between Boeing and Douglas made their jets artificially affordable to airlines in the late 1950s and early 1960s, thereby accelerating the replacement of piston-engine propeller aircraft.

The Boeing 707 was a product of the spiraling Cold War. In 1951, the US government launched the B-52, a long-range bomber meant for intercontinental missions. Powered by eight JT-3 engines, the B-52's demand for fuel would be incredible. To sate its thirst on long-range missions, the big bomber required in-flight refueling, but there was no tanker aircraft able to match either the bomber's minimum cruising speed or the altitude at which it would fly (Heppenheimer 1995: 153). Boeing proposed building a jet-powered tanker, which would eventually be known as the KC-135 and planned to simultaneously build a passenger jetliner based on the same prototype.

Boeing had an interesting set of reasons for moving earlier into the Jet Age than the other American aircraft manufacturers. First, Boeing was eager to get beyond the piston-engine, propeller combination. The company had been waging a losing battle with Douglas for two decades and its entrant in the fevered

Table 2.3 Jetliner deliveries by manufacturer, 1952–2008

Manufacturer	Home base	Still producing in 2009	Deliveries
Boeing	USA	Yes	13,105
Airbus	France/Germany	Yes	5,500
Douglas/McDonnell Douglas	USA	No	3,485
Tupolev	Soviet Union/Russia	Yes[1]	1,864
Bombardier	Canada	Yes	1,520
Embraer	Brazil	Yes	1,365
Yakovlev	Soviet Union/Russia	No	1,191
Ilyushin	Soviet Union/Russia	Yes[1]	668
British Aerospace/BAC/Avro	UK	No	635
Fokker	Netherlands	No	572
Sud	France	No	282
Lockheed	USA	No	250
de Havilland	UK	No	207
Fairchild-Dornier	Germany/USA	No	165
Convair	USA	No	102
Antonov	Soviet Union/Russia	Yes[1]	90
Three other manufacturers[2]		No	80
Total			**31,081**

Source: Airbus 2009b; Boeing Company 2009b; Embraer 2008; Bombardier 2009a; Airliners.net 2008.

Notes

1 Three Soviet heritage manufacturers, Tupolev, Ilyushin, and Antonov all had extremely small order books in 2008 as did Russian newcomer Sukhoi (*Flight International* 2009).

2 Vickers (UK), Aerospatiale (UK–France), and Dassault (France). None is producing today.

postwar competition among big piston-engine aircraft, the 377 Stratocruiser, had lost the company $15 million (Rodgers 1996: 147). Second, Boeing had more experience building and more confidence designing jet aircraft than any of its American rivals by the 1950s. By the early 1950s, Boeing had already developed two large jet-powered aircraft while its competitors, most notably Douglas, remained much more comfortably ensconced in the piston-engine era. Third, very high Korean War-era US tax rates on corporate profits gave Boeing an added incentive to pour money into the development of new airplanes since doing so would offset the company's profit and effectively reduce the opportunity cost of the new jets (Rodgers 1996: 157).

There were formidable reasons for caution, however. In particular, the financial stakes were huge. While developing the 707 and KC-135 programs, Boeing would have little capital to do anything else. Its fate would hinge on their success. Further, the tax benefits of investing in the new jets depended on Boeing actually being highly profitable. There were big questions about whether civil aviation authorities would certify the 707. Finally, the size of the anticipated passenger jet meant that if one crashed, it would be the biggest aviation disaster in history to that time and the resulting loss of public confidence might be calamitous for the company (Rodgers 1996: 162–3).

Having weighed the risks and opportunities, Boeing committed to building a prototype jetliner in April 1952, fewer than two weeks before the Comet entered commercial service (Anderson 2002: 349). Since 1949, the Comet, through its program of test flights, had been setting records for an airliner, providing an additional encouragement for American manufacturers to enter the jet business; and Pan Am's order for three Comets in 1953 was a clarion call to other carriers in the US to get on board. By the end of 1954, reluctant carriers had additional reasons to reconsider their position: BOAC had shown that the jet flights could be highly profitable, even at standard International Air Transportation Association (IATA) fares and given the Comet's prohibitively high costs. The combination of their speed, comfort, and modern image made jets enticing to passengers and therefore increasingly unavoidable for airlines. Buoyed by the confidence that airlines would buy jets, Boeing moved forward.

Douglas, at the time the world's largest airliner manufacturer, had no choice but to follow suit. In June 1955, the airframer committed to building a large jetliner called the DC-8. From a distance, the 707 and DC-8 were nearly identical. Each featured four jet engines hung in pods beneath highly swept-back wings. The two aircraft were roughly the same size too. But there were important differences between the two jets. The Douglas aircraft had wings swept back only 30 degrees versus 35 degrees for the Boeing. The smaller angle made the DC-8 easier to handle at low speeds but gave the 707 a 55-kilometer per hour higher cruising speed (Miller and Sawers 1970: 192; Serling 1992: 137). More importantly, the DC-8 was a bigger airplane as originally designed. Though both jets could conceivably accommodate six abreast seating, the three-inch wider fuselage of the Douglas aircraft provided for a more comfortable fit and a wider aisle more amenable to in-flight meal service (Serling 1992: 138). Finally, because Douglas started later it could more easily amend its design to accommodate the newer, more powerful engines then being developed by Pratt & Whitney.

The first head-to-head test for the big jets involved their most influential customer, Pan Am. In October 1955, just four months after Douglas had committed to building the DC-8 but three years after Boeing had started down the same road, Pan Am stunned the aviation community with an order for 20 707s and 25 DC-8s (Heppenheimer 1995: 165). The total order was worth nearly $270 million,[14] the largest in airline history to that date. To the two disappointed manufacturers who each wanted all of his business, Pan Am's Trippe explained that he had ordered the 707s so that he could be first in the sky with a big jetliner, but that his company believed the DC-8, which would be available about a year later, was the superior aircraft. Pan Am judged the 707 to be "underpowered, under-ranged, and undersized" (Serling 1992: 136).

Other airlines followed Pan Am in giving the DC-8 their collective nod. To stem the tide of customer sentiment, Boeing was forced to hastily refine the 707 in ways that eroded its commonality with (and therefore the degree to which it could be cross-subsidized by) the KC-135 (Heppenheimer 1995: 167–8). The fuselage was widened, its wings and fuel tanks were enlarged, and it was fitted with more powerful engines. To win specific customers, Boeing developed special variants, including, for instance, a version designed for takeoffs at the high altitude Andean airports in Braniff's network and a shorter, longer-range derivative for Qantas to use on transpacific routes. Boeing, it was joked, "possessed a Great Fuselage Machine that turned out one continuous fuselage from which the company cut off pieces as long as it wished." (Serling 1982: 71).

Initially, the DC-8 outsold the 707 in a contest that ranged around the world (partly due to broad established Douglas customer base), but Boeing had too many factors in its favor including a bottom-line price for the 707 that was $300,000 less than for the DC-8 (Rodgers 1996: 188). By the time production stopped on each line, nearly twice as many 707s as DC-8s had been produced.

The 707 and DC-8 were highly successful in service, giving substantial momentum to the nascent Jet Age. In the early 1950s, airlines in the US had feared that only the elite would be able to afford jet travel, as would later prove true of the Concorde (Rodgers 1996: 150). In fact, the operating costs proved to be lower for jets than for piston-engine aircraft for all but the shortest routes (Miller and Sawers 1970: 205). Even fuel costs, which had been expected to be punishing, turned out to be lower, on a seat-kilometer basis, than for piston-engine aircraft. The inherently superior energy efficiency of jet engines along with their reduced drag contributed to better fuel economy. Moreover, jet engines were relatively light in relation to the aircraft they powered, permitting more revenue-generating traffic to be carried. Finally, jet engines burned kerosene while the contemporary piston engines burned very high octane gasoline; in 1958, the prices of these two fuels were 9 cents and 16 cents a gallon, respectively (Miller and Sawers 1970: 187).

Most importantly, the productivity of the big jets was phenomenal. In a typical workday, a jet might be flown from Atlanta to New York to Houston to Chicago to Miami and then back to Atlanta again. Even if they flew the same number of hours per day, a 707 could do more than six times as much work (measured in passenger-kilometers per year) as a DC-6. However, because jets were easier to maintain and because they cost so much to purchase, they were worked much more intensively. Continental was able to keep its small fleet of four 707s in the air an average of 16 hours per day every day, a utilization rate that was double the then-industry average (Serling 1992: 147).

Rapid improvements in jet engine technology boosted the capabilities of later versions of the 707 and DC-8 well beyond what the first versions could do. Specifically, both aircraft were offered in versions equipped with turbofan engines after 1959. In a turbofan, also called a fanjet, a jet at the core of the engine not only provides thrust but also turns a large fan at the front of the engine in order to force air through and *around* the turbine. In this fashion, the bypassed air is heated indirectly and expands, adding to the pressure exerted on the internal surfaces of the engine and the consequent thrust produced. However, the bypassed air does not reach the same extreme temperatures as the air that moves through the engine directly nor does it exit the engine with the same velocity. The greater the proportion of air that is bypassed around the turbine, the cooler and slower the exhausted gases will be. Ironically, this is good from the standpoint of engine efficiency since much of the energy of hot, high velocity exhaust is simply dissi-pated into the surrounding atmosphere (Anderson 2002: 337). The turbofan engine translates more of the energy of combustion into forward thrust (Ander-son 2002: 339). By the end of the 1950s, both General Electric and Pratt & Whitney had developed engines with bypass ratios of about 1.5: 1 (Miller and Sawers 1970: 197) (Table 2.4).

Equipped with turbofans, both the 707 and the DC-8 could fly between almost any American city and European city and between Seattle and Tokyo along a high latitude great circle route (Heppenheimer 1995: 191). By the summer of 1961, there were 17 jet operators on the North Atlantic, 12 between Europe and Africa, 7 between North and South America, 8 across the Pacific, and 8 on polar routes – and almost all of these were using the DC-8 or 707 (Davies 1964: 488). A network of jet routes had encircled, squeezed, and shrunk the world in a high-speed web.

But the cost of spinning that web was staggering. Airlines bought, and they bought big, sometimes too big. As Davies (1964: 433) wrote in *A History of the World's Airlines*, "There is much to be said for the argument that air transport would have been better off financially if the inventors had been less inventive." But by the end of the 1950s, there was no holding back the Jet Age, if only because no airline boss wanted to risk being left behind on the tarmac while his competitors soared ahead. By the time Pan Am flew the first revenue flight with the 707 on October 26, 1958, Boeing had already sold 190 707s and Douglas had sold 131 DC-8s, and the development of other jetliners was well under way.

All in the family: the development of small and mid-sized jetliners

Up until the dawn of the Jet Age, individual airliner manufacturers offered narrow product lines. Until then, aircraft manufacturers had been straining at the limits of available speed, range, and payload. In the 1930s, for instance, after Douglas had developed the revolutionary DC-3, the California plane-builder sold almost nothing else to airlines but DC-3s. Jet engines offered such a leap in per-formance, however, that aircraft like the 707 and DC-8 were clearly inappropri-ate for some short-range, thinly traveled routes. Smaller jets, including some of the most successful aircraft ever manufactured, filled those gaps – or in industry parlance, "holes in the market" (Newhouse 1982: 18).

Europeans led the way in developing small jetliners. Following the lead of Britain and its Comet, France too decided to pursue a piece of the looming jet-liner business with a small passenger jet; and as in Britain, the French govern-ment selected the company that would build the jet and then heavily subsidized its national champion. The Sud Aviation Caravelle, which debuted in 1959, had a typical passenger load of 70 and a range of just 2,000 kilometers. The airlines that flew the Caravelle, beginning with Air France, rapidly captured business from competitors still flying slower, noisier piston-engine and turboprop aircraft. However, the Caravelle and three other small British jetliners – the three-engine

Table 2.4 Characteristics of selected jet engines

Manufacturer	Model	EIS[1]	Airliner example	Thrust (lbs)[2]	Fan diameter (inches)	Bypass ratio
De Havilland	Ghost	1952	De Havilland Comet 1	5,000	n/a	0
Pratt & Whitney	JT3	1958	B707	13,500	n/a	0
Pratt & Whitney	JT3D	1959	B707 Intercontinental	21,000	53	1.4
Pratt & Whitney	JT9D	1970	B747-100	45,600	93	4.8
General Electric	CF6-6	1971	DC-10-10	39,300	86	5.7
Rolls-Royce	RB211-22B	1972	L-1011	42,000	86	4.1
Pratt & Whitney	PW4056	1987	B747-400	56,750	94	4.9
Pratt & Whitney	PW4084	1995	B777-200	86,760	112	5.8
Rolls-Royce	Trent 500	2002	A340-500	53,000	97	7.6
General Electric	GE90-115B	2004	B777-200LR/300ER	115,300	123	9.1
Rolls-Royce	Trent 900	2007	A380	70,000	116	8.7
Rolls-Royce	Trent 1000	TBD[3]	B787	53,000–75,000	112	10–11

Sources: Rolls-Royce 2009; GE Aviation 2009; Pratt and Whitney 2009.

Notes
1 EIS = entry into commercial service
2 Thrust is usually measured in pounds of takeoff thrust at sea level.
3 TBD – as at the time of writing, the EIS was still to be determined.

de Havilland Trident, the twin-engine British Aerospace (BAC) One-Eleven and the Vickers four-engine VC-10 – never enjoyed the commercial success of their American rivals, partly because they lacked the synergy of the airliner families emerging on the other side of the Atlantic.

Boeing moved earlier than Douglas to add to its jetliner product line. Spurred by the sales won by small jets such as the Caravelle, Boeing developed the 720, which was a shortened version of the 707, and a far more important aircraft, the 727. The 727 was designed to meet the needs of United Airlines and Eastern Air Lines (Rodgers 1996: 208–9). United was interested in a medium range, mid-sized jetliner but wanted it to have four engines in order to ensure adequate power to take off from the carrier's high altitude hub at Denver's Stapleton Airport. Eastern wanted a lighter, more fuel efficient two-engine aircraft that could serve its lucrative New York–Miami market nonstop. As a compromise, Boeing developed the "three holer" 727 whose turbofans had ample power to take off from Denver even in the event of an engine failure.

Eastern also demanded that the plane be able to takeoff and land fully loaded from LaGuardia's runway 4-22. The runway was the only one at the important airport equipped with an instrument landing system (ILS) at the time; but it was just 1,480 meters long (Serling 1992: 183). The fruit of Eastern's demand was the remarkable system of triple-slotted flaps that distinguish the 727's wings. When fully extended at takeoff and landing, the flaps created a kind of "parasol" so that the wing could produce enough lift to takeoff and land at relatively low speed. The 727 entered commercial service with Eastern and United in 1964. Several stretched versions with more powerful engines were subsequently introduced. By the time production stopped in 1984, Boeing had turned out 1,831 727s (Rodgers 1996: 216), making it easily one of the most profitable airliners ever developed.

But in terms of its longevity, the 727 has been overtaken by the 737, the "Baby Boeing." The 737 entered service in 1968 with seating for about 100 passengers and a targeted stage length of just over 700 miles (1,125 kilometers) (Serling 1982: 254). Although the 737 would go on to become the most popular airliner ever developed, in its early years it faced very tough competition from the Douglas DC-9 which had a headstart of several years (Francillon 1979: 603). The first DC-9s were deliberately undersized, with fewer than 90 seats, in order to ensure that the aircraft did not exceed the Federal Aviation Agency (FAA) weight limit for aircraft flown by a two-pilot crew (Francillon 1979: 604). The 737 exceeded this limit from the start and therefore required a three-person crew, which made it unpopular with American carriers. Interestingly, it was the only major Boeing jet-liner program until the 787 for which a foreign carrier, Lufthansa in the case of the 737, served as launch customer. In 1974, amid a severe downturn in the airline industry, the FAA rule was relaxed (Serling 1982: 116); and by the end of the twentieth century, two-pilot crews operated even the largest aircraft.

Small and medium-sized jetliners, like the DC-9, could out-compete turbo-props and piston-engine aircraft because their speed and ease of maintenance translated into greater productivity. The powerful turbofans introduced in the

1960s were crucial to giving small and medium-sized jets their productivity advantage because a greater proportion of the takeoff weight could be revenue-generating passengers and freight. Moreover, quick turnarounds on the ground bolstered the jet's speed edge. The Boeing 377 Stratocruiser, for instance, required frequent changes of its 112 spark plugs (Solberg 1979: 318). Overall, operating costs for jets were dramatically lower than for comparably sized piston-engine aircraft by the mid-1960s, even for small and medium-sized airliners.

Beyond the compelling economic advantages of jets, traveler preference for the new technology drove the displacement of turboprops and piston-engine air-craft (Davies 1964: 487). Small jetliners like the 737, BAC-111, and DC-9 brought the Jet Age to cities and towns with too little traffic to warrant service by the big jets, such as Omaha and Hartford where United Airlines used Carav-elles in the very early 1960s. But these aircraft were also deployed on densely traveled routes linking major cities. In 1961, Eastern Air Lines had begun oper-ating an "Air Shuttle" service offering cheap fares and high frequency service with old aircraft that would otherwise have been unused (Davies 1964: 528). But by the mid-1960s, the shuttle services along the Atlantic Seaboard used newer, faster, more popular jets like the DC-9 (Francillon 1979: 612).

Meanwhile, on the other side of the Iron Curtain, jets were also introduced in the 1950s. Specifically, the Tupolev 104 debuted in 1956, and by the 1960s a jet shuttle service was in place between Moscow and Leningrad (St. Petersburg) where Aeroflot offered fifteen Tupolev 104 flights per day. In a market-based economy, the airliner, with just 50 seats (70 in a later version) and horrific fuel consumption would have been a failure; but in the Soviet Union, jet services were heavily subsidized by the state to such a degree that air fares for the one-hour flight were cheaper than the rail fare for an eight-hour journey on the ground (Davies 1964: 481).

Up, up, and away: the early jet age

It was in the US, however, not the Soviet Union that the jet was most fully embraced. Two years after the 707 first flew, Pan Am had a far-flung network of jet services that encompassed the globe (Figure 2.5). Incredibly, the proportion all revenue passenger-kilometers in the US accounted for by jets climbed from 0 in 1955 to 42 percent in 1960 and 82 percent in 1965, and over the same decade the sheer volume of air traffic increased phenomenally (Miyagi 1969: 25, 37).

The image of the jet began to permeate popular culture in the US and other advanced economies. Alastair Gordon (2004: 174) observes in his book *Naked Airport: A Cultural History of the World's Most Revolutionary Structure*,

> "The prefix 'jet' was used to sell products evoking speed and modernity and was attached to everything from laundry soap to vacuum cleaners. The Jetsons were the TV family of the future, while the New York Jets were the newest team in the National Football League."

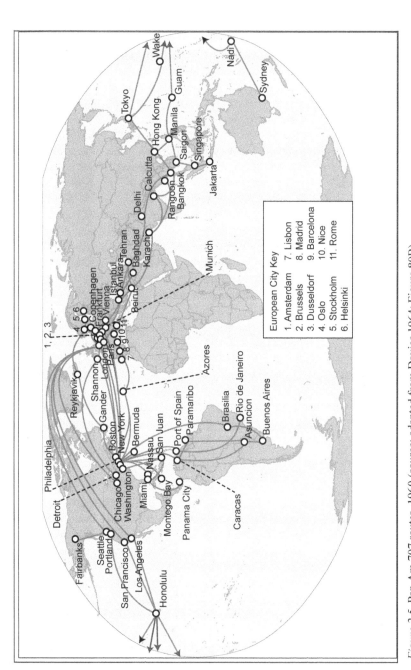

Figure 2.5 Pan Am 707 routes, 1960 (source: adapted from Davies 1964: Figure 80B).

Just two years after the 707 was introduced, Pan Am flew the jet around the world. The importance of European destinations and the absence of African ones reflected the distribution of wealth and American political interests at the time.

European City Key

1. Amsterdam	7. Lisbon
2. Brussels	8. Madrid
3. Dusseldorf	9. Barcelona
4. Oslo	10. Nice
5. Stockholm	11. Rome
6. Helsinki	

The Jets played in the nation's most important city; but jets helped less important cities, particularly in the south and west, to attract major league sports franchises. 1957, the Dodgers, having abandoned Brooklyn for sunny Los Angeles, relied on DC-7 charters to play teams still on the other side of the country; but the dispersal of baseball teams in earnest took off a decade later as United Airlines began offering jet charters to quickly deliver teams to their away games (Solberg 1979: 409–10) (Figure 2.6).

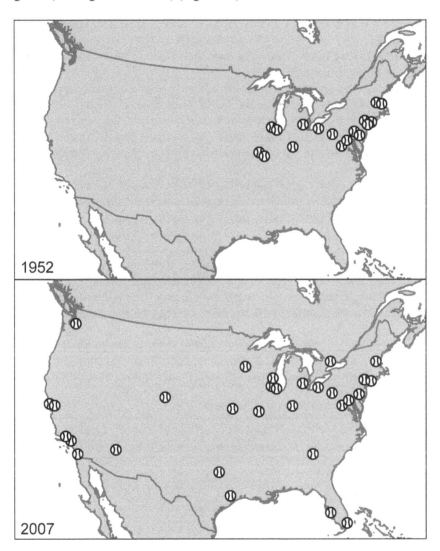

Figure 2.6 The changing geography of major league baseball teams (source: Cazeneuve *et al.* 2004).

Lower cost air transportation, especially by jet, permitted a more even distribution of teams in major league baseball.

Many businesses, not just sports leagues, stretched out their "tentacles" by jet. As a result, in the early 1960s, business travelers continued to fill most of the seats. *Time* magazine reported in 1964 that 86 percent of domestic airline travelers in the US were businessmen (Solberg 1979: 406). Many of these were in the air so often that they represented a harbinger of the frequent flyer at century's end. One Los Angeles leather salesman flew more than six million kilometers on United Airlines alone (Solberg 1979: 409). Reflecting the affluence of the pioneer jet-setters in the early Jet Age, a much higher proportion of seats were sold as first class than is true today. For American Airlines and TWA, for instance, a typical 707 configuration when the jets were first introduced was 66 seats in first class and 66 in coach (Serling 1992: 154). By the mid-1960s, the number of first class seats in the same plane was 44 and by the early 1970s just 12.

As the Jet Age progressed, space aboard airliners was increasingly packed with tourist and coach class travelers. The amazing productivity of jets, a result principally of their size and speed, allowed fares to drop so that jets brought not only faster transportation but also lower-cost transportation, a concurrence of positive trends evident in the falling costs of travel between New York and San Francisco (Table 2.5).

With capacity rising rapidly and real costs falling, the International Air Transport Association (IATA) and domestic regulatory agencies permitted carriers to introduce new, lower fare classes. Across the North Atlantic, TWA had begun offering "sky-tourist" fares in 1952 to fill its Super Constellations. In 1958, on the eve of the 707's debut, Pan Am offered new, even lower (after adjusting for inflation) "economy fares" (Sampson 1984). Pan Am found that 75 percent of those traveling on reduced fares had never flown before (Heppenheimer 1995: 193).

Meanwhile, the air cargo market began to grow more rapidly. A number of all-freight airlines emerged after World War II using surplus wartime transports, and by the 1960s the air cargo business was big enough to the purchase freighters new from manufacturers. Flying Tigers, for instance, acquired a fleet of 19 stretched and strengthened DC-8 freighters direct from Douglas (Francillon 1979: 596). The kinds of cargo carried in the 1960s were not entirely dissimilar

Table 2.5 Transcontinental travel times and costs

Year	Mode	Time	Nominal one-way cost[1]	Real one-way cost (2008 dollars)[2]
1854	Sea via Cape Horn	89 days	225	4,440
1872	Transcontinental rail	6 days	150	2,520
1932	Piston-engine airliner	31 hours	160	2,150
1963	Jetliner	5 hours	75	420
2007	Jetliner	5½ hours	145	148

Sources: relevant issues of Official Airline Guide, contemporary advertisements in the *New York Times*; www.orbitz.com.

Notes
1 Lowest cost available (e.g. economy class, roundtrip travel meeting advance purchase).
2 Converted to 2008 dollars using the GDP price deflator at S. Williamson (2008).

to those of today. In March 1960, for instance, the leading commodities imported to the US by air were, in order: beef, shrimps, cucumbers, automobile parts, and woolen fabrics. The top airborne exports were: hatching eggs, refrigerators, plastic kitchenware, automobile parts, and television sets (Sealy 1966: 70). In other words, air freight comprised mainly perishables and high value-to-weight goods – important characteristics of air freight decades later (see Chapter 9). Missing, however, was regular use of air freight across a broad selection of industries, and the volume of air freight was still small, but airborne commerce was growing rapidly, partly because jets increased the speed advantage of air cargo and eased some of the size restrictions that had confronted shippers loading goods aboard smaller piston-engine aircraft.

The growth of air traffic, both passenger and cargo, during the Jet Age was of course concentrated in the most important airports. As noted near the beginning of this chapter, the geography of jet travel was highly uneven. Remarkably, all but one of the 20 busiest airports in 1961 was in North America or Western Europe (Table 2.6).

To accommodate the surge in traffic in these and other cities, new airports and new terminals were built with designs celebrating speed, motion, and flight. The architectural gigantism of the Jet Age was perhaps most evident at New York's Idlewild. When the airport opened in the late 1950s, passengers had to make do with a functional concrete terminal, but the explosion of traffic in the early Jet Age was matched by the pace of construction at the new airport. Unlike

Table 2.6 The world's top passenger airports, 1961

Rank	Airport	Passengers (millions)
1	New York-Idlewild	10.3
2	Chicago-O'Hare	9.5
3	Los Angeles	6.9
4	London-Heathrow	6.1
5	San Francisco	4.8
6	Washington	4.5
7	Miami	4.1
8	Atlanta	3.7
9	New York-La Guardia	3.3
10	Chicago-Midway	3.2
11	Boston	3.2
12	Newark	3.0
13	Paris-Orly	2.9
14	Frankfurt	2.3
15	Philadelphia	2.2
16	Montreal	1.9
17	Toronto	1.9
18	Rome	1.9
19	Honolulu	1.8
20	Tokyo	1.8

Sources: ICAO 1963; FAA 1967; Nelkin 1974; Braden and Hagan 1989; *New York Times* 1962.

most other facilities of its stature elsewhere in the world, New York's principal airport did not strive for architectural coherence around a single theme. Instead, major airlines were permitted to develop their own terminals. The result was, depending on one's perspective, either an "architectural zoo" (A. Gordon 2004: 207) or the setting for several of the world's most spectacular structures. The latter included the vast umbrella roof of the Pan Am terminal and the graceful, soaring curves of the TWA terminal (Pearman 2004: 144–5).

Airports designed in the piston-engine era were quickly swamped when jets arrived. Chicago-O'Hare, for instance, was officially finished in 1963 and deemed overcrowded before the end of the decade. And at the same time that jets fostered more rapid traffic growth, they helped to marshal the gathering environmental movement which, with varying degrees of success, thwarted airport expansion projects. More and more airport neighbors shared the sentiment of the residents of a Ft. Worth apartment building who unfurled a sign reading "JETS GO HOME" after big jets began flying overhead (Serling 1992: 155).

Piston-engine aircraft had been noisy too, but the advent of commercial jets turned what had been a relatively minor issue into a matter of great public controversy. Jets exacerbated the problem of aircraft noise in several ways. First, they were louder. In a 1959 study, the noise of a four-engine propeller plane measured 490 meters away was about 85 dB(A); the corresponding measure for a 707-120 was 94 dB(A).[15] It is important to note that decibels are logarithmic so that the difference between 85 and 94 is not the modest 11 percent increase the numbers seem to imply; the actual difference in noise experienced by a person in this instance would be about twice as much. Second, beyond the difference in the noise volume, jets further compounded the problem of noise because they produced more shrill, high frequency noises than piston-engines. Third, jets produced significant noise both on takeoff and landing. Propeller aircraft are typically quiet as they glide into landing with their engines on idle but jets continue to use their engines to control the rate of descent and to maneuver all the way down. And jets equipped with thrust reversers to rapidly brake on the runway produced a burst of whooshing noise after touchdown.

Because the exhaust from a turbofan engine has a lower velocity than from a turbojet, the substitution of turbojets by turbofans brought some relief (Solberg 1979: 403). And the greater power of turbofans enabled aircraft to climb more rapidly after takeoff, reducing the noise "footprint" on the ground (Heppenheimer 1995: 191). Nevertheless, the problem of aircraft noise remained as the popularity of jets rose into the 1960s.

Noise, congested runways, the massive financial burden of building and buying jetliners – these were only the most obvious problems of expanded jet transportation. Striking a balance between the freedom of the air and those problems would prove even more difficult as the 1970s brought a new generation of jets that dwarfed even the largest that had flown in the first decade of the Jet Age. The next chapter turns to the era of wide-body jet transportation.

3   Far and wide

Wide-body jetliners and the growth of the global airline industry

Big time

The speed with which the Jet Age arrived and its concurrence with the Space Age fed fantasies about a still more astounding future. Around the time that the first manned lunar flights were making the once remarkable feat of jet travel seem mundane, aviation experts on both sides of the Atlantic forecast that supersonic passenger travel would become standard on international routes in the 1970s. By the mid-1960s, the Soviets, Americans, and Europeans all had supersonic transports in various stages of development.

Yet it was a different kind of innovative aircraft developed in the same period that would ultimately have a much larger impact upon the way the world works. For supersonic travel, despite its early promise, never attained anything like the heights that had been imagined, but new jetliners distinguished not by their speed but by their gargantuan size *did* take the airborne world to a new level. Foremost among this new class of wide-body jets was the Boeing 747 (Table 3.1). Indeed, the jet's bulbous nose became an icon of the Jet Age, an easily recognizable symbol for air travel. More than double the size of any preceding airliner, the 747 helped to lower the cost and broaden the accessibility of air travel much as the DC-3 had two generations earlier. The 747 was the "Everyman airplane" (Gandt 1995: 70). But the 747, which made a troubled first flight with launch customer Pan Am in 1970, would not so easily generate the traffic to fill its seats as had the DC-3.

The scale of the 747 respects was without precedent in all respects, including its cost. Combined, the financial commitments of Boeing, Pan Am, and the engine-builder Pratt & Whitney to the project made the jumbo the greatest private sector enterprise in history up to that time. Pan Am's launch order for 25 747s was worth $550 million, more than the world's most famous airline had made in any year. Pratt & Whitney had perhaps a billion dollars at stake in the development of engines powerful enough to meet the plane's performance specifications (Rodgers 1996: 246–7). And Boeing, which initially estimated its commitment to the project at $750 million before the first plane would fly with paying passengers, may actually have spent $2 billion,[1] several times its market capitalization at the time (Newhouse 1982: 115).

Table 3.1 Significant early wide-body jetliners

	Boeing 747	McDonnell-Douglas DC-10	Lockheed L-1011	Airbus A300	Boeing 767
Length (m)	71	56	54	54	48
Wingspan (m)	60	47	47	45	49
Engine number and type	4 turbofan	3 turbofan	3 turbofan	2 turbofan	2 turbofan
Total takeoff power (lb. s.t.)[1]	186,000	120,000	126,000	101,000	96,000
Typical passenger load	366	270	270	255	175
Cruising speed (kph)	895	965	890	915	915
Normal maximum range (km)	9,815	6,115	5,310	3,540	5,795
Date of first airline service	January 1970	August 1971	April 1972	May 1974	Sept 1982
First passenger airline	Pan Am	United	Eastern	Air France	United
First passenger route[2]	New York–London	San Francisco–Washington	New York–Miami	Paris–London	Chicago–Denver

Sources: Boeing Company 2008b; Airliners.net 2008.

Notes
1 lb.s.t. = pounds of static thrust.
2 First passenger routes identified through author's research of various sources.

The stakes involved in large commercial aircraft (LCA) development are so huge that *New Yorker* writer John Newhouse titled a book about the industry, *The Sporty Game* (Newhouse 1982). Companies that want to "play the game" have to bet big. Boeing did and came out a winner, but two of Boeing's rivals made wagers nearly as large and lost. Lockheed, which was late getting started in the jetliner business, and legendary Douglas both pursued what was predicted to be a vast market for a 250-seat wide-body aircraft. The aircraft they produced to fill that hole in the market, the L-1011 and the DC-10, respectively, were so similar that it was easy for airlines to play one manufacturer off another, with devastating financial consequences for both companies. The L-1011 was the only jetliner Lockheed would ever build and Douglas – whose already deep financial problems led to its merger with McDonnell in 1967 to create McDonnell Douglas (Newhouse 1982: 108) – never fully recovered from the DC-10 debacle. In 1997, McDonnell Douglas was acquired by its old nemesis in the airliner business, Boeing.

Of course, Boeing now faces a new competitor, Airbus.[2] In the late 1960s, as the 747, DC-10, and L-1011 were taking form, a different sort of modern marvel, the multinational conglomerate, was being crafted on the other side of the Atlantic. Across Europe, national governments and aircraft manufacturers were confronted by the same stark reality as Boeing, McDonnell Douglas, and Lockheed: to compete in the jet airliner business cost so much that only the largest (i.e., American) companies were likely to succeed. Yet at the same time, the business was made irresistible by the prospect of tens of thousands of high-paying jobs in an industry that, however routine air travel had become, was still at the technological frontier. Consequently, in late 1966, European leaders decided to form a consortium to produce an airliner designed for the continent's heavily traveled but relatively short routes (Mondey 1983: 17). Six years later, the Airbus A300 made its debut, the first aircraft in what would become the large family of airliners that now stretches from the A318 to the A380 Superjumbo.

The A300, L-1011, DC-10, and especially the 747 were not just big airplanes (see Table 3.1). They helped to make aviation itself a bigger part of everyday life. In 1979, the total number of passenger-kilometers on scheduled flights worldwide surpassed one trillion for the first time, up from one billion in 1935 (ICAO 1998; Davies 1964: Table 52). The new wide-bodies, while comprising a still quite small share of all airliners, helped to facilitate the expansion in traffic, even as the world economy reeled from the effects of spiraling oil prices (see Figure 12.2). For these jets brought savings through economies of scale. A pilot's salary, for instance, cost much less per passenger if spread across 350 rather than 150 passengers. In lowering the real cost of air travel, especially long-distance air travel, the wide-bodies helped to bring the airborne world to full flower. The supersonic visions of the mid-1960s never came to fruition, but the wide-body world was for real.

Jumbo

It is testament to the brief history of air transportation and the durability of commercial aircraft that the Boeing 747, of which 859 were still in service in 2008

(*Air Transport World* 2008c), sprang from the imaginations of two of the founding fathers of commercial aviation. In the summer of 1965, Juan Trippe, who had led Pan Am since its inception in 1927, and William Allen, head of Boeing since the end of World War II, went fishing on a yacht rented from the actor John Wayne. While on board, they dared each other into building the world's largest ever commercial jet. Trippe promised to buy it if Allen would build it, and Allen promised to build it if Trippe would buy it (Irving 1993: 195). Though the actual design and the two companies' colossal financial commitment to it would not be finalized for months, their mutual dare set in motion the creation of an airliner that served as the backbone of intercontinental air transportation for decades. The new airplane would have dramatically different consequences for their respective companies, however. Although Boeing barely survived the early years of 747 development, by the 1990s the jumbo jet was the top source of the company's profit. But Pan Am never recovered from its over-commitment to the 747 and flew its last flight – not one of the carrier's grand wide-bodies but rather a 727 from Barbados to Miami – on December 4, 1991 (Gandt 1995: 315–16).

Neither Trippe nor Allen would live long enough to see that grim day. Both men were near the end of their careers when they discussed the big jet in 1965. The two men had played similarly instrumental roles in the 707, Allen committing his company to build the world's first big jetliner and Trippe eagerly jumping to the head of the line to buy it. Trippe's belief in jets then had been crucial to the success of the 707 because other airlines, particularly on international routes, had bought jets at least as much out of fear of being trumped by Trippe as out of their own conviction in the new technology. Now the two would reprise their roles on a larger scale.

Boeing's exploration of a very large passenger jet had begun well before the fishing trip. The tremendous increase in passenger traffic in the early 1960s had sparked airline enthusiasm for aircraft larger than the 707 and DC-8 (Figure 3.1). Douglas had been able to respond to that interest with the stretched DC-8. The DC-8-60 series, for instance, featured a 36-foot fuselage plug that boosted the airplane's capacity about 60 percent (Francillon 1979: 598–9). The 707, however, could not be stretched so far mainly because the airplane had shorter landing gear than its Douglas rival; a stretched 707 would strike the runway as it rotated towards takeoff unless Boeing undertook an expensive redesign of this integral element of the airliner.[3] With the 707 already as long as feasible, Boeing began discussing several designs for a new, larger airplane with customers. To the company's surprise, there was considerable interest in the largest proposed size: 350 seats. And Trippe was keen on a 400-seat airplane (Rodgers 1996: 237).

An airplane of that size would require enormously powerful engines; but, somewhat fortuitously, in early 1965 the world's top engine-makers were developing a new class of engines that would generate more than twice the power of the turbofans used on the 707 and DC-8 (Irving 1993: 180; Davies 1964: Table 51). The new engines were for the gargantuan C5-A Galaxy, the US military's new jet transport. The C5-A actually began as an idea of Boeing's, which had hoped that a new civilian passenger transport could be piggy-backed on a new

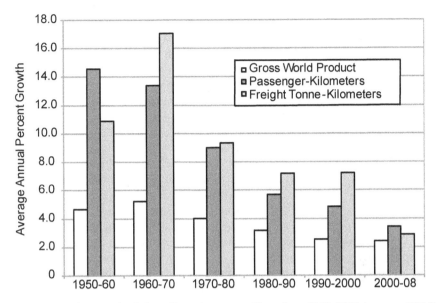

Figure 3.1 The growth of air traffic and gross world product, 1950–2008 (sources: ICAO 1998, 2008; Earth Policy Institute 2007).

Global air traffic, measured in terms of passenger-kilometers and freight tonne-kilometers, has steadily outpaced the broader growth of the world economy.

very large military jet – much as the 707 had begun as a sibling of the KC-135. Boeing did not get the contract and in the end the Galaxy had little in common with the 747, but the military transport did stimulate the development of engines suitable for the 747.

By spring 1966, Boeing and Pan Am had agreed on the specifications of the new airplane, which had been assigned its now famous model number: 747 (Rodgers 1996: 239–46). The airliner would weigh 655,000 pounds (nearly 300 tonnes), carry 350–400 passengers, be able to takeoff fully laden with just 8,000 feet (about 2,400 meters) of runway on a hot day, cruise at Mach 0.9, and have a range of 5,900 miles (almost 9,500 kilometers). The range would enable the 747 to fly nonstop from Rome to New York, which was already well within the capability of the 707 Intercontinental, against the strong prevailing west winds in the North Atlantic (Irving 1993: 214).

In accordance with a Pan Am requirement, the jet would have a hinged nose to allow front-loading of main deck cargo. Trippe, along with many others in commercial aviation at the time, believed that affordable supersonic travel was likely in the not-too-distant future. He saw the 747 as a stopgap until that time and when the much anticipated supersonic transport (SST) began to displace subsonic airliners, 747s could be easily converted for use as freighters. Trippe's conviction led to the familiar shape of the 747 as the cockpit was placed high above the main deck at the nose of the airplane (Heppenheimer 1995: 221).

Pan Am agreed pay $19 million[4] apiece for 25 747s (including two freight-ers), with two unusual conditions imposed by Boeing (Rodgers 1996: 246). Although the normal practice was for airlines to pay about a quarter of the pur-chase price before actually receiving a new aircraft, Boeing would pay half through a series of installments. And the price was indexed for inflation, reflect-ing the more general fear of inflation in an economy already made red-hot by Vietnam War spending (Newhouse 1982: 120). These conditions were unprece-dented at the time and had the effect of forcing Pan Am to bear a significant portion of the risk in the venture. Even so, the burden upon Boeing to finance the project was incredible. Boeing spent $200 million[5] alone on a new 747 assembly building in Everett, Washington, which featured a 43-acre roof.[6]

Boeing promised to deliver the first two aircraft in November 1969, giving the company just three and half years to manufacture and certify the largest ever jetliner. The challenge for Pratt & Whitney, the company Boeing selected to produce the initial engines for the 747, was even greater (Rodgers 1996: 242). Each engine would have to deliver 41,000 pounds of thrust and be comparatively quiet. Moreover, the development of a new engine typically takes a year longer than a new airframe, putting tremendous pressure on the engine manufacturer (Newhouse 1982: 117–21). In the end, the deadline proved too ambitious, and problems with the Pratt & Whitney JT9D would be the chief reason for the 747's troubled first year of service.[7]

Altogether, the airplane had 4.5 million parts drawn from suppliers that spilled across 48 of the 50 states (Serling 1992: 296, 305). Although the 747 assembly plant was immense, much of the actual manufacturing for the big jet occurred away from Everett. Boeing's Wichita, Kansas affiliate and Northrop in California, for instance, produced large sections of the fuselage. And that meant that, although the 747 would eventually play a substantial role in the develop-ment of airborne logistics, the logistics of *its* manufacture relied heavily upon the North American railroad network (Serling 1992: 289).

Boeing delivered the first 747 to Pan Am in December 1969, just over three years after the two companies had committed to the project. It was the fastest sprint in airliner development in Boeing's history (Rodgers 1996: 253). The first flight was scheduled to depart from New York's John F. Kennedy International Airport[8] bound for London-Heathrow at 7:00 p.m. on January 21, 1970, but Pan Am's *Clipper Young America* was forced to return to the terminal due to engine problems. The airline eventually sent the passengers to London seven hours late on an alternate jet, the *Clipper Victor* (Witkin 1970: 1). And thus, the age of wide-bodied air travel had begun, albeit behind schedule. Passengers generally raved about the new airplane, one likening its immensity to "Radio City Music Hall with wings" (Lindsey 1970: 151).

By the second anniversary of Pan Am's debut 747 flight, Boeing delivered just over 160 747s to 27 airlines, including 10 US carriers and 11 in Europe. The great majority of these new jets were deployed on the North Atlantic, especially after US domestic carriers discovered that the jets were too large to be practical on their networks. By 1972, Pan Am had extended jumbo operations to 29 cities across the world (Figure 3.2).

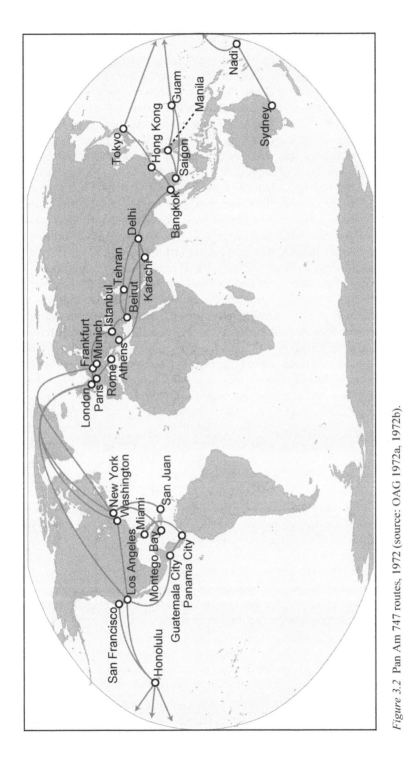

Figure 3.2 Pan Am 747 routes, 1972 (source: OAG 1972a, 1972b).

Two years after the debut of the 747, Pan Am's services had spread around the globe though they were not as extensive as the carrier's 707 services had been two years after that airliner was introduced (see *Figure 2.5*).

Boeing had enjoyed considerable success lining up airline customers for the 747 in the mid-1960s. In particular, international airlines contemplating competition with Pan Am fell in line behind the American giant. Indeed, Pan Am wanted foreign airlines to commit to the 747 in order to ensure that Boeing would go ahead with the project and that governments overseas would permit the jumbo to land and to spur the development of suitable facilities in those countries (Serling 1992: 287). The lengthening and strengthening of runways, terminal expansions, and purchase of larger ground equipment came just eleven years after airports had scrambled to get ready for the 707 and DC-8.

Ultimately, the injection of unprecedented numbers of seats into the market was ill-timed. Even before the launch of 747 services, the market had begun to weaken. By 1970, the situation had worsened, particularly as the US economy slipped into recession. The conjunction of weak demand and surging capacity threatened ruin for Pan Am and Boeing. Pan Am was paying $10 million a month just to finance its new fleet but could not fill all the new seats, partly because the airline had no domestic network to feed into its (Sampson 1984: 125). Incredibly, Pan Am exercised options on eight more 747s after it received the last of its original order of 25. But the enthusiasm of airlines in general waned rapidly in the early 1970s. Orders for the 747 evaporated amidst a sluggish market. From a peak of 83 orders in 1966, new 747 orders fell all the way to just seven for all of 1971 (Boeing Company 2009b). Boeing's other commercial aircraft ventures suffered similar setbacks, and the plane-maker was forced to cut its Seattle-area workforce drastically in 1969 and 1970. Two employees of a local real estate agency paid for a billboard plaintively asking, "Will the last person leaving SEATTLE – turn out the lights?" (Serling 1992: 335).

Yet the 747 would go on to become a great boon to Boeing and Seattle. By the 1990s, the big jet was the source of 70 percent of Boeing's commercial airplane profit (Rodgers 1996: 287). By then the 747 was the "Pacific airplane." In particular, the longer range, higher capacity 747-400, which first flew commercially in 1989, was especially well-suited for the heavily traveled routes to, from, and among the booming economies of East Asia and Southeast Asia. Peter Hugill (1993: 295–7) goes so far as to argue,

> The growth of the Asian economies within the world system almost depends on such a plane. Without it, managerial decisions will have to be made locally. With it, the level of integration achieved in the Atlantic with the four-engined, propeller-driven landplanes of the 1940s and 1950s will be possible.

Certainly the jet was phenomenally popular with Asian carriers. By 2008 nearly 40 percent of all 747s ever produced had been delivered to carriers in East and Southeast Asia (Bowen 2007) (Table 3.2).

Table 3.2 Southeast and East Asia share of airliner deliveries, 1958–2008

Boeing	Southeast and East Asia share (%)	McDonnell Douglas	Southeast and East Asia share (%)	Airbus	Southeast and East Asia share (%)
707	1.7	DC-8	8.1	A300	29.4
727	3.5	DC-9	4.9	A310	11.7
737	9.5	DC-10	11.0	A320	13.9
747	36.7	MD-80/90	10.3	A330	27.5
757	7.0	MD-11	27.0	A340	20.1
767	19.2	–	–	A380	46.2
777	38.1	–	–	–	–
All	**13.1**	**All**	**9.5**	**All**	**17.3**

Sources: Airbus 2009b; Boeing Company 2009b.

The Lockheed and McDonnell Trijets

Less than two years after Boeing launched the 747 program, two of its American rivals also jumped into the nascent wide-body market. Whereas the Boeing 747 was expected to *create* its own market through lower airfares, the more modest three-engined McDonnell Douglas DC-10 and Lockheed L-1011 were sized to *satisfy* the predicted market of the mid-1970s (Irving 1993: 229). Both were responses to a critically important letter to aircraft manufacturers written by Frank Kolk, the then-Chief Designer for American Airlines in April 1966 (Newhouse 1982: 122; Francillon 1979: 617). Kolk's letter called for a wide-bodied, two-engined airliner with seats for 220–230 passengers in mixed configuration, a range of 2,015 miles (about 3,240 kilometers) when operated from a full-length runway and 740 miles (about 1,200 kilometers) when operating from LaGuardia's short runway 4-22. The longer range would permit nonstop operations between American's Chicago hub and the West Coast, the shorter range would allow the airliner to fly nonstop between Chicago and LaGuardia (Francillon 1979: 617).

Other American domestic carriers were interested in similar aircraft, but their requirements led McDonnell Douglas and Lockheed to develop airliners around three engines rather than two. Eastern's key New York City–San Juan route included a long over-water section for which the Federal Aviation Administration (FAA) rules at the time mandated three engines; similarly TWA's transcontinental routes and United's high altitude hub at Denver also warranted a third engine given the technological limitations of the time (Heppenheimer 1995: 224; Francillon 1979: 618).

Although McDonnell Douglas had begun its program a few months later than Lockheed, by early 1968 both were fiercely pursuing their first orders; and much to their eventual detriment, they both won big orders early on. United and American placed massive orders for the DC-10, while TWA and Eastern ordered even more L-1011s (Newhouse 1982: 153; Francillon 1979: 619). The split between the big four US domestic carriers enabled both airliners to survive what had been expected to be a deadly early winnowing. Instead, both manufacturers continued to compete fiercely (and not always legally[9]) for each possible sale in a way that made it virtually impossible for either program to be profitable (Boulton 1978: 229). By the time production of the two jets had ended, Lockheed had sold 249 L-1011s but lost an estimated $2.5 billion on its Tristar (Rodgers 1996: 285) and was forced from the commercial jet business. McDonnell Douglas was the victor in the trijet battle; it sold 443 DC-10s but took too long to get to the magic number of 400 at which it started to earn profits on the aircraft.[10] By then, McDonnell Douglas, heir to the legacy of once-dominant Douglas, had been eclipsed by the new number two, Airbus Industrie.

All together now: Airbus and the wide-body twinjet

In the early 1960s, the European aircraft industry had, to its credit, produced several innovative jetliners, including the Comet and the Caravelle; but Europe's collective share of new aircraft sales was tiny. It made very few sales in the gigantic American market and even the formerly captive European carriers were being drawn into the arms of Boeing and Douglas. In 1962, European airlines operated 171 European jetliners versus just 105 American jetliners; but because the average American jet was twice as large, most of the capacity flown by European carriers was already manufactured by Boeing and Douglas (Davies 1964: Tables 50 and 51). Although jet technology had been born in Britain and Germany in the 1930s, the American eclipse of European aviation in the jetliner business was nearly complete by the late 1960s. France's Charles de Gaulle spoke of the "America's colonization of the skies" (quoted in Heppenheimer 1995: 203). It was amid these circumstances that Airbus Industrie was created.

A 1965 British government study, known as the Plowden Report, had found that the cost of producing aircraft in Britain was 10 to 20 percent higher than in the United States, due mainly to longer production runs in the latter (Newhouse 1982: 124). In an industry with such high development and learning costs, long production runs were crucial to reaching the point of profitability. The large American market, which Europeans had found difficult to penetrate, also gave American producers a substantial advantage in competing abroad. In the mid-1960s, the American commercial aircraft industry sold nine aircraft at home for every one sold abroad but nevertheless was able to export three to four times as many as its British counterpart (McIntyre 1992: 8).

The Plowden Report recommended overcoming the limitations imposed by a fractured European market through much stronger collaboration among the region's leading aircraft manufacturers. At the time, Sud Aviation (later Aerospatiale) and British Aircraft (later British Aerospace) had already been at work on the troubled Concorde for several years; but at the time the report was written, Concorde was one of only 28 aviation projects in which Britain and France were collaborating. Buried among those other projects was one that "was still not much more than a gleam in the eyes of a few enthusiasts, and the name it went by was propped up by inverted commas, as if to emphasize its speculative and fluid nature: 'Airbus'" (McIntyre 1992: 11).

The proposed Airbus was neither as technologically challenging nor as potent as symbol of national pride as Concorde. Yet the Airbus had a clear market. Air France had proposed a wide-body, short-range aircraft suitable for routes such as Paris–London and Paris–Amsterdam in 1963 (McIntyre 1992: 15), and subsequent discussions among aircraft manufacturers and airlines in Europe indicated broad support for such an airplane. From across the Atlantic, Frank Kolk, whose letter had helped to launch the DC-10 and L-1011, had given a similar set of specifications to Sud Aviation. Kolk's interest in a "jumbo twin" suggested that there could be a market for the Airbus in the critical US market.

The formation of Airbus Industrie took place in a political climate generally favorable to European cooperation. In particular, France and West Germany – antagonists in three wars during the preceding century – were the two largest economies in the European Economic Community (EEC), and each had much to gain from the project. For both France and Germany, the Airbus was a means of countering America's daunting economic penetration of Europe. For Germany, more specifically, Airbus would be a way back into the aircraft business after decades of dormancy. In France, the Airbus project and the jobs it could foster had taken on new political urgency after Sud Aviation had become one of the hotbeds of labor unrest during the tumult of 1968 (Heppenheimer 1995: 293–4).

The position of the United Kingdom towards the project was more ambivalent. By 1967, the British role in the planned aircraft was shaping up to be substantial. It would be powered by Rolls-Royce engines; and Hawker-Siddeley would design and build the wings. On the other hand, the already bitter experience of Concorde, which was on its way to racking up costs ten times those originally forecast, jaundiced the British government's appraisal of the new Airbus venture. Moreover, France had rejected the United Kingdom's application for EEC membership in 1963 (Heppenheimer 1995: 205).

So the French and West Germans went ahead on their own in 1970, forming Airbus Industrie as a *groupement d'interet economique* (GIE) under French law. The GIE combined the resources of Aerospatiale and Deutsche Airbus. Aerospatiale, formed in 1970 as a merger of SUD Aviation and two other French aerospace manufacturers, was almost 100 percent state-owned. Deutsche Airbus was a wholly owned subsidiary of Messerschmitt-Bolkow-Blohm (MBB), which was owned by a mixture of German state governments and private interests. Each of these companies would become the avenues for the strong, if indirect government role in Airbus Industrie's investments and operations. As a GIE, Airbus was an umbrella under which its constituent parts retained an important degree of independence. For Airbus Industrie products, however, the GIE made the key decisions on behalf of its member companies concerning design, manufacture, and marketing. An important advantage of the GIE arrangement was that it was free from the obligation to file public financial reports that would reveal the magnitude of the subsidies it received (Heppenheimer 1995: 295).

The first project for the consortium was the aircraft that gave it its name, the Airbus – specifically the Airbus A300. With a typical seating configuration of 255 passengers, the A300 had just 15 fewer seats than the basic DC-10; but the Airbus had only two engines whereas the McDonnell Douglas jet required three. Doing nearly as much work but with only two-thirds the engine power gave the Airbus a strong fuel efficiency advantage. Moreover, because the Airbus did not have a tail-mounted engine, its wings could be located farther forward and its tailfin and elevators could be smaller – further contributing to its superior fuel efficiency (Heppenheimer 1995: 297). Airbus made its maiden commercial flight in May 1974 between London and Paris (Mondey 1983: 17). By the end of the decade, Air France, the largest operator of the airplane, was using the A300 on routes linking Paris and other French metropolitan areas to one another and to destinations across the Mediterranean, in the Middle East, and over the Iron Curtain (Figure 3.3).

Despite its compelling advantages, Airbus Industrie had little success winning sales for its airliner beyond its home turf. In the program's first three years (1974–6), only 37 aircraft were ordered – mainly by airlines controlled by the

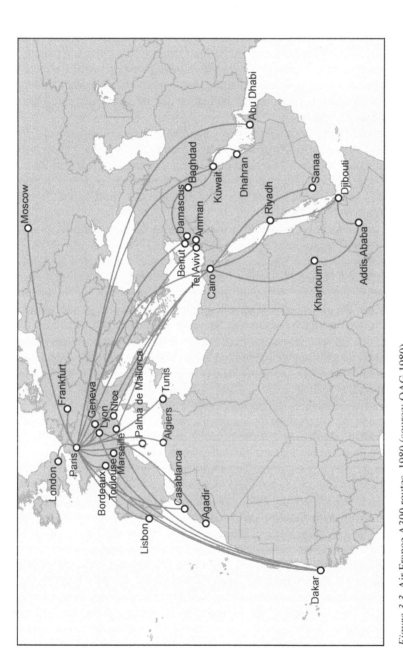

Figure 3.3 Air France A300 routes, 1980 (source: OAG 1980).

Air France flew the A300 twinjet on short- and medium-haul routes throughout Europe, North Africa, and the Middle East. Later, many of these routes in the Air France network would be replaced by smaller aircraft including variants of the Airbus A320.

same governments that backed Airbus (Heppenheimer 1995: 296). In those same three years, Boeing and McDonnell Douglas sold nearly 600 aircraft (Boeing Company 2009b). Airbus faced severe obstacles breaking into a market where most airlines with networks suitable for wide-body jets already operated either Boeing or McDonnell Douglas aircraft. Airlines tend to stick with manufacturers they know, some out of a sense of loyalty but more importantly because it lowers the cost of crew training and maintenance. Moreover, Airbus was saddled with the European aircraft manufacturers' reputation for inferior quality and poor service (McIntyre 1992: 34).

Nevertheless, Airbus was able to win a handful of orders in the early 1970s. A particularly important sale was to Korean Airlines, which pointed the way to Airbus Industrie's successful "Silk Route" strategy of targeting carriers in fast growing Asian markets. The Airbus was certainly priced to sell. In the mid-1970s, it was listed at about $6 million less than the $30[11] million DC-10 and L-1011 (McIntyre 1992: 34).

Airbus was able to break the American stranglehold on the big jet market through extremely aggressive marketing (McIntyre 1992: 44–5). In 1977, in order to win an order from Eastern Airlines, Airbus lent the carrier four A300s for six months at no cost to the carrier other than crew training and normal operating expenses (e.g., fuel). If Eastern did not like the airplanes, they could be returned when the six months were over. Instead, at the end of the world's longest test drive (or flight) Eastern was favorably impressed, but the carrier was still able to get further concessions from Airbus including loan guarantees from European governments and compensation from Airbus for the difference in the cost of operating the A300 versus the ideal (though nonexistent) 170-seat aircraft that Eastern really wanted. Finally, Eastern ordered 23 A300s, and Airbus had its first American customer (Heppenheimer 1995: 297).

A year later, the outbreak of the Iranian Revolution and the subsequent Iran–Iraq War pushed oil prices in 1981 to three times their level in 1978 (see Figure 12.2). The high oil prices cast the fuel-efficient A300 in a particularly positive light. Much as the oil crisis of the late 1970s and early 1980s helped the Japanese auto industry capture market share at the expense of American automakers, the same crisis helped Airbus capture sales that probably would have gone to its far larger American rivals. Boeing had decided to launch its own wide-body twinjet, the 767, in 1978; but that airplane would not fly until 1981 (Rodgers 1996: 346–7). Airbus, on the other hand, already had the proven A300 and in 1979 launched the 200-seat wide-body twinjet A310. Together they gave Airbus Industrie the first siblings in a family of jets.

Like its American counterparts, Airbus developed a sprawling supply chain; but the spatial fragmentation of the European plane-maker's production process was more exaggerated. The need to placate its big government investors and the smaller size of and uneven distribution of expertise among its member companies resulted in a more geographically dispersed pattern of production for major aircraft components. For the A300, Deutsche Airbus manufactured the forward and rear fuselage, the upper lobe of the center fuselage, and the tailfin.

Hawker-Siddeley and CASA (Construcciones Aeronáuticas, SA – the Spanish partner in the Airbus consortium) together built the wings, with the former manufacturing the main wing structures and latter producing the flaps and ailerons. Finally, Aerospatiale built the technologically demanding lower lobe of the center fuselage (from which the main landing gear operate), the nose and flight deck, and the engine pylons (McIntyre 1992: 35). The most important non-European contribution to the A300 came from GE, whose CF-6 engines were chosen after Rolls-Royce cast its lot with the L-1011.

The various elements were assembled in the southern French city of Toulouse, which had a long association with aviation (McIntyre 1992: 30). In the 1950s, Toulouse joined the far more selective roster of places manufacturing jet aircraft. From the moderately successful (at least by the standards of European airliners) Caravelle, Sud Aviation moved on to become the French wing of Concorde project. So as the Airbus project got underway, Toulouse already had a significant reservoir of local talent, abundant aviation-specific infrastructure, and – like Southern California – a climate conducive to aircraft testing.

The size of some components sent to Toulouse for assembly precluded shipment by rail or road (especially given the narrow streets of Europe's old cities) so Airbus used a modified version of the Boeing 377 Stratocruiser to carry out the shipments. The *Super Guppy* featured a hugely swollen fuselage (Heppenheimer 1995: 308). Airbus defended the expense of airlifting components across Europe by noting that components are rarely out of the production process and inventories are kept low – rationales familiar to other companies that have become dependent on air freight to tie together dispersed networks. Yet in the case of Airbus, achieving a politically palatable balance of work was critically important (McIntyre 1992: 74–5).

The politicization of Airbus may have complicated its operations, but without the generosity of its government backers, Airbus would never have gotten off the ground. For the A300 and the smaller wide-body A310, the British, French, and West German governments provided an estimated $2.6 billion in launch aids[12] (CRS 1992: 36). Over half that amount was provided by West Germany. Britain put up the smallest share because it was not a member of the consortium during the development of the A300. It reconsidered its position, however, and joined in 1979 to take part in the launch of the A310. By then Hawker-Siddeley had been absorbed into British Aerospace so the latter became the British component of the Airbus consortium (McIntyre 1992: 56–8).

The contrast between the wide-body jetliner experiences of Lockheed and Airbus during the 1970s is striking. The former, via its work on the C5-A military transport, already had a headstart in wide-body aircraft development and garnered 73 orders for the L-1011 within a year of launching the airplane. Airbus, in contrast, was formed as a consortium of companies with no wide-body experience, and it took Airbus seven years to reach 73 orders for its A300. Consequently, it is likely that the losses incurred by Airbus were at least as large as those suffered by the L-1011. Yet instead of being forced from the market like Lockheed, Airbus launched a smaller derivative of the A300 in 1979 and then moved on to launch two entirely new aircraft programs (the remarkably innovative A320 and A330/A340) in the early 1980s. Fundamentally, Airbus and Lockheed were playing by different rules in the "sporty game" of jetliner production (Tyson 1992: 173).

Wide-bodies in the world

By the end of the 1970s, the four wide-body plane-makers had delivered nearly 1,000 wide-body aircraft (Tyson 1992: Table 5.6). The insertion of so much capacity into a world economy weakened by the 1970s oil price hikes forced airlines to cut fares and air freight rates, at least in inflation-adjusted terms. At the same time, the difficult circumstances in the airline industry forced carriers into a desperate search for traffic. The discretionary traveler became more important than ever before. In 1969, in anticipation of the 747's debut, the International Air Transport Association (IATA) agreed to special bulk fares well below standard economy fares for passengers who traveled in groups and who agreed to spend at least $100 on ground arrangements (Lindsey 1969). The fares offered discounts of nearly 50 percent: cutting the New York–Rome roundtrip fare from a minimum of $409 to $220,[13] for instance. At least for 747 operators, the pressure on fares was somewhat offset by the lower per passenger cost of operating the jumbo. Pan Am, with by far the biggest fleet of 747s, claimed the aircraft cut costs by 23 percent compared with operating expenses for its 707s and 727s (Bedingfield 1971).

It was the promise of markedly lower operating costs that caused some to wax poetic in describing the airliner's broader consequences. One *New York Times* writer, for instance, saw grand import in the new jet:

> It will take time for internationally minded sociologists to assess what this expanding mobility and person-to-person fraternization among different peoples will mean to future international understanding. But the 747, by lowering the cost of air travel even more, or making it hold the line in face of inflation, will make it possible for more and more people to discover what their neighbors are like on the other side of the world.
>
> (Lindsey 1970: 151).

And there were many who did take advantage of the lower fares that the 747 helped foster in order to travel farther than ever before. Across the North Atlantic, the number of Americans visiting Europe swelled from 400,000 to 2.9 million between 1965 and 1970; and in the opposite direction European visitors to the US grew from 565,000 to 981,000 (quoted in Lindsey 1971).

A corollary to the democratization of air travel, however, was the dilution of the status it had once conveyed (Sampson 1984: 131). Physically, the dominance of the budget traveler was evident in aircraft interiors. Boeing's Stratocruiser had been popular with passengers for its sleeping berths and its lower-deck lounge reached by a circular staircase (Solberg 1979: 314). The Boeing 747 offered a far more cavernous interior and initially some operators did use the upper-deck space behind the cockpit for a modern rendition of the first-class lounge replete, in certain cases, with a "captain's table;" but as the 1970s and the ferocity of competition wore on, that space too was converted to seating on most 747s.

Yet even as the wide-bodies permitted more ordinary people to take wing, the airline industry's "caste system" deepened. In 1978, Pan Am became the first airline in the world to introduce a formally designated business class. Its Clipper Class was a separate cabin with product features positioned between economy class and first class. Within a matter of months, about a dozen other transcontinental and intercontinental carriers launched their own business class products (Grimes 1980). Like Pan Am, the other airlines tried to create a strong brand identity to distinguish the new in-between service from economy class. So TWA crafted Ambassador Class, El Al offered King Solomon Service, and Cathay Pacific introduced Marco Polo Class. The emergence of business class in the late 1970s is no accident, of course. Deregulation had opened some markets to new competitors, pushed down economy-class fares, and encouraged a greater emphasis on price discrimination. Neither is it any accident that the aircraft most associated with business class in the early years was the 747. The jumbo's deployment on long-range trunk routes meant that it carried a disproportionate share of the transnational capitalist class, and the plane's huge size lent itself to partition.

Meanwhile, below-decks the wide-bodies facilitated the expansion of air freight in several ways. First, wide-bodies offered much more lower deck space than had narrow-body jets. Second, their broad girth permitted a greater variety of goods to be carried; in particular wide-bodies could accommodate both palletized and containerized cargo. Third, passenger preference for wide-body comfort on long-range routes hastened the conversion of some 707s and DC-8s to freighters, providing a further boost in available capacity (Watters 1979: 156). In the 1970s, worldwide air freight traffic, measured in freight tonne-kilometers, grew at an average annual rate of nearly 10 percent even though fuel prices were markedly higher than in the 1960s (see Figure 3.1).

On the ground, the growth of air traffic, facilitated by the advent of new wide-bodies, mandated even larger airports, including new ones built even farther out. In Singapore, for instance, Changi Airport was built on reclaimed land at the northeastern edge of the island, completing a decades-long shift towards more distant airports. Although the earliest air transportation gateway to Singapore had been at a British colonial air base called Seletar in the far northern part of the island, the first specifically commercial airport opened at Kallang in 1937, immediately adjacent to the central business district (Figure 3.4). Kallang was replaced by Paya Lebar in 1955 still just 10 kilometers from the CBD and then by the still more distant Changi in 1980. Paya Lebar and Seletar remain active, primarily military, airports; but the old airport at Kallang has been replaced by a sports stadium and high-density housing.

By comparison with some other jumbo-era airports, Changi is close to the city it serves. In Japan, the New Tokyo International Airport, was built 65 kilometers

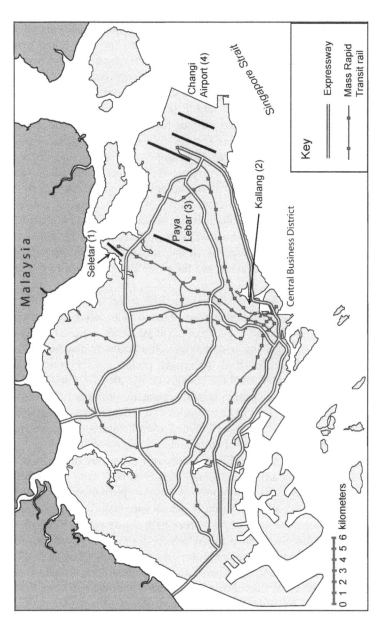

Malaysia

Seletar (1)

Paya
Lebar (3)

Kallang (2)

Central Business District

Changi
Airport (4)

Singapore Strait

Key

Expressway

Mass Rapid
Transit rail

0 1 2 3 4 5 6 kilometers

Figure 3.4 Changes in the location of Singapore's main airport (source: Bowen 1993).

As described in the text, over a five decade-long period in the mid-twentieth century, the city's main civilian airport moved from a location on the edge of the central business district to a massive expanse of reclaimed land in the northeast. The land transportation network displayed shown in the illustration was current at the time of writing.

from the Japanese capital amid the rice paddies of Narita. In a harbinger of an increasingly common problem, the site selection for the airport, though rational-ized in coolly bureaucratic and technical language, became wildly controversial. Narita was transformed into an ongoing battleground among local interests, the environmental movement, and the national government as issues ranging from noise to the loss of farmland defied easy resolution. Massive protests brought the massive project to a near standstill, but finally the airport opened in 1978, seven years late and four runways short of the original plan (Apter and Sawa 1984: 6, 82). With just one runway (until the early twenty-first century), the principal international gateway to the world's second largest economy became the ulti-mate wide-body haven as airlines made the most of limited takeoff and landing slots. Even in 2008, with two runways in operation, 88 percent of flights depart-ing Narita were wide-bodies (author's analysis of OAG 2008).[14]

Japan more generally has had a voracious appetite for wide-body jets; one out of nine 747s went to Japanese carriers, for instance. Boeing even sold a special version of the jumbo, the 747 Short Range, seating up to 560 people, to ANA and Japan Airlines (JAL). The latter operated the airplane every half hour during the day between Tokyo and Osaka in the early 1990s (Heppenheimer 1995: 302). It was one such jet that has the unfortunate distinction of having been the airliner involved in the worst single aircraft accident in history (Table 3.3). On August 12, 1985, a JAL 747 crashed into Mt. Ogura en route from Tokyo to Osaka, killing 520 of the 524 people on board. The only deadlier aviation accident also involved the 747, two of them in fact. On March 27, 1977, a Pan Am 747 and a KLM 747 collided on the runway at Tenerife in the Canary Islands. Overall, nineteen of the twenty deadliest airline crashes have involved a wide-body jet. Although safety has improved markedly, the sheer concentration of people on the 747, DC-10, L-1011, Airbus 300 and similar jets has contributed to single crash death tolls that would have been unimaginable before the Jet Age.

Of course, not all of the events listed in Table 3.3 were accidents. The Air India crash in the Atlantic Ocean and the downing of Pan Am 103 over Scotland, in particular, were acts of terrorism.[15] More generally, the introduction of wide-body jets coincided with the advent of terrorism directed against civil aviation, partly because the 747 and its confreres increased the size, visibility, and impor-tance of the airline industry – all of which made the industry an appealing target to the terrorist.

Although there were at least 20 (and probably more) instances of deadly viol-ence against civil aviation before 1970, most were cases of hapless airliners caught up in war zones or simple criminal activity.[16] In the past few decades, however, terrorism has moved to the forefront of threats to commercial air trans-portation (see Figure 11.1). Air terrorism was pioneered by the Popular Front for the Liberation of Palestine (PFLP), which in the late 1960s riddled two taxing El Al jets with gunfire, hijacked another El Al jet, and then a TWA jet. Those events were sprinkled over 13 months, but in September 1970, the PLFP carried out four nearly simultaneous hijackings, including a Pan Am 747[17] (Raab 2007). Like the 9/11 attacks 31 Septembers later, the terrorists were Muslim extremists

Table 3.3 Deadliest airline crashes

Rank	Year	Airline(s) and aircraft	Site of crash	Deaths
1	2001	American Airlines 767	Flown by terrorists into North Tower, World Trade Center, New York City	1,622[1]
2	2001	United Airlines 767	Flown by terrorists into South Tower, World Trade Center, New York City	655[1]
3	1977	Pan Am 747 and KLM 747	Collision on runway at Tenerife, Canary Islands	583
4	1985	Japan Airlines 747[2]	Crashed into Mt. Ogura, Japan	520
5	1996	Antonov 32 freighter	Crashed into busy market in Kinshasa, Congo	350+[1]
6	1996	Saudia 747 and Kazakh Illyushin 76 freighter	Mid-air collision near Delhi, India	349
7	1974	Turkish DC-10	Crashed near Paris, France	346
8	1985	Air India 747	Crashed in Atlantic Ocean off Ireland due to bomb	329
9	1980	Saudia Lockheed L-1011	Burned after emergency landing at Riyadh, Saudi Arabia	301
10	1988	Iran Air Airbus A300	Shot down by USS Vincennes over Persian Gulf	290

Sources: *World Almanac and Book of Facts 2005*; GlobalSecurity.org 2006a, 2006b.

Notess
1 Including those killed on the ground.
2 The aircraft involved was a special 560-seat version of the 747 designed for domestic travel in Japan.

hijacking airliners far from the Middle East to protest developments in that troubled region. In describing why the planes had been hijacked, George Habash, the PLFP's co-founder commented in a 2007 television program (*American Experience* 2007): "We said that the world does not understand or know about the Palestinian problem. This is how the idea of hijacking planes came about. Let the whole world know about the crisis that happened to us."

Yet while there are some similarities between the events of 1970 and 2001, their outcomes were very different. Four airplanes were blown up as cameras rolled, but none of the passengers was killed, though some (especially those passengers believed to be Jewish) were kept for as long as two weeks. The events of that September were a terrifying ordeal, but the hijackers were not prepared to kill innocent bystanders nor did they seek death for themselves. More sinister forms of air terrorism would burst upon the airborne world in the decades ahead.

Ultimately, the 747 and other very large jetliners had the ironic effect of making the world smaller: smaller for terrorists, smaller for tourists, smaller for business elites, smaller for exporters and importers of electronics, fresh seafood, and a host of goods traded by air. These jets shrank the world in two distinct ways. First, not only were these large aircraft; they were also long-range aircraft, especially versions developed in the 1980s. The 747-400 could fly more than 13,000 kilometers nonstop, meaning that it could link city-pairs such as Hong Kong and Chicago. At a different scale, the Airbus A300-600 could fly 7,500 kilometers nonstop and like the Boeing 767 brought the efficiency of the twin-engine wide-body to an increased number of city-pairs (including transatlantic) that might otherwise have required a connection en route. Second and more fundamentally, the efficiency of these big jets helped to make air transportation more affordable and thereby drew an increased variety and volume of traffic onto the world's skyways.

Those skyways are today dominated by planes produced by the two companies featured most prominently in this chapter – Boeing and Airbus. The competition between those two companies today, their product lines and production networks, and their futures are the subjects of the next chapter.

4 Space-makers and pace-setters

Boeing and Airbus

Foes: Boeing and Airbus

On October 24, 2003, the last commercial Concorde flight, British Airways flight 002 from New York-JFK, touched down at London-Heathrow (Parris 2003), evoking melancholic commentary from aviation enthusiasts who had seen it as a symbol of technological progress. Few are likely to notice or lament when other once great jetliners make their last flight in the next decade or so. In 2008, for instance, there were only five Lockheed L-1011s still flying, making it perhaps the most endangered airliner. Inevitably, Lockheed will join the ranks of de Havilland, Dassault, Vickers, and Convair as permanently grounded plane-makers. The last planes built by Douglas, Fokker, and Yakovlev will follow in a decade or two. Their demise will leave the skies still more firmly in the grasp of Boeing and Airbus. And so the title of this chapter refers to the fact that, more than ever before, it is these two plane-makers who shape the scope and speed of the airborne world.

Boeing and Airbus together accounted for 68 percent of the world jetliner fleet (Table 4.1) and a commanding 87 percent of the order backlog in 2008 (*Air Transport World* 2008c). Furthermore, because these two companies manufacture almost all new aircraft sold today with more than 100 seats, termed large civil aircraft (LCA) in the language of the industry, their share of actual air traffic is even higher than these figures indicate. This chapter tells the story of Boeing and Airbus – their families of airliners, their complex relationships with the national governments in their home countries, their partnerships with manufacturers of engines and other major aircraft components, and their competition – primarily with each other, but also with regional jet (RJ) manufacturers, and perhaps with new players based in China or some other part of the world.

Boeing and Airbus have very different origins but are rather similar today in many respects. Boeing first came to prominence as an airmail carrier, manufactured some innovative and important land planes and flying boats before World War II, and then defined and dominated the Jet Age. Airbus only got its start in the 1960s and introduced the world to the wide-body twinjet. Boeing has been a privately owned company throughout its history – although it has benefited from government largesse – while Airbus began as a consortium of government-backed and government-owned national aerospace champions.

Table 4.1 Jetliner[1] census, 2008

Manufacturer/ model	Operating	Orders	Manufacturer/ model	Operating	Orders
Boeing Total	8,427	3,542	Airbus Total	4,710	3,624
737	4,569	2,134	A320[2]	3,316	2,660
747	859	116	A330	524	366
767	843	48	A340	328	36
777	697	362	A350	0	369
787	0	882	A380	3	188
Other	1,459	0	Other	539	5
McDonnell Douglas	1,626	0	BAC/BAe/Avro	259	0
Lockheed	5	0	Fairchild Dornier	70	0
			Fokker	288	0
USA Total	**10,058**	**3,542**			
			W. Europe Total	**5,327**	**3,624**
Bombardier	1,377	185			
			Antonov	73	41
Canada Total	**1,377**	**185**	Ilyushin	319	27
			Tupolev	511	61
Embraer	1,261	509	Yakovlev	407	0
			Sukhoi	0	63
Brazil Total	**1,261**	**509**			
			Russia Total	**1,310**	**192**
AVIC	0	145			
China Total	**0**	**145**	**World Total**	**19,333**	**8,197**

Source: adapted from *Air Transport World* 2008c.

Notes

1 The focus of this chapter is on jet aircraft. However, it is worth noting that in 2008, the world's airlines operated about 5,500 turboprops and had 447 such aircraft on order. The small capacity and range of turboprops means that their actual significance in carrying passenger and cargo traffic is much smaller than their share of the world fleet.

2 Includes A318, A319, A320, A321.

Today, however, the rivals are not so different. In 2000, the four Airbus industry partners replaced the structure under which the consortium had grown since 1970 with a new, simpler business organization (Done 2000; Nisse and Discover 2001). The first step was the formation of the European Aerospace Defence and Space Company (EADS) through the year 2000 merger of the French, German, and Spanish pieces of the Airbus consortium. EADS, which owns Airbus and is also active in military aerospace and other defense systems as well as satellite technology, was born amid a spate of huge aerospace mergers at the end of the 1990s. Not long before launch of EADS, Aerospatiale had become Aerospatiale-Matra as the aerospace giant acquired a top French defense firm. Germany's piece in the EADS puzzle had become DaimlerChrysler Airbus, a company whose name alone portrayed the manner in which globalization slices through old industrial and political barriers. Meanwhile, Britain, whose commitment to Airbus was tepid from the beginning, no longer has a direct ownership stake in the company. British Aerospace (BAe) sold its stake in EADS in 2006, though the wings for all Airbus jetliners continue to be manufactured in the UK.

Unlike the old Airbus Industrie, the new Airbus has direct control over engineering and production as well. It also has a simpler management structure and a more transparent accounting system than the strange entity it has supplanted. The main headquarters of Airbus is now near Amsterdam's Schiphol Airport, and the company operates under Dutch law.

The new Airbus takes on a Boeing that has also been transformed in the past decade. Boeing's 1997 merger with McDonnell Douglas and its longer-term diversification away from airplane manufacturing have yielded a gigantic, complex company with expertise in defense, finance, and satellite technology among other fields. It was partly to reflect Boeing's breadth that the company moved its corporate headquarters from Seattle to Chicago. At the beginning of this century, Boeing earned less than 50 percent of its revenue from commercial aircraft, and that segment of its business is less profitable than the others (Fingleton 2005). Chicago also distances the firm from its highly unionized Seattle workforce, gives Boeing access to higher order business services, and strengthens the global accessibility of its headquarters (Bowe 2002). Indeed, both of the plane-builders have moved their headquarters to places with superior air accessibility

Thus, both Airbus and Boeing are now parts of larger corporations with deep stakes in other industries. Although their plane-making operations are concentrated in a handful of cities (Hamburg and Toulouse for Airbus, Seattle for Boeing), each is the focal firm in a complex global production network (Figure 4.1). Both are technologically innovative and fierce marketers, producing a wide range of airliners that continue to push down the real cost of air travel while making it steadily safer. Over the past decade, they have rarely been far from parity in terms of the number of airliners sold each year.

Families: Boeing, Airbus, and their airliners

Airbus and Boeing are also near parity in terms of the breadth and composition of their airliner family. In 2008, the Airbus product line (counting only aircraft that were for sale at the time) included, from smallest to largest, the A320, the A330, the new "extra wide-body" A350XWB twinjet, the A340, and the mammoth new A380 (Figure 4.2). Boeing's product line was broadly similar (Figure 4.3). Yet these handfuls of basic aircraft types belie the great variety of airliners actually produced by each manufacturer. Boeing offered four different basic models of the 737, for instance, with typical two-class seating capacities ranging from 110 to 180 passengers.[1] In total, Boeing's airliner product line comprised at least 16 different passenger airliners and 5 different freighters models with unique capacity and range combinations, while for Airbus the numbers were 14 and 2, respectively.

Aircraft drawn from a manufacturer's family have important commonalities that reduce costs both for the manufacturer and the airline (and indirectly for the passenger and air freight shipper). For the manufacturer, building a family creates new opportunities for attaining economies of scale and moving down the learning curve. For example, while developing the A320 in the 1980s, Airbus Industrie invested considerable sums in "fly-by-wire" technology – a system via which an aircraft's flaps, rudder, and other moving surfaces are controlled electronically rather than through mechanical and hydraulic systems linked to the yokes, pedals, and levers.[2] It later passed on the same technology to other airliners in the Airbus family (Tyson 1992: 163–5). For the carrier, the costs of training pilots, cabin crew, engineers, and mechanics on a new aircraft are lower as is the expense of maintaining spare parts if other aircraft from the same family are already in a carrier's fleet.

By the time the wide-body jets launched in the 1960s first flew, Boeing had already established an impressive aircraft product line, but all Airbus had was its A300. So the European consortium has expanded its product line dramatically over the past 30 years. Of course, Boeing did not stand still. Such is the cut-and-parry between the two plane-builders that a new product by one is often one-upped by a new offering from the other (Figure 4.4). In the first decade of this century, for instance, Airbus committed to the A380 and in 2004 Boeing sold its first 787. The cut-and-parry was on again. Airbus has taken on the 787 with the similar, though slightly larger, A350; and Boeing tried to weaken the competitive advantage of the A380 with an enlarged version of the 747.[3]

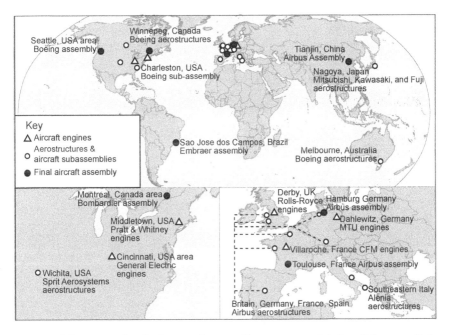

Figure 4.1 Important sites in the manufacture of large commercial aircraft (sources: Relevant manufacturer websites).

Note that sites associated with Russian and Chinese airliners are not shown, partly because they are not currently as important as the aircraft manufactured by firms based in the US, Canada, Brazil, and Western Europe.

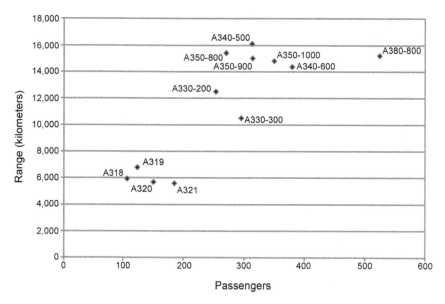

Figure 4.2 Airbus product line (source: Airbus 2009a).

Each symbol represents a major aircraft model (such as the Airbus A321) that was for sale by the manufacturer in mid-2009.

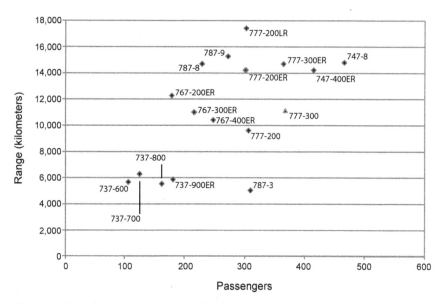

Figure 4.3 Boeing product line (source: Boeing Company 2009a).

Each symbol represents a major aircraft model (such as the Boeing 737-700) that was for sale by the manufacturer in mid-2009.

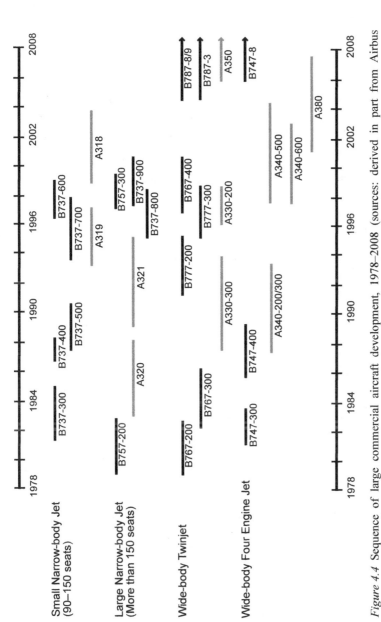

Figure 4.4 Sequence of large commercial aircraft development, 1978–2008 (sources: derived in part from Airbus (2009a); Airbus (2009b); Boeing Company (2009a); Boeing Company (2009b)).

Each line segment shows the interval between the formal launch of a new airliner and its commercial debut. For example, the Airbus A380 was formally given the go-ahead by the Airbus supervisory board in December 2000, and the airliner entered into service with Singapore Airlines in October 2007.

Despite the proliferation of Boeing and Airbus airliners, there are certain clear trends evident in commercial aircraft development over the past thirty or so years. First is the trend towards longer nonstop ranges, a trend that dates to the earliest years of aviation. There are now several airliners that can fly at least 15,000 kilometers nonstop – enough to connect almost any two cities on the planet – and in 2008 there were a handful of scheduled airline flights of more than 16 hours nonstop duration (Table 4.2). Yet the range of most airliners, not just the ultra-long-range ones, has been extended. The first 737 (introduced in 1968) had a range of fewer than 4,000 kilometers; the 737 Next Generation series has a typical range of about 6,000 kilometers, enough to operate many transcontinental routes in the US. The increased range of airliners, large and small, during the past few decades has facilitated the proliferation of so-called pencil routes (long, relatively thinly traveled routes such as Copenhagen–Atlanta) and has perpetuated the long-term trend towards fewer stops on air journeys (Figure 4.5).

Second and perhaps somewhat surprisingly, airliners are not any faster than those of the early Jet Age. Lower cruising speeds save fuel and as fuel prices have generally trended higher the appeal of faster jetliners has waned (Morrison 1984). Interestingly, the high fuel consumption of very fast aircraft was a key reason for airline disinterest in the Sonic Cruiser, an innovative airliner offered by Boeing between 2001 and 2003. Airlines showed little appetite for the Sonic Cruiser, which would have cruised at Mach 0.98. Boeing was left to wonder about the "value of speed" (Norris 2003), and in 2003 the plane was quietly dropped. In its place, Boeing began development of a new super-efficient airliner known provisionally as the 7E7 but now called the 787 whose cruising speed is Mach 0.85. Describing the change in plans, one writer put it this way: "If Boeing's Sonic Cruiser was meant to be the Lamborghini of commercial jets, the 7E7 is more like the Honda Civic. Its key selling points are fuel efficiency and low operating costs." (Talbot 2003: 40).

Third, new airliners have become enormously expensive, as airlines have traded higher acquisition costs for lower operating costs (Morrison 1984). The escalation of development costs (Table 4.3) has several basic causes: the greater and more complex knowledge embodied in commercial aircraft, the multiplication of interlocking systems (including in-flight entertainment systems on the most recent generation of airliners), and the industry's understandably obsessive concern with safety (McIntyre 1992: 132).

Fourth, the twinjet has become the dominant airliner form; in 2008, 85 percent of all jetliners flying and 95 percent of jets on order were twinjets (*Air Transport World* 2008c). The success of the twinjet should be no great surprise: early in the history of air travel, airplanes such as the Douglas DC-3 had demonstrated the inherent efficiency of the two-engine configuration. However, the contemporary popularity of the twinjet required both more powerful engines (see Table 2.4) and a significant change in policy. In the 1970s, American policy required that an alternate airport, to which the airplane could be diverted in the event of an engine failure, be no more than 60 minutes away from any point

Table 4.2 Ultra long-range nonstop routes, 2008

From[1]	To[1]	Airline	Aircraft[2]	Flying time	Distance(km)
Singapore	Newark	Singapore	A345	19:00	15,239
Los Angeles	Singapore	Singapore	A345	17:30	14,096
Los Angeles	Bangkok	Thai Int'l	A345	17:30	13,275
New York	Bangkok	Thai Int'l	A345	17:35	13,916
Dubai	Houston	Emirates	B772	16:20	13,116
Vancouver	Sydney	Air Canada	B772	16:00	12,493
New York	Hong Kong	Cathay Pacific	B773	15:55	12,965
Mumbai	New York	Air India	B772	15:55	12,525
Newark	Hong Kong	Continental	B772	15:50	12,955
Mumbai	New York	Delta	B772	15:50	12,525
Atlanta	Shanghai	Delta	B772	15:40	12,299
Tel Aviv	Los Angeles	El Al	B772	15:30	12,162
Washington	Johannesburg	South African	A346	15:25	13,086
Chicago	Hong Kong	United	B744	15:25	12,519
Toronto	Hong Kong	Air Canada	B772/B773	15:15	12,545
Los Angeles	Melbourne	Qantas	B744	15:15	12,751
Dubai	Atlanta	Delta	B772	15:05	12,202
Vancouver	Sydney	Air Canada	B772	15:00	12,493

Source: author's analysis of data in OAG 2008.

Notes
1 Each of the routes is also flown nonstop in the opposite direction. The direction shown above is the one for which the flying time is longer. For instance, the flying time from Newark to Singapore aboard Singapore Airlines A345 is 18:50.
2 A345 = Airbus A340-500; A346 = Airbus A340-600; B772 = Boeing 777-200ER/LR; B773 = Boeing 777-300/ER; B744 = Boeing 747-400.

along a route flow by a twinjet (Serling 1992: 403). The 60-minute rule dated from the piston-engine era, a time when the four-engine Lockheed Constellation was nicknamed "the most reliable three-engine airplane flying" given its engines' propensity to fail. However, jet engines proved to be about twenty times more dependable in service; and in 1985, partly due to lobbying by Boeing, the US Federal Aviation Administration (FAA) and its European counterpart, the Joint Airworthiness Authorities (JAA), formally agreed to new rules, permitting 120 minute Extended Twin-engine Operations or ETOPS[4] provided certain conditions were met by the airplane and the operating airline. About a decade later, the 777 not only became the first airliner to have FAA ETOPS approval upon its entry into service but was certified for 180 minute ETOPS, opening up the possibility of nonstop twinjet service over the Pacific, too.

But it is over the Atlantic that ETOPS has most helped to fragment intercontinental travel among more city-pairs (Figure 4.6). In 2008, there were 272 city-pairs from the US and Canada to destinations on the other side of the Atlantic (in Europe, Africa, the Middle East, and South Asia) by nonstop scheduled passenger flights, with wide-body twinjets such as the 767 accounting for about 65 percent of departures. Across the Pacific, conversely, the 747 was still the single most important airplane, accounting for 41 percent of transpacific flights but its

Table 4.3 Development costs for selected airliners

Aircraft	Year of first service	Development costs constant 2008 dollars[1]
Douglas DC-3	1936	3,800,000
Douglas DC-6	1947	123,000,000
Boeing 707	1958	1,100,000,000
Boeing 747[2]	1970	4,440,000,000
Boeing 777	1995	5,310,000,000
Airbus A380	2007	17,900,000,000

Sources: Miller and Sawers 1970; Newhouse 1982: 115; *Economist* 1994; Done 2007.

Notes
1 Costs converted to 2008 dollars using information available from S. Williamson (2008).
2 As noted in Chapter 3, it is estimated that the 747 may have cost Boeing as much as $2 billion in current dollars to develop. The inflation-adjusted figure shown above is based on a more conservative estimate of $1 billion in current dollars.

importance is declining. Already, the 777 has facilitated the opening up of some ETOPS routes such as Shanghai–Atlanta, Seoul–Dallas, and Guangzhou–Los Angeles. Will transpacific travel remain concentrated or will it fragment as happened over the Atlantic? The answer will have far-reaching implications.

Before leaving the subject of ETOPS, it is worth pausing to elaborate upon the long-term trend towards increased air safety that has made such flights not only feasible but widely accepted by the traveling public. As has been oft-noted, aviation is extraordinarily safe (Table 4.4). In the 1990s, for example, approximately 8,000 people were killed while passengers on scheduled airline services, meaning that about one out of every 1.6 million airline passengers died during the decade[5] (*ICAO Journal*, various issues), and the death rate for the first decade of the twenty-first century is on pace to be less than half that of the 1990s. Of course, aviation safety today is spatially uneven. In the 1990s, 72 percent of the people who died in commercial airplane crashes worldwide were aboard airlines registered in developing countries – despite the fact that airline traffic is strongly concentrated on carriers from wealthy countries. Old aircraft and poor maintenance by financially distressed carriers go far to explain the markedly higher accident rate in the developing world (Bisignani 2006). Yet even in the poorest countries, aviation is generally safer than alternative modes; and Boeing, Airbus, and the other manufacturers discussed in this chapter are partly responsible.

Table 4.4 Fatality rate for major passenger transportation modes in the US, 2004

Mode	Passenger-kilometers (Billions)	Fatalities	Fatalities per billion passenger-kilometers
Highway	7,795	36,702	4.71
Urban public transit	79	219	2.77
Intercity rail	9	3	0.34
Certificated air carriers	898	14	0.02

Source: derived from data in BTS 2007.

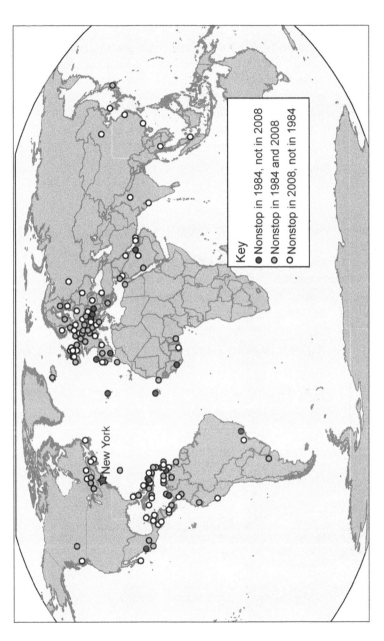

Figure 4.5 Cities connected by nonstop services to New York City (sources: OAG 1984a, 1984b, 2008).

Between 1984 and 2008, the number of foreign cities served nonstop from the New York City area (i.e. via JFK International or Newark Liberty International) more than doubled, due to a combination of liberalization, air traffic growth, and the increased range of commercial aircraft.

Friends: the plane-builders and their suppliers

The 777 has been described as "four million parts all moving in close formation" (Anderson 2002: 353); other airliners incorporate a similarly dazzling number of parts. Boeing and Airbus actually manufacture few of those parts – though at least until recently, they made many of the most technologically demanding and critical structures. Hundreds of different suppliers make most of the components. The most important suppliers by far are the engine manufacturers, but other major component manufacturers matter, and they matter more than ever before. It is worth briefly examining these companies, their geographies, and their evolving relationships with Boeing and Airbus.

Transatlantic
272 city-pairs

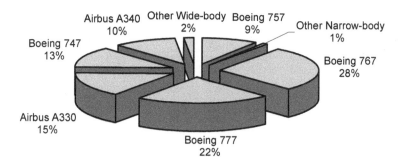

Transpacific
85 city-pairs

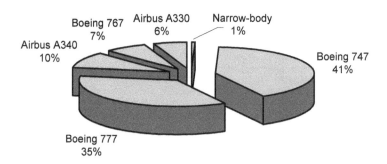

Figure 4.6 Aircraft used on transatlantic and transpacific routes (sources: author's analysis of data in OAG 2008).

Each graph shows the share of weekly frequencies for passenger flights accounted for by aircraft types on routes from Canada and the USA to points across the Atlantic and across the Pacific. The number of transpacific city-pairs excludes six links between Honolulu and cities in the mid-Pacific (e.g. Nadi, Fiji).

At the beginning of aviation's second century, the LCA engine business is split (Figure 4.7). A pair of international consortiums dominates the narrow-body engine market, and a pair of industrial giants controls most of the wide-body engine market. Overall, the two biggest players are General Electric and Rolls-Royce, but the company that made most of the engines at the beginning of the Jet Age, Pratt & Whitney, is still a significant, albeit fading force in the industry. The head of United Technologies, Pratt & Whitney's parent corporation, has described the LCA engine business as "uninvestable" because the combination of massive development costs and pricing at or below cost make profitability elusive (Michaels *et al.* 2005). So Pratt has retreated from independently developing new LCA engines. However, Pratt is part of one of the two consortiums that manufacture engines for narrow-body jets; and via another alliance, Pratt has a stake in engines that power the biggest of all airliners, the A380.

Pratt's old rivals, GE and Rolls-Royce, are also integrated into several different consortia. GE's newest engine, the GEnx, is the product of a consortium linking GE (which owns 64 percent of the project) with five companies from Japan, Italy, and Sweden (Ranson 2005). The GEnx is one of two choices available to airlines for the 787. Boeing expects the new, lighter-weight engines to contribute as much as 8 percent of the 787's predicted 20 percent gain in efficiency over earlier, similar-sized airliners (Harvey 2006). GE's main rival for engines on the 787 is the Rolls-Royce Trent 1000, whose manufacturer also makes claims of great leaps in efficiency and environmental sustainability. Rolls-Royce also manufactures the only engine that was available for customers of the A350 at the time this book was written.[6] Interestingly, both GE and Rolls-Royce, while highly internationalized and technologically innovative, continue to have their main operations in old industrial areas of the US and England, respectively (see Figure 4.1).

While Rolls and GE carve up most of the wide-body jetliner market, both companies (and Pratt) are involved in two consortiums dominating the other end of the business. The larger of the two, in terms of market share, is Commercial Fan Moteur (CFM). CFM was formed in 1971 as 50/50 joint venture between GE and the French state-owned engine manufacturer SNECMA. Its product, the CFM 56, has been very popular on narrow-body aircraft, powering about 60 percent of A320 series aircraft and all Next Generation 737s. For both partners, the alliance was meant to increase their share of the civil aircraft market at a time when Pratt was still overwhelmingly dominant. For GE, more specifically, its partnership with a French firm was meant to burnish its bona fides as it attempted to get its engines on Airbus jets (*Economist* 2007b). In both respects, CFM has been very successful. The actual operational arrangement between GE and the now privatized SNECMA is straightforward: the former makes the engine core and the latter makes the fan and low-pressure turbine.

The other international engine consortium was formed in 1982 in response to CFM's success. International Aero Engines combines the resources of Pratt & Whitney, Rolls-Royce, the German manufacturer MTU, and an alliance of three

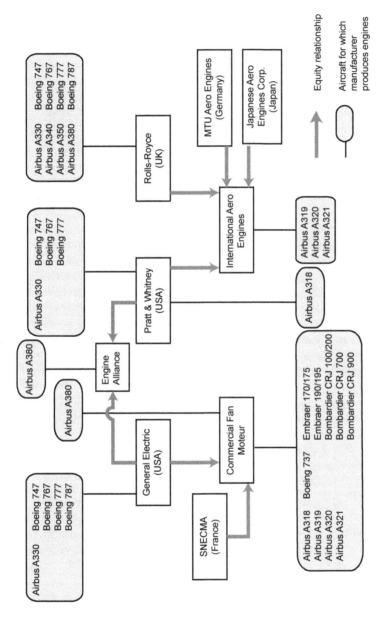

Figure 4.7 Major jetliner engine manufacturers (sources: relevant manufacturer websites).

The middle of the diagram shows the companies involved in the manufacture of engines for most commercial jets in production today. Arrayed along the top and bottom of the diagram are the names of the specific wide-body models and narrow-body models, respectively, for which each manufacturer or consortium provides engines. For most aircraft, there is a choice of engines.

Japanese companies (Thornton 1995: 117). The crisscross pattern of alliances in the LCA engine industry is testament not only to the huge development costs and risks involved but also to the politicization of the industry. The airline industry, despite decades of deregulation and privatization, remains strongly influenced by national governments across the world and, for an engine-maker, flying the flag of more than one country helps to win business.

The same mixture of marketing and financial considerations helps to explain the increased dependence of Boeing and Airbus upon tier-one suppliers for airframe structures themselves – not just the engines. For every airliner there is a long supply chain reaching around the world and fed by myriad manufacturers of components large and small. The evolution of the plane-makers' dependence on such suppliers, especially foreign suppliers, can best be seen in the progression from the 767 to the 787. Launched together with the 757, the more technically demanding 767 put an enormous financial burden on Boeing (Newhouse 1982: 20). To ease that burden, the plane-maker for the first time outsourced a large share of an airplane to foreign manufacturers, specifically the Italian firm Aeritalia (which was later folded into a company called Alenia) and a consortium of Japanese companies called the Japan Aircraft Development Corporation (JADC). JADC combined several of the giants of Japanese industry: Mitsubishi, Kawasaki, and Fuji. Aeritalia and JADC each manufactured about 15 percent of the 767, working mainly on its fuselage (Rodgers 1996: 349). The choice of partners was significant. Italy was the largest European economy not directly involved in Airbus Industrie; and Japan had become, by the late 1970s, the world's second largest economy, an economy already noted for its excellence in precision manufacturing. Japan's importance as a market for Boeing was a relevant consideration too.

For the 777, launched in 1990, Boeing's dependence on foreign suppliers increased. The Japanese share of the airframe, in particular, climbed to 21 percent (Bowermaster 2005) but was still limited mainly to the fuselage. Other parts sourced abroad included wing flaps from Italy, ailerons from Spain, and landing gear doors from Singapore (McMillin 2003). Nevertheless, Boeing designed the airplane, including most of its smallest details, and retained control over the key technologies in the airframe. Moreover, Boeing manufactured the wing of the 777 largely on its own (Pritchard and MacPherson 2004).

For the 787, on the other hand, Boeing has taken the role of systems integrator as it spreads design, manufacturing, and financial risk across its global network of suppliers (Pritchard and MacPherson 2004; *Economist* 2005a). Most importantly, Mitsubishi Heavy Industries (MHI) manufactures the main structures in the wings, making the Dreamliner the first Boeing "to fly on foreign wings" (Fingleton 2005, quoted in Pritchard and MacPherson 2005). Because the wing is the most technologically demanding part of an airframe, its outsourcing to a Japanese manufacturer has been met by fierce criticism. And MHI is only the most important among a constellation of Japanese firms involved in the 787 (Gates 2005). Kawasaki Heavy Industries (KHI) builds a section of the fuselage forward of the wing and the wing's trailing edge. Fuji Heavy Industries

(FHI) has responsibility for the center wing box, the part of the lower lobe of the fuselage to which the wings are attached and within which the landing gear are housed. These same "heavies" were also involved in the 767 and 777; but their role in design, manufacturing, and development financing is substantially broader on the 787. With respect to design, for instance, on the previous airliners, the Japanese were engaged in a "build to print" relationship with Boeing whereas they now have responsibility for design specifications (Pritchard and MacPherson 2005: 5; Duvall and Bartholomew 2007). Moreover, the very large Japanese role in the 787 does not stop with the "heavies" (Pritchard and MacPherson 2005: 8, 10). Two other Japanese firms are first-tier suppliers and many more are second- and third-tier suppliers. In total, Japan's share of the Dreamliner fuselage is about 35 percent (Bowermaster 2005).

The Dreamliner, therefore, represents a big step towards the realization of Japan's dream of developing an industry capable of independently designing and manufacturing airliners (Pritchard and MacPherson 2005: 4, 11). During World War II, one of Japan's few military advantages had been in naval aviation (including the Mitsubishi A6M Zero). Defeat in the war and the subsequent American occupation of Japan cast the Japanese aircraft industry into decades of technological inferiority, especially after Britain, the Soviet Union, the US, and France led the world into the Jet Age. West Germany had faced problems similar to those of Japan and found a way out through the creation of Airbus Industrie, for which it provided a disproportionate share of the crucial early launch aid. For Japan, conversely, the way out of the shadows has come through its role as a subcontractor, especially to Boeing. This is an ironic development, for Boeing-built bombers contributed enormously to the American victory in the war. A Boeing B-29, the *Enola Gay*, dropped the atomic bomb on Hiroshima. Now, more than 60 years later, a very different airplane has brought the two countries closer together.

Japan is only the most important of at least eleven countries in which first-tier suppliers for the 787 program are located (Figure 4.8). So dispersed is the production of the jet that one industry trade journal deemed the 787 the "flat-earth airplane," referring to Thomas Friedman's conception of globalization in *The World Is Flat* (Mecham 2006). That is, the Dreamliner is the product of a horizontally organized production network in which design and manufacturing spill over national boundaries and are linked by sophisticated information technology systems. Because Dreamliner program suppliers will do so much of the work, final assembly is expected to take as few as three days (Gates 2005) and employ just 1,000 people in same Everett, Washington complex that assembles the 747, 767, and 777 (Gates 2003).[7]

Interestingly Boeing investigated the prospect of moving final assembly to a different, lower cost location in the US spurring the State of Washington to extraordinary lengths. It provided tax breaks worth $3.2 billion over 20 years to any company manufacturing a "250-seater, economical aircraft" in Washington (*Economist* 2005a). In the end, the Seattle area's advantages,[8] augmented by the state's new tax incentives, kept the 787 in Washington.

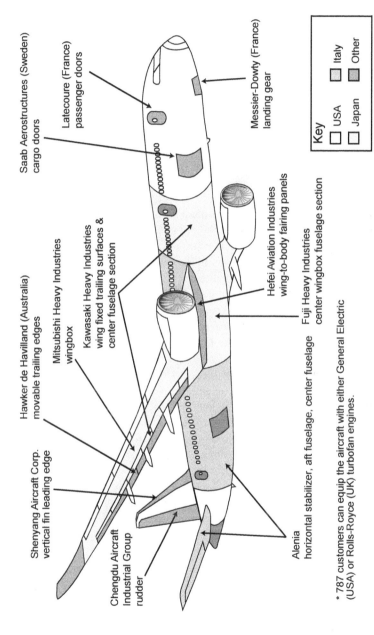

Saab Aerostructures (Sweden) cargo doors

Latecoure (France) passenger doors

Messier-Dowty (France) landing gear

Hawker de Havilland (Australia) movable trailing edges

Mitsubishi Heavy Industries wingbox

Kawasaki Heavy Industries wing fixed trailing surfaces & center fuselage section

Hefei Aviation Industries wing-to-body fairing panels

Fuji Heavy Industries center wingbox fuselage section

Shenyang Aircraft Corp. vertical fin leading edge

Chengdu Aircraft Industrial Group rudder

Alenia horizontal stabilizer, aft fuselage, center fuselage

Key

☐ USA   ☐ Italy
☐ Japan   ☐ Other

* 787 customers can equip the aircraft with either General Electric (USA) or Rolls-Royce (UK) turbofan engines.

Figure 4.8 Boeing 787 Dreamliner components by national origin (sources: adapted from Gates 2005 with additional information from Boeing Company 2007b).

The foreign content of the Boeing 787 is unprecedented, with the Japanese contribution being particularly significant. Many of the plane's interior elements (e.g. its in-flight entertainment system) not shown in the diagram are also foreign in origin.

Meanwhile, the politicization of Airbus operations has prevented the plane-builder from outsourcing and internationalizing its production to the same degree as Boeing (*Economist* 2006f). That is changing, however. For the same reasons that have motivated Boeing – tapping foreign talent, lowering production costs, winning overseas sales – Airbus will outsource a significant share of the A350 (approximately 5 percent to China and 3 percent to Russia) and in 2009 began assembling A320s at a jointly owned plant in Tianjin, China – the first Airbus assembly line outside Europe.

Favorites: government subsidies and the plane-builders

The aircraft industry generally, and not just Airbus, has been showered with gifts in the form of protectionist policies, contracts from captive military and civilian clients, government-funded technology, and the like. In the early decades of aviation history, favoritism towards plane-makers was justified because aircraft manufacturing was an infant industry that needed nurturing and because civilian aircraft often had cross-over significance in national defense. Today, favoritism is more likely to be justified by the high-paying jobs the industry creates and its position along the technological frontier. Further, the aircraft industry is a major source of export earnings, a particularly important concern in the US. In fact, Boeing's plane-making operations have made the Seattle area the top exporting metropolitan region in the US (Paulson 1999).

Airbus and Boeing both have benefited enormously from government support; but over the past quarter century, an increasingly acrimonious transatlantic dispute has arisen between the US and the European Union (EU) over subsidies to the aircraft industry. It has been an odd conflict, with both sides often mired in hypocrisy. The American government has contended that the massive state aid provided to Airbus is unfair and fundamentally at odds with the principles of free trade. And yet, the American champion in this fight, Boeing, has been assisted for decades by its own massive, albeit less direct government help. For its part, Airbus alleges that US aid to foreign governments has biased aircraft purchases by those governments' flag carriers – which is true, of course, but European governments have proven adept at the same game.

Although LCA subsidies had been a cause of disagreement between the two sides since at least the 1970s, the conflict became more serious in the early 1980s. Sales of the A300 and A310 ate into the market share of the big American trijets, and European consortium launched three aircraft programs (A320, A330, and A340) during a decade in which no entirely new American airliner was launched.[9] So in the early 1990s the US pushed hard against subsidies at the same time that the market success and maturation of Airbus made the Europeans amenable to reform. The result was the 1992 US–European Community Bilateral Agreement, which limited the government share of Airbus launch costs to 33 percent and forbid even that amount unless there was a reasonable expectation that the aid would be repaid within 17 years (Tyson 1992: 207–10). The agreement also set the interest rate that would be applied to launch aid for Airbus, specified the manner in which Airbus would repay government aid, and called for transparency in accounts of government aid.

The 1992 agreement provided the rulebook for the LCA industry for more than a decade; but in 2004 the disagreement over subsidies erupted yet again. The trigger for the new round of charges and countercharges was the launch of the A350. Lacking the munificent support given Airbus, Boeing has launched just two airliner programs in the past twenty-five years (the 777 and 787). In the same period, Airbus introduced five (the A320, the A330, the A340, the A380, and the A350). The American position was that the 1992 agreement was to have been only a starting point for the further reduction in Airbus subsidies. The pre-amble of the agreement had included a vague statement pointing in that direction; but the specifics referred only to the fixed levels described above. From the American perspective, the Europeans institutionalized those levels, with no reduction in government support in the offing.

In October 2004, the US unilaterally terminated the 1992 agreement, and in May 2005 referred the dispute the World Trade Organization (WTO). If the WTO rules in favor of the US in its suit against the European plane-maker and the Airbus-backers fail to make the necessary amends, the US could be author-ized by the WTO to levy countervailing duties against Airbus aircraft purchased by American carriers and perhaps even punitive duties against other American imports from the four European countries concerned (*Economist* 2005a). In response to the US action, the European Union (EU) countered with a suit of its own against the subsidies that it claims Boeing receives. The latter subsidies are more complex than those given to Airbus and illustrate why it will be so difficult to extricate the commercial aircraft industry from its dependence upon govern-ment aid. Airbus alleges that Boeing has received $23 billion in subsidies to research and development since 1992, including research by the National Aero-nautics and Space Administration (NASA) on composite materials, for instance.

More intractable are the subsidies that Boeing receives directly or indirectly from local and state governments in the US and from foreign governments. Like major manufacturers in other industries (e.g., the automobile industry), Boeing has adeptly played different states and municipalities against one another to win tax concessions in return for the high-paying jobs that the plane-maker has at its disposal. Airbus points in particular to the $2.6 billion in tax breaks that Boeing has received from the city of Wichita to keep its fuselage manufacturing opera-tions there (*Economist* 2005a).[10] Boeing's dependence on foreign subcontractors is even more problematic. Trade experts David Pritchard and Alan MacPherson at the University of Buffalo estimated that the Japanese government would provide $1.6 billion in subsidies to the 787 in the form of both grants (30 percent) and repayable loans (70 percent) (Pritchard and MacPherson 2005: 9). Ironically, the loans from the Japanese government have generous repayment terms similar to those applying to the repayment of European aid to Airbus.

As the production networks of Boeing and, to a lesser extent, Airbus, become ever-more internationalized, the difficulty of resolving the subsidies issue is likely to grow. With manufacturers from nearly a dozen countries involved in the 787 production network as first-tier suppliers and the number connected to Airbus expected to rise, it is less likely that a bilateral solution like that signed in 1992 will defuse the current crisis over subsidies to the aircraft industry. More-over, the greater tolerance and even eagerness for government intervention in the economy because of the 2008–9 global financial crisis further weakens the prob-ability that the LCA industry will be free of the subsidies issue soon.[11]

The ultimate beneficiaries of government intervention in the industry have been passengers and air freight shippers. For there is a case to be made that, given the massive returns to scale in the industry, there would by now be only one large commercial aircraft manufacturer left standing in the absence of government inter-vention. But governments have intervened, especially in Europe; and both Airbus and Boeing have survived and even thrived. Their fierce competition with one another has helped the airline industry and its customers in two ways. First, the aircraft manufacturers have been compelled to develop more kinds of jetliners more rapidly than would otherwise have been the case (Tyson 1992: 166). Second, the high level of competition in the aircraft industry has created a buyer's market. And in that sense the relentless struggle between Boeing and Airbus has redounded to the benefit of the broader airborne world. By one reckoning, the cost of com-mercial jets is 40 percent lower than they would be if government-backed Airbus were not in the market (*Economist* 2005a).

Futures: the superjumbo and the super efficient

While American and Europeans lob charges back and forth assailing each other's intervention in the LCA market, both believe that the overall market is poised for rapid growth in the early decades of the twenty-first century. Boeing's 2008 *Current Market Outlook* predicted that between 2008 and 2027, an estimated 29,400 new large commercial jet planes, worth $3.2 trillion, will be delivered (Boeing Company 2008a). Airbus has its own similarly bright forecast (Airbus 2007).

Although they share an optimistic outlook for the business in general, Airbus and Boeing differ in the predicted geography of future air travel and the correspond-ing makeup of new jetliner sales (Mecham 2005a). Airbus envisions a future domi-nated by travel between very large cities. The company notes that the number of so-called megacities (i.e., metropolitan areas with more than 10 million people) will swell from just four when the Boeing 747 was introduced to 24 by 2015. The growing number of such cities (and of more modest sized metro areas, too) augurs well for travel via very large aircraft, or so Airbus argues. So too do increased con-cerns about the environmental costs of air transportation and congestion on highly trafficked routes. Thus, Airbus began the twenty-first century by launching the largest ever Western jetliner. Boeing on the other hand believes the future lies in fragmentation, perpetuating the trend discussed earlier in this chapter (e.g., the dis-placement of the 747 by aircraft such as the 767 over the Atlantic). And it has an aircraft to suit such a future – the ultra-long-range, mid-sized twinjet 787. Because they are premised on such different visions of the future of the airborne world, it is worth examining more carefully the development of these two aircraft (Table 4.5).

Table 4.5 Significant turn-of-the-century airliners

	Airbus A320	Boeing 777	Canadair CRJ	Airbus A380	Boeing 787
Length (m)	38	64	27	73	57
Wingspan (m)	34	61	21	80	60
Engine number and type	2 turbofan	2 turbofan	2 turbofan	4 turbofan	2 turbofan
Total takeoff power (lb s.t.)[1]	50,000	186,000	18,500	280,000	140,000
Typical passenger load	150	301	50	525	225
Cruising speed (kph)	875	895	785	950	905
Normal maximum range (km)	5,560	14,260	1,815	15,195	15,000
Date of first airline service	April 1988	June 1995	November 1992	October 2007	TBD[2]
First passenger airline	Air France	United	Lufthansa CityLine	Singapore	ANA
First passenger route	Paris–Frankfurt	Washington–London	Cologne–Barcelona	Singapore–Sydney	TBD[2]

Sources: Segal 1995; *Aviation Week & Space Technology* 1988; Airliners.net 2008.

Notes
1 lb.s.t. = pounds of static thrust.
2 To be determined.

The A380 Superjumbo

The A380, like other significant jetliners before it, was meant to fill a hole in the market. In the early 1990s, both Airbus and Boeing began exploring the feasibility of what the industry called an ultra high capacity aircraft (UHCA) and what people outside the industry nicknamed the Superjumbo (Lynn 1997: 204–9). For Airbus, specifically, the Superjumbo was appealing because it would trap the then-uncontested 747 in a "pincer movement," eating into the 747's sales with the A330 and A340 on one side and with the new Superjumbo on the other. In 1996, therefore, Airbus embarked on what it provisionally called the A3XX, the double X suggesting the extra, extra large size of what was to come. Airbus considered a variety of designs but ultimately settled on a relatively lightweight design featuring a three-deck fuselage, though the plane is nevertheless the heaviest jetliner ever built. The design reflects a balance among several objectives: to provide ample space for more than 500 passengers in a three-class configuration, to lower the direct operating costs per seat to at least 15 percent below those of the 747-400, and to require as few changes to existing airport infrastructure as feasible. The result was a kind of skyscraper approach in which the airliner minimizes its footprint on airport tarmacs by building up. In passenger versions, the plane has two full decks (main deck and upper deck) of twin-aisle seating atop the usual lower deck for cargo and baggage.

Although the A380 is by far the largest airplane ever built by Airbus, the basic geography of its production carries on the seemingly unwieldy spatial division of labor established for previous models (Pae 2005; Bowie 2005). The case of the wings is particularly striking (Pae 2005). The wings are put together at Airbus' Broughton, Wales wing assembly plant, with much of the work done by robotic riveters to limit the use of expensive labor and to attain higher precision in crafting the most aerodynamically refined shape possible. Stuffed with fuel flow systems, hydraulics, and electrical wiring, the partially finished wings are then sent on a purpose-built 96-wheel trailer to a port about 20 kilometers from the wing assembly plant. There they are loaded, along with fuselage components that have been delivered from Germany via the A300-600ST *Beluga* (the jet-powered successor to the *Super Guppy* mentioned in Chapter 3), on another customized vehicle – this time a modified car-carrying ship built in China. From Wales, the ship travels south to the Bay of Biscay and then into the mouth of the Garonne River, upon the banks of which lie Toulouse, hundreds of kilometers upstream. To get there, the A380 components are transferred to a river barge at a port near Bordeaux. Finally, a convoy of three tractor-trailer trucks completes the final 245 kilometers of the journey. Through medieval villages and over Airbus-built bypasses, the nighttime convoy moves at 16 kilometers per hour through intersections closed by the police. Fortunately for Airbus, the initial rate of A380 production is low enough to require this logistical obstacle course just twice a month.

Airbus has at least two important reasons to continue assembling wings in Wales rather than closer to Toulouse. First, the British expertise in Airbus, and in the global aircraft industry more generally, has long been wing design and manufacturing. Second, keeping wing manufacturing in Wales gives Britain a very compelling reason to continue supporting Airbus politically and financially. Germany has wanted to move into wing production for years and reiterated its demands after BAe sold its share of Airbus (Evans-Pritchard 2007), but to date, Airbus has rejected Germany's requests in favor of maintaining the British "center of excellence" (Butterworth-Hayes 2006b). Keeping wing production in Britain was a principal justification for the $530 million in British launch aid to the A380 project (Barrie 2005). Beyond the issue of government subsidies, developing a new wing facility from scratch elsewhere could cost Airbus $500 million so a certain industrial inertia makes it likely that at least the next few Airbus airliners will fly on British wings. Yet the anticipated shift to all-composite wings, which the British factory has not yet done, may provide an opening for a new facility elsewhere to pry the wings away from Wales.

Although the dispersed production of Airbus has created logistical headaches, the biggest nightmare for the A380 came from its dispersed design. Like every large airliner since the 777, the A380 was the designed mainly on computer. Engineers used computer-aided design (CAD) software called Catia to draw the airplane's components, test their performance, and model how they would fit together. A separate system was used to disseminate drawings and other specification among the thousands of engineers, technicians, and other professionals working on the project at Airbus, its suppliers, and subcontractors. When they work well, such systems can save time and money; but in the case of the A380, the "paperless airplane" proved very costly (Duvall and Bartholomew 2007). On October 3, 2006, Airbus announced that the A380, which was already a year behind schedule at the time, would be delayed a further year due to problems with its design (Done 2006). Specifically, wiring bundles designed on one version of Catia by Airbus engineers in Germany did not fit the spaces into which they were supposed to go – spaces that had been designed by Airbus engineers in France using a different version of Catia.

Of course, it is worth recalling that earlier airliners such as the 747 had their own teething problems commensurate with the scale of their ambition (and so has the 787 as discussed below). The A380 may yet recover from its early stumbles and go on to become as important in the early twenty-first century as the 747 was in its prime. Perhaps. To have the same kind of giant impact as the 747, however, the A380 will have to sell well. In the first eight years after the airplane was formally launched, Airbus had recorded a total of just 198 orders from 16 customers. By comparison, in first eight years after the launch of the 747, at a time when the airline industry was much smaller, Boeing recorded 247 orders from 36 customers. The comparison is not entirely fair, of course. Airlines have many more choices today, including other wide-body airliners in Airbus' own family. Moreover, as discussed in the opening pages of this book, the first decade of the twenty-first century has been a troubled one for the airline industry.

In the meantime, the number of copies that Airbus needs to sell to break even had risen from an estimated 250 to 420 by late 2006 (*Seattle Times* 2006). Interestingly, it was generally understood in the industry that at least one reason

Singapore Airlines (SIA) ordered nine more A380s in 2006 to go with the ten it had ordered in 2001 was to ensure the survival of Airbus and prevent the emergence of a near Boeing monopoly. Through the end of 2008, SIA ranked third in A380 orders, far behind the hugely ambitious Dubai-based Emirates (Table 4.6). Because the A380 is premised on the future importance of travel via hubs, it is unsurprising that its big customers have been carriers that funnel huge numbers of passengers on long-range routes through a single or very small number of hubs, such SIA and Dubai-based Emirates.[12]

It was launch carrier Singapore Airlines that won the honor of flying the A380 first. As noted in Chapter 1, there was something remarkable in where the A380 began its journey: the A380 is the first significant Western commercial aircraft to make its debut not on routes from Europe or the United States, but on one commencing in Asia. The 747, the Boeing 707, the de Havilland Comet, and the Douglas DC-3 all got their start on routes that began either in New York or London. The A380 on the other hand began its commercial career in Singapore.

The flight itself was packed with aviation enthusiasts and journalists from across the world, with many of the seats having been won via an online lottery – the proceeds of which went to several charities (Bleach 2007). Although the A380 has a design capacity of 525 passengers, SIA fitted just 471 seats on its two decks, 399 of which are in what one British writer described as "the ominously familiar-looking economy area." (Bleach 2007: 20). Conversely, the accoutrements for those traveling in one of the airplane's 12 first class suites were extraordinary; each contained a fold-out full-size bed, a separate leather chair, and a 23-inch LCD entertainment screen all concealed behind a sliding door (Pae 2007).

The maiden commercial flight brought congratulatory attention to Airbus, yet the first travails of the A380 were not over. It remains to be seen whether Airbus will be able to make the venture profitable. As described above, the A380 is aimed squarely at the thick routes linking the world's primary hubs, a fact already evident in the skeletal distribution of Superjumbo services in mid-2009.

Table 4.6 Top customers for the Airbus A380 and Boeing 787 through 2008

Airbus A380			Boeing 787		
Rank	Customer	Number	Rank	Customer	Number
1	Emirates	58	1	ILFC[1]	74
2	Qantas	20	2	Qantas	65
3	Singapore	19	3	All Nippon	50
4	Lufthansa	15	4	Air Canada	37
5	Air France	12	5	Etihad	35
6	British Airways	12	6	Japan Airlines	35
10	other customers	62	50	other customers	582
Total		**198**	**Total**		**878**

Sources: Boeing Company 2009b; Airbus 2009b.

Note
1 ILFC = International Lease Finance Corporation.

In the longer term, the A380 is likely to see heavy service at important, capacity constrained hubs (Figure 4.9). Specifically, Airbus has predicted that the Narita and Heathrow will rank first and second, respectively, in the number of A380 operations in 2019 (Norris *et al.* 2003).

The 787 Dreamliner

Boeing's 787 traces its lineage to the stillborn Sonic Cruiser. Boeing took the size and range specifications of a Sonic Cruiser model that many airlines had liked and turned it into what was then called the 7E7. The purpose of the new airliner was to edge out the competition not in terms of speed but efficiency. Specifically, the airliner, known as the 787 Dreamliner since its formal launch in April 2004, was designed to be 20 percent more fuel-efficient than similarly sized aircraft and to have 10 percent lower seat-kilometer costs (Boeing Company 2007a). In other words, Boeing's response to the Superjumbo was the Superefficient.

The 787's vaunted efficiency comes from several sources. First, as noted earlier in this chapter, the 787 is powered by new engines (8 percent of the efficiency gain) from either Rolls-Royce or GE that are path-breaking in their own productivity. Second, the plane is streamlined to a greater degree than previous airliners and features a wingspan on one version nearly as broad as that of a 747.[13] The most interesting source of the 787's efficiency is its use of lightweight, very strong composite materials including carbon fiber-reinforced plastics (CFRP) (Holmes 2005). Composites are not new in the commercial aircraft industry, but the degree to which the 787's primary structures comprise composites is unprecedented. Composites in the fuselage, wings, and empennage (vertical tailfin, rudder, and horizontal stabilizer) make up half the airplane's weight. By comparison, the 777 was only 12 percent composites by weight (Boeing Company 2007a). The greater use of composites in the 787 is offset by far less reliance on aluminum than in any airliner since just after the "all-vegetable" era of the aircraft industry's infancy. Indeed, the aluminum share of the 787's weight (20 percent) is only moderately higher than the share of titanium (15 percent).

The advantages of composites are several. First, Boeing claims the use of composites alone deliver a 3 percent improvement in the aircraft's fuel efficiency (Talbot 2003). A second advantage is the reduction in the number of fasteners and, concomitantly, the complexity and cost of the assembly process (Holmes 2005). Third, the greater strength of composites and their reduced propensity to corrosion translate into lower anticipated maintenance costs. For passengers, the 787's embrace of composites could mean not only lower real airfares but also greater comfort. The strength of the composites permits the Dreamliner to have larger windows and higher cabin pressurization. Specifically, the interior of the 787 can be flown at cruising altitude with an air pressure comparable to that at 1,800 meters instead of the usual 2,400 meters (Holmes 2005).

The fuel efficiency of the 787 is fundamental to the Dreamliner program's goal of "bringing big-jet ranges to mid-size airplanes" (Boeing Company 2007a); indeed, its range is nearly the same as the much larger A380. As noted earlier,

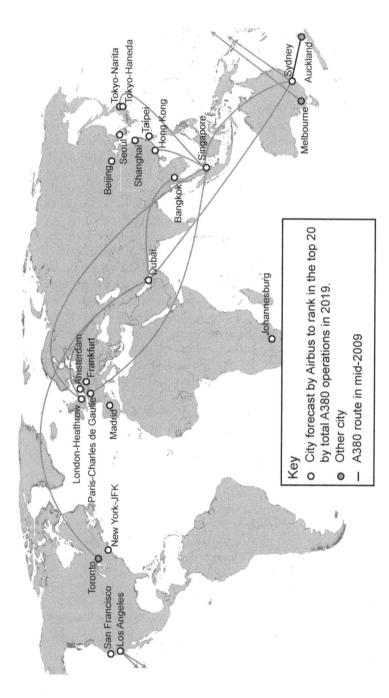

Figure 4.9 The geography of A380 operations in 2009 and the future (sources: Norris *et al.* 2003 and relevant carrier websites).

Airbus predicts that the ten of the top 20 cities ranked by Airbus to rank in the top 20 by total A380 operations in 2019 will be in Asia-Pacific, a regional emphasis that was already evident in the operations of the first three A380 operators (Singapore Airlines, Emirates, and Qantas) in 2009.

Boeing is convinced the future of air travel lies in further fragmentation. The company pins particular hope on the Chinese market, noting that it has 12 cities with at least five million people and that as the market develops, people in those and many other cities will demand direct flights (Mecham 2005a).

China has been one of the best markets in the early sales effort for the Dreamliner. By the end of 2008, five Chinese airlines and one China-based leasing company had ordered a combined total of 62 787s (Boeing Company 2009b). The very presence of five Chinese carriers on Boeing's customer list is testament to the partial deregulation of that country's airline industry. However, the biggest early market for the 787 program was not China but rather Japan. All Nippon Airways (ANA) was the launch customer for the 787 and Japan Airlines later placed an order for 787s as well. The prominence of Japanese carriers among the customers for the 787 is mirrored, of course, in Japan's unprecedented significance in the manufacture of the airplane.

Through the end of 2008, 56 customers placed a total of 878 orders for the 787, making it the fastest selling new model in the history of the industry. However, like the A380, the 787 has encountered significant delays. The first jet, which was supposed to have been delivered to ANA in May 2008, is not expected to make its commercial debut before early 2011. The stumbling blocks for Boeing have been several: a logistical breakdown in the 787 supply chain, a major labor strike in early 2009, and unexpected weakness in the join where the wing meets the fuselage (Anselmo 2008a; Mecham 2009).

Meanwhile, Airbus has responded to the 787 with the aforementioned A350. It initially tried to meet the 787 challenge with a similar long-range, wide-body twinjet that was heavily based upon the A330. Potential customers were not impressed. In particular, the powerful head of International Lease Finance Corporation (ILFC), Steven Udvar-Hazy, encouraged Airbus to go back to the drawing board (Ott *et al.* 2006). The plane-maker relented and the result was the A350XWB. The jet, which is expected to make its maiden commercial flight in 2013, will look much like a 787 and have an even greater dependence on composite materials. And as the "XWB" in its moniker indicates, a distinctive attribute of the jet will be its extra wide body. Interestingly, the A350 will have a range similar to that of the 787 so that it will be, to some degree, a rejection of the "4 for the long-haul" principal that has guided Airbus Industrie's long-haul aircraft design since the A340 (Mecham 2005b). But to the extent that the A350 becomes the Airbus platform for the future, it will return the company to its roots as a manufacturer of wide-body twinjets.

Two for the future

The contest between the 787 and the A350 and between the A380 and 747-8 will profoundly affect the two plane-makers for decades to come. In particular, their ability to pay for the next and most important battle, the one that will pitch Boeing's replacement for the 737 against the successor to the A320, will be helped or hindered by the performance of their new wide-body contenders. Developing those new narrow-body workhorses will, of course, cost billions of dollars and euros and take years. To give the new jets the expected 15 percent efficiency edge over the 737 and A320 will almost certainly require much greater use of composites, new engines, more sophisticated avionics, and the like. The risks involved will be great and made all the more so if Boeing and Airbus are joined by a third competitor, a distinct possibility. In fact, many in the industry believe that the Boeing and Airbus LCA duopoly will be broken in the decades ahead (Condom 2007). Where will the next big LCA player be based? The two most obvious possibilities are China and Japan (Vencat and Caryl 2006).

Japan may be the nearer term threat. It has long coveted a slice of the LCA business, and its significant position as a supplier to Boeing has served as a conduit for technology transfer from the US. And yet that very position in Boeing's supply chain may make it hard for any of the "heavies" to go it alone. In particular, MHI, FHI, and KHI are tier-one suppliers to the 787, a hot-selling airliner likely to be in production for decades. Severing a connection to Boeing in pursuit of an independently designed and produced airliner would be very costly and risky – and out of tune with an aircraft industry moving towards greater international collaboration. Furthermore, the commercial aircraft industry is not particularly profitable (Boeing's profit on its defense systems, for instance, tends to be substantially better than its profit on commercial airplanes), and the creation of an independent Japanese competitor in rivalry with Airbus and Boeing would likely suppress profits further. Boeing and, to a lesser extent, EADS are able to balance the cyclical commercial aircraft business with the sale of military hardware. Japan's smaller armed forces would make it difficult for any Japanese aerospace firm to do the same.

China may be a more significant long-term threat to Boeing and Airbus. China has already carved out a position, albeit much less significant than that of Japan, in the supply chains of both Airbus and Boeing, and the country has made no secret of its aspirations to build a "Peoples' Airplane." Moreover, continued government dominance of the airline industry there creates a potentially huge captive market. The country's aviation market is expected to be the world's second largest by 2022 (Vencat and Caryl 2006). However, the shortage of aerospace talent in China, combined with its growing importance in jetliner assembly (e.g., from the new Airbus plant at Tianjin) and airplane component manufacturing for foreign firms, may actually slow its development of an independent plane-making capacity. There may simply not be enough talent to spread around (Zanger 2006).

Interestingly, it is the regional jet business that has attracted several new entrants, rather than the much bigger LCA business. Like the LCA business, the RJ business is nearly a duopoly today, with Brazil's Embraer and Canada's Bombardier accounting for almost all sales. However, in the next decade, new RJs built by Mitsubishi, China's AVIC 1 Commercial Aircraft Company,[14] and Russia's Sukhoi will make their debut. Interestingly, the Mitsubishi MRJ, for which ANA gave the launch order, will debut in 2013 with an innovative new engine design called a geared turbofan (GTF). The GTF, which is under development by Pratt & Whitney, promises significant noise and emissions improvements over more traditional designs and could ultimately power the replacement for the Boeing 737 and Airbus A320 (Searles 2009).

In the meantime, each of these new RJs can expect substantial sales in its home market, and in the longer-term one or more of these companies might conceivably move into the manufacture of larger jets. Yet the economies of scale in the LCA business are colossal, placing a new manufacturer not far down the learning curve at a massive disadvantage. Airbus, of course, overcame that problem, but it did so with enormous government aid and, perhaps more importantly, by exploiting a big hole in the market. There was no wide-body twinjet before Airbus. Today, it would be harder for a new challenger in China or Brazil or any other country to get away with aid on the scale provided to Airbus at the beginning; and there are almost no holes left in the market.

Nevertheless, the LCA market is too dynamic to make definitive long-term predictions. A generation ago, the prospect of Airbus' annual airliner sales repeatedly topping those of Boeing would have seemed preposterous to many; but it happened. The demise of McDonnell Douglas, the 787's Japanese wings, and the A380's multibillion dollar wiring problems would have also seemed unlikely. The decades ahead could be just as surprising; but for now at least, the foreseeable future belongs to Airbus and Boeing, though an Airbus will not be quite as European or a Boeing quite as American as was true in the past.

It is not just that their planes are increasingly dependent upon foreign components, but also that airliners today are designed with markets beyond Europe and America in mind. As the preceding chapters have indicated, historic US airliners like the DC-3, 707, the DC-10, and even the 747 were designed primarily to suit the networks of American customers; and the first Airbus was designed to suit intra-European routes. All of those airplanes found use in the fleets of airlines from other regions, of course. The difference today is that Boeing and Airbus give high priority to the needs of foreign customers from the very beginning of the design process as evident in the launch carriers for recent airliners (Table 4.7). Asian carriers have become especially influential, and their preponderance to buy higher capacity, larger airliners has powerfully shaped the trajectory of new jetliner development during the past decade and a half (Figure 4.10).

One Asian airline in particular exercises a great deal of influence on Boeing and Airbus. Singapore Airlines (SIA) has been the most consistently profitable airline since the early 1990s, and its rapid growth has made the carrier a big customer for new jets – especially wide-body jets. Yet it is not just SIA's own fleet purchases that given the airline such singular power in the industry. The carrier's reputation for "technical and financial scrutiny" (Mecham 1995) compels other airlines to pay attention to SIA's aircraft choices. SIA has become, according to one trade journal, the new "gold standard," playing the roles once filled by Pan Am and TWA (Thomas 2000).[15]

Pan Am and TWA can no longer play those roles because they are gone. Both succumbed to the brutal economics of an airline industry transformed by liberalization. SIA, on the other hand, has thrived in the liberalized industry. The effects of liberalization have extended far beyond these three carriers, affecting for better or worse virtually every airline, airport, plane-maker, passenger, and shipper. For liberalization has meant that the heavy but protective hand of government has been lifted from the airline industry; and free to change, the industry has. Indeed, it is fair to say that liberalization has replaced technological change – the theme that has run through the past three chapters – as the primary catalyst to the development of the airborne world in the past two decades. It is to liberalization that we next turn.

Table 4.7 Launch airlines for selected Boeing and Airbus airliners

Aircraft	Airline	Year[1]	Aircraft	Airline	Year[1]
B707	Pan Am	1955	A300	Air France	1969
B727	Eastern/United	1960	A310	Lufthansa	1978
B737	Lufthansa	1965	A320	Air France	1984
B747	Pan Am	1966	A340	Air France/Lufthansa	1987
B757	Eastern Airlines	1978	A330	Air Inter	1989
B767	United Airlines	1978	A380	Singapore Airlines	2000
B777	United Airlines	1990	A350	US Airways	2005
B787	ANA	2004			

Sources: derived in part from Airbus 2009b; Boeing Company 2009b.

Note
1 The year indicated is the year the first order was placed.

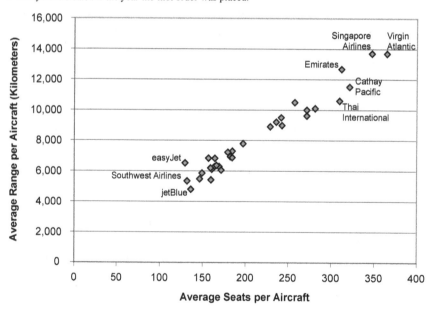

Figure 4.10 Average fleet performance for selected airlines (sources: based on figures in *Air Transport World* 2008a; Airbus 2009a; Boeing Company 2009a).

Each symbol shows the average range and seat capacity for passenger fleets of 32 large airlines in 2008. The averages were produced by weighting the typical performance characteristics of each airplane type (e.g. 301 seats and a range of 17,446 kilometers for the Boeing 777-200LR) by the number of such aircraft in a particular carrier's fleet.

Part II

Open skies and a crowd of competitors

5 Letting go

The liberalization of the airline industry

The new freedom in the air

In mid-1972, the makers of the Anglo-French Concorde received very good news from China. The People's Republic had agreed to the purchase of three of the new supersonic transports. The Chinese made their announcement in the same two-month period as Air France and the British Overseas Airways Corporation (BOAC), the flag carriers of the countries building the pace-setting airliner, committed to a total of nine Concorde supersonic transports and the government of Iran decided, after the Shah piloted a personal test flight, to buy two for Iran Air (Trubshaw 2000). The Concorde seemed to be on a roll.

Thirty-three years later, it was Boeing's turn to be blessed with welcome Chinese orders for a new airliner. In early 2005, China's government announced orders for 60 new 787s (Yu 2005). The good news for Boeing came during a two-month period in which two European airlines, Blue Panorama Airlines from Italy and First Choice Airways from the United Kingdom, also placed orders for ten 787s. The new orders seemed to augur well for the Dreamliner.

The similarities in the two stories belie the enormous changes in the aircraft and airline industries in the intervening few decades. The preceding section of this book dealt primarily with changes in aircraft and with the companies that build them. In this and the next two chapters, we turn our attention to changes in the airline industry. Consider, for example, the difference between Air France and BOAC on the one hand and Blue Panorama and First Choice on the other. In the early 1970s, Air France and BOAC were state-owned airlines of long lineage. They purchased the Concorde under some duress as they fulfilled their obligation to support their governments' prestige project. Ultimately, they were the only airlines to buy the Concorde (the Chinese and Iranian orders were never consummated). Blue Panorama and First Choice, conversely, were new carriers in 2005, part of the huge expansion in the number of airlines competing in the skies over Europe. The changes in China have been no less spectacular. At the time of the Concorde order, there was only one Chinese airline, the fully state-owned Civil Aviation Administration of China (CAAC), which was also charged with operating the country's airports and its air traffic control system (B. Graham 1995: 191). The China of the early 1970s wanted the Concorde for the esteem it would earn, not because the supersonic transport made commercial sense. The Chinese government ordered the 787s, conversely, on behalf of six different carriers that very much needed additional capacity.[1] Indeed, China had become the fastest growing major commercial aircraft market on the planet – a distinction rooted in a variety of factors, including the increasingly competitive Chinese airline industry.

The changes in China and in Europe convey a measure of the dynamism in an industry rife with new carriers and emboldened by new freedoms – the freedom to choose routes, to determine what aircraft will be used on those routes and at what frequency, and to set fares and air cargo rates. Over the past two decades in particular, the change in government policies towards the airline industry has been more dramatic than that in aircraft technologies. The last revolutionary advance in aircraft technology was the introduction of the jet engine more than fifty years ago – or perhaps the advent of fly-by-wire in the mid-1980s. Conversely, the changes in the airline industry, including the privatization of dozens of carriers and the removal or relaxation of rules governing where and how airlines operate – developments that have been strongly concentrated in the thirty years since 1975 – do comprise a genuinely revolutionary transformation.

The Malaysian carrier, AirAsia, for instance, has broadened the scope of the traveling public in Southeast Asia; but it has done so using a fleet comprising rather unremarkable Boeing 737s and Airbus A320s. What makes AirAsia's success and that of other low-cost carriers (LCCs) possible is not the development of new airliners, but the development of policies that permit competition with the full-service network carriers from the industry's past. LCCs have taken advantage of that freedom to introduce new ways of running an airline that dramatically lower the cost of air travel. In this manner the liberalization of the airline industry has liberalized access to the sky. AirAsia emblazons the audacious claim, "Now everyone can fly" upon every one of its aircraft. That is still not true, but in countries like Malaysia where only 6 percent of the population had ever flown in 2005 (*Aviation Week & Space Technology* 2005a), the arrival of LCCs is having a significant effect.

Yet it is not just the LCCs and the other startups that have been affected by the new freedoms in the global airline industry. Although the past two decades have witnessed the demise of storied names like Pan Am and SABENA, the more nimble of the network carriers, like British Airways and Malaysia Airlines, have not only survived but even thrived, at least during the industry's cyclical upswings; for the successful carriers of the past have been the airlines best positioned to take advantage of the globalization of the airline industry. It was Malaysia Airlines, not AirAsia, which operated to 61 foreign cities on six continents in 2008;[2] and it was British Airways, not its LCC rival easyJet, that became a founding member of the oneworld alliance, a group of airlines whose schedules are meshed to create an integrated network commensurate with the scale of the global economy.

New and old carriers alike operate in an industry made more relentlessly competitive by the partial withdrawal of the state. The "Airbus governments" will almost certainly not let their plane-maker fail just as the US government could not be expected to sit idly by if Boeing were to teeter on the brink; but few airlines are so sacrosanct. The brutality of competition in the industry is not good news for airline employees but for many travelers and cargo shippers, liberalization has helped to make air transportation routine, unremarkable, and less expensive.

America first: the deregulation of the US airline industry

For much of the brief history of commercial aviation, the typical airline was a state-owned carrier, which often had a monopoly on domestic routes and was its home country's sole representative on international routes. There are still carriers that fit that profile in 2009: carriers such as Air Malawi, Turkmenistan Airlines, and North Korea's Air Koryo; but their ranks have been dramatically thinned in the past two decades. Dozens of carriers have been privatized; and during the same period, scores of new airlines have taken wing. In most countries, state-owned carriers and privately ones alike enjoy greater freedom to decide which routes to fly and when to fly them, what kinds of aircraft to use, what passenger fares and air cargo rates to charge, what to pay their employees, and when to get in or get out of the airline business. That is, the airline industry, to a considerable degree, has been both privatized and deregulated. Together, privatization and deregulation make up the two wings of liberalization.

Liberalization has not been a linear, one-way process; some privatized carriers, for instance, have returned to high levels of state ownership (e.g., Air New Zealand). Yet the overall trajectory of the relationship between government and the airline industry is unmistakable: government has less direct control over the industry than at any time since World War II and perhaps even since World War I. The result has been a freer airline industry, better able to grow to meet the unprecedented demand for the space-shrinking and time-saving technology of air transportation.

Although liberalization is by now a worldwide phenomenon, the US was clearly the most important early arena for reform of the industry. Other countries, such as Singapore, had liberal air transport regimes early on; but because the US airline industry was easily the world's largest, its deregulation at the end of the 1970s was enormously influential. Moreover, the US government later became a prominent global advocate for liberalization, seeking the freedom for its carriers to operate abroad that it had failed to secure at the 1944 Chicago Conference. And so it is worth considering the American experience in some detail.

Government regulation had been both a blessing and a burden for the US domestic airline industry. On the one hand, regulation had the effect of ensuring the overall profitability of the industry. That assurance was particularly important in allowing US carriers to quickly replace their fleets with expensive new jets beginning in the late 1950s. On the other hand, regulation hamstrung the ability of better-run airlines to grow at the expense of poorly-run ones. No significant airline went bankrupt under regulation (Heppenheimer 1995: 315).

The four largest carriers in 1938 ranked among the five largest in 1978 (Table 5.1), but the largest airlines were unable to expand much either. United Airlines, for instance, was awarded only one new route between 1961 and 1978; and Pan Am had been prevented from establishing a domestic network to match its far-flung international operations (Brown 1987: 104).

Moreover, by the 1970s, it was clear that the US airline industry was not as efficient as it could be. The lightly regulated intrastate carriers offered lower fares than interstate carriers did on routes of comparable length (Heppenheimer 1995: 316) (Table 5.2). For example, it cost less to fly from Dallas to San Antonio than from Cleveland to Chicago, despite nearly identical distances between each pair of cities. Southwest Airlines had pioneered fares so low that the airline challenged bus companies on the carrier's intra-Texas routes (Petzinger 1995: 33).

Interstate airlines, by comparison, were faltering under the weight of too much capacity as 747s, DC-10s, and L-1011s ordered in the 1960s rolled off the plane-makers' assembly lines, too few passengers in an economy mired in recession, and spiraling fuel costs. The remedy adopted by the Civil Aeronautic Board (CAB) was to authorize sharp increases in airfares and to further constrain competition among the carriers. The result was a fierce political backlash as the CAB's actions angered interest groups ranging from Ralph Nader's Aviation Consumer Action Project to Sears Roebuck, which was dependent upon air services to deliver goods ordered from its catalog (Brown 1987: 103). Deregulation advocates, especially Senator Edward Kennedy, leveraged this groundswell of opposition to the CAB to marshal political support for stripping the CAB of its

Table 5.1 Largest US airlines, 1938–2008

Rank	1938		1978		2008	
	Airline	*RPKs[1] (millions)*	*Airline*	*RPKs[1] (millions)*	*Airline*	*RPKs[1] (millions)*
1	American	227	United	66,669	American	211,730
2	United	167	American	41,026	United	176,869
3	TWA	116	Delta	36,766	Delta	169,856
4	Eastern	114	Eastern	33,419	Continental	129,355
5	Pan Am	72	TWA	28,898	Southwest	118,330
6	Northwest	34	Western	15,884	Northwest	115,134
7	Penn Central	36	Pan Am	14,404	US Airways	97,331
8	Braniff	23	Continental	13,768	jetBlue	41,893
9	Western	18	Braniff	11,747	AirTran	30,193
10	Panagra	13	Republic	9,791	Alaska	30,076
	Other	31		37,649		201,465
Total		**851**		**310,021**		**1,322,232**

Sources: Davies 1972, Appendix 3; E. Bailey *et al.* 1985: Appendix F; BTS 2009a.

Note

1 RPKs = Revenue passenger-kilometers systemwide (domestic and international).

Table 5.2 Intrastate and interstate fares, January 1975

Intrastate routes			Interstate routes		
Route	Distance (km)	Lowest fare ($)	Route	Distance (km)	Lowest fare ($)
Dallas–Houston	373	30	Atlanta–Charlotte	365	48
Dallas–San Antonio	393	30	Chicago–Detroit	383	50
Los Angeles–San Diego	175	14	Cleveland–Pittsburgh	191	34
Los Angeles–San Francisco	584	34	Baltimore–Boston	595	66

Source: author's analysis of data in OAG 1975.

powers. They were aided in that effort by the consensus among academic economists that deregulation would improve the industry's efficiency and its financial health and by two successive chairman of the CAB who also favored deregulation. Finally, while most of the major airlines remained opposed to the initiative, first United and then a handful of other carriers endorsed deregulation for the expansion opportunities it seemed to promise.

Although deregulation later came to be associated with conservatives in the US and elsewhere, Democrat Jimmy Carter signed the Airline Deregulation Act (ADA) into law in October 1978 (Brown 1987: 123). The ADA effectively ended government control over domestic routes and fares and over the entry and exit of carriers from interstate services. By the early 1980s, the CAB no longer existed. That said, the US federal government has retained important powers to regulate air safety and to regulate airline mergers. And via the Essential Air Services (EAS) program, the government continues to subsidize – often heavily – services to small cities and towns that might otherwise be abandoned in the deregulated market (DOT 2009). In 2008, the US subsidized services to 152 communities in 34 states and Puerto Rico (Figure 5.1).

Despite precautions such as the EAS program, the US experience with deregulation can best be described as sweeping and epochal. It spurred waves of mergers and acquisitions as big airlines devoured smaller ones, freed airlines to expand nationwide, facilitated the emergence of hub-and-spoke systems, and stimulated the development of computer reservations systems and frequent flyer programs – all of which helped big network airlines become bigger and all of which are discussed more fully in the next chapter. In the longer term, however, deregulation created a context favorable to the emergence of low-cost carriers (LCCs), whose revolutionary impact upon the industry is examined in Chapter 7. The rapid growth of LCCs has been instrumental in pushing the cost of air travel down in real terms. One estimate is that Americans save $20 billion dollars per year because of deregulation (Gessing 2005). Yet it is important to emphasize that these savings vary geographically. Those markets with the greatest intensity of competition, especially competition from LCCs, have benefited disproportionately while those places where a single network carrier is dominant, unsurprisingly, have benefited much less (Goetz and Sutton 1997).

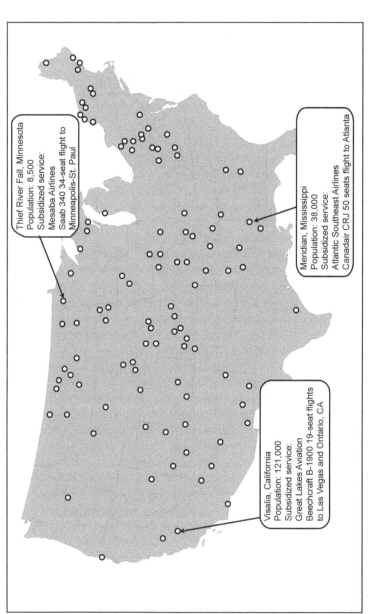

Thief River Fall, Minnesota
Population: 8,500
Subsidized service:
Mesaba Airlines
Saab 340 34-seat flight to
Minneapolis-St. Paul

Meridian, Mississippi
Population: 38,000
Subsidized service:
Atlantic Southeast Airlines
Canadair CRJ 50 seats flight to Atlanta

Visalia, California
Population: 121,000
Subsidized service:
Great Lakes Aviation
Beechcraft B-1900 19-seat flights
to Las Vegas and Ontario, CA

Figure 5.1 US communities receiving subsidized air services, 2009 (source: DOT 2009).

In mid-2009, 105 communities located in the lower 48 states of the US received subsidized Essential Air Services (EAS). The greatest concentrations of such communities were in Appalachia and in the Great Plains. In addition, 45 communities in Alaska and 2 in Puerto Rico were subsided under the EAS program.

Nevertheless, the overall effect was to foster the further growth of air travel. In the first 25 years after deregulation, passenger enplanements in the US grew at a robust average annual rate of about 4 percent (based on data at BTS 2009b). Admittedly, traffic had grown more than twice as fast in the quarter century before deregulation, but that period had witnessed the transformative impact of jets and then wide-body jets. Further rapid growth of traffic in the absence of such technological breakthroughs was impressive and much of the credit was due to deregulation.

The diffusion of deregulation: false starts and true gains

Kingfisher Airlines. Wizz Air. Gol Linhas Aereas. These could be giants in the airline industry of the future or they could disappear into the depths of bankruptcy and collapse that have claimed so many new entrant airlines in the past. There was a remarkable proliferation of new carriers in the 1990s and first few years of the twenty-first century, including Gol in Brazil, Wizz Air in Eastern Europe, and Kingfisher Airlines in India. In *Flight International*'s 2006 World Airline Directory, nearly 1,600 airlines were listed, up from just over 500 in 1984 (*Flight International* 1984, 2006a, 2006b, 2006c). In the mid-1980s, dozens of countries – from South Korea to Jamaica, from Afghanistan to Bulgaria – had just one homegrown airline apiece. Today, in these four countries and many others across the world, new airlines have sprung up. The growth in the number of competitors promises to extend the fruits of greater choice to literally billions of travelers and tens of thousands of air freight shippers in markets that were once monopolies.

Figure 5.2 provides a measure of the increased competitiveness of airline markets around the globe. Each symbol represents one the 100 largest national aviation markets measured by the total available seat-kilometers (ASKs) produced by airlines domiciled there in 2008. The horizontal axis measures the 1998 share of total national ASKs accounted for by the largest carrier in the market (e.g., Air Canada's share of all ASKs performed by airlines domiciled in Canada); the vertical axis shows the comparable figure for 2008. Most national markets fall below the diagonal indicating they became more competitive. In Indonesia, for instance, Garuda Indonesia's share of the national airline market fell from 78 to 39 percent. Even some markets above the diagonal (e.g., Canada) became more competitive due to increased competition from foreign carriers.

Although deregulation swept the US industry in the 1970s, its arrival in other countries is more recent. There are some markets where it has still barely begun. In the first decade after the passage of the ADA, domestic markets were deregulated at least partially in Canada (beginning in 1984), New Zealand (1986), Australia (1990), the United Kingdom, Japan, and China (1988) (Kasper 1988: 1). In most of these countries, the early proliferation of competitors gave way to sharp increases in market concentration later on. In Canada, for instance, mergers involving five carriers created Canadian Airlines International in 1988. The mergers were expected to yield an airline strong enough to battle Air Canada;

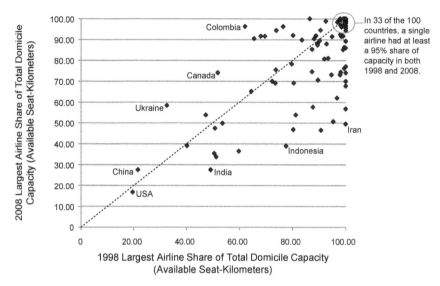

Figure 5.2 The competitiveness of national airline markets, 1998–200 (source: author's analysis of data in OAG 1998, 2008).

Most national aviation markets became more competitive as measured by the top airline's share of total capacity. See text for an explanation of the graph.

and, in fact, Canadian had an important advantage in the western part of the country as well as over the Pacific. Yet by the end of the 1990s, the Canadian government's concern was competition on another scale, as the liberalization of cross-border services with the US exposed Air Canada to keener competition from the American giants. Accordingly, the government relaxed restrictions that had prevented the further consolidation of Canada's aviation industry clearing the way for Air Canada's acquisition of Canadian in 2000.

By the 1990s, deregulation had spread to many developing countries but did so in an often uneven, halting fashion. The case of China is particularly important. The break-up of CAAC in the late 1980s yielded the newly christened flag carrier Air China and five new regionally based carriers: China Eastern Airlines, China Northern Airlines, China Northwest Airlines, China Southern Airlines, and China Southwest Airlines (S.-L. Shaw *et al.* 2009). Later, many more provincial and municipal governments also established airlines of their own. Unfortunately, the sudden surge in competitors came at a cost. During the 1990s, the new Chinese airlines that resulted from the breakup of CAAC had 11 fatal crashes that together killed more than 800 people. In response, the Chinese government in 2000 shepherded the ten airlines under its direct control into three groups organized around Beijing-based Air China, Shanghai-based China Eastern Airlines, and Guangzhou-based China Southern Airlines. However, other province-based and municipality-based carriers survive as independents outside these umbrellas.

The Chinese government's aggressiveness in reshaping the structure of the country's airline industry after its putative deregulation is a defining characteristic of deregulation in developing economies. Governments in poor countries have proven reluctant to fully release the industry to unfettered competition. In India, for instance, a dozen new entrant domestic carriers were given permission to launch services in the early 1990s (Ionides 2005b); but the government's continued interference in the industry doomed most to failure. The airlines were compelled to deploy at least 60 percent of their capacity on non-trunk routes, including 10 percent on "social" routes to remote regions and 10 percent to particularly destitute regions (Hooper 1998). The government further compounded the new entrants' difficulties by dictating that any new entrant's fleet had to include at least three jets, limiting the number of pilots they could hire away from the state-owned carriers, and restricting their sources of capital.

Nevertheless, by 2008, seven airlines created under India's airline liberalization provided more than 70 percent of the country's domestic air capacity[3] (Figure 5.3). New carriers have pioneered scheduled air services to places such as hill resorts like Kandhla and Dharamsala (which is also the headquarters of the Dalai Lama and the Tibetan government in exile) and have they have expanded services to giant, but underserved cities like Raipur and Bhubaneswar. The latter city, for instance, has a population of two million and is the capital of India's Orissa state; but in 2003, state-owned Indian Airlines – the only carrier in the market – offered just 20 flights per week. By 2008, six airlines provided 127 flights per week.

Perhaps the most audacious of the Indian start-ups is Kingfisher Airlines, which, like other new Indian carriers, was favored by a fortuitous mixture of liberalization and sustained development that boosted the Indian middle class to an estimated 200 million people by 2005 (Mathews 2005). The grand ambitions of Kingfisher specifically, which began flying in May 2005, were evident in the 79 aircraft including five A330s, five A340s, five A350s, and five A380s it had on order in 2008 (*Air Transport World* 2008a). Unlike most other recent Indian start-ups, Kingfisher aims to be a full-service network carrier extending from New Delhi, Mumbai, and the Indian high-tech capital of Bangalore to destinations throughout the world, including the US (*Aviation Week & Space Technology* 2005b). Yet for several years after the carrier was formed by a beer industry magnate, Kingfisher was bottled up inside India by a government rule requiring an airline to have at least five years' service on domestic routes before commencing international operations. Kingfisher vigorously lobbied against the rule and in September 2008, it opened its first international route: from Bangalore to London-Heathrow (Boles 2008); but by then it was too late in a sense for the global downturn had struck the air travel market, including the market in India. By mid-2009, Kingfisher was in precarious financial straits (Timmons and Bajaj 2009).

Kingfisher's international ambitions are shared by new entrant airlines in countries across the world; and that brings us to another basic feature of deregulation in developing countries: deregulation of domestic markets often provides too little scope for new carriers to survive. Juan Maggio, the founder of the Argentine new entrant Southern Winds, complained to *Airline Business* in 2002, "In the USA you can be only a regional carrier and have 300 airplanes. You cannot do that here. A domestic airline in Argentina cannot survive without having international services." (quoted in Knibb 2002). International routes

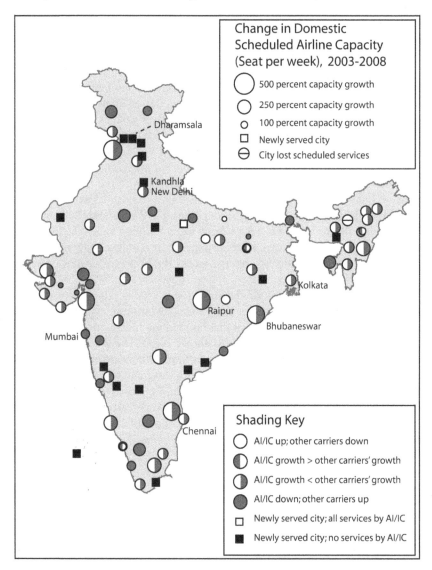

Figure 5.3 Capacity by airline in India's domestic market (source: author's analysis of data in OAG 2003, 2008).

Most of the rapid expansion of airline capacity between 2003 and 2008 was attributable to new carriers rather than the state-owned Air India (AI) and Indian Airlines (IC) (the latter two carriers merged in 2007). New carriers were also instrumental in inaugurating service to new cities.

provide critical traffic feed for domestic routes and can cross-subsidize loss-making domestic operations (Hooper 1997). Because the liberalization of international routes requires the cooperation of more than one country, however, domestic deregulation has often advanced further and faster than international deregulation.

Yet now, at the beginning of the twenty-first century, the liberalization of international routes is catching up with the reforms at the domestic level. Southern Winds, for instance, got its chance at international routes. The carrier was chosen by the Argentine government to break the international monopoly of Aerolineas Argentinas (Knibb 2002); and by 2003, Maggio's creation was operating alongside the flag carrier to distant destinations including Miami and Madrid. Like many other new entrants, Southern Winds proved to be short-lived, as it failed in 2005.[4] Still, the liberalization of international airline routes continues to gain momentum – in Latin America and Asia, even in the Middle East and parts of Africa, and especially on the world's heavily trafficked intercontinental and transcontinental routes. The implications for the airline industry and its importance to the global economy are enormous.

Breaking the rules: the deregulation of international air transportation

One of the watershed events in international airline regulation began with a volcanic eruption. On June 15, 1991 Mount Pinatubo erupted in fury 90 kilometers north of Manila. The second most powerful volcanic eruption of the twentieth century inundated a vast area with ash and mud and killed 800 people. At the time of the eruption, Subic Bay Naval Base and Clark Air Field, both located within 50 kilometers of the volcano, were the two largest US military bases on foreign soil. They had been key bulwarks in the American effort to contain the Soviet Union during the Cold War; but at the time of the eruption the American and Philippine governments were entangled in negotiations over the bases' lease renewal. Pinatubo brought the negotiations and the Pentagon's interest in the bases to an abrupt end. Once home to thousands of sailors and airmen and tens of thousands of Filipino workers, the bases were evacuated and fell silent.

The Americans did not stay away for long, though. By 1995, American planes were once again arriving and departing at Subic's seaside runway; but this time they were not painted in the drab gray of military aircraft. Instead, the jets descending through the night sky were marked with the distinctive red, white, and indigo livery of FedEx. Initially connected to 14 cities, a decade later the FedEx AsiaOne hub at Subic was linked to nearly 20 cities throughout Asia as well as gateways in Europe and America. UPS followed the FedEx lead and established its own intra-Asian hub at Clark in 1998. Compared to the massive FedEx hub at Memphis or UPS hub at Louisville, the Subic and Clark operations were small. Yet in one way, these transformed military bases were significant because FedEx and UPS were American airlines but they had been given permission to operate hubs on Philippine territory, an action that would once have been anathema to countries jealous of their sovereignty and protective of their own carriers (Bowen *et al*. 2002). The Philippine government, intent on rejuvenating the economy of the region where the bases were once situated, was one of the pioneers in permitting a foreign carrier to operate a hub on its soil, but its lead has now been followed by several other countries around the world. For instance, both of the American express giants have hubs in Europe (FedEx at Paris; UPS at Cologne) and both will have their intra-Asian hubs in China by 2010[5] (see Figure 9.1).

The foreign cargo hubs are cracks in the old edifice of international airline regulation, a system that emerged in the aftermath of World War II. The signs are not just in air freight. Passenger carrier Air Berlin, for instance, operated 56,000 seats per week in 2008 on *domestic* routes in Spain (author's analysis of data in OAG 2008). Remarkably, there were no restrictions to prevent the German carrier from carrying domestic passengers between the two Spanish cities, a practice called cabotage (see Figure 2.3). Since World War II, cabotage has almost always been forbidden in the airline industry. Yet in 2008, the Air Berlin route from Madrid to Palma de Mallorca, for instance, was just one among more than 140 cabotage routes within Europe served by foreign airlines (Figure 5.4).

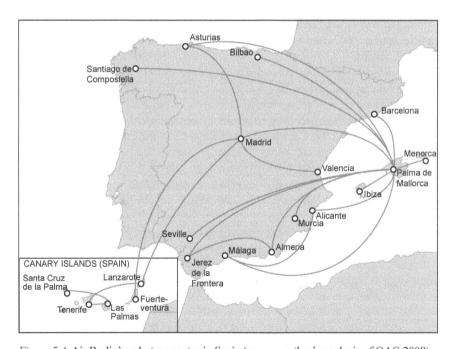

Figure 5.4 Air Berlin's cabotage routes in Spain (source: author's analysis of OAG 2008).

In 2008, Air Berlin was one of several carriers operating cabotage routes in Spain. The routes served mainly linked coastal tourist destinations to Palma de Mallorca where the airline has a hub well-connected to the rest of the Air Berlin network (see *Figure 8.4*).

Meanwhile, on opposite sides of the South Pacific, extraordinary new relationships have emerged among airlines located in different countries. Virgin Blue, an Australian LCC set up by Richard Branson's Virgin Group, owns 100 percent of Pacific Blue, a New Zealand-based LCC that flies domestic routes as well as links to nearby countries. And in South America, Chile's LAN has stakes in a bevy of subsidiaries in other countries, from LAN Argentina to LAN Dominicana (*Flight International* 2006a, 2006b, 2006c).

Although hubs in foreign countries, cabotage routes, and wholly owned foreign subsidiaries are among the fruits of liberalization, the multiplication of international competitors is a more important but less dramatic way in which the international airline industry has changed. Less dramatic because on some international routes the presence of several competitors is not new. More important because the proliferation of international airlines gives customers, whether they are passengers or freight shippers, more choices and – as in more competitive domestic markets – lower air fares and freight rates.

The US initiative

The plot of *Airport '77*, the most exciting of the four movies in the air disaster series, is about the crash of a 747 in the Bermuda Triangle. The movie is far-fetched but it deftly tapped into the 1970s' public fascination with the famed zone of ship and aircraft disappearances. By coincidence, Bermuda was on the minds of many airline executives in 1977, too. Not the Bermuda Triangle, but the 1946 Bermuda Agreement that had established the first air service agreement (ASA) – see Chapter 2 – between the US and the UK. Britain terminated the Bermuda Agreement in 1976 because it claimed that US carriers enjoyed too many fifth freedom or "beyond" rights through London and Hong Kong. Britain also wanted its airlines to capture a higher share of traffic on the North Atlantic sector. The negotiations that followed culminated in a generally more restrictive agreement, Bermuda II, which was signed in 1977. Although the agreement did grant six more US gateways to British carriers, it also restricted most US–UK routes to a single US carrier each except those linking London to New York and Los Angeles (and later Boston and Miami). US carriers also lost most beyond rights through London and Hong Kong (B. Graham 1995: 171–2).

The angry reaction in the US prodded the Carter Administration to push its policy of airline industry deregulation overseas. In pursuit of that policy, the US used a "beachhead" strategy of negotiating much more liberal ASAs with favorably disposed European and Asian countries and then leveraging the threat of traffic diversion to force other countries to bend to the same liberalizing drive. The new agreements typically included provisions for multiple designation (i.e., more than one carrier from each side could fly each route), much freer competition in airfares and cargo rates, new gateways, and minimal controls on capacity. Across the Atlantic, the US concluded new agreements with the Netherlands, Belgium, Israel, and Germany beginning in 1977. The agreement with the Dutch helped make the connection between the US and the Netherlands the fastest growing transatlantic route. In response, Britain loosened restrictions on US carriers in order to protect the primacy of London. Interestingly, Britain's withdrawal from Bermuda I had been motivated by the desire to promote the interests of British Airways but the American strategy forced Britain to retreat in order to protect something more important: its privileged place in the geography of international air transportation.

The US used the same strategy in Asia. Liberal ASAs were negotiated with South Korea, Singapore, the Philippines, Thailand, and Taiwan to put pressure on Japan (Kasper 1988: 82–7). Japan's complaints were similar to those of Britain: it claimed that American carriers had a disproportionate share of the bilateral traffic and too many "beyond" rights through Tokyo (e.g., to China) and that Japanese carriers had too few gateways in the US. Moreover, the Japanese argued that the ASA between the two countries had been concluded during the US occupation of Japan after World War II and therefore the agreement had not fairly represented Japanese interests. In the late 1970s and early 1980s, the two sides went through a series of bruising negotiations, but their overall outcome was additional rights for American and Japanese carriers.

In the 1990s, the US government went further in negotiating new so-called "Open Skies" agreements with foreign partners, beginning with the Netherlands. The US–Netherlands agreement had provisions that have since become standard in Open Skies deals (Doganis 2006: 40):

- multiple designation
- full traffic rights for airlines from each country on routes to any point in the other country
- unlimited fifth freedom rights
- no limits on frequencies or capacity
- permission to break gauge (e.g., to fly from Amsterdam to Detroit with a 747 and then on from Detroit to Mexico City with a 757)
- permission to code-share (e.g., to sell seats on a KLM flight from Amsterdam to Detroit under the codes of both KLM and Northwest, making the flight appear in computer reservations systems as a Northwest flight; code-sharing is discussed more fully in Chapter 6).
- minimal controls on passenger fares and air freight rates

The fact that the Netherlands was once again the first partner in the US drive to liberalize air transportation is not coincidental. With only a relatively small domestic hinterland, the Netherlands relies upon international traffic to feed its hub at Schiphol. Netherlands therefore had much to gain from liberalization. The same could be said of Singapore, helping to explain why the city-state, too, has been an ardent advocate of liberalization in general and Open Skies in particular. In 1997, it became one of the first Asian countries to sign such an agreement with the US. By mid-2009, the American government had signed Open Skies agreements with 94 countries (Figure 5.5), although there were some notable absences, including Japan and China.

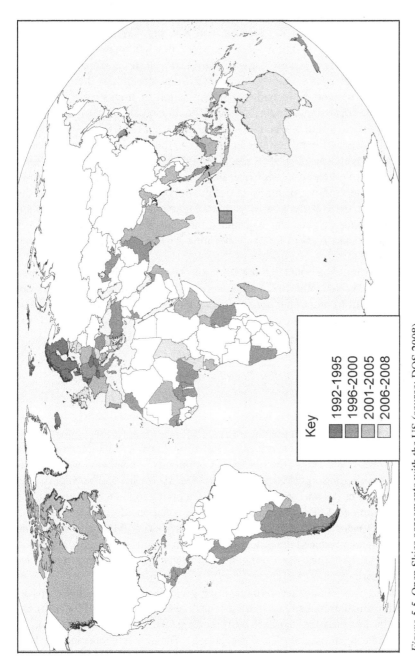

Figure 5.5 Open Skies agreements with the US (source: DOS 2008).

By 2009, the US had working Open Skies agreements with nearly half the countries in the world.

US advocacy of international airline liberalization has had several important results. First, it facilitated the internationalization of large US network carriers formerly confined to domestic routes. The three flag carriers that had represented the US abroad for decades, Pan Am and TWA worldwide along with Eastern Airlines in Latin America, were first complemented and then replaced by likes of American, United, and Delta – airlines which could feed their international routes with traffic drawn from throughout their domestic hub-and-spoke networks. Second, the liberalization of transatlantic and, to a lesser degree, transpacific routes precipitated the emergence of many new American gateways and a trend towards smaller aircraft (B. Graham 1995: 178). In this respect, liberalization complemented the development of Extended Twin-engine Operations (ETOPS) discussed in Chapter 4. Third, the US liberalization initiative helped to spur liberalization in other countries. In Taiwan, for instance, the granting of multiple designation on transpacific routes to the US meant that there were unused rights available for new entrants. Taking advantage of those rights was a primary rationale for the creation of EVA Airways, an upstart rival to flag carrier China Airlines (Bowen and Leinbach 1995).

Finally, it should be noted that the US has not been alone in advocating Open Skies. Australia, New Zealand, Singapore, and the United Arab Emirates are among a handful of other countries that have aggressively pursued reform. And perhaps the most important exponent in the spread of international airline liberalization today is not the US at all but rather the European Union.

Neighbors without fences: airline liberalization in Europe and other regions

Although the US has been an influential advocate for liberalization across the world, the greatest progress towards fully deregulated international air transportation has not been made on routes to and from the US but rather on routes within Europe. In the 1980s, the European Community's member countries committed to forming a Single European Market (SEM) by 1993. The SEM would mean that most tariffs and other trade barriers applying to intra-community trade would be eliminated. The creation of a Single Aviation Market (SAM) was a part of that broader agenda (B. Graham 1995: 141). The SEM in general and the SAM in particular reduced the power of European countries to regulate aviation as the increasingly muscular Community and later the European Union (EU) grew in authority.[6]

The SAM was established through three progressively more liberal "packages" of reforms introduced in 1988, 1990, and 1993 (B. Graham 1995: 142). By the time the last package had been fully implemented in 1997, air transport in Europe had been almost completely deregulated. The new freedoms included:

- virtually unrestricted pricing on intra-EU routes although member countries could reject fares so low that they amounted to dumping.

- unrestricted access for any EU airline to any route connecting two EU countries, including fifth freedom routes
- limited cabotage between 1993 and 1997 and full cabotage thereafter
- full freedom for any majority EU company or person to form an airline in any EU state provided certain financial and safety prerequisites are met

The three packages made Europe the first large region in the world where airlines not only enjoyed unfettered third, fourth, and fifth freedom rights but also seventh freedom and cabotage (eighth freedom) rights (see Figure 2.3). Some explanation of these rights is necessary here. Sixth freedom rights refer to the carriage of traffic between two foreign countries via an airline's home country. For instance, Air France carries traffic between the Sweden and Italy via its Paris hub. No specific granting of sixth freedom rights is necessary, and so the sixth freedom is often referred to as unofficial. Seventh freedom rights, on the other hand, must be formally granted. They enable a carrier to serve a route between two foreign countries that neither begins nor ends in its home country. Effectively, this means basing aircraft in a foreign country – as in the case of the FedEx hub at Subic Bay or, to use a European example, the Irish LCC Ryanair's hub at Frankfurt-Hahn. All airlines within the European Common Aviation Area (ECAA), which in 2008 comprised the 27 member countries of the European Union along with Iceland and Norway in the north and several countries in the Western Balkans, enjoy this right (Doganis 2006: 50).

Interestingly, relatively few carriers have taken advantage of either the seventh freedom or cabotage rights available in the SAM. In 2008, 33 carriers operated just under 4,800 cabotage flights per week; but more than half of those flights were operated by an airline from one Scandinavian country serving domestic routes in another Scandinavian country. As evidenced by the long-time status of SAS as the shared flag carrier of Denmark, Norway, and Sweden, Scandinavia had a relatively integrated airline industry even before the European liberalization packages were put in place. More generally, the number of cabotage flights was dwarfed by the nearly 48,000 domestic flights flown in 2008 by home market airlines (e.g., the 17 daily flights flown each way by Spanish carriers from Madrid to Palma de Mallorca versus Air Berlin's once daily flight) (author's analysis of data in OAG 2008). Home market airlines' deeply entrenched advantages, ranging from the control of premium airport gates to national pride, will take a long time to erode.

In the meantime, the expanded power of the EU and its institutions in aviation has also had a profound effect upon the sixty-year-old system of bilateral air service agreements. In 1997, the European Commission (EC) challenged the right of eight member states to individually negotiate ASAs with the United States, arguing that their doing so violated the principles of the SEM. The case dragged on for years, but in 2002 the European Court of Justice (ECJ) ruled that the EC did not have the right to negotiate ASAs on behalf of member states. In the same ruling, however, the court deemed illegal the nationality clauses that are intrinsic to most ASAs. Nationality clauses limit traffic rights to carriers that are majority-owned by nationals of the states concerned, meaning, for instance, that for a carrier to use rights granted to the Netherlands in an ASA with the US that carrier must be majority-owned by Dutch interests. Because nationality clauses discriminate against carriers from other EU countries, they were found incompatible with European law. The rejection of nationality clauses was seen by airline industry insiders across the world as a staggering blow to the post-World War II bilateral regulatory system (Doganis 2006: 54–9). The renegotiation of ASAs to remove nationality clauses will undermine the commercial value of the agreements. When Spain, for instance, negotiated ASAs around the world under the old system, it did so knowing the traffic rights it won would redound to the benefit of Iberia and other Spanish airlines. Now, the rights may end up being used by a German or a Portuguese or a Hungarian carrier.

Although the court rejected the claim by the EC for "exclusive competence" in negotiating ASAs, the ruling against nationality clauses so undermined the bilateral system that the EC essentially got what it had sought anyway. The ECJ decision meant that every ASA involving an EU country would eventually have to be renegotiated, and the Commission argued that it should be the one to do so (*Flight International* 2002). The EU had already negotiated bloc aviation agreements with Norway and with Switzerland. Moreover, the fact that member states could no longer engage in the usual horse-trading in favor of their own carriers made negotiating as a bloc more palatable and even attractive. So in 2003, the EC was authorized by EU member countries to negotiate on their behalf. A top objective of the EC has been to use this power to extend the scope of the ECAA to the European Union's neighbors beginning, in 2006, with Albania, Serbia, Bosnia-Herzegovina, Croatia, and Macedonia. In 2008, agreements with Ukraine, Israel, and Jordan were under negotiation as further steps toward the creation of a single pan-European aviation market encompassing not just Europe but much of Central Asia and North Africa, too (European Commission 2008).

As impressive as these achievements have been, they comprise only one scale of the EC's efforts to promote and spread liberalization. The organization has also become a very important actor in intercontinental markets, including the biggest – the transatlantic.

From "Open Skies" to "Clear Skies"

The spread of liberalization, both through the renegotiation of bilateral ASAs and through multilateral initiatives like that in Europe, has done much to free the airline industry from the restraints put in place after World War II. Yet there is farther to go, at least in the eyes of liberalization advocates. For the airline industry is still beset by practices that make it unlike *any* other part of international trade. To "normalize" the industry or, to put it in the terms of airline industry expert Rigas Doganis (2006: 52–4), to move from "Open Skies" to "Clear Skies" would require two sorts of reforms. First, airlines would have to enjoy broader route rights. In particular, cabotage and seventh freedom rights would have to be freely available. Currently, very few ASAs beyond Europe include such rights.

Second and more importantly, restrictions on the foreign ownership of airlines would have to be lifted and greatly loosened.

As noted above, most ASAs include nationality clauses that require that an airline be owned by citizens of the signing country. As Doganis notes (2006: 57), this practice – like most aspects of the relationship between airlines and governments – has had some salutary effects. For example, it has precluded the kind of "flag of convenience" system that has emerged in maritime transportation where companies register ships in Panama or Liberia, for instance, to limit regulation and taxation. Accordingly, a primary justification for national ownership rules is that they make clear which government has the right and obligation to enforce an airline's conformance to safety, labor, and financial probity standards (*Flight International* 2003).

Moreover, it is hard to break from the decades-long tradition of flag carriers as symbols of national identity (Raguraman 1997). The colors and symbols used in a flag carrier's livery, the uniforms worn by its flight crew, the languages used on board, and the food served in flight all tend to reinforce nationalist sentiment. As a result, nationalistic opposition to foreign ownership in the airline industry is common. In a survey of New Zealanders, for instance, 72 percent agreed with the statement, 'New Zealand should have its own national airline." and only 10 percent agreed that "The Government of New Zealand should allow full foreign ownership of any New Zealand-based airline." (Duval 2005).

Nationality clauses have made it difficult for airlines to merge across international boundaries, making it hard for some carriers to attain the economies of scale that US carriers draw upon in their huge home base. Instead, too many small airlines from small and medium-sized markets have tried to sustain sprawling international networks – often duplicating the services of airlines based in neighboring countries. It is no coincidence that the merger between Air France and KLM and the acquisition of Swiss by Lufthansa took place after the ECJ ruling against nationality clauses.[7] Removing nationality clauses elsewhere in the world would likely clear the way for fewer, larger, and presumably more efficient airlines to emerge. Similarly, the relaxation of nationality rules would make it easier for airlines to raise capital abroad.

These issues are at the heart of the liberalization of air services between Europe and the US. Interestingly, the American refusal to give ground on the ownership issue has been a stubborn obstacle to progress. Indeed, the US, despite decades of advocating liberalization, has a more restrictive ownership standard than most other countries. American law requires that no more than 25 percent of the voting rights in a US-registered airline be held by foreigners. The European position has been that the US must lift this ceiling to balance what was seen as a profoundly unequal relationship. US airlines have long enjoyed extensive fifth freedom rights to and from European gateways (e.g., see Figure 3.2), but domestic routes in the US remained strictly forbidden to foreign airlines.

The fact that the EC, rather than 27 individual countries, negotiated with the US after 2003 enhanced the European bargaining position. In the past, the US had been able to "pick off" European governments one-by-one, using concessions granted by more liberally minded countries to put pressure on more recalcitrant ones. The EC represented a more formidable and unified foe on the other side of the bargaining table. The discussions between the EC and US unfolded over years of shuttle diplomacy. Twice, the talks collapsed, but in early 2007, the US and the EU took the first significant steps towards a Transatlantic Common Aviation Area (TCAA).

The agreement gave the US a great deal. It extended Open Skies provisions to 11 more European countries, the most important being the UK. One important result was that services between Heathrow and the US were opened to more than the four carriers that had such rights under Bermuda II (United and American for the US; British Airways and Virgin Atlantic for the UK). The new agreement went into effect in March 2008 when Heathrow's new Terminal 5 provided additional capacity to parcel out.

Europe's gains under the agreement were somewhat more limited. European carriers did win the right to establish franchises in the US, meaning that a European airline could contract with a US-owned airline to fly US domestic routes in the European carrier's livery and under its brand. Air France might contract, for instance, for franchised services from New York to Los Angeles. European carriers also got seventh freedom rights on routes between the US and Europe. The first seventh freedom service established under the new agreement was a short-lived Air France flight between London-Heathrow and Los Angeles. In 2008, a wholly-owned British Airways subsidiary called Open Skies (discussed more fully in Chapter 8) commenced seventh freedom flights between Paris and the United States (Wall 2008a). However, European carriers did not get cabotage rights nor did the American government significantly change its position on ownership of US carriers (Bond and Wall 2007). However, the 2007 agreement was only the first step. The second phase talks began shortly after the first phase went into effect.

The stakes are huge. One study of the economic benefits of airline liberalization reported, for instance, that liberalization in the trans-Tasman Sea market (Figure 5.6) had made both the Australian and New Zealand economies more than US$700 million larger than would have been the case in the absence of any liberalization (InterVISTAS-ga 2 2006: 51). Further liberalization of the transatlantic market is expected to have similarly favorable economic consequences (Robyn 2003). Furthermore, if the TCAA ever comes to fruition, the effects will not be limited to the countries directly involved. The overall result will be to denationalize the airline industry. Much as a Hyundai assembled in Alabama or Slovakia is not exactly a Korean car and an airliner assembled in Washington is not American in the way it once was, many airlines will not fit neatly in national containers in the future either. The airline industry, which has been so instrumental in globalization, will have been globalized itself.

Cutting the strings: airline privatization across the world

To a greater degree than at any time since the earliest years of aviation, the airlines that ply the world's skyways, including the routes opened by deregulation,

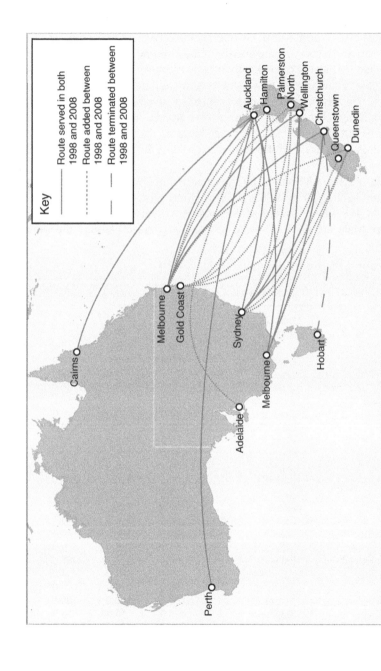

Figure 5.6 Nonstop scheduled airline services across the Tasman Sea (sources: adapted from a similar illustration in InterVISTAS-ga2 2006 with new data from OAG 1998 and 2008).

Since the Australia–New Zealand Open Skies Agreement became effective in 2002, the number of city-pairs served nonstop across the Tasman Sea has proliferated, with many of the new routes attributable to new carriers such as Pacific Blue.

are privately owned. Indeed, deregulation has been paralleled by a wave of privatizations (Table 5.3). And, of course, the legions of new carriers competing for traffic are overwhelmingly privately owned.

As Chapter 2 noted, state ownership in the airline industry was pervasive in the decades just after World War II. Government involvement in the industry did have some positive effects upon the growth of the airborne world, but state ownership also made for bloated carriers only weakly responsive to the needs of customers. The routes and aircraft flown, the employees hired and fired, the fares and air freight rates levied have all been subject to government manipulation in state-owned airlines. An extreme instance was Burma Airways. In 1989, the ruling junta fired all of the airline's pilots and replaced them with copilots whose loyalty was less suspect. The effect on the airline's safety performance was predictable.[8]

Yet Burma (renamed Myanmar by the same junta) was out of step with its time and region by then for the 1980s were when the great airline sell-off gained momentum. In 1985, both Singapore Airlines (SIA) and Malaysia Air System (MAS – later Malaysia Airlines) were partially privatized. Around the same

Table 5.3 State ownership of selected flag carriers, 1984–2005

Carrier	Nationality	1984	1995	2005
Aer Lingus	Ireland	100.0	100.0	85.1
Aeroflot RIA	Russia	100.0	100.0	51.2
Aerolineas Argentinas	Argentina	100.0	5.0	5.0
Air Canada	Canada	100.0	0.0	0.0
Air China	China	100.0	100.0	69.0
Air India	India	100.0	100.0	100.0
Air New Zealand	New Zealand	100.0	0.0	80.2
Avianca	Colombia	0.0	0.0	0.0
British Airways	United Kingdom	100.0	0.0	0.0
Cathay Pacific	Hong Kong	0.0	0.0	0.0
Egyptair	Egypt	100.0	100.0	100.0
El Al	Israel	100.0	100.0	20.0
Ethiopian Airlines	Ethiopia	100.0	100.0	100.0
Japan Airlines	Japan	37.7	0.0	0.0
Kenya Airways	Kenya	100.0	100.0	22.0
LAN Chile	Chile	100.0	0.0	0.0
LOT Polish Airlines	Poland	100.0	100.0	68.0
Mexicana	Mexico	58.0	35.0	0.0
Pakistan International	Pakistan	100.0	57.4	87.0
Philippine Airlines	Philippines	99.7	33.0	4.0
Qantas	Australia	100.0	0.0	0.0
Royal Jordanian	Jordan	100.0	100.0	100.0
Singapore Airlines	Singapore	100.0	54.0	54.0
South African Airways	South Africa	100.0	100.0	98.2
United Airlines	USA	0.0	0.0	0.0
Sample Average		*83.8*	*51.4*	*41.8*

Sources: *Flight International* 1984, 2006a, 2006b, 2006c; *Airline Business* 1995.

time, Japan Airlines was fully privatized, partly because the horrific 1985 crash referred to in Chapter 3 gave the then-prime minister the clout to install a new management team favorable to the government's privatization plan (Whymant 1986). By the late 1980s, major carriers had been privatized in Europe, Latin America, and Canada. In the 1990s, carriers ranging from giants like Lufthansa and Qantas to small fry like Uruguay's Pluna were added to the mix.[9]

Perhaps the most famous and influential of the early privatizations was that of British Airways (BA). BA had been created in 1974 through the merger of BOAC and British European Airways (Sampson 1984: 87–9). From BOAC, BA inherited an enviable network of international routes; but BOAC had always been hobbled by the politicization of its operations. The airline was overstaffed and spent lavishly at the same time that its position was undermined by the loss of Britain's overseas colonial empire. BOAC lurched between "politicians ignorant of airlines and professionals bewildered by politics" (Sampson 1984: 88). As a result, BA figured prominently in the privatization initiative of Prime Minister Margaret Thatcher. The airline was privatized in 1987 via a highly successful public offering of shares in Britain and several overseas stock markets. BA thus became first European flag carrier in which the state held no direct financial interest (Hanlon 1996: 7; Morrell 2007: 131–4).

Even before its formal privatization, BA – whose initials had been derided as standing for "Bloody Awful" – began to change under the pressure of its impending transition in ownership. Stewardesses were taught to smile more warmly and to exercise greater care in maintaining their personal appearance. Personnel throughout the airline who worked in contact with customers were trained in the finer points of "Putting People First." Together, these changes made more believable BA's new advertising claim to be "The World's Favourite Airline." At the same time, however, BA slashed the airline's labor force.

Newly aggressive, British Airways also embarked upon a significant expansion spree. In 1987, BA bought British Caledonian (BCal), its main competitor in Britain. The acquisition gave BA a much stronger presence in Africa and at Gatwick, London's second airport (Doganis 1991: 99). By 1990, BA served 164 cities in 76 countries, an almost unrivalled global reach. The carrier's bottom line had improved markedly, too.

More broadly, BA became a prime example of the merits of privatization. In the decades since, airlines have emerged as favored targets in the broader privatization movement across Latin America, East Asia, and the countries making the transition from communism to capitalism. The airline industry seemed better suited for privatization than many other arenas of heavy state involvement because there were already decades of evidence that privately-run airlines could perform well. In contrast, privatization initiatives in other arenas, such as elementary education, were more experimental. Moreover, the assets of a state-owned airline could be relatively easily valued. And the airline industry was in the midst of a great boom precisely when privatization was taking the world by storm.

There is another factor, however, that accounts for the high profile of airlines in "the greatest sale" (Yergin and Stanislaw 1998: 13). A century on from the

Wright Brothers, air transportation still evokes an aura of daring and exhilaration absent from most other parts of the economy. Perhaps no other industry has attracted such massive, and often fruitless, investments from such an assortment of already successful individuals including Richard Branson (whose fortune was made in media), Kingfisher's Vijay Mallya (beer), Gol's Constantino Oliveria (buses), and Carlos Slim, the highly diversified Mexican billionaire who is a major investor in the LCC startup Volaris.

Airline privatization took several forms during the crucial decade from 1985 to 1995. In high- and middle-income countries, such as Britain and Mexico respectively, shares in flag carriers were offered to the public and the airlines were listed on stock exchanges. In a number of poorer countries, however, air-lines were essentially sold to elite insiders. For example, a controlling 67 percent share in Philippine Airlines was sold to a consortium controlled by a tobacco and beer magnate Lucio Tan. Third, airlines as diverse as BWIA International (Trinidad's flag carrier) and Aeroflot were privatized in part by selling stakes to employees. This particular form of "popular capitalism" mitigates the hostility with which employees typically regard the privatization of their employers. Finally, privatization created openings for a frenzy of international trade sales among carriers as airlines from richer countries bought up strategic stakes in air-lines from poorer countries such as KLM's 26 percent stake in Kenya Airways[10] (Morrell 2007: 139–42). In conjunction with the 1995 purchase, the two carriers also formed a marketing partnership in which Kenya Airways drew on its African network to feed KLM's Nairobi–Amsterdam flights while KLM with-drew from all African markets south of Nairobi except South Africa. Kenya Airways' privatization was actually a mixture of methods in that the trade sale to KLM was complemented by the allocation of shares to the African carriers' employees and the flotation of about a third of Kenya Airways' shares on the Nairobi stock market. By 2006, the Kenyan government had just a 23 percent share in its flag carrier (Morrell 2007: 142).

Yet in much of the developing world, state ownership remains pervasive. In South Asia, the Middle East, sub-Saharan Africa, and the island nations of the Pacific, most flag carriers have remained fully state-owned for decades and there are only dim prospects for privatization over the horizon. In India, decades of state intervention in the economy have snarled Air India in a web of government strictures from which escape seems remote (Ionides 2004). In the Middle East, meanwhile, the tradition of repressive and authoritarian one-man rule has hardly been conducive to privatization.

Sub-Saharan Africa is perhaps the region where the state-owned airline's dominance was least challenged through the 1980s and 1990s. The only large African flag carriers with majority private shareholdings in 2005 were Kenya Airways[11] and Air Mauritius. It was no coincidence that these two carriers oper-ated substantially larger networks and younger fleets than state-owned African flag carriers. Kenya Airways, for instance, flew to 25 foreign destinations stretching from London to Hong Kong to Johannesburg and featured the 777 in its long-haul fleet. In contrast, state-owned Nigerian Airways on the other side of the continent was a spectacular failure, culminating in its collapse in 2003. What happened next in Nigeria is the more interesting part of this story. Instead of further propping up Nigerian Airways, the government allowed the carrier to sink under the weight of its debt and mismanagement. Since then, a very different airline has been allowed to fill at least part of the void left by the collapse. In June 2005, Virgin Nigeria began flying repainted Airbuses borrowed from Virgin Atlantic (Mahtani 2005). The new carrier is a joint venture between Virgin Atlantic Airways, which owns 49 percent, and a group of Nigerian investors.[12]

New carriers like Virgin Nigeria are representative of a shift in the primary dimension of change in the airline industry. For a decade beginning around 1985, the industry was swept by privatization; but now new privatizations continue at a trickle. Instead, the energy in the industry has shifted to new entrants. In India, for instance, well-funded start-ups now represent a major challenge to Air India (as evidenced in Figure 5.2). More importantly, those new entrants dramatically increase the choices for travelers and air cargo shippers and lower their costs.[13]

6 Survival of the fittest

Network carriers in the global airline industry

Different directions, same destination

In late 1980s, Aeroflot operated perhaps the most globally dispersed airline network the world has ever seen (Davies 1992: 86–7). Its international routes stretched around the world: 45 destinations in Europe, 36 in Asia, 36 in Africa, 9 in Latin America, and 4 in the USA and Canada. The carrier's winged hammer-and-sickle logo was seen from Kolkata (previously Calcutta) to Kingston, Bujumbura to Buenos Aires. Two decades later, most of that sprawling network was gone (Figure 6.1). In 2008, a much shrunken Aeroflot, operating from Russia rather than the Soviet Union, served only one city in Latin America (Havana) and only one city in Africa (Cairo). In all, the number of destinations beyond the former Soviet Union fell by about half. In contracting so dramatically, Aeroflot ran counter to the broader trend in the airline industry. Aeroflot has retreated while many carriers have expanded aggressively abroad. The explanation is simple: Aeroflot's old network, especially the inclusion of places like Bujumbura, was driven by geopolitics. The demise of the Soviet Union left the carrier without the rationale or funds to continue flying to so many far-flung, economically unattractive destinations. Conversely, for many other airlines, the loosening of the links between the airline industry and governments has meant the freedom to expand.

Before deregulation, for instance, Delta Air Lines was largely confined to the Southeastern US; by the late 1980s, the carrier had taken advantage of deregulation to literally spread its wings across the US yet it still had a minimal presence internationally – just a dozen points located primarily in Canada and Mexico. Then the spread of liberalization abroad and the sagging fortunes of Pan Am created new opportunities abroad for Delta. By 2008, the carrier flew to 111 destinations outside the US,[1] including Moscow (author's analysis of data in OAG 2008). And in late 2008, Delta merged with Northwest Airlines creating the largest airline in the world (measured by revenue, passenger-kilometers, fleet size, and other criteria), a status once enjoyed by Aeroflot.

Aeroflot and Delta, despite the seemingly contrary directions in which they have changed, are both full-service network carriers, the type of airline that is the focus of this chapter. A network carrier is an airline that flies a mixture of

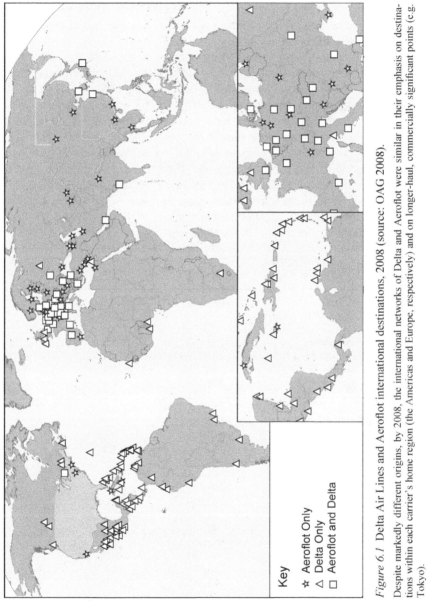

Figure 6.1 Delta Air Lines and Aeroflot international destinations, 2008 (source: OAG 2008).

Despite markedly different origins, by 2008, the international networks of Delta and Aeroflot were similar in their emphasis on destinations within each carrier's home region (the Americas and Europe, respectively) and on longer-haul, commercially significant points (e.g. Tokyo).

Key

☆ Aeroflot Only
△ Delta Only
☐ Aeroflot and Delta

short-, medium-, and long-range routes, operates diverse fleets, and generally has at least one hub. In-flight and on the ground, network carriers tend to offer better services than most other airlines, but ultimately what such a carrier sells is its network. Both Aeroflot and Delta have responded to the new realities of the airline industry by trying to build more economically competitive networks; for one, that has meant an overall contraction, for the other expansion; but the ultimate goal is the same.

Although low-cost carriers (LCCs) have drawn much admiring attention in recent years, it is network carriers, especially those with networks stretching around the world, that actually do much of the airline industry's work. Of the 20 largest airlines, measured by traffic in 2007, 19 were network carriers (Table 6.1). Together, the 19 accounted for just over 50 percent of all revenue passenger-kilometers worldwide (based on *Air Transport World* 2008d and ICAO 2007). The only LCC to break into the top 20 was Southwest Airlines. LCCs *are* important and becoming more so. Their rise and significance are discussed in the next chapter. For now, our interest is in network carriers, specifically the geography of their operations, their alliances with one another, the daunting problems many face, and the implications of those problems for those who make their living at more than 10,000 meters.

Table 6.1 The world's top 20 passenger airlines, 2007

Rank	Airline	RPKs[1]	Average annual growth, 2002–2007 (%)
1	American Airlines	222,868	2.6
2	Air France-KLM	207,227	5.5
3	United Airlines	188,983	1.4
4	Delta Air Lines	166,529	1.8
5	Continental Air Lines	135,653	7.3
6	Lufthansa	117,656	5.8
7	Northwest Airlines	117,550	0.3
8	Southwest Airlines	116,416	9.8
9	British Airways	113,016	2.5
10	US Airways Group	98,618	0.5
11	Emirates	94,346	25.6
12	JAL Group	92,173	2.0
13	Singapore Airlines	90,900	5.0
14	Qantas	84,366	2.3
15	China Southern	81,728	30.6
16	Air Canada	81,462	3.3
17	Cathay Pacific Airways	74,303	8.7
18	Air China	66,986	22.8
19	Thai Airways	61,619	4.9
20	ANA	61,219	2.9

Source: *Air Transport World* 2008d.

Note
1 RPKs = revenue passenger–kilometers.

Hubs, spokes, and the American network carriers

In the more competitive industry shaped by liberalization, geography is one of the most decisive factors determining who wins and who loses. More specifically, the places an airline serves and the spatial organization of the network that draws those places together matter more than they did before liberalization. Some airlines, such as British Airways (BA), inherited strong networks from the era of pervasive state ownership and regulation and thrived in the liberalized market; other carriers, like BA's rival Virgin Atlantic, took advantage of the opportunities opened up by liberalization to build strong networks; and still other airlines were never able to surmount the weaknesses of their networks and they disappeared.

Pan Am, for instance, was the world's most prominent airline in the mid-twentieth century, but it did not survive deregulation. Many factors, geography among them, conspired to bring Pan Am down. Favored by the US government abroad, Pan Am spun a vast international network (not so different from that of Aeroflot), but was prevented by the same government from developing any domestic network. When US domestic carriers were cooped up inside the country's borders, Pan Am's imbalanced network was no great liability. Gateways like JFK served as transfer points from other airlines' domestic services to Pan Am's international network. However, when liberalization freed US domestic airlines to begin adding international services to their own networks, Pan Am was forced to try to compete on their turf, too. It bought National Airlines at an inflated price and then began paying the former staff of National the elevated wages to which Pan Am's employees were accustomed. The National merger compounded Pan Am's already difficult financial circumstances stemming from its massive wide-body purchases. The rash of terrorist attacks against the airline industry, including the 1989 bombing of Pan Am 103 over Lockerbie, Scotland, only deepened Pan Am's woes. Along the way, the carrier sold off its international crown jewels (Table 6.2). The airlines that replaced Pan Am on those overseas routes – especially United, American, and Delta – had geography on their side.

Deregulation, hub-and-spoke networks, and the ascent of the mega-carriers

The survivors, such as Delta, had significant domestic networks when deregulation began and then took advantage of deregulation to establish sprawling nationwide and ultimately international hub-and-spoke networks that became a cornerstone of their competitive advantage. By "bundling" traffic at its hub, an airline can draw on a number of incoming flights to "feed" each outbound flight, and similarly a number of outbound flights will draw more traffic feed onto each incoming flight. As a result, the hubbing carrier is likely to enjoy at least one of three advantages:

- a higher load factor, meaning a greater percentage of seats or cargo space is filled with revenue-generating traffic;
- larger aircraft, which typically have lower per passenger-kilometer costs than smaller aircraft;
- higher frequency service, which is more likely to match the travel plans of potential customers.

Further, the hub-and-spoke system is a means of efficiently serving lightly traveled markets by bundling traffic at the hub. In 2006, fewer than 2 percent of the 47,000 airport-pair markets in the US generated more than 200 passengers per day.[2] (Table 6.3).

There *were* hub-and-spoke systems in the US before deregulation. As described in Chapter 2, for instance, Delta hubbed at Atlanta, giving rise to the wry comment in the southeastern US that whether one was bound for heaven or hell, you had to pass through Atlanta first. However, the vagaries of the Civil Aeronautics Board (CAB) route awards prevented the development of nation-wide hub-and-spoke systems. In 1977, for instance, under regulation, Atlanta was linked by nonstop flights to only 47 of the 81 cities in the Delta's network. The busiest route for Delta did not involve Atlanta at all but instead linked Chicago and St. Louis, a route Delta had gained through its merger with Chicago & Southern Air Lines in 1953. Yet apart from this connection, Delta had almost no presence in St. Louis (Bowen 1991).

Table 6.2 Purchases of US flag carrier routes

Date	Seller	Buyer	Routes	Millions of dollars
1985	Pan Am	United	US–Asia/Australia/New Zealand	$750
1990	Pan Am	United	New York/Washington–London	$400
			San Francisco/Los Angeles/Seattle–London	
			London–Europe fifth freedom routes	
1990	Pan Am	Lufthansa	Intra-Germany	$150
1991	Pan Am	Delta	US–Europe	$416[1]
			(except London routes and Miami–Paris)	
1991	Pan Am	United	US–Latin America	$135
			Miami–Paris	
1990	Eastern	American	US–Latin America	$310
1991	TWA	American	Chicago–London	$110
1991	TWA	American	Boston/New York/Los Angeles–London	$445
1991	TWA	USAir	Baltimore–London	$50
			Philadelphia–London	
2001	TWA	American	Remainder of TWA international network	[2]

Source: contemporary media accounts of route purchases.

Notes
1 This amount also includes Pan Am's US East Coast shuttle.
2 American took control of the rest of TWA's international network, including New York–Paris vv (vice versa), via a 2001 merger valued at $4.2 billion, which also included TWA's extensive US domestic network, TWA's fleet, ground infrastructure and other resources.

Table 6.3 Top airport-pairs in the US, 2006

Rank	Airport 1	Airport 2	Passengers (thousands)[1]
1	Chicago-O'Hare	New York-La Guardia	1,680
2	Los Angeles	New York-Kennedy	1,592
3	Atlanta	New York-La Guardia	1,568
4	Honolulu	Maui	1,524
5	Ft. Lauderdale	New York-La Guardia	1,482
6	Newark	Orlando	1,387
7	Las Vegas	Los Angeles	1,356
8	Orlando	Philadelphia	1,257
9	New York-Kennedy	Orlando	1,207
10	Honolulu	Los Angeles	1,200
11	New York-La Guardia	Washington-Reagan	1,199
12	Denver	Phoenix	1,178
13	Ft. Lauderdale	New York-Kennedy	1,169
14	Los Angeles	Oakland	1,167
15	Oakland	San Diego	1,137
57 other airport pairs with at least 2,001 passengers per day			51,213
1,226 airport-pairs with 201–2,000 passengers per day			260,502
4,114 airport-pairs with 21–200 passengers per day			95,232
41,309 airport-pairs with 1–20 passengers per day			32,102
Total			**459,151**

Source: BTS 2009a.

Note
1 The number of passengers shown is the annual sum of the number of passengers traveling in either direction (e.g. the Honolulu–Maui figure is the total of those traveling from Honolulu to Maui and from Maui to Honolulu).

After the Airline Deregulation Act (ADA) was passed, Delta restructured its network in ways that greatly increased the importance of Atlanta and the airline's other hubs. By 2008, despite the carrier's massive expansion across the US and the world, the share of its flights accounted for by the Atlanta hub had grown from 18 percent on the eve of deregulation to 24 percent. Further, by 2008, more than two-thirds of the cities in the airline's network were linked by nonstop Delta flights to Atlanta, and the busiest link was between Atlanta and New York (author's analysis of data in OAG 2008).

Not only did carriers such as Delta establish more sharply defined hub-and-spoke systems after deregulation, they also tried – with varying degrees of success – to extend those networks nationwide and internationally. For if a hub-and-spoke network confers important advantages to the airline that operates it, a larger network confers even larger benefits. The greater the number of cities an airline has in its network, the greater the number of onward flights each arriving flight can "feed" through the hub amplifying a hubbing airline's load factor, aircraft size, and frequency advantages. Higher density traffic along each spoke drives down the cost per passenger for gates, ticket counters, and other fixed costs on the ground. Moreover, each new spoke exponentially increases the number of possible city-pairs the network can mediate. A network of 20 cities has 380 possible city-pairs, for instance, but a network of 21 cities has 420 city-pairs.

To grow their networks, many airlines have relied upon mergers and acquisitions. In particular, mergers combining airlines with very different geographies offer the potential for significant synergies, although Pan Am's difficult digestion of National showed that it was not so simple. Some mergers, however, *have* worked. Delta, for instance, has been involved in two massive mergers. In 1987, it merged with Western Airlines. As the name of the latter implies, its home market was the western US, which it served from its Salt Lake City hub. The merger helped to increase the number of cities in Delta's network west of the Mississippi from 19 before deregulation to 59 by the late 1980s (Bowen 1991). More recently, of course, Delta merged with Northwest in 2008; that merger is discussed more fully below.

The geographic expansion of top airlines has been matched by the development of multi-hub networks. By the late 1980s, for instance, the Delta hubs at Salt Lake City and Atlanta were complemented by Dallas-Ft. Worth and Cincinnati. Other carriers also established multi-hub networks. The advantage of multiple hubs was in mitigating the circuitousness of trips involving connections at key hubs. Passengers – particularly time-sensitive business travelers – thereby avoided the diversions that a single national hub would have required for city-pair combinations as diverse as Buffalo–Tampa, Des Moines–Tucson, and Milwaukee–El Paso.

In the 1980s, network carriers amplified the advantages of bigness with two new marketing tools, both pioneered by Robert Crandall at American Airlines. First, Crandall oversaw the development of a new approach to yield[3] management using the company's Sabre computer reservations system (CRS). Even before deregulation, Sabre and two other systems helped to make the airline industry the single biggest private user of computing power in the US. Under Crandall's leadership, American Airlines turned its CRS into an even more valuable asset as Sabre became a weapon wielded against competitors. Drawing on the power of Sabre, for instance, American carefully released only a limited number of seats at its lowest fares (Belobaba 1987; Petzinger 1995: 281). Upstart rival PEOPLExpress, a forerunner of today's LCCs, was filling up entire economy class cabins at the same low fares.[4]

Crandall's other key innovation was the frequent flyer program (FFP). The AAdvantage FFP built brand loyalty, while at the same time leveraging both the sophistication of American's computer systems and the scope of its network (Petzinger 1995: 139). The larger network of American increased both the earning and redemption opportunities available to members, and the cost of the FFP was minimized by using the same yield management system described above to carefully limit where and when frequent flyers could redeem the free tickets they earned as rewards.

Together, hub-and-spoke networks, yield management systems, and frequent flyer programs made for a lethal trident in the arsenal of the largest airlines, which soon became the so-called mega-carriers. Between 1977 and 1982, the market share of the four largest US carriers (in terms of revenue passenger-kilometers) had fallen from 56 percent to 54 percent; but it then climbed steeply to 65 percent by 1987 (Taaffe *et al.* 1996: 149). An industry that had had 11 heavily regulated trunk carriers before 1978 now had a handful of mega-carriers whose services blanketed the nation in a way that no airline's network ever had. The ascent of the mega-carriers challenged a key argument used to justify deregulation (Goetz and Sutton 1997). Economists had argued that the market for airline services was contestable, meaning that it cost so little for an airline to enter a new market that even if a particular carrier had a monopoly on a route between two cities it would not abuse its position because doing so would only invite in the competition. The massive expansion of carriers such as American and the demise of challengers such as PEOPLExpress seemed to refute contestable markets theory and lent credence to the thesis that "some degree of market power will be necessary for carrier survival in trunk markets" (Viton 1986: 367[5]).

The rationalization and internationalization of US network carriers

Then came a new wave of low-cost carriers (LCCs) along with one, Southwest Airlines, which had been growing all along since the early 1970s. By 2008, the domestic market share of the four largest US airlines, again measured in domestic revenue passenger-kilometers, had fallen to 49 percent (based on BTS 2009a). And ranked among the big four was LCC Southwest Airlines. If only network carriers are considered, then the four largest US domestic airlines in 2008 (American, United, Delta, and US Airways) had a combined share of 44 percent and overall network carriers and their regional airline affiliates had about 75 percent of the US domestic market in 2008 (based on BTS 2009a); LCCs held the rest and their share was still growing. The outlook for other developed markets, including Canada, Australia, and much of Europe, is similar in direction if not in degree; and over a longer timeframe, the same shift in the balance of power is likely to affect the airline industry in developing countries.

In response, the network carriers have been forced to adapt and that has meant changing the structure and operation of hub-and-spoke networks, at least in the US. First and most importantly, between the LCCs and the old network carriers, a third category of airline has become more important than ever – especially in the US. American Eagle, Atlantic Southeast Airlines (ASA), and Comair are three of more than a dozen regional carriers in the US. The network airlines formed relationships with the regional carriers in the 1980s, relying on the latter to feed their key hubs using smaller aircraft on short-haul routes. The regional airlines' services were code-shared with those of the larger carriers so that in a CRS, an ASA flight from Savannah to Atlanta would be listed with the carrier code "DL", giving a passenger traveling from Savanna to Stuttgart via Atlanta the impression of seamless Delta services. The advantage for Delta and other network carriers in such arrangements included the regional airlines' lower labor costs (e.g., for their pilots) and the flexibility permitted by the arm's length relationship with regional airlines. Big airlines could more easily terminate a contract with the former than cut back their own unionized operations.

In the 1990s, the network carriers became even more reliant on their regional carrier partners as the latter took on increasingly long-haul codeshare services. Critical to this transformation was the development of regional jets (RJs), which first flew in 1993. During the following decade, two kinds of constraints that had circumscribed RJ operations were loosened: their range increased to make possible nonstop routes well in excess of 1,500 kilometers and several of the network carriers successfully renegotiated "scope agreements" with their pilot unions to allow larger RJs. Before the September 11, 2001 attacks and ensuing financial calamity for the industry, scope agreements commonly required an airline to use its mainline staff for aircraft with more than 50 seats; but in the ensuing financial distress, unions agreed to greater flexibility to stave off the collapse of their employers (Abbey 2005). These two changes permitted network carriers to assign RJs to many more routes, including routes so long that they make misnomers of the terms "regional jet" and "regional carrier" (Figure 6.2). By 2008, regional carriers together mounted more domestic US flights than either the network carriers they served or the vaunted, up-and-coming LCCs – though the small size of the aircraft flown by regional carriers meant that their share of revenue passenger-kilometers was small (Table 6.4).

Second and related to the previous point, US airlines have eliminated some hubs[6] (Figure 6.3). In particular, recent major airline mergers have been followed by hub rationalization. American Airlines scrapped the St. Louis hub it acquired through its merger with TWA, and several of the hubs operated by US Airways – especially Pittsburgh[7] – and America West (e.g., Columbus) have been abandoned or downsized since their merger in 2005. The merger of Delta and Northwest is likely to have the same outcome, further reducing the number of network carrier hubs. There were about two dozen remaining major hub and intercontinental gateways in the US in 2008 (Figure 6.3).

Third, during the same period in which the surviving network carriers have rationalized their hub-and-spoke systems in the US, they have become more aggressive in extending those systems globally, partly to generate still more traffic feed over their networks and partly to escape the depredations of the LCCs (Table 6.5). The growth of Continental abroad has been particularly stunning. In the summer of 2005 alone, for instance, it introduced nonstop service from Newark to Beijing, Stockholm, Hamburg, and Berlin (Connelly 2005). The expansion of the carrier featured throughout this chapter, Delta, has been nearly as impressive (Figure 6.4). It has added dozens of destinations in Latin America, Europe, Asia, the Middle East, and even long-neglected Africa. Delta's African routes by 2008 included Atlanta–Lagos, Atlanta–Dakar–Johannesburg, and New York-JFK–Accra.

China has proven an especially attractive foreign market as its surging economy has fuelled traffic growth. US carriers leaped at the expanded traffic rights opened up via new agreements with China, particularly a landmark 2004 deal (Bond 2004). By 2009, American, Continental, Delta, and US Airways had joined Northwest and United in offering passenger services to China (Figure 6.5). And, as noted earlier in Chapter 5, FedEx and UPS will both have their principal intra-Asian hubs in China by 2010.

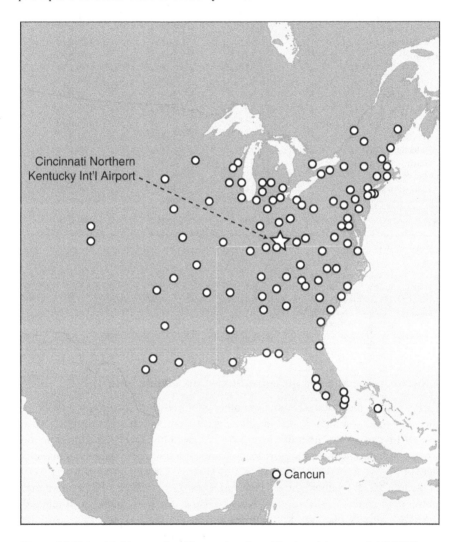

Figure 6.2 Delta Air Lines regional jet services from Cincinnati (source: OAG 2008).

In 2008, regional carriers (primarily Comair) flew regional jets (RJs) from Cincinnati Northern Kentucky International Airport to 101 destinations nonstop. The farthest destination was Cancun, Mexico, 2,000 kilometers to the south. Overall, RJs accounted for nearly 85 percent of Delta's flights at its Cincinnati hub.

Table 6.4 Domestic traffic for US network, low-cost, and regional carriers, 2008

Carrier	Passengers (thousands)	Flights (thousands)	RPKs[1] (millions)
American	71,539	590	131,158
United	51,661	441	100,196
Delta[2]	59,276	448	97,914
US Airways	48,504	448	75,686
Other Network Carriers	98,507	903	171,072
All Network Carriers	**329,487**	**2,830**	**576,025**
Southwest	101,921	1,191	118,250
JetBlue	20,479	193	38,856
AirTran	24,571	260	30,154
Frontier	10,071	96	14,629
Other LCCs[3]	14,995	290	27,026
All LCCs	**172,037**	**2,030**	**228,916**
Skywest	19,454	557	16,050
Expressjet	12,847	355	12,553
American Eagle	15,575	474	10,964
Atlantic Southeast	11,916	278	8,861
Other Regional	72,037	1,804	51,593
All Regional	**131,829**	**3,468**	**100,020**
Other carriers[4]	16,555	993	10,998
All carriers	**649,908**	**9,321**	**915,959**

Source: BTS 2009a.

Notes
1 RPKs = revenue passenger-kilometers.
2 The figures for Delta do not include Northwest, with which Delta merged in late 2008. If the two carriers are combined, then the 2008 figures are: passengers (thousands) 97,725; flights (thousands) 796; and RPKs (millions) 156,380.
3 LCCs = low cost carriers.
4 Other carriers include, for example, small airlines providing intra-Alaska services.

Liberalization and the globalization of the airline industry

Liberalization has freed airlines from other countries, too, to add more spokes to their networks. Lufthansa, for instance, grew from 102 foreign destinations in 1979 (the eve of the liberalized era) to 172 in 2008. Over the same interval, SIA's international network grew from 32 cities to 63, LAN Chile's international network grew from 14 to 25, and that of Cyprus Airways grew from 12 to 30 (Bowen 1993 and author's analysis of data in OAG Max 2008). Not every carrier grew of course. Some former Warsaw Bloc carriers, such as Romania's TAROM, shrank like Aeroflot, and some Western carriers, too, (e.g., Alitalia) contracted in the face of a more competitive market.

The international network of Qantas also shrank over the period 1979 to 2008 (from 28 to 21 cities) but not because the carrier was too weak. Rather, the network realignment by Qantas was an effort to harness the strengths of other carriers and in that sense Qantas points towards what is sure to be an important

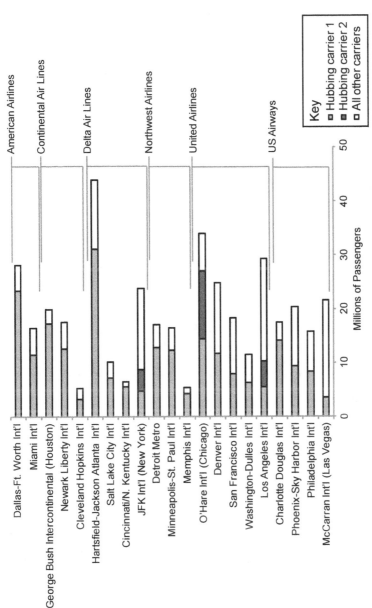

Figure 6.3 US network carrier hubs 2008 (source: author's analysis of data in BTS 2009a).

The diagram shows the share of passenger traffic accounted for by carriers with major hub or intercontinental gateway operations at the indicated airport. American Airlines was the second-ranked hub or gateway carrier at JFK International, O'Hare International, and Los Angeles International.

Table 6.5 The internationalization of US network carriers

Carrier	International destinations		Top ranked[1] international destinations, 2008
	2003	2008	
American	81	91	London, Santo Domingo, Toronto, Cancun, Port au Prince
Continental	70	130	London, Cancun, Tokyo, Mexico City, Toronto
Delta	65	107	London, Cancun, Paris, Toronto, Mexico City
Northwest	39	46	Tokyo, Amsterdam, Cancun, Osaka, Nagoya
United	34	43	Tokyo, London, Frankfurt, Hong Kong, Vancouver
US Airways	20[2]	48	Cancun, Toronto, Nassau, London, Montego Bay

Source: author's analysis of OAG 2003, 2008.

Notes
1 Ranked by scheduled seats per week.
2 The total number of foreign destinations served by US Airways and America West Airlines, who merged in 2005, was 27 in 2003.

pattern in the twenty-first century: airlines relying upon their partners to cover the global market rather than attempting to do so alone.

Although international alliances are increasingly common in other industries, their importance as a form of globalization in the airline industry is unprecedented. Alliances take several basic forms (Tretheway and Oum 1992: 104–10):

- Type I – a narrow, route-by-route alliance;
- Type II – a much more ambitious commercial alliance involving coordinated flight schedules, common ground handling arrangements, integrated frequent flyer programs, and joint advertising and promotion;
- Type III – an equity alliance involving some or all the elements associated with Type II plus a significant equity stake in one alliance member by another.

Equity alliances, as explained below, have created airline families with increasingly global scope. First we consider the development of commercial alliances.

My friend is your friend and your friend is mine: commercial alliances

The development of alliances began in earnest during the late 1980s and early 1990s (B. Graham 1995: 100–1). By 1990, Northwest was already linked to

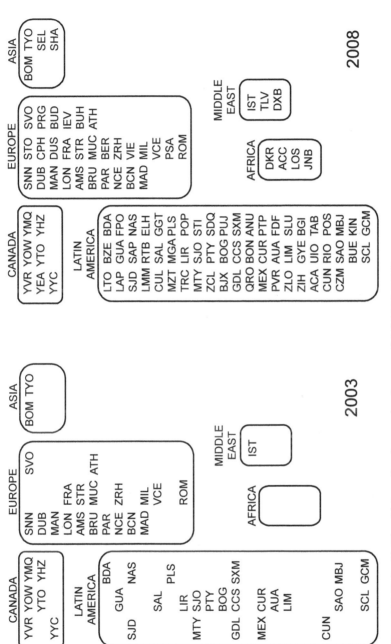

Figure 6.4 Delta Air Lines' international expansion (sources: OAG 2003, 2008).

Each three-letter code represents a single city (e.g. TYO = Tokyo). Between 2003 and 2008, the number of international destinations served by Delta more than doubled with particularly rapid expansion in Latin America.

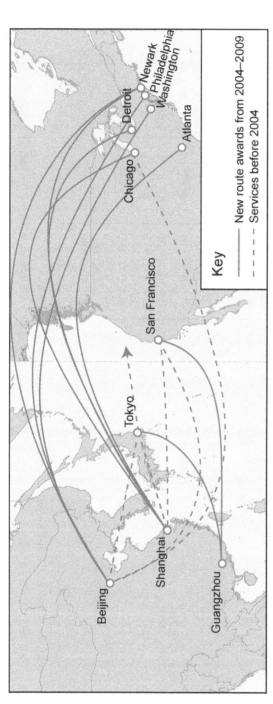

2004: United, Chicago–Shanghai vv[1]
Northwest, Detroit–Tokyo (Narita)–Guangzhou vv
2005: Continental, Newark–Beijing vv
2006: American, Chicago–Shanghai vv
2007: United, Washington (Dulles)–Beijing vv
Delta, Atlanta–Shanghai vv

2008: United, San Francisco–Guangzhou vv
2009: Northwest, Detroit–Shanghai vv
Continental, Newark–Shanghai vv
US Airways, Philadelphia–Beijing vv

Key

——— New route awards from 2004–2009

– – – Services before 2004

Figure 6.5 New passenger route awards from the US to China (sources: various press releases by the US Department of Transportation).

New traffic rights have greatly increased the number of airlines and gateways accommodating the burgeoning volume of traffic between the US and China. It should be noted that US carriers had rights to serve China nonstop from Los Angeles and other cities that were unused during the time period shown.

KLM through cross-investments and code-sharing; and Delta, Swissair, and SIA had formed what they described as the world's first global aviation network (Westlake 1990). The scope and importance of alliances have increased dramatically since then. Today's leading alliances link airlines from every significant world market, providing fairly well-integrated networks whose global extent would be impossible for any one carrier to match given the persistence of regulatory barriers.

The seeds of the largest alliance today were sown in 1994 when United and Lufthansa launched a major marketing alliance. At the time, the two airlines together operated more than 3,000 flights per day but had only one route in common, pointing to the potential synergy between the giants (B. Graham 1995: 101). By code-sharing, United and Lufthansa were able to tap deep into each other's respective networks. In this way, the partnership was like that between Northwest and KLM. Another similarity is that both partnerships were granted antitrust immunity (ATI) by the US Department of Transportation. ATI permitted the partners to coordinate their schedules and fares without fear of prosecution. For the US government, the alliances between putative international competitors were acceptable because code-sharing greatly expanded the destinations easily available to American consumers while reducing competition on very few sectors.

There was, however, an important difference between the United-Lufthansa and Northwest-KLM alliances. The absence of an equity link in the former case made it easier for the two partners to add other carriers to their alliance because the threshold for participation was more easily met. So while Northwest and KLM remained tightly linked but had few alliances in common with other airlines of comparable size, United and Lufthansa became the founding members of the Star Alliance in 1995, which grew to 21 members by 2009 (Table 6.6).

The Star Alliance draws together carriers from every major world market. It is worth noting, however, that the Star Alliance overwhelmingly serves high- and middle-income countries. From the ten poorest countries in the world in 2008 (whose combined population was more than 230 million people), the Star Alliance airlines operated a total of 30 flights per week, versus 5,343 from the ten richest countries (with a combined population of just over 50 million).[8]

There are two other global passenger airline alliances: the Skyteam alliance, which has been greatly enlarged through the addition of KLM and Northwest following the Air France/KLM merger; and oneworld, which is led by American Airlines and British Airways. In 2008, the three alliances accounted for just under half of all capacity in the airline industry, measured in seats per week and were particularly important in the important transatlantic market (Figure 6.6). Membership in the alliances is contingent mainly upon a carrier's overall traffic volume and especially the strength of its hub or hubs. All of the members of the three alliances are network carriers, although some have LCC subsidiaries.

The alliances are most evident to passengers via code-sharing. In 2008, for instance, Air France was code-shared on nearly 1,300 Delta Air Lines flights per week via which it gained access to dozens of routes and many cities not it its

Table 6.6 The members of major passenger airline alliances (date of membership in parentheses and founding members in italics)

Star Alliance (1997)	oneworld (1999)	Skyteam (2000)
North America	**North America**	**North America**
Air Canada (1997)	*American Airlines* (1999)	*Delta Air Lines* (2000)
United Airlines (1997)		Northwest Airlines (2004)
US Airways (2004)		
Continental Airlines[1]		
Latin America	**Latin America**	**Latin America**
TAM Airlines (b)	LAN Airlines (2000)	*Aero México* (2000)
Western Europe	**Western Europe**	**Western Europe**
Lufthansa (1997)	*British Airways* (1999)	*Air France* (2000)
SAS (1997)	Finnair (1999)	Alitalia (2001)
Austrian Airlines (2000)	Iberia (1999)	KLM Royal Dutch (2004)
bmi (2000)		
TAP Portugal (2005)		
Swiss (2006)		
Spanair (2003)		
Aegean Airlines[2]		
Brussels Airlines[2]		
Eastern & Central Europe	**Eastern & Central Europe**	**Eastern & Central Europe**
LOT Polish Airlines (2003)	Malev (2007)	Czech Airlines (2001)
	S7[2]	Aeroflot Russian (2006)
East, Southeast & South Asia	**East, Southeast & South Asia**	**East, Southeast & South Asia**
Thai Airways Int'l (1997)	*Cathay Pacific Airways* (1999)	*Korean Air* (2000)
ANA (1999)	Japan Airlines (2007)	China Southern Airlines (2007)
Singapore Airlines (2000)		Vietnam Airlines[2]
Asiana Airlines (2003)		
Air China (2007)		
Shanghai Airlines (2007)		
Air India[2]		
Southwest Pacific	**Southwest Pacific**	**Southwest Pacific**
Air New Zealand (1999)	*Qantas* (1999)	
Middle East & North Africa	**Middle East & North Africa**	**Middle East & North Africa**
Turkish Airlines (2008)	Royal Jordanian (2007)	
Egyptair (2008)		
Sub-Saharan Africa	**Sub-Saharan Africa**	**Sub-Saharan Africa**
South African Airways (2006)		

Sources: Star Alliance 2009; oneworld 2009; Skyteam 2009.

Notes
1 In 2008, Continental announced that it would move from Skyteam to the Star Alliance (Field 2008).
2 Membership is expected to be formalized in 2010.

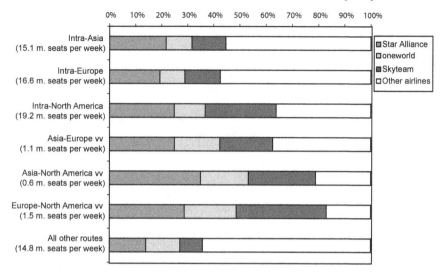

Figure 6.6 Alliance capacity by route region (source: author's analysis of OAG 2008).

The three major alliances are particularly important in the lucrative transoceanic markets. In 2008, Star Alliance led in terms of capacity over the Pacific, and Skyteam was number one over the North Atlantic, though the shift of Continental from Skyteam to Star Alliance will likely change the balance of power in the latter market.

own network including places like Grand Rapids, Mobile, and Kahului. In turn, Delta was code-shared on Air France flights to destinations like Montpellier, Ouagadougou, and Hanoi. Code-sharing between global alliance partners, like code-sharing between a network carrier and its regional affiliates, generates traffic feed.

Yet each of the big three alliances includes but goes well beyond code-sharing. To begin, their schedules are meshed at the members' respective hubs to facilitate passenger connections (Figure 6.7). Connections are made even easier when alliance members share terminals at key hubs – a goal which several significant recent airport infrastructure projects have borne in mind. Following the opening of Heathrow's new Terminal 5, for instance, airline assignments at the crucial hub were reshuffled so that members of the oneworld alliance are co-located in Terminal 3 (all alliance members other than British Airways) and Terminal 5 (British Airways), the Star Alliance members are clustered in Terminal 1, and Skyteam is situated in Terminal 4 (Flottau 2006; *Business Travel News* 2007).

Frequent flyer programs (FFPs) comprise another important area of cooperation among alliance partners, so that passengers can earn miles by flying one airline and redeem them on another. Much as the huge extent of the American mega-carriers' hub-and-spoke systems augmented the appeal of their FFPs in the 1980s, so too the global extent and hundreds of cities served by the alliances make their members' FFPs more appealing than those of unallied airlines.

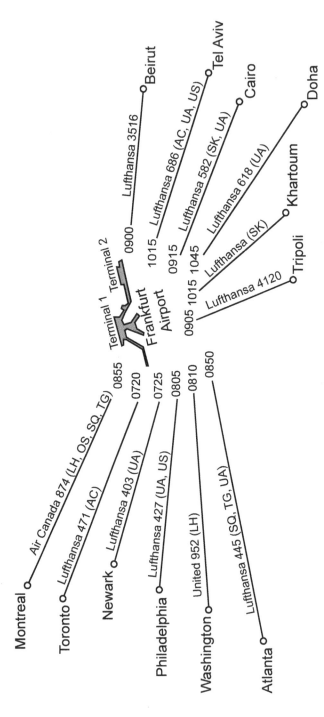

Figure 6.7 Star Alliance connections at Frankfurt (source: author's analysis of OAG 2008).

The co-location of Star Alliance partners in Frankfurt's Terminal 1 and schedule meshing among the carriers facilitate connections between, for example, arriving flights from North America and departing flights to the Middle East and North Africa. The airlines listed in parentheses code-shared on the indicated flight.

Code-sharing, schedule-meshing, and integrated frequent flyer programs are three principal means via which alliances deliver more traffic and higher yielding traffic to their members. In a survey of alliance participants (Iatrou and Alamdari 2005), every respondent reported that alliance membership had increased his or her carrier's revenue; and almost all of the respondents credited alliance membership with boosting the volume of traffic carried and load factor. Interestingly, the survey revealed that about 30 percent identified fare increases as one impact of alliance membership (Iatrou and Alamdari 2005). Especially on routes connecting alliance members' hubs where two or more alliance members provide competing services, the potential for fare-gouging is real. From a broader perspective, however, alliances have been given credit for lowering fares. Specifically, alliances have lowered interline fares, such as the combined fare for Des Moines to Chicago on United and Chicago to Cairo on Lufthansa, by 18–28 percent (Robyn 2003).[9]

Passenger alliances are likely to become increasingly significant as the industry moves further into its second century. Crucial to that greater significance is wider antitrust immunity (ATI) to coordinate the activities of alliance members. In a landmark decision in 2008, the US Department of Transportation granted ATI to Skyteam partners on transatlantic routes, permitting them to pool revenue and coordinate fares, schedules, and services (Compart 2008). The decision was important because it marked the first time that ATI had been granted to two US carriers in the same alliance (Delta and Northwest in this case). Star Alliance and oneworld members have applied for the same immunity. Yet the matter is not settled: by mid-2009, the European Commission was engaged in multiple investigations of practices by the alliances (Arnott 2009).

Meanwhile, at the time of this writing there is only one active global air cargo alliance: Skyteam Cargo, which in 2009 linked eight airlines[10] also found in the Skyteam passenger alliance. A once prominent cargo alliance called the WOW Alliance that linked JAL Cargo, Lufthansa Cargo, SIA Cargo, and SAS Cargo has faded away, partly because the members proved unwilling to share information with one another (Conway 2008). In the cargo business, more than in the passenger business, a relative handful of major customers determine a carrier's success; sharing information that might undermine a carrier's hold on those customers is anathema. Furthermore, cargo cannot walk from one airline's terminal to another airline's terminal at a hub where alliance members' networks interface, and this constraint alone complicates the challenge of interlining cargo. Shippers strongly prefer that a shipment be carried from the origin airport to the destination airport on a single carrier.

Despite their limitations, alliances have had important effects on the geography of international air transportation. Already by 1997, for instance, Northwest's hubs had raced to the top ranks of transatlantic passenger gateways partly due to the alliance with KLM (Pearson 1997). In just five years in the mid-1990s, Detroit's transatlantic traffic tripled. Some industry analysts forecast that, in order to save costs, alliance traffic – and therefore global traffic in general – will be increasingly concentrated in fewer than a dozen hubs worldwide. A study by Boston Consulting Group identified nine future "super hubs": Chicago-O'Hare,

Dallas-Ft. Worth, Atlanta, London-Heathrow, Frankfurt, Paris-Charles de Gaulle, Tokyo-Narita, Singapore, and Hong Kong (Mecham 2004) (Figure 6.8). There is an appealing symmetry to this forecast: three hubs each for the US, Europe, and Asia and close to three hubs for each of the main passenger alliances: O'Hare (United), Frankfurt (Lufthansa), and Singapore (SIA) for the Star Alliance; Dallas-Ft. Worth (American), London (BA), and Hong Kong (Cathay Pacific) for oneworld; and Atlanta (Delta) and Paris (Air France) for Skyteam. Narita does not fit so neatly into this scheme. Seoul is the main hub for Skyteam's largest Asian member (Korean); but Narita is the hub for both Star Alliance member ANA and oneworld member JAL.

Capulets and Montagues: airline families

Between 1984 and 2006, the number of airlines around the world swelled from just over 500 to nearly 1,600 (*Flight International* 1984, 2006a, 2006b, 2006c). To some degree the tripling in the number of airlines since the mid-1980s is illusory because many of today's airlines are subsidiaries of other carriers, drawn together in families with as many as a dozen members. Consider the case of SAS (*Flight International* 2006c). In 2006, the Scandinavian flag carrier had a wholly-owned freight subsidiary (SAS Cargo), an LCC (Snowflake), and a

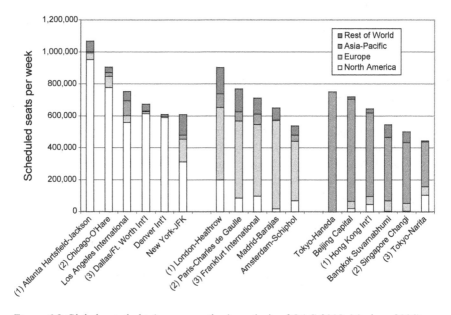

Figure 6.8 Global superhubs (sources: author's analysis of OAG 2008; Mecham 2004).

The figure shows the regional composition of capacity for the most important airports, measured by total scheduled seats per week, in each region. The airports identified with numerals in parentheses are those identified as likely "superhubs" in the Boston Consulting Group study referred to in the text. Note that in almost all of these cases, capacity is overwhelmingly concentrated on routes within the airport's home region.

Finnish feeder carrier (Blue1). SAS also owned in whole or in part nine other airlines, stretching from Air Greenland in the west to Estonian Airlines in the east and Spanair in the south. Altogether, the SAS family numbered thirteen, including the parent carrier. SAS was rather prolific in this regard, but other airlines linked by equity ties to at least eight other airlines in 2006 included Air France/KLM (19 linked carriers), LAN (nine), Lufthansa (nine), and Qantas (nine) (*Flight International* 2006a, 2006b, 2006c).

As in the case of SAS, many of these airline families spilled over international boundaries. There is a long tradition of such investments dating back to the earliest decades of the airline industry's storied history. In particular, the two most important international carriers before World War II, Pan Am and British Overseas Aircraft Corporation (BOAC), each had stakes in carriers around the world. In the 1930s, for example, Pan Am had a 40 percent stake in each of five different carriers in Central America (Davies 1964: 334). The difference today is that it is many more airlines, including medium-sized ones like LAN, that have invested abroad.

In examining the patterns of international ownership of one airline by another, a number that pops up again and again is 49 percent. In mid-2006, SIA owned 49 percent of Virgin Atlantic, SAS owned 49 percent of Estonian Airlines, the Malaysian LCC AirAsia owned 49 percent of Thai AirAsia and Indonesia AirAsia, and the list went on and on (*Flight International* 2006c). Forty-nine percent is the maximum stake that foreigners can hold in an airline in most countries. The 49 percent cap reflects the historic association between the air transportation and national defense. More practically, as explained in Chapter 5, if foreigners own more than half of an airline, it may not be able to use its home country's traffic rights. For example, LAN Ecuador began life as a wholly-owned LAN subsidiary, but the US Department of Transportation did not recognize the airline as Ecuadorian, forcing the sale of 55 percent of the carrier to a local company, so that it could use Ecuador's traffic rights to America.

Why do dozens of airlines own shares of carriers in other countries? There are several reasons. First, if a carrier's own market is relatively mature and characterized by slow growth, other countries' domestic and international markets may present greener pastures. Singapore Airlines' futile quest for a stake in Air India in the 1990s was motivated by the prediction, borne out in fact, that India would experience rapid traffic growth in the future. Second, an investment in another market provides a means of hedging the risks associated with one's own home base. Third, investing in another carrier can solidify marketing coordination and, more specifically, ensure traffic feed. Fourth, like McDonalds, a carrier may want to exploit its brand image or proven formula for success in markets across the world. Richard Branson's Virgin Group (Figure 6.9), for instance, has investments directly or indirectly in Europe (Virgin Atlantic and Virgin Express), the USA (Virgin America), Africa (Virgin Nigeria), and the Southwest Pacific (Virgin Blue plus two smaller affiliates). On a more regional scale, in the first few years of the twenty-first century LAN, one of the most successful Latin American carriers, established subsidiaries including LAN Dominicana, LAN Ecuador, and LAN Peru.

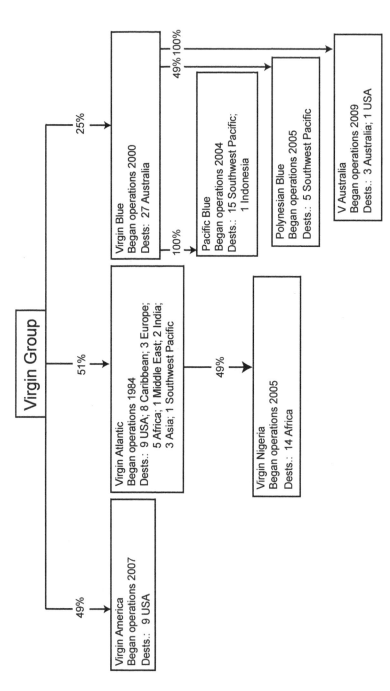

Figure 6.9 Virgin Group members (sources: various relevant company press releases).

In 2008, airlines directly or indirectly linked to the Virgin Group were scattered across much of the world. The percentage figures indicate the relevant ownership share such as Virgin Group's 51 per cent share in Virgin Atlantic (the other 49 per cent was held by Singapore Airlines).

Finally, foreign acquisitions may be strategic in nature as evident in the union of Air France and KLM. In 2004, the two carriers were placed under a common holding company, but Air France, as the much larger of the two airlines, essentially acquired KLM. The merger not only increased the presence of Air France globally and vaulted the carrier to first place among European airlines, it also prevented any of Air France's rivals, especially British Airways, from merging with KLM. The merger was also appealing from a network standpoint. The two airlines' networks spanned 208 cities in 2003, with only 72 points in common (author's analysis of data in OAG 2003). The rationalization of services to common points – such as the withdrawal of Air France from Manila and KLM from Caracas – was expected to yield significant savings (Sparaco 2004). So too, the rationalization of their fleets. A primary objective of the merged enterprise is to reduce the number of aircraft types to cut the costs of spares, maintenance, and training. Still, the continued politicization of the airline industry – and more specifically national pride – has prevented more fully merging the two carriers and realizing the resulting efficiencies and synergies. The two airlines have kept their separate identities and retained both the hub at Paris and at Amsterdam.

In 2009, the leadership of Air France-KLM among European carriers was bolstered when the holding company took a 25 percent stake in Alitalia (Flottau 2009). The investment in the struggling Italian carrier is to be complemented by joint marketing and cooperation on routes, particularly between Italy and France and between Italy and the Netherlands. Interestingly, Alitalia decided after the agreement with Air France-KLM to downsize its Milan hub (Nativi 2009); the old Alitalia had maintained large hubs at both Rome and Milan, a politically motivated division of labor that had hobbled the airline.

The moves by Air France-KLM have spurred similar actions by its big European rivals. The Lufthansa empire is particularly impressive (Table 6.7). In 2005, Lufthansa acquired Swiss International (O'Toole 2005b). At the time, Swiss was in financial distress, and Lufthansa acquired the carrier for a bargain price. Perhaps equally important, Lufthansa prevented any of its rivals from acquiring an airline with a hub (Zurich) so close to the hinterland for Munich, Lufthansa's second hub.[11] Lufthansa's acquisition of controlling shares in Austrian Airlines and Brussels Airlines[12] and a proposed merger between British Airways and Iberia are likewise strategic moves to develop more fully continental home markets while simultaneously blocking rivals from doing so. Further, British Airways' potential tie-up with Iberia is meant to prevent it from being even further eclipsed by Lufthansa and Air France-KLM. Once the largest international carrier in Europe, by 2008, BA had fallen to number three (*Economist* 2008).

In for the long haul

A number of industry experts have argued that further consolidation among network carriers is inevitable (Doganis 2006: 266; Tretheway 2004). Recent mergers in the US and Europe seem to substantiate those expectations and point

Table 6.7 Airline subsidiaries of the Lufthansa Group

Airline	Domicile	Type	Lufthansa Share (%)
Austrian Airlines	Austria	FSNC[1]	—[2]
British Midland	UK	FSNC[3]	30
Brussels Airlines	Belgium	FSNC	45[4]
Swiss International	Switzerland	FSNC	100
Germanwings	Germany	LCC	100
jetBlue	USA	LCC	16
Air Dolomiti	Italy	Regional	100
Eurowings	Germany	Regional	100
Lufthansa Cityline	Germany	Regional	100
Lufthansa Italia	Italy	Regional	100
Luxair	Luxembourg	Regional	14
Sun Express[5]	Turkey	Regional	50
Aero Logic[6]	Germany	Cargo	50
Jade Cargo Int'l	China	Cargo	25

Sources: Lufthansa 2009 and subsequent corporate news releases.

Notes
1 FSNC = full-service network carriers; LCC = low-cost carrier.
2 The merger between Lufthansa and Austrian was pending before European competition authorities at the time this book was completed. Lufthansa's goal is to acquire a majority of the shares in Austrian.
3 British Midland owns bmibaby, an LCC.
4 Under the terms of the agreement between Lufthansa and the parent company of Brussels Airlines, Lufthansa has the option to acquire the remaining 55 percent of the Belgian carrier after 2011, by which time the traffic rights of Brussels Airlines are expected to permit its complete German ownership.
5 Sun Express is a joint venture with Turkish Airlines.
6 Aero Logic is a joint venture with DHL.

to some of the possible survivors in any shakeout. If consolidation does take place, it will likely reinforce the aforementioned trend towards greater importance for a relative handful of hubs. The consolidation of hub-and-spoke systems within Europe has already increased the dominance of the continent's four main hubs. London-Heathrow, Paris-Charles de Gaulle, Frankfurt, and Amsterdam increased their share of intercontinental scheduled seats from 44 percent in 1990 to 50 percent by 1998 and 54 percent by 2008 (Burghouwt and Hakfoort 2001; and author's calculations[13]).

Interestingly, their amplified dominance of Europe's external connections happened at the same time that liberalization and the development of long-range twinjets facilitated the proliferation of new intercontinental linkages. Working against the fragmentation of traffic, however, have been the the consolidation of Europe's elite global carriers and the growth of the alliances, which have funneled traffic into key hubs (e.g., oneworld to Heathrow, Skyteam to Charles de Gaulle and now Amsterdam, the Star Alliance to Frankfurt).

Europe's elite carriers are of course dominated by the triumvirate of Air France/KLM, Lufthansa, and British Airways. By virtue of its network, scale, and scope economies, Air France/KLM would likely survive the coming shakeout among network carriers. Lufthansa also appears well-positioned, its strong position at the center of Europe bolstered by acquisition of Swiss and probably Austrian. British Airways has the advantage of operating from the world's most important international hub, but its control of the limited slots at Heathrow will diminish as the 2007 US-EU agreement takes effect.

It is worth noting that the big European network carriers are not particularly vulnerable to LCCs, despite the massive expansion of Ryanair, easyJet, and newer upstarts in the region. BA, Lufthansa, and Air France have faced fierce competition from charter operators for decades, forcing the former to become more reliant on business traffic decades ago (R.J. Gordon 2004). Further, rail has long been a real alternative to air travel for short-haul trips within Europe; so the threat LCCs pose on short-haul routes is not especially new. And related to the last point, major European airlines fly a greater proportion of long-haul routes compared to their American counterparts, placing more of the traffic carried on airlines like BA beyond the reach of LCCs (at least as LCCs have operated to date). For instance, in 2008, more than 30 percent of BA's weekly capacity (in seats per week) was on flights of at least 5,000 kilometers in length (author's analysis of data in OAG 2008); only 6 percent of American Airlines' capacity fit this profile.[14] So it is not so surprising that BA and its large counterparts have been generally profitable even as the LCCs have expanded.

The future for Europe's smaller network carriers is less assured. SAS, for instance, announced in 2009 that it would divest from most of the carriers described above as comprising its "family." And it will trim both its fleet and its network, withdrawing from some thinly traveled long-haul markets such as Copenhagen–Seattle. The ultimate effect of these changes will be a sharply increased Nordic market focus for the carrier (Kaminski-Morrow 2009; Scandinavian Airlines 2009).

In Asia-Pacific, too, the gap between the region's largest, most efficient competitors and the rest of the network carriers seems to be widening. In particular, SIA, Korean Airlines (KAL), and Cathay Pacific operate fleets comprised of disproportionately large, long-range airliners (see Figure 4.10) and fly a lot of sixth freedom traffic over networks with relatively few short-haul sectors. The result is very high productivity because they are able to keep their aircraft in the air longer each day, because they use relatively large aircraft, and because they generate substantial traffic feed for each link in their networks via well-positioned hubs (Windle 1991; Doganis 2006: 124–32) (Table 6.8). High productivity translates into cost competitiveness and a degree of insulation from the LCC threat. These airlines also share locations amid Asia's galloping economies – or at least they were galloping until the 2008–9 global financial crisis.

As for China, while its domestic market is poised for greater growth than anywhere else on the planet, it is not clear that any of its international carriers will survive as a global network airline. The exposure of Air China, China Southern, and China Eastern to unfettered competition has been too limited, both in duration and degree, for them to take on the likes of SIA and KAL. Moreover, the hubs of the Chinese are precariously close to those of their stronger rivals.

Table 6.8 The productivity of selected airlines

Airline	Total tonne-kilometers performed[1] (000)	Operating costs (000 dollars)	Unit cost (dollars per tonne-kilometer)	Weight load factor (%)
Emirates	15,764,086	9,386,104	0.60	66.4
Singapore Airlines	16,495,404	10,208,179	0.62	67.7
Korean Air	13,960,149	9,560,576	0.68	73.0
Ethiopian	1,610,070	1,132,160	0.70	59.6
Malaysian	5,727,372	4,038,360	0.71	67.7
Cathay Pacific	16,446,405	11,760,000	0.72	72.3
Air France/KLM	30,386,694	32,108,418	1.06	73.8
Royal Jordanian	860,510	948,322	1.10	54.6
British Airways	15,228,809	16,896,000	1.11	68.0
Qantas	11,712,745	13,182,168	1.13	75.6
Delta Air Lines	17,086,104	21,667,877	1.27	59.0
Air India	3,330,081	4,540,585	1.36	51.5
Iberia	5,910,497	8,090,140	1.37	63.5
US Airways	9,281,308	14,017,217	1.51	61.6
TAROM	210,978	340,565	1.61	49.6

Source: author's analysis of data in IATA 2009.

Notes:
1 Sum of passenger, freight, and mail traffic measured in tonne-kilometers. It would be preferable to analyze productivity for a single kind of traffic (e.g. passengers) but the IATA data used do not permit such an analysis.

Guangzhou (China Southern), for instance, is about 175 kilometers from Hong Kong. The Chinese carriers do have the advantage, however, of lower-cost labor.

The other Asian market poised for massive future growth is India, but Air India remains stymied by the vestiges of heavy state intervention in the economy, including limits placed on foreign investment in Indian aviation. Moreover, Air India faces tough competition from a pair of new Indian network carriers: Jet Airways which began scheduled services in 1995 and Kingfisher Airlines which commenced operations in 2005. The former already had a substantial international network by mid-2009 with nearly 20 foreign destinations, while the latter was present throughout India but had only begun to make forays abroad (as noted in Chapter 5) beginning with London-Heathrow, Colombo, Dhaka, and Dubai.

Ultimately, Dubai-based Emirates may be the airline best positioned to profit from India's rise. The state-owned flag carrier rose from its creation in 1985 to become the 11th largest airline in the world, measured by revenue passenger-kilometers, in 2007 (*Air Transport World* 2008d). By 2008, Emirates flew to 97 cities stretching from São Paulo to Christchurch and Johannesburg to Nagoya. Its fast-growing fleet included no narrow-body aircraft, and the average range of Emirates' fleet was higher than almost any other airline. In 2004, the carrier introduced nonstop A340-500 services from Dubai to New York and has subsequently added nonstop flights to São Paulo, Houston, and Toronto, too. Once, it was feared that aircraft like the A340-500, which have removed the need for technical stops in the Middle East for flights between Europe and East Asia, would undermine the significance of Dubai in the global airline industry. On the contrary, the A340-500 and A380 (for which Emirates has placed by far the largest orders) make it possible to fly between any two points on earth with just one stop in the Middle East, and Emirates therefore has a significant cost advantage linking spoke cities like Barcelona and Trivandrum, India that might otherwise require two stops en route (Flottau 2007). Traffic feed through Dubai is one factor supporting Emirates' remarkable productivity (see Table 6.8).

And then there is the United States. It should be emphasized that the American carriers are less internationalized than carriers based in other regions, although their expansion abroad since 2003 is obviously changing that; but for now, they remain strongly domestic in orientation. If its merger with Northwest is successful,[15] Delta will be well-positioned to benefit from the further internationalization of the air travel market. Delta's goal is to become the new US flag carrier (Figure 6.10). It made great strides in that direction on its own, and the merger with Northwest will make it the largest US carrier in Europe, East and Southeast Asia, and Africa; a close rival with Continental for first place in the Middle East and South Asia; and essentially tied with Continental for second place in Latin America (behind American).[16]

A further point that should be made about US carriers is that all of them except American have been through Chapter 11 bankruptcy at least once since deregulation and have emerged leaner and stronger on the other side. Competitors both inside and outside the US have attacked the "revolving door" (Bond 2005) of bankruptcy because it allows an inefficient carrier to shed obligations to workers and creditors while pricing below its costs during the months and oftentimes years that an airline remains under Chapter 11. Some, like Continental, have been through that door more than once. The consequences for their employees have often been drastic, including severe job cuts and pension benefit cutbacks.[17] In total, the big six American network carriers (American, United, Delta, Northwest, Continental, and US Airways) cut their combined employment from 443,000 to 273,000 between 2000 and 2008, a drop of 40 percent (Table 6.9). However, the concomitant increase in productivity has permitted the real cost of a ticket to the airborne world to fall still further. Indeed, one can argue that American bankruptcy policy has effectively shifted wealth from airline employees, retirees, and investors to frequent flyers (Pilling 2005).

The only large US passenger network carrier that has not cycled through bankruptcy is American Airlines. It is noteworthy that American has been the first or second largest US carrier since the dawn of commercial aviation. Its persistence in so tumultuous an industry is a credit to good luck, a good geography,[18] and effective leadership (e.g., Robert Crandall as discussed above).

And yet, American is hardly the only network carrier to survive the industry's repeated travails. Consider the past decade: in 1997, the twenty largest passenger network airline enterprises accounted for 59 percent of all revenue earned in the

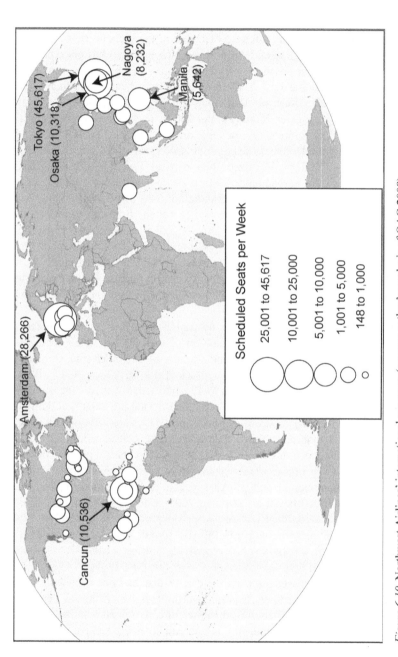

Figure 6.10 Northwest Airlines' international presence (source: author's analysis of OAG 2008).

The sizes of the symbols are proportional to Northwest's capacity (measured in seats per week) in early 2008. Four of the airline's top six foreign destinations (which are labeled) were in Asia, a traditionally weak area for Delta.

Table 6.9 Airline jobs (full-time and part-time) in the US, 2000–2008

	Bankruptcy protection after 2000	2000	2008	% change
United Airlines	2002–6	101,814	48,571	−52.3
American Airlines	–	101,199	75,074	−25.8
Delta Air Lines	2005–7	80,390	48,248	−40.0
Northwest Airlines	2005–7	53,899	29,137	−45.9
Continental Airlines[1]	–	45,944	37,720	−17.2
US Airways[2]	2002–6	59,634	33,809	−43.3
All other airlines	–	289,169	315,552	+9.1
Total		**732,049**	**588,111**	**−19.7**

Source: BTS 2009c.

Notes
1 Continental was in bankruptcy protection from 1983 to 1986 and from 1990 to 1993.
2 The figure for 2000 for US Airways is the sum of US Airways and America West Airlines employment.

industry worldwide; by 2007, the share of the top 20 was 65 percent (Table 6.10). The somewhat surprising expansion of their combined share is partly explained by the fact that these are shares for airline enterprises some of which, such as the SIA Group, have large stakes in LCCs, foreign airlines based in fast-growing markets, and/or cargo carriers. In other words many network carriers

Table 6.10 The largest passenger network airline enterprises, 1997 and 2007

Rank	1997		2007	
	Enterprise[1]	Revenue (millions USD)	Enterprise[1]	Revenue (millions USD)
1	UAL (United)	17,378	Air France/KLM	38,083
2	AMR (American)	16,903	Lufthansa	32,971
3	British Airways	14,342	AMR (American)	22,935
4	Delta Air Lines	13,946	JAL Group	22,461
5	Lufthansa	12,800	UAL (United)	20,143
6	Northwest Airlines	10,226	Delta Air Lines	19,154
7	Air France	9,772	British Airways	17,506
8	Japan Airlines	9,604	ANA	14,983
9	US Airways	8,514	Continental Air Lines	14,232
10	Swissair	7,300	Qantas	12,852
	Total Industry[2]	**291,000**	**Total Industry**[2]	**485,000**
	Top 10 Share (%)	41.6	Top 10 Share (%)	44.4

Sources: *Air Transport World* 1998a, 1998b; Flint 2008; *Air Transport World* 2008b.

Notes
1 The revenue figures include subsidiaries (e.g. Lufthansa's subsidiaries described in *Table 6.7*). Note that only passenger network airlines are listed in keeping with the theme of the chapter. In 1997, FedEx ranked sixth in revenue among all airlines, and in 2007, the company ranked fourth.
2 All airlines including full-service network carriers, low-cost carriers, and others.

have harnessed the more dynamic parts of the airline industry for revenue and profit growth. Still, the basic significance of the passenger network carrier is not going to go away. Fifty years from now, a person traveling from Maputo to Manila or Riga to Rio – and there likely will be many more such passengers then – will make the journey, or at least most of it, on a carrier like Lufthansa or SIA. But those making shorter trips such as Maputo to Mombasa or Riga to Rome – and chances are there will be even more of them – will perhaps be as likely to be aboard one of the burgeoning number of LCCs. We turn to the LCCs and their effect upon the airborne world in the next chapter.

7   A world taking wing

Low-cost carriers and the ascent of the many

New chicks in the flock

In the beginning, airlines were named like railroads: Chicago & Southern Air Lines, Transcontinental & Western Air, Queensland and Northern Territorial Aerial Service (QANTAS). The names were almost invariably geographical, telling the public on the ground where an airline flew. Later, the names were geographical in a different way, celebrating the name of the country whose flag the airline carried: Garuda Indonesia Airways, Société Tunisienne de l'Air (Tunisair), Aerolineas Argentinas. Informative, serious, ambitious names. Leap forward to the early twenty-first century. The names of new airlines are often neither geographical nor serious: bmibaby, Baboo, Jet4you, One-Two-Go. And everywhere the sky is blue: Air Blue, Blue Air, Atlas Blue, jetBlue, Virgin Blue, Pacific Blue, Blue Panorama, and – for variety – Azul Linhas Aéreas Brasileiras and IndiGo.

These are the names of low-cost carriers (LCCs) – a rapidly growing group of carriers that have helped to make air travel a commodity. In a world where one airline is about as good as another and customers often have many carriers from which to choose, having a cool or fun image is an edge. Hence the creativity in name choice. What was once Jersey European Airways became Flybe, and Aero-caribe was re-branded as Click Mexicana (*Flight International* 2006b).

Of course, the largest LCC, Southwest Airlines has an old-fashioned, rather boring name (Table 7.1). But Southwest does share in common with other LCCs most of ten operational characteristics that help to account for the fact that the typical LCC has per-seat costs less than half those of the typical network carrier. These ten characteristics (Doganis 2006: 170–8) merit careful consideration at the beginning of this chapter devoted to the LCC phenomenon:

1   *Higher seating density:* LCCs squeeze more seats onto their aircraft. Malaysia's AirAsia, for instance, is one of many LCCs that fit 180 seats on each of an A320 aircraft. Conversely, United Airlines flies the same airplane with 138 seats each. The downside of higher seating density is less legroom and more specifically a shorter seat pitch (i.e., the distance from the back of one seat to the back of the seat in the next row). AirAsia has one of the industry's lowest standards for seat pitch at just 29 inches. In fairness, it should be noted that many hard-pressed network carriers also have very tight economy class seating; United, for instance, has a 31 inch seat pitch (Skytrax 2009).

Table 7.1 The world's largest LCCs by 2008 traffic

Rank	Carrier	Passengers (million)	RPK (million)	Base	Fleet Boeing 737 Family	Airbus A320 Family	Other
1	Southwest Airlines	88.5	118,248	USA	525	–	–
2	Ryanair	57.6	61,983	Ireland	163	–	10
3	Air Berlin	28.6	44,310	USA	57	44	34
4	JetBlue Airways	21.9	41,948	USA	–	107	–
5	Thomsonfly	12.2	33,640	UK	22	1	24
6	AirTran Airways	24.6	30,500	USA	53	–	87
7	easyJet	44.6	27,448[1]	UK	30	115	–
8	Gol Transport	25.7	25,308	Brazil	79	–	–
9	WestJet	14.3	22,093	Canada	73	–	–
10	Virgin Blue	16.7	18,764	Australia	49	–	6
11	TUIfly	10.6	18,309	Germany	47	–	–
12	Aer Lingus	10.4	16,655	Ireland	–	32	9
13	Frontier	10.6	15,828	USA	62	–	–
14	Jetstar Airways	9.2	15,701	Australia	–	19	6
15	AirAsia	11.8	13,485	Malaysia	9	35	–

Sources: *Airline Business* 2009; *Air Transport World* 2008a.

Note
1 Figure is for 2007.

2 *Higher aircraft utilization:* By minimizing in-flight services and therefore the need for time-consuming catering on the ground, by flying only narrow-body airliners that can be loaded and unloaded quickly, and by dispensing with assigned seats, LCCs are able to keep their aircraft in the air for more hours each day. Frequently, LCCs are able to load and unload a jet in as few as 25 minutes.

3 *Lower flight and cabin crew costs:* LCCs use fewer cabin crew and get more work out of both their cabin and flight crews by operating more flights per day. Moreover, because most LCCs are brand-new, their staff often has little experience and is paid accordingly.

4 *Use of less expensive secondary airports:* Where feasible, LCCs often avoid high-cost primary airports. Romanian LCC Blue Air, for instance, is based at a secondary airport serving Bucharest (Figure 7.1). Secondary airports have two further advantages: lack of competition, and uncongested runways, taxiways, and terminals that facilitate rapid turnarounds.

5 *Lower maintenance costs:* LCCs tend to focus on a single aircraft type or fly at most a few basic types in contrast to the much more diverse fleets flown by network carriers, as evident, for example, in the comparison between Korean Air and Southwest Airlines, which are roughly the same size in revenue terms (Table 7.2). Fewer aircraft types translate into lower mainte-nance costs. Moreover, most LCCs operate very young fleets with concomi-tantly fewer maintenance problems. Outsourcing, a common strategy among LCCs, is still another means of lowering maintenance costs.

Table 7.2 Fleets of Korean Air and Southwest Airlines, 2008

Korean Air			*Southwest Airlines*		
Aircraft	*In Fleet*	*On Order*	*Aircraft*	*In Fleet*	*On Order*
Airbus A300-600R	8	0	Boeing 737-300	187	0
Airbus A330-200	3	0	Boeing 737-500	25	0
Airbus A330-300	16	0	Boeing 737-700	313	100
Airbus A380	0	8			
Boeing 737-800	16	0			
Boeing 737-900	16	0			
Boeing 737-900ER	0	4			
Boeing 747-400	23	0			
Boeing 777-200ER	16	2			
Boeing 777-300	4	0			
Boeing 777-300ER	0	10			
Boeing 787-8	0	10			
Airbus A300-600F	2	0			
Boeing 747-400F/SF	13	0			
Boeing 747-400ERF	8	0			
Boeing 747-8F	0	5			
Boeing 777-200LRF	0	5			
CASA 212	1	0			
Total	**127**	**44**	**Total**	**525**	**100**

Source: *Air Transport World* 2008a.

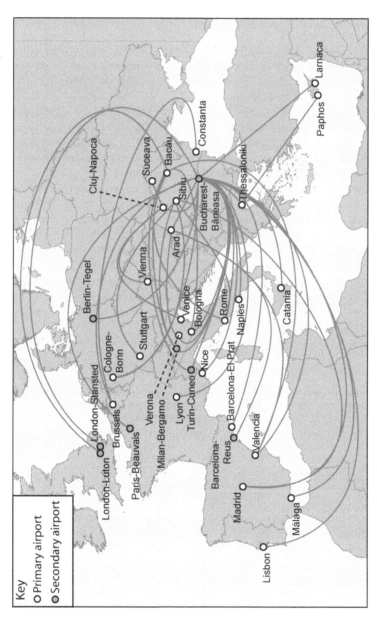

Figure 7.1 Blue Air network, 2009 (source: Blue Air 2009).

Blue Air, a Romanian low-cost carrier (LCC), illustrates several features of the typical LCC network. It serves many secondary airports, including its home base of Băneasa near Bucharest (the main airport of Bucharest is Otopeni); it operates many point-to-point services (e.g. the many nonstop international flights to smaller cities such as Bacău), and its network emphasizes tourist destinations.

6 *Lower station costs:* Outsourcing also helps to reduce station costs, such as aircraft cleaning. In some cases, LCCs get their own cabin crew to clean aircraft on arrival – a task made easier by the lack of in-flight meals. Some carriers even encourage passengers to help clean up, an imposition which aptly expresses how LCCs have changed the experience of flying. A *Boston Globe* editorial observed, "[T]he announcement telling passengers to clean up the trash around their seats to 'keep ticket prices down' on a no-frills airline can be as jolting as turbulence." (*Boston Globe* 2005: 14).

7 *Fewer passenger services:* Not only do LCCs provide minimal in-flight services, many of them now charge for what once would have been considered the most rudimentary offerings. In early 2009, Ryanair's chief executive Michael O'Leary raised eyebrows when he suggested that the carrier might charge passengers extra to use airplane lavatories (Calder 2009). That suggestion seems to have been in jest, but some LCCs have gone far in stripping away passenger services once taken for granted (e.g., free pillows and blankets for use in-flight).

8 *Minimal agent commissions:* In the past, most passengers bought airline tickets through travel agents, and agent commissions were a significant cost for carriers. In the US, agent commissions fell from as high as 20 percent in the 1980s to an average of 6 percent in the first decade of the twenty-first century (Doganis 1991, 2006); but LCCs are able to avoid even this lower cost since they overwhelming deal directly with the public via the Internet, a fact evident in the number of LCCs that prominently display their website on every jet in their fleets.

9 *Reduced sales costs:* Relying on sales via the Internet positively affects LCCs in other ways too. For one, LCCs require few reservations staff. Internet sales have helped to make e-tickets popular in much of the developed world, saving carriers still more money. IATA has estimated that an airline's cost of processing a paper ticket is $10 versus just $1 for an e-ticket (Doganis 2006: 203). Of course, network carriers, too, have now moved onto the Internet but LCCs were earlier and more aggressive in doing so. The reliance on e-commerce also greatly simplifies accounting for LCCs, requiring fewer staff and saving more money. And the combination of widespread Internet access, proven software, and inexpensive computing power have gone far to neutralize the yield management advantages of the full-service network carriers.

10 *Smaller administrative/office staff:* LCCs have fewer headquarters staff and emphasize flexibility in job responsibilities so that a single person might do the work of several people at an established network carrier. Partly this difference is a function of the LCCs' rapid growth while the network carriers have been contracting. Some network carriers, for instance, built up large headquarters departments in the years before office automation made many such staff (e.g., secretaries) redundant.

Together, these advantages make for a wide disparity in average costs (Table 7.3). It should be emphasized, however, that, first, not all of these distinctions are sustainable and, second, some of the LCCs' strategies have already been embraced by network carriers. So in the future it is likely to become harder to clearly separate the two kinds of airlines. We will return to this point in the final section of this chapter, but first we turn to the story of the LCCs' origins and how they have spread.

Beginnings: intrastate airlines and charter operators

The roots of today's LCCs reach back to ancestors in the 1960s and 1970s on either side of the Atlantic. In the US, intrastate carriers were not subject to regulation by the Civil Aeronautics Board (CAB) and developed more efficient business models before passage of the Airline Deregulation Act (ADA) (see Table 5.2). After deregulation had been made law, some of the formerly intrastate carriers carried their successful strategy to interstate routes, Southwest Airlines being by far the most important example. Meanwhile, in Europe, charter operators developed their own successful business models in the 1960s based on extremely low fares and near 100 percent load factors. Some of the charter operators' practices, such as collaboration between carriers and entrepreneurial airports, have become important to many contemporary LCCs, and a few charter airlines, such as Air Berlin, have become significant LCCs with hundreds of scheduled routes. The American roots of this family tree are arguably the more influential in shaping today's global LCC phenomenon, and so we turn first in that direction

Table 7.3 Seat costs for selected US carriers (cents per available seat-kilometer)

	Airline	Second quarter 1997	Second quarter 2002	Second quarter 2007
Network carriers	US Airways	8.1	8.8	10.1
	United Air Lines	5.9	7.0	8.1
	Northwest Airlines	5.6	6.2	8.1
	Delta Air Lines	5.6	6.3	8.9
	Continental Air Lines	5.7	6.5	8.4
	American Airlines	5.8	6.7	8.0
	Alaska Airlines	5.3	6.1	7.3
LCCs	America West Airlines	4.6	4.8	8.1
	Frontier Airlines	5.7	5.3	6.7
	AirTran Airways	5.0	5.3	5.8
	ATA Airlines	–	–	5.8
	Southwest Airlines	4.5	4.7	5.6
	Spirit Airlines	4.5	4.6	5.3
	JetBlue Airways	–	3.9	5.0

Source: BTS 2009a.

A different way: Southwest Airlines as the model LCC

There is some irony in the significance of Southwest Airlines in an era when the airline industry had become so important to the global economy and when the industry itself is beginning to globalize. Southwest flies to no foreign destination, not even to the many Mexican destinations close to the carrier's traditional core in the southwestern US. International flights, particularly in an age of heightened security precautions, require too many time-consuming clearance procedures on the ground. Likewise, Southwest has so far eschewed membership in any of the global airline alliances discussed in Chapter 6. Nevertheless, Southwest has been an important factor in driving down the cost of air transportation, both through its own services and more importantly through the demonstration effect it has provided. A part of that demonstration effect has been to show that well-run upstarts can capture the market from established carriers, and a growing number of carriers in countries other than the US have done just that on their own home turf.

As noted in Chapter 5, Southwest Airlines got its start on intrastate routes in Texas that were not subject to regulation by the Civil Aeronautics Board. Still, the airline faced a difficult challenge in getting state approval to commence services on the "golden triangle" linking Dallas, Houston, and San Antonio (Freiberg and Freiberg 1996: 15). The carriers already serving those routes (Braniff, Continental, and Texas International) contended the routes among the three cities were saturated, forcing Southwest to slog through three years of legal challenges and administrative proceedings before finally taking off in 1971. Two years later, the carrier again was in court successfully fending off suits intended to force it to move its Dallas operations from Love Field to the new Dallas-Ft. Worth International when the latter airport opened in 1974[1] (Freiberg and Freiberg 1996: 16–25).

The fact that Love Field was 18 kilometers closer to downtown Dallas than Dallas-Ft. Worth was not the only reason for Southwest's attachment to the older airport serving the Metroplex. "Love" with its myriad connotations to be played upon, not always tastefully, was prominent in the company's early advertising. One television ad featured a stewardess asking, "How do we love you? Let us count the ways." She then listed the airline's many departure times, emphasizing the Southwest's characteristic high-frequency service; but many viewers would have been at least as struck by the image of a Southwest Airlines' jet moving suggestively towards the fading image of the stewardesses lap as the ad drew to a close (Petzinger 1995: 29). Like most airlines across the world, Southwest is more circumspect in its image-making today.

One of the constants in Southwest's now nearly 40 years in the air has been its dependence on the Boeing 737. Southwest originally planned to use less expensive turboprops as fellow intrastate carrier Pacific Southwest had done in California; but by the 1970s, the public appetite for jets was too great to be ignored (Petzinger 1995: 24, 27). The selection of the 737 was a fateful choice because every aircraft Southwest has flown since then has been a "baby Boeing," and the carrier's success has helped to popularize the 737 among other LCCs.[2] For example, bmibaby, Ryanair, and Gol in Brazil were among the carriers operating strictly 737s in 2008 (*Air Transport World* 2008a). The development of multiple versions of the 737 (with the 600, 700, 800, and 900ER currently on offer) enables LCCs to standardize on the 737 without severely restricting the airlines' flexibility to serve different kinds of routes.

For Southwest in the early 1970s, route flexibility was not a pressing concern because the Texas state line circumscribed the carrier's operations. After deregulation, Southwest was free to spread beyond those borders but it did so in an unusually deliberate fashion. The all-at-once nature of deregulation in the US was like a spark that set off a wildfire of frantic expansion by old carriers such as Braniff and new ones such as PEOPLExpress. Southwest's first foray beyond Texas – to nearby New Orleans – was much more modest. Over this small and slowly expanding network, Southwest operated very high frequency services. And the carrier cut its turnaround time to 10 minutes, achieving extremely high aircraft utilization as result and apportioning the cost of a 737 across many more passengers each year.

By 1985, the carrier had spread as far west as Los Angeles and as far north as St. Louis, but still no further east than New Orleans (Figure 7.2). The slow expansion precluded the need to take on the debt that had proved so crushing a burden to other airlines after deregulation; and by adding cities at a judicious pace, Southwest could restrain the growth of its labor force in order to protect the integrity of its corporate culture, which blended a penchant for fun with "an underdog spirit" (Petzinger 1995: 287). Even in 2008, when Southwest ranked as one of the largest airlines in the world in terms of passengers carried, its network included just 64 airports in 33 US states, a far less pervasive presence than that attained by its major US rivals (author's analysis of data in OAG 2008).

Apart from its modest number of destinations, Southwest's network is distinguished by three features: its de-emphasis of hubbing, its unusually high frequency of flights per city, and its use of well-positioned secondary airports as gateways to some large metropolitan areas. First, while Southwest does do some hubbing through Las Vegas, Chicago-Midway, Phoenix, and Baltimore, these four airports combined accounted for only 24 percent of Southwest's flights in 2008 (Table 7.4). By comparison, the top four airports in Delta's 2008 network (Atlanta, Cincinnati, Salt Lake City, and New York-JFK) accounted for 44 percent of all Delta departures despite the fact that Delta served five times as many cities as Southwest. Southwest's network emphasizes point-to-point services so that even relatively small cities like Boise and Little Rock were linked by nonstop services to seven cities each (with only Las Vegas in common).

The advantage of point-to-point services over hubbing is faster turnaround times. An arriving aircraft can begin boarding for the next destination almost immediately after the last inbound passenger steps onto the jetway, with the result that the number of hours the airplane is in the air earning revenue is maximized. If a passenger does transfer at one of Southwest's pseudo-hubs, it is the

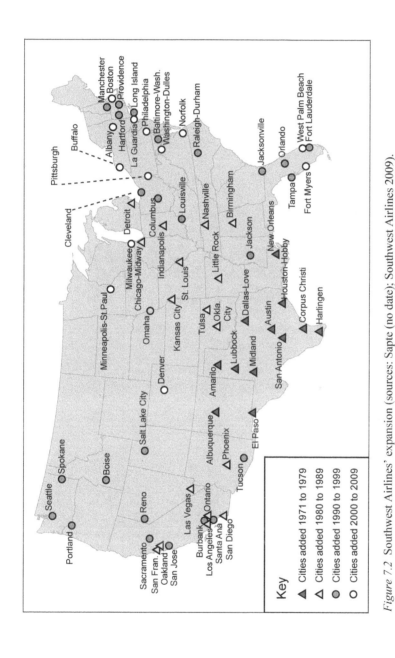

Figure 7.2 Southwest Airlines' expansion (sources: Sapte (no date); Southwest Airlines 2009).

It should be noted that Southwest first entered the Denver market in 1983, withdrew in 1986, and reentered in 2005. Similarly, the carrier served San Francisco International from 1982 to 2001, when it withdrew citing high costs and excessive fog-related delays, but it resumed services to the airport in 2007. Southwest has withdrawn permanently from three airports that it served in the past: Beaumont, Detroit City, and Houston Intercontinental.

Table 7.4 Top Southwest Airlines and Delta Air Lines cities, 2008

Southwest Airlines

Airport	Flights per week	Share of airline total
Las Vegas	1,667	7.1
Chicago-Midway	1,539	6.7
Phoenix	1,360	5.8
Baltimore-Wash.	1,156	4.9
Houston-Hobby	960	4.1
Oakland	943	4.0
Dallas-Love	906	3.9
Los Angeles	832	3.6
Orlando	830	3.6
San Diego	723	3.1
54 other airports	12,493	53.4
Total	**23,409**	**100.0**

Delta Air Lines

Airport	Flights per week	Share of airline total
Atlanta	6,711	23.7
Cincinnati	2,433	8.5
Salt Lake City	2,246	7.9
New York-JFK	1,141	4.0
New York-LaGuardia	776	2.7
Boston-Logan	636	2.2
Los Angeles	570	2.0
Orlando	562	2.0
Washington-Reagan	362	1.3
Fort Lauderdale	294	1.0
306 other airports	12,711	44.6
Total	**28,492**	**100.0**

Source: author's analysis of data in OAG 2008.

traveler (whose selection of the carrier is likely motivated more by its low fares rather than its convenience) that waits rather than the aircraft. Point-to-point services are a feature of many LCC networks, including that of Blue Air (see Figure 7.1).

Southwest maximizes its use of aircraft, personnel, and infrastructure on the ground by not only by minimizing turnaround times, but also by scheduling an unusually high number of flights per day to most points in its network (Sorenson 1991). To return to the contrast between Delta and Southwest, in 2008 Delta flew five or fewer flights per day to 189 airports in its network, a threshold beneath which no Southwest city fell. Corpus Christi, Texas was the least frequently served city in the Southwest network but even there the carrier had five or six daily departures depending on the day or week. The high frequency of Southwest operations per city per day further lowers the carrier's cost per passenger because it dilutes the fixed costs on the ground (e.g., leased gates) across many more passengers; these cost savings are termed density economies (Sorenson 1991).

Southwest is able to attain density economies *without* relying heavily on traffic feed from throughout its network. As explained in Chapter 5, hub-and-spoke systems operated by network carriers make sense because such systems bundle traffic feed permitting higher frequency service, larger aircraft, and/or higher load factors. Southwest has attained the same advantages without a strong emphasis on hubbing (and without incurring the costs that large hubbing operations entail) because it serves only markets that can support fairly high frequency service and because its low fares help the carrier to capture much of the business in any market it targets. The density economies that Southwest enjoys and its cost leadership in the airline industry are mutually reinforcing: Southwest's low fares are a magnet for cost-conscious passengers, and the more of those passengers the airline is able to put in its seats the more flights per day it can profitably schedule.

Still another factor contributing to Southwest's cost leadership is its use of secondary airports. For example, Southwest services Chicago via Chicago Midway Airport instead of O'Hare International. Interestingly, the airline's brand image is now so strong and its cost advantage so compelling that travelers drive hours to use its services. Although Southwest still serves Dallas via Love Field instead of Dallas-Ft. Worth, the airline is less dependent upon the convenience of the airports it uses than it is to those airports' compatibility with a business model based on rapid turnarounds and low infrastructure costs. Still, before leaving this point, it should be emphasized that Southwest *does* fly to some large hub airports such as Los Angeles International and San Francisco.[3]

Southwest has been able to maintain its cost advantage despite having one of the most highly unionized labor forces of any airline in America (Gittell 2003: 166). Furthermore, its employees earn wages that compare well with their counterparts at network carriers. In late 2007, for instance, the average pay for a Southwest Airlines 737 captain with 10 years' experience was $194 per hour versus $162 at American, $149 at Delta, $137 at jetBlue, and $130 at United for similarly experienced captains flying the same size aircraft (Airline Pilot Central 2007). But Southwest's strong and steady growth has kept the seniority of its workforce relatively low so it has few personnel at the high end of the pay scale. The same steady growth has been instrumental in maintaining Southwest's characteristic *esprit de corps* while the incumbent network carriers' reputations have been jeopardized by the employee bitterness engendered through massive layoffs. In fact, in the American Consumer Satisfaction Index produced by the University of Michigan, Southwest Airlines has finished first every year since 1995 (ACSI 2009).

High employee morale. Strong branding. Fleet standardization. An emphasis on point-to-point flights and a predilection for secondary airports. Very high frequency services to achieve density economies. All of these are elements of the Southwest model, a model that has influenced new airlines and old ones, both within the US and beyond. Not every one of those elements is found in other LCCs. For instance, not only is Southwest less reliant on any hub than its network carrier rivals; it is also less hub-dependent than any other American LCC (Reynolds-Feighan 2001). The shares of Frontier's enplanements at Denver, those of AirTran's at Atlanta, and Spirit's at Detroit are all markedly higher than Southwest's in Las Vegas McCarran International (Table 7.5). Nevertheless, much of what defines Southwest *is* characteristic of other LCCs.

Finally, the contribution of Southwest to what has become the LCC phenomenon is not just to have drawn the blueprint for later copycats. Equally important is Southwest's success: its stature as the most profitable US passenger airline over the past decade or so (Table 7.6) has been a catalyst for the venture capital invested in new LCCs in the US and beyond since the late 1990s (Morrell 2007: 116–17). For example, Oaktree Capital, a private investment firm, has been a long-term large investor in Spirit Airlines. Oaktree's investments of $125 million in 2004 and, with Goldman Sachs and Spirit's management, another $100 million in 2005 enabled the Florida-based LCC to replace its old aircraft with Airbus A320s and to expand in the Caribbean (Baldanza and Field 2006).

Filling the seats: Britannia Airways and its low-cost legacy

Although LCCs have made in-roads into the business travel market as described later in this chapter, a disproportionately large number of those flying on LCCs are leisure travelers. In tapping the large and growing leisure market, the LCCs – especially in Europe – are building upon the foundation laid down by charter operators. In particular, just as one early intrastate carrier in the US was clearly the most important, one European charter carrier was more influential than its rivals: Britannia Airways. The airline was one of several charter operators that took advantage of the network carriers' rush to sell their piston-engine and turboprop aircraft at the dawn of the Jet Age. In 1961, Britannia – then called Euravia – began flying offloaded Lockheed Constellations in a high-density 82-seat configuration between Britain and holiday destinations in Southern Europe. Euravia was part of a vertically integrated enterprise controlling both the airline and what would eventually be thousands of hotel rooms in places like Palma de Mallorca. The goal was to fill 100 percent of airline seats and the hotel

Table 7.5 Hub dominance at selected US airlines, 2008

Airline	Airport 1	% carrier's scheduled flights	Airport 2	% carrier's scheduled flights	Number of other airports	Combined share of other airports
AirTran	Atlanta	31.0	Orlando	8.4	53	60.6
Alaska	Seattle	26.9	Portland, OR	12.5	87	60.1
American	DFW	18.6	O'Hare	12.1	247	69.3
Continental	Bush (Houston)	24.0	Newark	14.2	283	61.8
Delta	Atlanta	23.7	Cincinnati	8.5	315	67.7
Frontier	Denver	49.1	Las Vegas	2.5	58	48.5
JetBlue	New York-JFK	27.9	Boston	10.1	51	62.1
Northwest	Detroit	19.7	MSP	18.6	240	61.8
Southwest	Las Vegas	7.1	Midway (Chi.)	6.6	62	86.3
United	O'Hare	17.2	Denver	12.0	221	70.9
US Airways	Charlotte	16.1	Philadelphia	12.4	219	71.6
Virgin America	San Francisco	40.3	Los Angeles	19.6	5	40.1

Source: author's analysis of data in OAG 2008.

Table 7.6 Most profitable airlines, 1998–2007

Rank	Airline	Cumulative net income (millions of dollars)
1	Singapore Airlines	8,179
2	Air France/KLM	8,044
3	FedEx	6,673
4	Lufthansa	5,885
5	Emirates	4,919
6	Southwest Airlines	4,667
7	British Airways	4,643
8	Cathay Pacific	4,051
9	Qantas	3,419
10	Ryanair[1]	2,718

Source: based on various editions of *Air Transport World.*

Note
1 Ryanair's figure is based on data for 2001–2007 only.

beds by wooing discretionary travelers with as low a package price as possible for a two-week getaway (Cuthbert 1987: 10–15). Today's LCCs rely upon a similarly virtuous cycle between low-fares and high load factors.

In 1964, Euravia began flying surplus turboprop Britannias and took that name as its new moniker; but as the company's traffic grew so did its fleet, and by the late 1960s, Britannia was flying jets (Cuthbert 1987: 10, 22, 147). Britannia's network grew to encompass not just sun and sand destinations in the Mediterranean but also the Caribbean, Australia and New Zealand, and the USA as well as winter destinations in Europe. It was relatively easy for Britannia to add destinations because as a nonscheduled operator it did not need the kind of traffic rights its scheduled brethren required. Finally, in 1985, the airline commenced scheduled operations, beginning with the link between Manchester and Palma de Mallorca (Cuthbert 1987: 137), a route on which it had operated charters for two decades. Many other carriers have similarly built upon the traffic, especially leisure traffic, cultivated by charter operations.

Partly as a result of the charter carrier-to-LCC evolution, the charter business is slowly becoming less important. In 1985, for instance, non-scheduled services accounted for 17 percent of all international passenger-kilometers; the corresponding figure for 2005 was 11 percent (*ICAO Journal* 1986, 2006). Still, charter operators are not going to disappear altogether for they have a number of advantages versus LCCs that will keep them relevant in some markets, particularly those more than three hours in flight duration. Charter airlines fly bigger planes with lower per-seat costs; they fly only when there are enough passengers to fill the great majority of seats; and because their services are part of inclusive tours, the carriers' marketing costs are minimal (Doganis 2006: 184–5). Against these advantages, the LCCs have a few of their own, including high frequency (and therefore passenger-pleasing) services. Moreover, the development of an Internet-savvy, well-traveled populace reduces the appeal of inclusive tours. A growing number of travelers prefer to craft their own custom-made vacations.

As for Britannia, its evolution took another step forward when it was re-branded as Thomsonfly in 2004 (*Flight International* 2006c). Thomsonfly is primarily an LCC with a network of scheduled services extending throughout Europe (but many charter services besides). The airline's headquarters remains Luton, an airport that Britannia essentially developed. In the 1960s, Britannia agreed to base its operations there in the 1960s in exchange for the airport's agreement to upgrade its facilities to handle larger aircraft and to have no duty-free sales that might cut into Britannia's own airborne commerce (Cuthbert 1987: 19). In the partnership between the upstart airline and the ambitious airport, Britannia served once more as a model for LCCs.

LCCs worldwide

By 2006, the LCC phenomenon had gone global (Table 7.7). Low interest rates, the ease of securing leased aircraft from the likes of ILFC (see Chapter 4), and Internet-based marketing and management software are among the factors that have lowered entry costs in the entry. Moreover, Southwest and other veteran LCCs have given new entrants models to emulate (*Economist* 2004). The impact of the new carriers upon the airborne world, especially in poor countries, could be huge; but LCCs face formidable odds to their success, precisely in those countries that could benefit most from less expensive air transportation.

LCCs in developed markets

The greatest number of LCCs is found in Europe where about 50 budget airlines had a combined market share of 19 percent in 2005, up from just 5 percent in 2000 and on the way to a predicted 33 percent in 2009 (Thomas 2005b; *Economist*

Table 7.7 LCCs by region, 2006

Region	Low-cost carriers[1]
Africa	6
Europe	47
Middle East	3
South Asia	8
Southeast Asia	16
East Asia	9
Southwest Pacific	6
Latin America	12
North America	15
Total	**122**

Sources: based on *Flight International* 2006a, 2006b, 2006c.

Note

1 There is no consistent definition of an LCC. The numbers listed here reflect the number of carriers described as "low-fare," "low-cost," or "budget" in *Flight International*'s 2006 World Airline Directory.

2006e). Europe is an especially promising market for LCCs. The region has a large middle class, a cultural predisposition to take vacations too far away to drive, dozens of enticing cities and holiday destinations (e.g., ski and beach resorts) located well within the nonstop range of the narrow-body jets favored by the LCCs, widespread Internet access and credit card use, and rich capital markets that have poured money into this component of the airline industry.

Further, the single aviation market (SAM) in Europe since 1997, described in the Chapter 5, provided an environment favorable to the growth of international airline services within Europe. A few LCCs have been especially aggressive in exploiting the new fifth and seventh freedom and cabotage rights opened up by the SAM. An extreme case is Ireland-based Ryanair, which relied upon such rights for 71 percent of its routes, enabling the carrier to escape the confines of its small home market (Dobruszkes 2006). Other features of Europe's economic unification, including the simplification of immigration and customs clearance procedures, have facilitated the quick turnarounds that are basic to the LCC formula.

Ryanair is the largest of Europe's LCCs. The Irish carrier took wing in the mid-1980s, along with another important start-up from the British Isles, Virgin Atlantic Airways. Ryanair shared a low-fare strategy with Virgin; and the emergence and survival of both depended on the first stirrings of liberalization in European aviation. The similarities end there, however. While Virgin tackled high density, long-haul networks, Ryanair focused on the short-haul. In particular, its most significant early route linked Dublin and London. The market, previously a high-fare duopoly shared by BA and the Irish flag carrier Aer Lingus, had tremendous potential for Ryanair. The large Irish immigrant and guest worker population in Britain and the substantial number of travelers then crossing the Irish Sea by ferry made the market fertile ground for the upstart LCC. With Ryanair's entrance, the number of discount fares skyrocketed as the average yield on the route fell by a third. The result was predictable: in the five years before Ryanair launched its low-fare service, London–Dublin traffic grew at less than 3 percent per year. In the next three years, traffic doubled (Doganis 1991: 104–5). By 2008, the Dublin–London link was the second most heavily trafficked international city-pair in the world (see Table 8.2).

Ryanair's network has long emphasized secondary airports and initially the carrier served the crucial London market from the same Luton airport that Britannia had helped to create. Ryanair's chief rival, Aer Lingus heaped sarcastic praise upon Luton in one radio advertisement:

> Fly to fabulous Luton Airport. Right in the middle of Luton. Cosmopolitan Luton Airport, a stone's throw from an absolutely fabulous bus stop where you will wait for a bus to take you directly to the train station. Glamorous Luton Station, where you will wait for a train to take you to another train station.
>
> Why fly to Luton for more when you can fly to London for less?
>
> (quoted in Creaton 2004: 27)

Perhaps in part because of such advertising salvos, Ryanair later made Stansted its principal gateway to London. Several other LCCs have chosen Stansted, too – so much so that at the end of 2006 it had 237 LCC arrivals per day, more than twice as many as any other European airport (Table 7.8) (Eurocontrol 2006).

Although Ryanair specifically tried to imitate Southwest beginning in the early 1990s, its network resembles a conventional hub-and-spoke system rather than the point-to-point network flown by Southwest. In 2008, the concentration of flights in its main hubs (especially London-Stansted, Dublin, Gerona, and Milan-Orio al Serio) was more like the network of Delta than that of Southwest. And of course, the most basic difference is that while Southwest operates entirely with the US, almost all of Ryanair's routes are international.

Like many other LCCs, Ryanair has big ambitions. In 2008, the carrier had outstanding orders for nearly as many 737s as the total number of aircraft already in its fleet. UK-based easyJet had a similarly huge number of A319s on order (*Air Transport World* 2008a). Filling all those planes will require a vast expansion in the number of passengers at the same time that dozens of new European LCCs are challenging the big players. Ryanair's head has forecast a "bloodbath" and has complained about the crazy pricing of new rivals – prices so low that the airport tax sometimes exceeds the fare collected by the carrier (*Economist* 2004). The industry consensus is that most of the new entrants will ultimately disappear and that the winners in the "European shootout" will include Ryanair (Thomas 2005b).

The American LCC market is less fractured, and Southwest already has a strongly dominant position. Yet the grandfather of today's LCCs does face a number of significant domestic rivals. The largest is jetBlue, which grew rapidly from its first flight in 2000. JetBlue was launched at a time when financial markets were awash in venture capital, and the previous achievements of the airline's founder, David Neeleman,[4] in the industry helped to attract the attention of powerful financial interests, including financier George Soros whose fund took a

Table 7.8 European airports ranked by LCC flights

Rank	Airport	*Average daily LCC flights arrivals*
1	Stansted (London)	237
2	Gatwick (London)	114
3	Dublin	111
4	Luton (London)	102
5	Palma de Mallorca	100
6	Amsterdam-Schiphol	99
7	Cologne/Bonn	92
8	Manchester	78
9	Barcelona	73
10	Málaga	73

Source: Eurocontrol 2006: 12.

24 percent stake in the new airline (Wynbrandt 2004: 100). In total, the new venture raised $130 million even before getting its airline certificate, airport slots, and aircraft. It was the best-capitalized new airline in the history of the industry in the US. The abundance of capital meant that, unlike many short-lived LCCs, jetBlue could afford to buy a substantial fleet of new, low-maintenance aircraft, flood the market with advertising, withstand the price-slashing attacks of incumbent carriers, and absorb losses while building up traffic density. JetBlue continues to be well-funded; in 2007, Lufthansa paid $300 million for a 19 percent stake in the carrier (Maynard 2008a).

Though an LCC, jetBlue defied some of the defining characteristics of the LCC model described earlier in this chapter. To begin, the carrier's main base is New York-JFK rather than some secondary airport. JFK is in the midst of one of the richest markets in the world; and, prior to jetBlue's arrival, the international gateway airport was used only at certain times of the day (e.g., between 6 p.m. and midnight for departures to Europe). In 2008, jetBlue moved into a new $800 million terminal at New York-JFK which incorporates with Eero Saarinen-designed TWA terminal whose soaring avian lines made it an icon of the early Jet Age (Maynard 2008a).

Labor relations were another area where jetBlue departed from the Southwest model. While Southwest had prospered despite its very high level of unionization, jetBlue regarded unions as anathema to a business model that prized flexibility – expecting pilots, for instance, to help with cleaning an aircraft upon arrival in order to minimize ground time between flights. JetBlue tried to undercut the appeal of unions through a profit-sharing plan and by dispersing its workforce; in its early years, the airline relied almost exclusively on telecommuting for reservations staff who worked from their homes scattered in the Salt Lake City area (Wynbrandt 2004: 132). Another difference: jetBlue has not followed the example of the established carriers in setting up a defined-benefit retirement system, opting for a less costly defined-contribution system.

JetBlue has also distinguished itself with superior in-flight services. In particular, it was a pioneer among LCCs in placing satellite television screens in every seatback. LiveTV was crucial in differentiating jetBlue in the transcontinental markets that comprise much of its network.[5]

Now it is JetBlue's success that has inspired imitation. One of the newest LCCs in the world, Virgin America, has embraced key elements of the jetBlue model. Based in San Francisco and partly owned by Richard Branson's Virgin Group, Virgin America has targeted heavily trafficked and competitive trunk routes like San Francisco–Los Angeles, San Francisco–New York-JFK, and Los Angeles–Washington-Dulles. Virgin America's Airbus A320 aircraft are fitted with outsized seatback in-flight entertainment screens and the option to order food from one's seat. Virgin America is also like jetBlue and a number of other new LCCs in the ample capital with which it has entered the fray.

Virgin America is just one of several LCCs in the loosely knit Virgin empire (see Figure 6.9). On the other side of the Pacific, Virgin Blue grew so fast that in just four years, it captured about one-third of the Australia's domestic market

(Knibb 2005). And yet, during the same period Qantas thrived. In part, the simultaneous success of the old and new players was attributable to the collapse of a third. Not long after Virgin Blue's debut, the country's second-largest airline, Ansett, fell into a financial abyss from which it could not extricate itself. Its grounding left underserved markets and unused airport slots. Furthermore, Virgin Blue and Qantas have served different markets, at least until recently, with the former strongly focused on the domestic market and nearby international destinations (e.g., in New Zealand and Indonesia) while the latter operated an expansive intercontinental network. Yet already, this basic difference in their networks has narrowed, and it is likely to narrow further in the future. Like flag carriers elsewhere in the world, Qantas has tried to harness the LCC phenomenon to its own advantage through an LCC subsidiary:[6] in 2003, it established Jetstar Airways with a fleet of A320s. And Virgin Blue has formed a long-haul subsidiary, V Australia, which competes on routes between Australia and the US.

LCCs in developing countries

Qantas' involvement in the LCC market includes a joint venture with Singaporean investors called Jetstar Asia. The Singapore-based Jetstar Asia was one a few dozen or so LCCs flying in Asia by 2006 (see Table 7.7), and the significant investment by Qantas is indicative of the region's perceived promise. Until recently, a number of factors militated against the success of LCCs in Asia. Most important has been the relatively restrictive ASAs which still govern many Asian bilateral markets (Kua and Baum 2004). Yet those barriers are coming down. For example, the 300-kilometer route from Singapore to Kuala Lumpur has characteristics that would make it ideal for LCCs, but until 2008, the route was a virtual duopoly[7] shared by Singapore Airlines (SIA) and Malaysia Airlines because the ASA between the two countries provided only for single designation on the route. Finally, in early 2008, those restrictions were relaxed and a trio of LCCs (SIA subsidiary Tiger Airways and Qantas subsidiary Jetstar Asia from Singapore, and AirAsia from Malaysia) commenced services on the route. Still, despite the spread of liberalization in the region, many other routes within Asia remain off-limits to LCCs.

Moreover, Asia is home to a handful of very competently managed, high productivity network carriers (see Table 6.8) (Lawton and Solomko 2005). SIA, Cathay Pacific, and other Asian carriers are not immune to the LCC threat, but neither are they as vulnerable as their American counterparts in particular. Furthermore, the culture of flying in Asia has resisted the commoditization of air travel upon which most LCCs have been premised (Ionides 2005a). More so than in other parts of the world, Asian airline passengers are accustomed to a high level of in-flight service. The lean LCC business model runs against the grain of the expectations carriers such as SIA and Thai, with their free drinks and elaborate in-flight entertainment offerings, have helped to cultivate. Furthermore, Asia-Pacific flag carriers generate a very significant share, averaging more than 20 percent, of their business from freight; this source of revenue is difficult for LCCs flying only narrow-body aircraft to tap. Still another obstacle to the LCCs is the lower proportion of discretionary local passengers on many routes within Asia compared to Europe and the US.

Despite these problems, however, LCCs began to sprout in Asia in the late 1990s and early years of the twenty-first century. In fact, the rapid ascent of budget airlines in the region prompted Boeing to revise its vision of the future global aircraft market by shifting the predicted balance of narrow-body airliners and wide-body airliners in favor of the former[8] (Coppinger 2004). Boeing had assumed that the plodding pace of liberalization in Asia would constrain and delay the growth of LCCs compared to Europe and North America; but by 2004, it was apparent that Asian LCCs were, to some degree, forcing liberalization as at least some governments in the region latched on to and sought to accommodate and even harness the LCC phenomenon – through, among other things, the construction of special LCC terminals at places such as Singapore's Changi Airport and the opening up of old or distant airports, such as the former Clark airbase near Manila, to LCCs.

The most successful Asian LCC so far has been Malaysia's AirAsia (Figure 7.3). Begun as a regional carrier to complement Malaysia Airlines, AirAsia was re-created as an LCC in 2001. Just a few years later, it claimed the highest daily utilization in the world for any airline with a 737 Next Generation series fleet (Hooper 2005). And, taking a page from LCCs elsewhere, AirAsia sold 45 percent of its tickets online as early as 2005, an achievement helped by widespread Internet usage in a country that has made "multimedia" a cornerstone of its development strategy.

Ironically, the Asian financial crisis of 1997–8 helped to foster conditions favorable to the LCCs. The crisis left newly built airports (e.g., Kuala Lumpur International Airport) and recently expanded ones (e.g., Singapore Changi) with excess capacity, easing LCC access to needed gates. The downturn also prodded the region's governments to further unshackle the airline industry, opening up new spaces for LCCs. In Indonesia, for instance, more aggressive domestic deregulation cleared the way for Lion Air. Created in 1999, the airline flew to 27 Indonesian cities and a handful of foreign destinations, including Singapore, by 2008 (OAG 2008). Around the time that the carrier commenced services on the Singapore–Jakarta market, Lion Air claimed its fares were 60 percent lower than those of SIA (Hooper 2005).

India is perhaps the most promising market for LCCs in Asia. India's newly buoyant middle class, large physical size, traditionally high airfares, numerous cities spaced one to two hours flying time apart, heavy ground (especially rail) transportation flows, and relatively aggressive deregulation (in contrast to China) comprise ingredients favorable to LCCs. And the industry has responded. IndiGo, an upstart funded by one of India's many information technology firms, had a fleet of 18 A320s and 82 more Airbus narrow-bodies on order in 2008, and altogether five Indian LCCs had 133 jetliners on order in 2008 (*Air Transport World* 2008a).Yet filling all those planes will be a daunting challenge, and there has already been significant consolidation in the Indian LCC sector.[9]

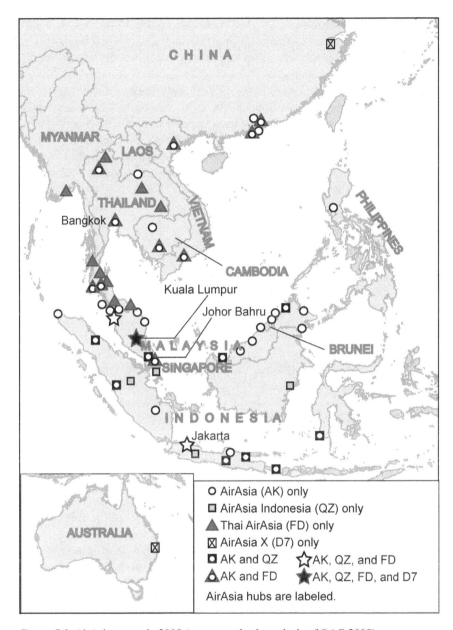

Figure 7.3 AirAsia network, 2008 (source: author's analysis of OAG 2008).

AirAsia has circumvented the regulatory limitations of the Asian market by forming subsidiaries based in Thailand and Indonesia (AirAsia has a 49 per cent share in each carrier). AirAsia X, meanwhile, is similar to Virgin Blue's long-haul subsidiary V Australia.

More generally, the airline industry's troubles of 2008 and 2009 proved fatal to a substantial number of LCCs. The American carrier ATA, New Zealand's Freedom Air, Indonesia's Adam Air, and Sterling Airlines in Denmark were among the budget carriers that failed in 2008. In that sense, the adverse market conditions may have hastened the "bloodbath" forecast by Ryanair's O'Leary – not just in Europe but across the LCC universe. Nevertheless, this crisis, like the one a decade earlier, may prove conducive to the rise of the LCC phenomenon as well-financed, well-run LCCs gain at the expense of hobbled network carriers (and weak LCCs). Most obviously, Southwest Airlines, the biggest LCC of all, captured more of the US domestic market through the crisis, with its market share climbing from 11.9 percent in the 12 months ending March 2007 to 13.2 percent in the 12 months ending March 2009 (BTS 2009a).

Low cost = high impact

The person who could not otherwise have flown is a standard element of news coverage of the LCC phenomenon. In a story about Air Deccan (which was acquired by Kingfisher in 2007), a Delhi shopkeeper likened his first flight to a fairground ride (Ramesh 2005). In another story, a woman described how she was finally able to take a long-awaited vacation to Thailand with her family because of AirAsia's $90 round-trip fare from her Johor Bahru hometown in southern Malaysia to Bangkok (Balfour 2004). The chief executive of Thailand's Nok Air claimed in an interview, "We're creating an entirely new business. We're flying people who have never flown before." (quoted in Barnes 2004).

In the US, there is a name for the LCC-engendered increase in air travel: it is called the "Southwest Effect" (Vowles 2001; Morrison 2001). Southwest Airlines' entry into a market, particularly one not already served by another LCC, is associated with a significant fall in average fares and an increase in traffic. Southwest fares are often so low that travelers drive 100 miles (about 160 kilometers) or more to reach an airport the airline serves. In a 1996 column, consumer advocate Clark Howard (1996) advised his *Atlanta Journal-Constitution* readers to use the "west Atlanta airport" – two hours' drive west in Birmingham, Alabama in order to avail themselves of Southwest's $25 one-way fares.

The alacrity with which travelers get in their cars and drive to a Southwest airport means that the "Southwest effect" is not limited solely to those airports it serves. One study based on analysis of the 1,000 most heavily traveled US routes (Morrison 2001) found that:

- on routes that Southwest actually flew, fares were 46 percent lower than they would otherwise have been;
- on routes where Southwest flew between an airport near the origin and an airport near the destination but not between the origin and destination airports themselves (e.g., Southwest's effect on fares between New York-JFK and Chicago-O'Hare, which the airline did not serve, via the carrier's

services between Long Island Islip MacArthur Airport and Midway Airport), fares were 15 percent lower than they would otherwise have been;

- on routes where Southwest was present at both airports but did not actually fly directly between them (e.g., Southwest served both Seattle and Portland, Oregon but had no direct route linking them), fares were 33 percent lower – due at least in part to other carriers' fear that Southwest could enter the market;[10] and
- on routes where Southwest was a competitor only via faraway airports (e.g., the effect of Southwest on the Atlanta–Chicago market via the carrier's service between Birmingham and Chicago-Midway), fares were 12 percent lower than they would otherwise have been.

Economist Steven Morrison estimated that in 1998 Southwest saved consumers $6.6 billion on routes that it actually served, another $3.0 billion on routes where Southwest served alternative airports but was not present itself, and a further $3.3 billion on routes where Southwest was a potential competitor. The total savings attributable to Southwest thus amounted to $12.9 billion, which Morrison further estimated to be half of all the savings that year to American consumers creditable to airline deregulation. In this regard, the results were troubling since so much of the gain from deregulation depended on a single airline. Still, in the years since then several other substantial LCCs have emerged in the US, most notably jetBlue and Virgin America, so that the welfare gains attributable to LCCs are not likely to be so narrowly based.

The effects of LCCs have been similarly great in Europe. LCCs have made possible weekend holiday trips from one side of a continent to another, ultra-long-distance commuting, and the devoted pursuit by fans and groupies of their favorite touring sports teams and rock stars (Capell 2006). Or, given the incredibly low fares offered by some LCCs, to fly for no particular reason at all. In July 2005, the website for Ryanair listed 84 destinations for which it offered one-way fares below US$18 to passengers who booked flights at least 14 days in advance and avoided certain peak travel periods. From the airline's perspective, such promotional fares make sense by exciting interest in its services, attracting new passengers, building market share, and filling seats that might otherwise go empty.

From a broader perspective, however, a cut-rate one-way fare as low as US$0.30 (before taxes), for instance, from London to Stockholm creates a vast gap between what the traveler pays for a trip and what that trip really costs society. In Britain, *The Independent* noted the contradiction between a pair of government white papers released there in 2003: one advocating reduced emissions of carbon dioxide by industry and transportation and a second envisioning a huge increase in affordable air travel (*Independent* 2005). The environmental sustainability of air transportation, to which I return in Chapter 11, is a critical issue facing not just Britain but the airborne world more generally.

There is another way in which the LCC phenomenon has been expensive in ways few of its beneficiaries are likely to consider: thousands of once well-paid airline employees have lost their jobs. Consider the story in the US: there, the total number of revenue passenger-kilometers performed by all airlines combined grew 72 percent between 1990 and 2006, but the number of airline industry employees barely budged. Many flight crew and cabin crew are still well-paid compared to most service sector workers but not as well-paid, relatively speaking, as they used to be. As recently as the late 1990s, for instance, the average flight attendant earned 8 percent more than the average nurse; by 2006 the average nurse earned 6 percent more (BLS 2007). Moreover, because pilots and flight attendants are more likely to live in major metropolitan areas (Table 7.9) with fast-rising costs of living, the erosion in their relative pay is steeper than these numbers suggest.[11]

A distinction without a difference?

LCCs have so saturated short-haul markets in some parts of the developed world that they have little choice but to look farther afield and that will mean, at least for some, an expansion onto long-haul routes. The addition of long-haul routes, in turn, may necessitate the diversification of fleets beyond the 737s and A320s and a greater reliance on traffic feed through hubs. In other words, some LCCs will become more like network carriers. AirAsia may be showing the way forward in this regard. In 2007, it launched long-haul services via its subsidiary AirAsia X (see Figure 7.3). By mid-2008, AirAsia X operated its small fleet of Airbus A330 aircraft to Australia and China, and by March 2009 the carrier introduced nonstop services from Kuala Lumpur to London-Stansted using leased Airbus A340s. Similarly, as noted above, Virgin Blue, which prefers to call itself "a new world carrier" rather than an LCC (Dorman 2006) has launched intercontinental services (using Boeing 777-300ERs) via its subsidiary V Australia.

Table 7.9 US metro areas ranked by pilot and flight attendant populations

Occupation	Metropolitan statistical area	Occupation employment	Annual mean occupation wage ($)	% total MSA employment
Pilots, copilots, and flight engineers	Louisville, KY-IN	3,300	—[1]	0.534
	Anchorage, AK	680	107,760	0.413
	Fort Worth, TX	3,440	—[1]	0.395
	Detroit, MI	2,700	—[1]	0.354
	Atlanta, GA	6,480	110,830	0.269
Flight attendants	Atlanta, GA	9,060	—[1]	0.377
	Honolulu, HI	1,260	28,270	0.284
	Charlotte, NC-SC	2,130	40,690	0.243
	Chicago, IL	8,490	33,410	0.222
	Denver, CO	2,770	27,840	0.221

Source: BLS 2009.

Note
1 Information withheld at source.

To date, most LCCs have avoided such routes because their cost advantage over conventional network carriers is much smaller than on short-haul routes, where, for instance, quick turnarounds make a bigger difference. Moreover, some elements of the LCC model, such as minimal in-flight service, become less tenable the longer passengers are on board. An analysis of long-haul routes of more than six hours duration (Francis *et al.* 2007) found that the typical LCC was likely to enjoy only about a 20 percent cost advantage versus a conventional network carrier, compared to a 50 percent advantage on short-haul routes. Still, 20 percent is significant, both for the network carriers that might face new competitors on their treasured long-haul routes and for the passengers to whom that advantage will ultimately redound.

Even Southwest Airlines is outgrowing the LCC model. As one financial analyst put it, "Southwest is morphing more and more into a regular airline." (quoted in Schlangenstein 2007). In 2007, Southwest announced that it would cut capacity on some routes, drop one route (El Paso to Midland, Texas) altogether, and defer some airplane deliveries. Slower growth will, by itself, erode the carrier's cost advantage. Even before the 2007 announcement, Southwest's costs had been rising quite rapidly; the cost per available seat-kilometer grew 20 percent in four years (Schlangenstein 2007), a sign of the carrier's maturity and the paucity of as-yet-underserved, overpriced short-haul routes that have been the LCC's low-hanging fruit. Partly in response, Southwest is adapting to better serve higher-yielding business travelers, which already account for 40 percent of its business. Abandoning its decades' old cattle-car seating in favor of assigned seats is one expected change directed at business travelers that will please Southwest's leisure passengers, too.

Indeed, Southwest is hardly alone among LCCs in setting its sights on business travelers. EasyJet, for instance, regularly fills half of its seats with such passengers (Mason 2000). Interestingly, a comparison of business travelers using network carriers at London-Heathrow and business travelers using easyJet at London-Luton found few differences (Mason 2001). Those flying on easyJet were somewhat more likely to work for small and medium-sized companies, to place a high importance on the price of air travel and to attach less importance to such amenities as in-flight service and frequent flyer programs, and to have booked their travel via the Internet. Overall, however, the study found that among business travelers, the market for the two different kinds of carriers had become blurred.

Attracting business travelers for that first trip and then keeping them as future flyers is made all the easier by the proliferation of LCC networks. Ultimately, the expansion of Southwest, Ryanair, easyJet, and other large LCCs has created airlines defined as much by their networks as by their low costs. And over time the balance, for some of these airlines, is likely to shift more towards emphasizing their networks, which will mean – as in the case of Virgin Blue – diverse fleets, more than just one class of service, and improved in-flight and airport services.

Meanwhile, some network carriers are "morphing" in the opposite direction. The clearest example is Aer Lingus, which under heavy pressure from Ryanair, essentially became an LCC itself through a transformation begun in 2001. The Irish flag carrier consolidated its fleet, eliminated business class on most routes, greatly increased its emphasis on Internet ticket sales, and cut its costs and fares (C. Baker 2003). However, Aer Lingus kept its transatlantic routes, upon which it offers mixed class services with wide-body aircraft; so Aer Lingus is something of a hybrid rather than a narrowly defined LCC. Other network carriers are evolving in a broadly similar direction.

Ultimately, then, the classification of airlines into either network carriers or LCCs is likely to lose some of its purchase as cost-cutting network carriers and network-building LCCs fill in the spaces in between.

Part III

Life aloft and on the ground in the airborne world

8 People on the move at 1,000 kilometers per hour

The airborne populace

In 2006, 21-year-old Tobias Gutt booked an airline ticket on the Internet to what he thought was Sydney, Australia. He departed from his native Germany on December 23 lightly clad in preparation for what he expected to be a four-week holiday in the balmy Australian summer. He was surprised that his itinerary took him to the US en route to Australia; but only realized his mistake when, after having first stopped in Portland, Oregon and then Billings, Montana, he was directed to board a 19-seat commuter flight to Sidney, Montana – 14,000 kilometers from his intended destination (CNN 2006)! Such incidents are not exactly common, although a Sydney, Australia-bound British couple ended up in Sydney, Nova Scotia in 2002 via a similar mistake. Yet what is emblematic about Mr. Gutt's experience is how *fast* he ended up so *far* off-course. Less than 24 hours after his departure, he was 14,000 kilometers astray. Going far and going fast are the defining qualities of the airborne world – even if that occasionally means going far and fast in the wrong direction. Of course, most people go in the right direction. Ending up in Sidney instead of Sydney was a beginner's mistake. The frequency of air travel today is such that most travelers to Sidney and Sydney – and Sydney, Nova Scotia, too – are aviation veterans, frequent flyers quick to recognize that "SDY" is not "SYD."

This chapter is about people in the airborne world. In 2007, the total number of passengers reached nearly 2.3 billion, up by more than 50 percent in just a decade (Flint 2008). The increased number of flyers has been matched by the increased diversity of trip purposes. In the US, just over 50 percent of airline trips are pleasure-related; another 8 percent are for personal business; and, incredibly, 3 percent of trips are undertaken by commuters (BTS 2006a). A minority of air journeys is now work-related. The endless variety of reasons that motivate airline trips is testament to the penetration of aviation deep into the interstices of the lives of millions.

For the world's Muslims, for instance, air travel has transformed the pilgrimage to Mecca. A journey that once took months on foot or at sea is now made mainly by air. Furthermore, inexpensive air charters have made the journey affordable to believers even in some of the poorest countries; in 2002, the pilgrims numbered

2.5 million (versus 300,000 in 1965) and included more Indonesians than Saudi citizens (Bukhari 2002). In the United States, the images associated with Thanksgiving now include not only roasted turkey and the cartoon balloons of the Macy's parade but also airports teeming with people rewinding some of the family ties that air travel has helped to stretch. In China, meanwhile, air travel is beginning to challenge the country's trains as the principal means via which the millions of migrants to the booming cities in the east return to their provincial villages for the Chinese New Year celebration (Chiu 2005). And in Bangalore and Bangkok (among other developing world destinations), thousands of "medical tourists" arrive by air each year for surgical operations that are either higher in quality or lower in cost than what is available in the patient's home country.

Despite the growth of myriad kinds of air traffic across the world, the everyday importance of flight remains highly uneven. An estimated minimum of 84 percent of American adults have flown at least once (Greenberg 2001); conversely, in India, less than 1 percent of the population had in 2005 (Mathews 2005). The US and Europe are part of the "fast world;" most of Africa and India belongs to "the slow world." The marginalization of the poor in the world's airline networks is not surprising. For the same pattern is evident in the sea freight networks, telecommunications networks, and that most celebrated of networks: the Internet. Unequal access to the latter has fueled discussions of a global "digital divide" (Hammond 2001), but the older inequality in physical accessibility is a more intractable problem. In the Philippines, for instance, cell phones and Internet cafes are common even in the country's poorest regions, but the sky remains beyond the means of the great majority of Filipinos. To put matters in perspective, for the nearly 50 percent of Philippine population that lives on less than $2 per day, the typical airfare from Manila to San Francisco represents at least two years' income. In the poorest countries of Asia, Latin America, and especially Africa, the network of air services remains remarkably thin because too much of the population on the ground simply cannot afford the ticket to join the world aloft.

Thus it is unsurprising that the busiest hubs and most heavily trafficked passenger routes are found in upper- and middle-income countries (Table 8.1). It is hubs and routes such as these that mediate the increasingly global scale flow of passenger traffic. The writer Pico Iyer (1995) discovered that the Traveler's Aid desk at the Los Angeles International Airport (LAX) dispensed help in Pangasinan, Waray-Waray, Dari, and dozens of other languages (Iyer 1995). It is no coincidence that all five of the Disney theme parks are located near one of the world's thirty busiest airports (see below). Neither is it a coincidence that each of the four flights hijacked on September 11, 2001 originated from or was destined to one of these 30 hubs; nor is it surprising that the international spread of Severe Acute Respiratory Syndrome (SARS) in 2003 only began in earnest when the disease reached Hong Kong (Bowen and LaRoe 2006).

With these far-reaching implications in mind, this chapter deals with three kinds of airline passengers: business travelers, tourists, and immigrants. The first two groups fill most airline seats. The last group is far smaller in number but potent in influence.

Flying business class: the world is a workplace

Most business trips are not globe-trotting adventures. In the US the median one-way distance for business trips is just 123 miles (198 kilometers), a distance that hardly makes a diversion to the airport worthwhile (BTS 2003). Accordingly, American businessmen and businesswomen make more than 80 percent of their work-related trips by car. Nevertheless, the airborne share of business travel is large enough and so lucrative that it has become the ambrosia of airline executives' dreams. It has been said, only half in jest, that airlines lose money on economy class, break-even on first class (because low load factors and the high cost of having such capacious seats so far apart offset the high fares), and make whatever profit they can on business class. More precisely, in the late 1990s, it was estimated that, for large network airlines, business travelers occupied only a fifth of the seats on scheduled flights but generated about half of the carriers' revenue (*Economist* 1998a).

Table 8.1 The world's top passenger hubs, 2007

Rank	Airport	Passengers (million)	Average annual growth since 2000 (%)
1	Hartsfield-Jackson Atlanta Int'l	83.4	0.6
2	Chicago-O'Hare Int'l	76.2	0.8
3	Heathrow (London)	68.1	0.8
4	Haneda (Tokyo)	66.8	2.4
5	Los Angeles Int'l	61.9	(1.0)
6	Paris-Charles de Gaulle Int'l	59.9	3.2
7	Dallas-Ft. Worth Int'l	59.8	(0.2)
8	Frankfurt	54.2	1.3
9	Beijing Capital Int'l	53.6	13.8
10	Madrid-Barajas Int'l	53.6	7.2
11	Denver Int'l	49.9	3.7
12	Amsterdam Airport Schiphol	47.8	2.7
13	John F. Kennedy Int'l (New York)	47.7	5.4
14	Hong Kong Int'l	47.0	5.3
15	Las Vegas-McCarran Int'l	47.0	3.5
16	George Bush Intercontinental (Houston)	43.0	2.9
17	Phoenix-Sky Harbor Int'l	42.2	2.3
18	Suvarnabhumi (Bangkok)	41.2	4.8
19	Changi (Singapore)	36.7	3.6
20	Orlando Int'l	36.5	2.5
21	Newark Liberty Int'l	36.4	0.9
22	Detroit Metro	36.0	0.2
23	San Francisco Int'l	35.8	(1.9)
24	Narita Int'l (Tokyo)	35.5	3.8
25	Gatwick (London)	35.2	1.3
26	Minneapolis-St. Paul Int'l	35.2	(0.6)
27	Dubai Int'l	34.3	15.8
28	Munich-Franz Josef Strauss	34.0	5.7
29	Miami Int'l	33.7	0.0
30	Charlotte Douglas Int'l	33.2	5.3

Source: ACI 2008.

Table 8.2 The world's top passenger city-pairs,[1] 2008

Rank	Domestic	Weekly Scheduled Seats (000)	International	Weekly Scheduled Seats (000)
1	Sapporo–Tokyo vv[2]	217	Hong Kong–Taipei vv	180
2	Osaka–Tokyo vv	199	Dublin–London vv	122
3	Rio de Janeiro–Sao Paulo vv	186	London–New York vv	120
4	Fukuoka–Tokyo vv	182	Seoul–Tokyo vv	97
5	Melbourne–Sydney vv	174	Amsterdam–London vv	84
6	Jeju–Seoul vv	170	Jakarta–Singapore vv	78
7	Beijing–Shanghai vv	165	Bangkok–Hong Kong vv	76
8	Cape Town–Johannesburg vv	127	Madrid–Paris vv	73
9	Barcelona–Madrid vv	123	Bangkok–Singapore vv	71
10	Milan–Rome vv	122	Hong Kong–Singapore vv	61

Source: author's analysis of data in OAG 2008.

Notes
1 It is important to note that *Table 8.1* and *Table 8.2* show airline traffic in different ways. *Table 8.1* shows the actual number of passengers who traveled through various hub airports. *Table 8.2* shows airline capacity between various city-pairs; the actual number of passengers between each pair of cities would of course be less than the capacity.
2 vv = vice versa.

A people set apart: the development of business class services

Even in the earliest decades of air travel, airlines targeted business travelers as the industry's "bread-and-butter" (Hudson 1972: 39). In a 1935 report on aviation, a United Airlines traffic manager cited a simple statistical analysis showing that for any one earning more than $1.00 per hour ($15 in 2007 dollars), travel by air was more economical than by rail or bus (Hudson 1972: 50). Interestingly, the analysis was premised on air travel being four times faster than travel by train and six times faster than bus.

With the advent of jets, air travel enjoyed an approximate ten-to-one speed advantage over ground transportation; and airlines were no longer trying to convince businessmen (and they were overwhelmingly men) to fly but rather to fly in first class. A BOAC advertisement early in the Jet Age advised corporate executives, "If you want a man to do a first-class job, give him a first-class ticket." The ad went on to argue:

> Economy class travel looks like sound company policy. On paper.
> In practice, just how sound is it?
> Think of what you're asking your man to do.
> Make decisions that could affect the future of your company. Decisions that rely on clear thinking.
> He'll need to be as rested and relaxed as possible.
> Ready to go into action as soon as he reaches his destination.
> And that's how first class will get him there.

More relaxed, because he's traveling in greater space and comfort. More rested because there are fewer people and fewer disturbances.

And, psychologically, that first class ticket does a lot for his image and yours. It tells him you think he's the best man for the job.

So give him a first class ticket. And he'll do a first class job.

(quoted in Hudson 1972: 126)

Today, many businesspeople continue to travel in first class, but more travel in business class (and, it is fair to say, even more in economy class). The history of business class draws together the main themes of this book so far, and therefore warrants some attention. That is, technological change and liberalization have been enabling factors in the development of the airborne world in general and in the creation of business class in particular.

As noted in Chapter 3, large flag carriers, led by Pan Am, began introducing business class in 1978, the same year of course as the Airline Deregulation Act was passed and one year after the approval of the Bermuda II air service agreement between the US and Britain. Pan Am's Clipper Class, a separate cabin with product features positioned between economy class and first class, was advertised as "a sensible alternative for the business traveller." In its early years, business class was available primarily on transatlantic and to a lesser extent transpacific routes. In most short-haul markets, it took longer for the new class to take hold, though SAS was a pioneer in offering business class on shorter-haul routes within Europe.

By the end of the twentieth century, business class was available almost worldwide, yet business class and first class seats still accounted for a small share of airline capacity. In early 2008, for instance, the world's scheduled airlines offered approximately 69 million seats weekly (author's analysis of data in OAG 2008); and of these, just under 5 percent were in business class cabins and a little less than 2 percent were in first class. Of course, the significance of the upper classes (first and business combined) varies spatially. To begin with, there is a clear association between the percentage of seats in upper classes and stage length. Long-haul routes between Europe and North America ranked first and between Asia and North America second in the percentage of upper (first or business) class seats, at about 15 percent for each route-region. Conversely, within Latin America, fewer than four percent of seats were in business or first class (author's analysis of data in OAG 2008).

Nevertheless, although business class travel is associated with long-haul trips and the iconic globe-trotting business executive, when city-pairs are ranked by the number of seats in the two upper classes combined, short-haul linkages predominate (Table 8.3). This is partly due to distance decay – that is, the tendency for interaction between two places near one another to be greater than two places that are far apart – even in a globalized world. Indeed, Table 8.3 attests to the fact that, despite the contemporary fascination with the global economy, most international economic connections remain confined within regions, including Europe (Poon 1997). That said, it should be emphasized the quality of business class and first class on short-haul routes tends to be quite different from that on long-haul routes. British Airways' Club World product, for instance, is distinctly superior to its Club Europe product.

There have been two, seemingly contradictory directions in the development of long-haul services with respect to class. Some carriers have shifted to a two-class service on some routes, while others have not only retained the conventional three-classes but have inserted a fourth class. Both of these developments can be credited to the relentless upward creep in the size and accoutrements of business class seats (Table 8.4). In 2000, British Airways, for instance, became the first carrier to put lie-flat seats in business class (Mills 2006), and since then the top European and Asian carriers have been leap-frogging one another to be the first with the next generation of lie-flat (or nearly flat) seats. In 2006, Singapore Airlines (SIA) inaugurated a new high-tech, amazingly capacious business class seat as part of a more general $360 million overhaul of its in-flight amenities (Pae 2006). It is striking that fifty years ago, the early jets rendered sleeper seats – which were once common across the US, for instance – obsolete because a traveler got to his destination too fast to need to rest in the air (Jakle 1985: 182); but by the 1980s very long-range travel – particularly to and from the booming economies of Asia – was common enough to make sleeper seats popular again.

The result has been a narrowing of the gap between first and business class so that some carriers have decided to eliminate the former, and the widening of the gap between business and economy class into which other carriers have inserted a new economy plus service (Shifrin 2005). Several large carriers now pursue a mixture of geographically varying class strategies as exemplified by Singapore Airlines' services to the US (Figure 8.1). The carrier introduced its ultra-long-haul A340-500 services to the US in 2004 with 64 lie-flat Spacebeds in its Raffles business class and 117 Executive Economy seats, but in 2008 the carrier converted its A345s, as they are commonly known in the industry, to an all-business class con-

Table 8.3 The world's top upper class city-pairs, 2008

Rank	Route	Weekly business class seats	Weekly first class seats	Upper class (business and first) seats
1	Paris–Toulouse vv[1]	14	40,936	40,950
2	Nice–Paris vv	0	38,682	38,682
3	London–New York vv	7,226	21,998	29,224
4	Marseilles–Paris vv	66	25,228	25,294
5	Sapporo–Tokyo vv	2,408	22,869	25,277
6	Bordeaux–Paris vv	8	24,270	24,278
7	Hong Kong–Taipei vv	1,824	21,753	23,577
8	Milan–Rome vv	156	21,344	21,500
9	Osaka–Tokyo vv	2,134	19,166	21,300
10	Paris–Rome vv	192	17,898	18,090

Source: author's analysis of data in OAG 2008.

Note
1 vv = vice versa.

Table 8.4 Long-haul business class seat pitch on three airlines

British Airways		Singapore Airlines		United Airlines	
Year[1]	Pitch (inches)	Year[1]	Pitch (inches)	Year[1]	Pitch (inches)
1980	32	1987	38	1983	38
1987	38	1993	42	1990	40
1995	50	1999	52	1996	49
2000	73[2]	2002	78[3]	2001	55
–	–	2006	78[2]	2007	76[2]

Sources: contemporary media accounts.

Notes:
1 The first date shown for each airline indicates when it introduced business class. The other dates indicate when conversion to a new business class seat pitch standard began; the conversion process for an entire long-haul fleet often takes years to complete.
2 Full-flat sleeper seats.
3 Angled lie-flat sleeper seats.

figuration with 100 seats. In contrast, the carrier's Boeing 747-400 transpacific services to the US, which stop either in Northeast Asia or Europe en route, are operated with 12 First Class, 50 Raffles Class, and 313 Economy Class seats. And then there are Boeing 777s flown with either two or three classes.

Meanwhile, as noted above, a growing number of carriers have inserted a less expensive and less luxurious economy plus class between rock-bottom economy and Business Class. On British Airways 747-400s, for instance, BA offers World Traveler Plus with a seat pitch of 38 inches between World Traveler (31 inches) and Club (73 inches).[1]

Interestingly, there were four classes across the Atlantic in the 1950s, too, but the disparities among them, both with respect to service quality and airfares, were much smaller (Table 8.5). It is striking that, after adjusting for inflation, economy class travel across the Atlantic is far less expensive today than a half century ago but first class travel – at least on the best airlines – is more costly. The huge range of air fares today corresponds to the huge range of services on board as evident in, for instance, the 47-inch gap in the seat pitch between BA's First and World Traveler classes. The gap between the upper and lower classes is more pronounced on BA than on some of its rivals, but all long-haul full-service carriers are under unremitting pressure to improve the quality of their business class products. So the caste system deepens.

Meanwhile, like Singapore Airlines, a handful of carriers have introduced all-business class (ABC) services (Figure 8.2). All of these are operated either by or on behalf of network carriers.[2] The pioneer in this segment of the market was Lufthansa. In June 2002, the carrier joined with Geneva-based Privatair to launch an all-business class Airbus A319 service between Newark and Düsseldorf. Lufthansa had operated a three-class Airbus A340 on the route but suspended that service in response to poor loads after the September 11, 2001 terrorist attacks. The ABC service allowed Lufthansa to lower its costs while

Table 8.5 Four transatlantic classes, 1958 and 2008

	Fare (US dollars)	Real fare[2] (2008 US dollars)	Seat pitch (inches)
1958[1]			
First, sleeperette	485	2,895	–
First	435	2,596	42
Tourist	315	1,880	39
Economy	252	1,504	34
2008[3]			
First	16,337	16,337	78
Club World	4,028	4,028	73
World Traveller Plus	1,173	1,173	38
World Traveller	698	698	31

Sources: Friedlander 1958; www.britishairways.com.

Notes
1 IATA approved.
2 Converted to year 2008 dollars using the price deflator data available from S. Williamson 2008.
3 For travel on British Airways between New York-JFK and London-LHR, departing October 24 2008 and returning October 31 2008 with a one-month advance purchase.

simultaneously retaining a foot in the lucrative business market on this sector (Bond 2002). Lufthansa subsequently resumed mixed class A340 services on the route, but in 2009 it offered ABC services on several routes in conjunction with Privatair. Inspired no doubt by Lufthansa's success with this concept, Swiss and KLM also contracted with Privatair for ABC services between Zurich and Newark and between Amsterdam and Houston, respectively. The latter service was directed specifically at the oil industry (*Airline Business* 2005). On the other side of the world, ANA became the first conventional airline in Asia to launch an ABC service (Sanchanta 2007) when it deployed Boeing 737-700ER between Tokyo and Mumbai. And then in 2008, SIA became the first airline to launch transpacific ABC services with nonstop A345 flights between Singapore and Los Angeles and Singapore and Newark. It is worth noting that the same two new flights also rank among the longest range nonstop flights in the world (see Table 4.2), a reflection of the lengthening of business ties.

Stretch: air travel and transnational corporations

Across the world in 2007, there were approximately 79,000 transnational corporations (TNCs), controlling 790,000 affiliates and directly employing 82 million people (UNCTAD 2008: xvi). Many of the largest TNCs operated business networks of such geographic scope and complexity that they enveloped the globe. Most such corporations make their headquarters in or near major hubs, though some were well-established before the advent of aviation and remain ensconced in somewhat peripheral locations[3] (Table 8.6). In either case, such firms could not function in the absence of air transportation.

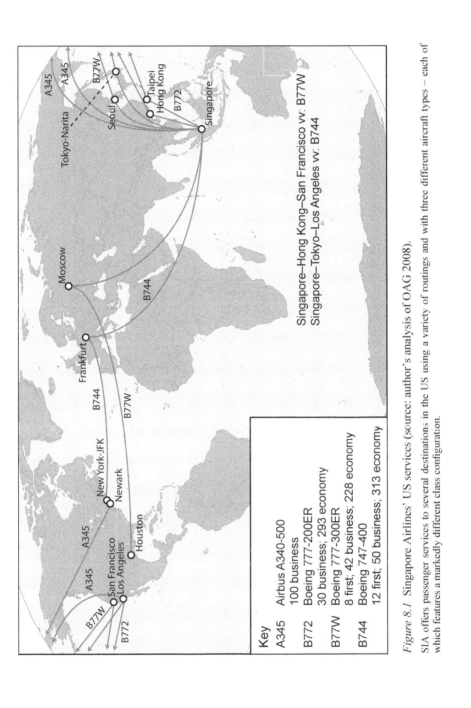

Figure 8.1 Singapore Airlines' US services (source: author's analysis of OAG 2008).

SIA offers passenger services to several destinations in the US using a variety of routings and with three different aircraft types – each of which features a markedly different class configuration.

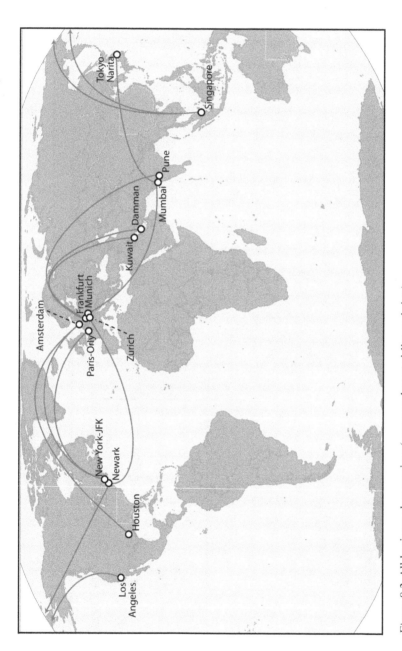

Figure 8.2 All-business class services (source: relevant airline websites).

In mid-2009, several network airlines offered all-business class services as a supplement to their conventional, mixed class services. Most of the services depicted were on special versions of the Boeing 737 or Airbus A319.

Table 8.6 Most geographically widespread TNCs

Company	Main headquarters	Nearby hub airport	Host countries[1]
Deutsche Post AG	Bonn	Dusseldorf (83 km)	111
Royal Dutch Shell	The Hague	Amsterdam Schiphol (48 km)	98
Nestle SA	Vevey, Switzerland	Geneva (88 km)	96
Siemens AG	Berlin and Munich	Munich F.J. Strauss (37 km)	89
BASF	Ludwigshafen	Frankfurt (74 km)	88
Proctor & Gamble	Cincinnati	Cincinnati N. Kentucky Int'l (22 km)	75
GlaxoSmithKline	London	Heathrow (10 km)	74
Linde	Munich	Munich F.J. Strauss (38 km)	72
Bayer AG	Leverkusen	Dusseldorf (45 km)	71

Sources: UNCTAD 2008: 28; various corporate websites; Google Maps.

Note
1 Only those countries in which a company had a least one-majority owned affiliate are counted.

Or at least they would function differently (Hugill 1993: 100–1). Ford, for instance, became a multinational corporation as early as 1913 but the breadth of the Atlantic Ocean and the tedium of crossing it by sea meant that the automaker's British subsidiary in Dagenham, England was effectively an independently run enterprise for decades. When nonstop transatlantic commercial air travel finally became common after World War II, Ford brought its European operations much more directly under the control of its Dearborn, Michigan, headquarters (Hugill 1993: 283). Today, of course, it is far easier and far less expensive in real terms to travel from Dearborn to any outpost in the Ford dominion than in the late 1940s. In response, a legion of executives, sales staff, engineers, accountants, supplier representatives and other personnel have taken to the skies to keep the wheels of the automaker's empire rolling. In 2004, Ford spent $62 million on air bookings in the US and $134 million company-wide (Meyer 2005).

The numbers look impressive but Ford's company-wide air bookings amounted to just 0.08 percent of the company's total operating expenses for the year. In fact, for most companies, air travel is a small expense. For Wal-Mart, air travel was just 0.02 percent of total operating expenses, for ExxonMobil 0.10 percent, and for Dell 0.13 percent. Each of these companies spent enough on air travel to rank in the Corporate Travel 100, a list annually compiled by *Business Travel News* (Table 8.7), but so little in relation to their overall operations that the cost of air transportation was no impediment to their globalization.

There were firms in the Corporate Travel 100 for which air travel *did* comprise a much higher share of total operating expenses. For Accenture and BearingPoint, two consultancies, company-wide air travel represented more than 2 percent of total expenses. Unsurprisingly, producer services firms – especially those providing knowledge-intensive services – require many more air-miles to do their work than old-line manufacturing and retail companies. So Accenture

Table 8.7 Air travel by selected firms from the Corporate Travel 100, 2004

Company	Companywide air travel (millions of dollars)	Operating expenses (millions of dollars)	Air travel percent
Accenture	363	13,354	2.72
BearingPoint	90	3,893	2.31
Cisco Systems	147	15,753	0.93
Johnson & Johnson	272	35,017	0.78
Microsoft	191	27,801	0.69
Goldman Sachs	140	23,163	0.60
Bristol-Myers Squibb	82	14,962	0.55
Walt Disney	140	27,013	0.52
Merrill Lynch	137	26,783	0.51
Intel	120	24,079	0.50
General Electric	455	113,994	0.40
General Mills	36	9,046	0.40
Pepsico	80	24,002	0.33
FedEx	84	26,892	0.31
Dell	60	44,951	0.13
ExxonMobil	260	256,794	0.10
Ford Motor Co	134	169,450	0.08
Wal-Mart Stores	48	267,010	0.02

Source: Meyer 2005.

spent more on company-wide air travel than ExxonMobil and systems engineering and consulting firm SAIC spent nearly twice as much as Wal-Mart. Services firms like these cater to an increasingly international clientele, a clientele with which they need regular face-to-face contact to do their work.

For a growing number of businesspeople, such as those featured in a study of the Irish software industry, "to work is to travel" (Vecchi and Wickham 2006). The study found, as one would expect, that foreign firms in the industry generated more business air travel and travel to more widely dispersed destinations than locally-based firms. This basic difference reflected the fact that Irish firms were better integrated into the local software cluster while foreign firms were more dependent on their links to distant "hotspots" for resources and opportunities. The amount of business travel also depended on the degree to which a company employed a team-based, collaborative strategy as well as the complexity of its products and the diversity of its customer base. The study identified the most travel-intensive individual in each sample company. The high flyers were those at or near the top of each business: CEOs, managing directors, R & D managers, and customer relations managers. One interviewee working for an Irish company involved in the video game industry described his company's frequent travelers this way:

> The people who travel the most are the CEO, the CTO and the Sales Director. Either myself of the CEO travels every two weeks to our R & D facility in Munich. We all travel to the US (San Francisco) every six weeks to meet

up with the publishers and when they go they stay there at least for a week. The technical staff also travels quite intensively both as trouble-shooters (to San Francisco) and to undertake specific training (mostly in Munich).

(quoted in Vecchi and Wickham 2006)

The costs of such globe-trotting are high, of course; but as an R & D manager for a large TNC interviewed for the same study explained, "Business travel is seen as a necessary evil. The company cuts back from time to time but it needs to be done, to create networks, which is how work is often done most effectively." (quoted in Vecchi and Wickham 2006).

Business air travel is not simply functional, however. Rather, "[i]t is a combination of social needs, wishes and dreams that *necessitates* flight." (Adey *et al.* 2007: 786, emphasis in original). Businesspeople travel not just for the sake of their companies but also because flight brings status, release from the ordinary, and the pleasures of mobility itself. It is unsurprising then that videoconferencing and similar telecommunications alternatives, though long extolled as substitutes for actual physical travel, have little apparent impact in reducing passenger-trips. Research shows that instead telecommunications complement rather than substitute for travel. A study in Norway, for instance, found that videoconferencing reduces total business air travel there by just 2.5 to 3.5 percent (Denstadli 2004). Among companies that actually used this alternative technology, the reduction was greater, of course; but relatively few companies do so. Further, about 16 percent of the respondents in the Norway study stated that videoconferencing increased the need for face-to-face meetings.

Unable to eliminate or even very much reduce their dependence on air travel, firms in many industries have instead sought to reduce the cost of air travel, both in money and time, in several ways. For instance, a growing number of firms have appointed travel managers to more tightly administer expenses on the road and in the sky (Mason 2000). A sample of firms in the European Union (EU), for instance, found that the proportion employing travel managers rose from 36 percent in 1992 to 43 percent just five years later. Also, many firms, including Airbus and Boeing as discussed in Chapter 4, have moved their main headquarters to hub cities in order to mitigate the costs of airborne commerce.

The costs of business air travel are borne not just by the corporations who pay for the tickets, hotel rooms, restaurants, and the like. Globe-trotters are prone to special health problems, for instance. The most obvious is jet lag, a pox upon travelers whose body clocks, like misdirected suitcases, are stranded several time zones behind the passengers to which they belong. Far less common but also more dangerous is deep-vein thrombosis (DVT), a medical condition in which the blood clots in the legs of a person who has been still for a long period of time.[4] While high-tech seats and the like can counter the physical effects of frequent long-range travel,[5] there is little airlines can do about the psychic costs. For having helped to free businesses to spread the tentacles of their corporate networks and commercial dealings across continents and oceans, inexpensive air transportation has helped to make long-distance air travel obligatory (S. Shaw and Thomas 2006). The consequences are, of course, not altogether good for the travelers involved. Several studies done by the World Bank concerning its own staff found that business travel was associated with increased medical claims, especially for psychological disorders. The studies also found that stress related to business travel permeated staff members' families, adversely affecting spouses and children. The difficulties faced by World Bank travelers are exacerbated by the length of time they typically spend away from the Washington, DC, headquarters, but other – more anecdotal – evidence points to the ordinariness and poignancy of such concerns (Stoller 2006). For instance, an executive interviewed in a story in *The Gazette*, a Montreal daily, described buying two copies of children's books so that she could read along with her young daughter on the phone during frequent business trips away from home (Whittaker 2006).

Of course, like most of us, the woman in the *Gazette* story had a single home from which her long-distance business travel inevitably took her away. A growing number of people, however, live lives that are anchored in two widely separated places at once. In the US, it is called bicoastalism. Largely an offshoot of the 1990s tech boom, bicoastalism linked dispersed innovation centers, especially Silicon Valley and Boston's Route 128 corridor with a still-small number of entrepreneurs, programmers, analysts, and their associates living on both coasts at once, literally flying over "flyover country" on a regular basis (Kirsner 2005). In Europe, a somewhat similar phenomenon has been facilitated by the rise of LCCs. Small business entrepreneurs circulate among branch offices sprawled across Europe, émigrés keep their jobs in high stress capitals like London but continue to live in the provincial communities from which they originated, and skilled personnel from low-wage countries fly to and from wealthier markets with critical labor shortages (Capell 2006). For each, low fares make it possible to live in one country and regularly work in another hundreds of kilometers away.

Flying tourist class: the world is a playground

On September 20, 2005, the pilot of an airborne L-1011 declared an emergency shortage of fuel near Piura, a city in northern Peru. The plane was allowed to land even though the flight had entered Peruvian airspace without permission (*Washington Post* 2005). It turned out, however, that there was no emergency, just a planeload of 289 Gambians hell-bent on watching a Gambian team compete in Piura in the Under 17 Federation of International Football Associations (FIFA) World Championship against Qatar. So routine is such sports tourism today, even from countries as poor as Gambia, that the story would hardly have attracted any notice had it not turned out the fuel emergency was a ruse. Once on the ground, the plane was met first by emergency crews and then by angry Peruvian officials after the scam was discovered; but ultimately the fans got to see their team defeat the Qataris 3–1.

The Gambian gambit was stunning for its boldness but the number of fans involved was tiny compared to the flow of soccer aficionados to Germany for the FIFA World Cup the following year. A year in advance, supporters of 32 national teams began making arrangements to travel to Germany in the summer of 2006 for the FIFA Men's World Cup (H. Williamson 2005). Fortunately, as a result of the liberalization of air travel, to, from, and especially within Europe, getting to Germany would not be as much of a problem as getting to Piura. LCCs and network carriers had so much capacity into Germany that the problem for airlines was not so much how to accommodate the inward flow of sports fans but rather how to fill the seats out of Germany during the month-long football fest. One solution: airline-promoted getaways for "soccer widows" (Carvajal 2006).

Soccer fans and soccer widows are but one current in the ever-mounting flow of tourists moving to and fro via the world's airways. Today, tourism is by some estimates the largest industry in the world, employing directly and indirectly one out of every ten people (*Economist* 1998b). Air travel has been instrumental to the expansion of tourism, especially long-distance tourism. In 2008, there were 924 million international tourist arrivals, up from 50 million in 1950 (G. Shaw and Williams 1994; *UNWTO World Tourism Barometer* 2009) (Figure 8.3); and more than 40 percent of international tourists now arrive by air (A. Graham 2006).

The intertwined development of aviation and tourism

Fundamentally, tourism in much of the world depends upon aviation; and, in turn, the airline industry depends and has long depended upon tourists. Indeed,

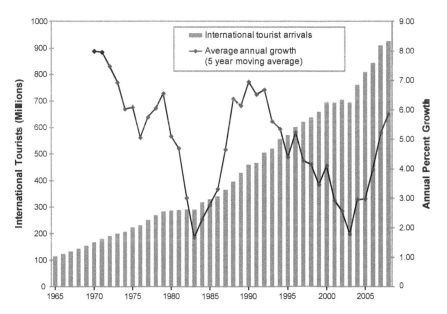

Figure 8.3 Growth of international tourism (sources: various issues of the *United Nations Statistical Yearbook*; *UNWTO World Tourism Barometer* 2009).

International tourist arrivals have grown rapidly during most of the past forty years, partly due to lower real airfares made possible by technological change in aviation and the liberalization of the airline industry.

the first paying airline passengers in the world were tourists. They flew on a short-lived route across Tampa Bay in 1914 (Jakle 1985: 176–83). In the early decades of heavier-than-air flight, seaside tourist resorts became an early market for the infant industry; the well-heeled patrons could afford the fares and the proximity of water provided ample takeoff and landing space for the then-dominant seaplanes. The symbiotic relationship between air travel and tourism deepened after World War II (L. Turner and Ash 1976: 93–108). The war left thousands of surplus aircraft and an archipelago of underused airfields, many of which were fortuitously located on tropical isles and other tourist-ready destinations.

As described earlier in this book, the war also hastened the advent of the commercial jet. In slashing the cost of distance, both in terms of time and money, jet travel – especially wide-body jet travel – brought the rest of the world closer and changed the geography of the "pleasure periphery" – the edge of the world to which tourists repair for recreation (L. Turner and Ash 1976: 100–7). Where once Europeans ventured little farther than to the Mediterranean and Americans to Mexico and the Caribbean, cut-rate fares since the 1960s have dramatically pushed the pleasure periphery outwards. By the end of the 1960s, for instance, thirty Club Méditerranée (Club Med) resorts had opened, and many were nowhere near the Mediterranean (A. Gordon 2004: 176).

Islands demonstrate especially well the way in which air transportation has brought the once-remote within the compass of the tourist (Butler 1997). In 1959, the year Hawaii welcomed both statehood and its first jet flights, Waikiki Beach sported just 3,900 hotel rooms. By the early 1960s, the total was 8,000 (C. Turner 1959; Cunningham 1960). Only about 300,000 tourists visited Hawaii in 1960, partly because the roundtrip jet airfare from New York was $571, or 25 percent of annual US per capita income at that time (Folsom 1961). By 2006, the number of visitors had reached 7.5 million[6] and getting to Hawaii had never been so affordable, with the typical airfare from New York equal to less than 3 percent of per capita income (State of Hawaii 2009).

The case of the Maldives is even more dramatic. In 1972, the newly independent country comprising 1,200 small islands spread in the Indian Ocean had only one hotel, no banks, and no bars (*New York Times* 1972). In that year, just 325 tourists visited the islands. Five years later, after the country's president decided to promote tourism and air services to the outside world were established, the number had swollen to 20,000. In the 1980s, a Kuwait-sponsored extension of the capital city's runway led to direct flights from Europe and East Asia (Borders 1977), and by 2007, annual tourist arrivals – virtually all by air – reached 676,000, more than the country's own population (UNWTO *World Tourism Barometer* 2008).

Improvements in aviation technology have not, however, been uniformly advantageous for tourism-dependent places. Long range versions of the 747, especially the 747-400, for instance, eliminated the need for refueling stops on most transpacific routes (Butler 1997: 52). In 1975, the segment between Sydney and Fiji was part of a heavily traveled transpacific corridor, with more scheduled aircraft seats per week than the link between Sydney and Auckland (Taylor and Kissling 1983); today there is four times more capacity on the latter route than the former (author's analysis of data in OAG 2008). Airlines no longer need to stop in the mid-Pacific and in general they do not.

Something from nothing: airlines and tourism in Dubai, Las Vegas, and Orlando

The advent of long-range and ultra-long-range aircraft has also reduced the need for refueling stops in the Middle East on trans-Eurasia routes; and some airports there are, at least in relative terms, less important that they were in aviation's early years. Yet the Middle East is also home to the city that has translated, more successfully than perhaps any other place, its former status as a refueling stop into a contemporary position as putative tourist mecca. Dubai, in the United Arab Emirates (UAE), cultivated a small tourism industry based on duty-free shopping by passengers passing through the emirate aboard refueling airliners. Today, Dubai has become a destination in its own right. The city sports championship golf courses and horse tracks, tony shopping districts, and the world's tallest hotel. Yet these only hint at the staggering scope of Dubai's tourism ambitions (Tosches 2006). The country has become a Rhode Island-sized construction site. By 2010 it will lay claim to the world's largest shopping mall, indoor snow-blanketed slopes for pseudo-skiing, and a sextet of housing developments based on super-sized facsimiles of spectacles like the Leaning Tower of Pisa and the Taj Majal. Offshore in the Persian Gulf, there are hundreds of manmade islets arranged in the shape of a world map (Tosches 2006). The "World," the malls, the theme parks, and myriad smaller developments are all in pursuit of the goal set by Dubai's emir, Sheik Mohammed bin Rashid al-Maktoum, that the emirate should attract 15 million visitors by 2010,[7] more than three times the number that visit New York City and about ten times Dubai's population. If that vision is realized, the attractions on the ground and in the sea will draw the masses to the desert metropolis, but they will arrive by air – especially on Emirates, Dubai's hometown airline and the largest customer for the A380.

In the sheer scale of its tourism ambitions, in its use of imitations to reel the visitors in, and in its dependence upon air travel, Dubai now has much in common with two otherwise very different places: Las Vegas and Orlando. Decades ahead of Dubai, these two cities piloted their way to prominence in an airborne world. In 2007, Las Vegas ranked 15th in the world in air passenger traffic (not just because of arriving and departing tourists but also because US Airways, via its merger with America West, has a transcontinental hub there), and Orlando ranked 20th (see Table 8.2). The flow of tourists to each of these cities is now global in scope. In 2008, for instance, Las Vegas had nonstop flights to Seoul, Dusseldorf, Frankfurt, London, and many cities in Canada and Mexico (OAG 2008).

Despite the links to distant continents, Las Vegas remains most dependent on the same market that got the gambling center off the ground in the early twentieth century, nearby California. At the end of the 1990s, the Golden State accounted for about 30 percent of Las Vegas visitors (Thompson 1999: 110). Many Californians arrive and depart via the 440-kilometer stretch of Interstate 15 that links the desert oasis to Los Angeles; but many fly even that short distance. In April 2008, for instance, airlines offered 70 flights per day from the five airports in the Los Angeles area (LAX, Long Beach/Daugherty Field Airport, John Wayne Orange County, Ontario International, and Burbank-Pasadena-Glendale Airport) to Las Vegas, one every few minutes during the peak hours of the day. In total, Las Vegas was linked by nonstop scheduled services to 117 US cities and 18 foreign ones, with a combined total of nearly 4,000 arriving flights per week (author's analysis of data in OAG 2008). McCarran International Airport has become a linchpin of the Las Vegas economy. Although the city's critical dependence upon the water and hydropower from the Colorado River and the Hoover Dam have been properly emphasized by Mark Reisner (1986: 125–6) in his celebrated book *Cadillac Desert*, Las Vegas could not keep its famous neon lights ablaze without the steady influx of arriving airliners (Thompson 1999: 95).

Much the same is true in Orlando. Before Disney World opened in 1971, Orlando's chief tourist attractions were a Tupperware museum and an alligator park. Since the Disney park opened, however, the landscape around Orlando has been blanketed with theme parks, including three additional gigantic parks in Disney's kingdom alone. In retrospect, the opening of Disney World was well-timed to take advantage of the deregulation of the airline industry. In 1979, when ground was broken for a new terminal at Orlando's airport, only four airlines served the city. By the time it opened in 1981, the number had jumped to 15 (*Aviation Week & Space Technology* 1981). Later in the 1980s and 1990s, international liberalization opened up Orlando to direct service by foreign airlines. By 2007, the number of passengers using the airport was more than 400 times higher than it had been the year Disney World opened (ACI 2008; Krotz 1996: 204).

Airborne tourism in developed and developing countries

The newest Disney Park – and the smallest – opened in Hong Kong in 2005 and is closer to a large airport than any of its predecessors (Table 8.8). The new park's site, at Discovery Bay on Lantau Island, is strategically positioned between the brand new Hong Kong International Airport and the city it serves. Like other new Asian tourism developments – including for instance two massive casino complexes in Singapore – the theme park in Hong Kong is aimed at the growing volume of Asian tourists. China alone is expected to generate 100 million outbound tourists in 2020 up from 12 million in 2001; and the great majority will travel by air (Tretheway and Mak 2006). Chinese tourism is being propelled primarily by the country's galloping economy, but an important

Table 8.8 Air accessibility and the five Disney parks

Park	Year opened	Nearest hub airport	Hub rank[1]	Distance (km)[2]
Disneyland	1955	Los Angeles Int'l	5	53
Disney World	1971	Orlando Int'l	20	41
Tokyo Disney Resort	1983	Tokyo-Haneda	4	23
Disneyland Resort Paris	1992	Paris-Charles de Gaulle Int'l	6	41
Hong Kong Disneyland	2005	Hong Kong Int'l	14	16

Sources: *Globe and Mail* 2005; ACI 2008; Google Maps.

Notes
1 Rank is by passenger volume among all the world's airports. See *Table 8.2*.
2 Road distance from park to airport.

enabling factor is the greater number of destinations to which the Chinese government permits its people to travel without an exit visa. The importance of this policy change in amplifying the effects of economic growth echoes the earlier experience of Japan in the 1970s and South Korea in the 1980s. India and other large developing economies will also become increasingly large sources of outbound tourists (Tretheway and Mak 2006).

In the meantime, one factor that may sustain robust tourism growth, even from countries with lackluster economic growth and declining populations such as Germany and Italy, is the proliferation of new airlines, especially LCCs (Bieger and Wittmer 2006). Their low fares have been credited with generating a significant number of new airborne leisure travelers. Air Berlin, for instance, flew to 19 points in Spain alone (including destinations in the Balearic and Canary Islands) in 2008 as well as more distant tourist destinations in the Caribbean, Southeast Asia, and the Indian Ocean (Figure 8.4). Moreover, new carriers have repeatedly taken the lead in pioneering new tourist destinations in order to fill their seats and to escape markets dominated by established carriers, which are often under the protection of governments. In Thailand in the 1980s, for example, Bangkok Airways was denied the right to directly challenge flag carrier Thai International on routes the latter already served in Thailand, so Bangkok Airways developed its own airport and tourist resort on Koh Samui, an island in the Gulf of Thailand (*Asian Aviation* 1989).

Indeed, an important aspect of air transportation is the relative ease with which new points can be added to a network. In this respect, air travel is both a fast means for an individual tourist to arrive at his destination and for a destination to "arrive." In the case of Spain, for instance, it took just twenty years, from the 1950s to the 1970s, for the country to evolve from "a snob destination" to a "mass-market position" (L. Turner and Ash 1976: 98). For decades, Spain has been the second most popular international tourist destination in the world, behind only France (Table 8.9). And Koh Samui by 2009 was linked to Bangkok by more than 30 flights per day and also had nonstop services to several other Thai cities as well as Hong Kong, Kuala Lumpur, and Singapore.

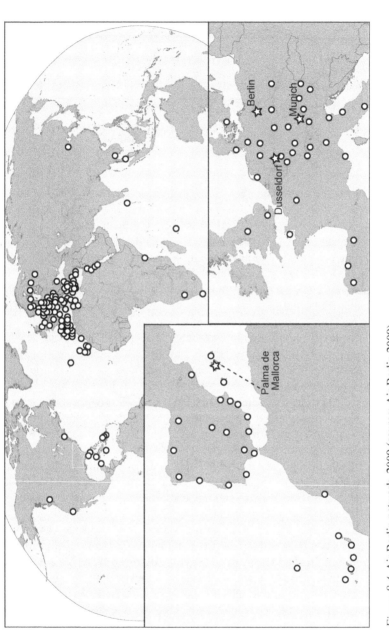

Figure 8.4 Air Berlin network, 2009 (source: Air Berlin 2009).

By mid-2009, Air Berlin had expanded into the intercontinental market (mainly by merging with Dusseldorf-based LTU in 2007). Neverthe-less, the carrier's network emphasizes tourist destinations.

Table 8.9 The world's top tourism destinations, 2007

Rank	Country	Tourist arrivals (millions)
1	France	81.9
2	Spain	59.2
3	United States	56.0
4	China	54.7
5	Italy	43.7
6	United Kingdom	30.7
7	Germany	24.4
8	Ukraine	23.1
9	Turkey	22.2
10	Mexico	21.4
11	Austria	20.8
12	Russian Federation	20.2[1]

Source: *UNWTO World Tourism Barometer* 2008.

Note
1 Figure is for 2006.

The popularization of existing tourist havens compels the more adventurous and/ or deep-pocketed to move on, to destinations too far in time or too dear in expense for the masses to follow. At first, at least; but then the avant-garde depart again to the more distant reaches of the receding pleasure periphery or the undiscovered interstices of the ground already covered. Among the countries recording at least a quintupling of visitor arrivals between 1990 and 2007 were Cambodia, Peru, and Oman (Table 8.10). And of course China, which has experienced explosive growth in both inbound and outbound tourism, with both flows borne primarily by air.

Heavy landing: the impact of tourism

With nearly a billion tourists traveling internationally annually and more traveling domestically, the realm of the undiscovered and untouched continues to shrink. For the countless places over which the great tide of tourists has already swept, the effects have been, in many cases, stunning. To return to the example of Spain, the travel writer John Bishop marveled in a 1972 issue of *Travel Trade Gazette*,

> It somehow seems impossible to believe that in the last twenty or so years the travel industry has been responsible for changing the way of life of the Mediterranean people in a way never equaled by Alexander the Great, Julius Caesar, the Greek philosophers, the Christian church, nor any single event during more than 2,000 years of history.
>
> (quoted in L. Turner and Ash 1976: 101)

Bishop wrote more than 30 years ago. The scale of tourism along the Mediterranean today dwarfs that of his time. And so tourism continues to remake the

Table 8.10 Fastest growing tourism destinations, 2000–2007

Country[1]	Tourist arrivals (000)		Average annual % growth
	1990	*2007*	
Cambodia	17	1,873	31.9
Vietnam	250	4,172	18.0
Iran	154	1,659[2]	17.2
Oman	149	1,195[2]	14.9
United Arab Emirates	973	7,100[2]	14.2
South Africa	1,029	9,090	13.7
Syria	562	3,368[2]	12.7
Cuba	327	2,119	11.6
Jordan	572	3,431	11.1
Peru	317	1,812	10.8
Saudi Arabia	2,209	11,531	10.2
China[3]	10,484	54,720	10.2

Source: *UNWTO World Tourism Barometer* 2008.

Notes
1 Excluding all countries with fewer than one million tourist arrivals in 2007.
2 2005 figure.
3 Excluding Hong Kong and Macau.

region's landscape, its economy, and its culture. The same can be said, more or less, of the world's other tourist destinations.

Tourists arrive laden with their own cultural baggage, an observation that is hardly novel; but air travel, chief among a variety of post-World War II enabling factors, has permitted tourists to arrive in such numbers that their imprint in the receiving countries is more durable and pervasive than ever before. Moreover, the very speed of air travel has so eased the experience of tourism – especially international tourism – that tourists are less likely to be transformed by the experience than the destinations they visit. And the sheer scale of tourism has contributed to an unprecedented degree of homogenization of tourist destinations across the world (Gottdiener 2001: 145–6). Examples abound: the thousands of McDonald's franchises abroad, the familiar hotel and car rental chains, CNN and Fox News on television, and the ubiquity of English. In his book *Tourists*, Larry Krotz (1996: 195) writes, "If you are American, it is more and more difficult to leave America behind."

Of course, the homogenization is only partial and often just superficial. Indeed, there are other changes wrought by tourism that sharpen the differences between the sending and receiving lands. The uneven geography of sexual liberty, for instance, has been artificially magnified by tourism as a growing number of places across the world have been branded as destinations for sex tourism where virtually anything goes. Sex has long run like an undercurrent through tourist flows, hidden from view but a powerful motive force neverthe-less. Today, the relationship between tourism and sex has many facets, from "Singapore girl" stewardesses beautifully clad in form-fitting *sarong kebayas* (and the less subtle uniforms of the now-defunct Hooters Air) to honeymooning couples to college students on orgiastic Spring Break getaways (McKercher and Bauer 2003: 5–7). Sex tourism, however, is different in the degree of exploitation involved. And while it predates air travel, only with inexpensive air transportation linking relatively wealthy men to poor women and children on a global scale could it have become the multibillion-dollar industry of today.

Thailand is particularly prominent in the global sex tourism industry. Though many of the patrons of the country's brothels and go-go bars are Thais themselves, many are foreigners who take a six- or eight- or twelve-hour flight to escape the strictures of home. An estimated 60 percent of visitors to Thailand are men; but it is unknown what proportion of the "excess" male tourists are in the country primarily for sex (Renton 2005). Some of Thailand's visitor arrival statistics, however, do give hints. For example, among British citizens arriving in Thailand for non-business purposes (as stated on their entry forms) men outnumber women by 28 percent. For comparable Japanese visitors, the imbalance is even greater at 35 percent (Renton 2005). No other major destination has such imbalanced in-bound tourist flows.

Whether sex tourism is condoned or condemned, it is likely to continue. Alex Renton ends his account of the Thai sex industry in the British journal *Prospect* with this prognosis:

> Travelling to Thailand for sex will continue. The brand is established. The beautiful young woman wrapped in silk with her demure but inviting smile is a feature of Thai travel posters across the world. The promise is of "happiness on earth" – the delights of paradise a cheap flight away. Most of the traditional tourist attractions are disappearing. The country's beaches are overexploited, its forests shrinking and the islands poisoned by tourists' waste. But Thailand and its neighbors retain one renewable resource for the tourists that is not in danger of running out – the supply of poor, smiling women.
>
> (Renton 2005: 62)

Here then is a darker side of the airborne world. The speed and affordability of air travel bring the distant closer and facilitate the exploitation of the poor and the weak by the rich and the strong.

And yet, almost every country on earth seems intent on attracting more tourists. Indeed, so pervasive is the pursuit of the "Golden Horde" (L. Turner and Ash 1976) that the one stark exceptional country – a place that could be a tourist magnet but has so far refused to get on board – seems almost mythical. Bhutan deliberately restricts inward tourism as part of the country's policy of maximizing "gross national happiness" instead of gross national product (Henly 2007). International visitors – there were only 21,000 in 2007,[8] about the same number as arrived in Thailand every 12 hours (*UNWTO World Tourism Barometer* 2008) – pay hefty fees of about $200 per day, in addition to the normal costs of tourism in so remote a place, to the Bhutanese government in order to slow the growth of tourism in order to protect the country's environment and Buddhist culture. The relative isolation of the country is evident in its air linkages. From the capital of Paro, the flag carrier Druk (Dragon) Air offered just 11 flights per week in 2008, none of which went farther than Kolkata, and Druk Air was the only airline to offer schedule services to the country.

So Bhutan remains a land apart for now. Seemingly every other place on the planet, however, has already thrown high its welcome: "Come on in. You are cleared to land."

New Ellis Islands: LAX, JFK, and airborne migration

There is a different kind of passenger traffic that has also escalated rapidly, which most countries regard with decidedly more ambivalence. The period since World War II has been characterized by an expansion not only of tourism, but also of immigration. And just as many of today's tourists transit the world's skyways en route to their pleasure peripheries, so too immigration is increasingly an airborne phenomenon.

There is a difference, however, in that today's great tide of leisure visitors has no precedent, but the scale of immigration, at least to some countries, was as enormous at the beginning of the last century as at the beginning of the present. In the case of the US, the world's top immigrant destination for most of the past two hundred years, the number of legal permanent residents admitted in 1905 was 1,026,499 or about the same as the 1,122,373 admitted in 2005. In the intervening years, however, immigration fell precipitously – all the way to 23,068 in 1933 – before growing briskly after World War II in tandem with the airline industry. The fact that the number of US immigrants crested at one million when only a literal handful of people had ever flown in an airplane is clear evidence that air travel was not the prerequisite for the growth of immigration that it appears to have been for the growth of tourism, especially long-range international tourism.

And yet, air travel has profoundly affected the experience of immigration. In the case of migration to the US, for instance, a transatlantic immigrant of a century earlier spent at least ten days to make a crossing by sea that now demands fewer than ten hours by air. For many immigrants in the "First Great Wave" (Brimelow 1995: 30–1), moreover, the time at sea was only a part – often a small part – of the total journey. Weeks might be spent traveling by land across Europe and then across America. Today, of course, the thousands of airports across the world mean that an immigrant seldom has to travel far by land at either end of their flight.

A fair estimate is that as many as 90 percent of legal migrants to the US arrive by airplane.[9] It is for this reason that LAX and JFK can be thought of as the new Ellis Islands. Of course, not even these two airports together are as dominant as gateways for today's US immigrants as Ellis Island in New York harbor was during its run from 1892 to 1924. Airline industry liberalization has helped to make Miami International, San Francisco, Chicago-O'Hare, and other major airports important entry points, too. Meanwhile, for other top immigrant-receiving countries such as Canada and even more obviously Australia, the importance of air transportation is at least as important in delivering new arrivals.

Air travel is also important in the flow of illegal migrants. To return again to the US, about 45 percent of illegal migrants there were visa over-stayers – people who arrived in the US as tourists, students, or businesspeople; and of course many such visitors arrive on airplanes. Other illegal immigrants are smuggled into the US aboard airliners. Air travel is not necessarily a particularly fast or easy way to America for such immigrants. A study of Chinese smuggled to the US by air found that, on average, they took 106 days to get to the US, having stopped for days or weeks at multiple transit points along the way[10] (Chin 1999: 50).

The flow of migrants, legal and illegal, to the US comprise only one channel (albeit a thick one) in the rising tide of immigration globally (Castles and Miller 1993: 124–67). Migrants are on the move from North Africa, Turkey, and Eastern Europe to Western Europe; from North Africa, South Asia, the Philippines, and oil-poor Middle Eastern countries to oil-rich Middle Eastern countries; from their poor neighbors to Asia's newly industrializing economies. The enormous scale and vast scope of international migration are attributable to the stark difference in wages and population growth rates across the world, combined with the easy mobility afforded by contemporary transportation systems, particularly air transportation.

And, in turn, migrants are becoming important to the airline industry. The flow of migrants is too small in relation to the overall volume of air traffic to have much effect on most airlines on the great majority of routes. If the estimate that approximately 90 percent of US legal immigrants arrive by air is about right, for instance, then on average about one out of every hundred seats on a flight arriving in America is occupied by an immigrant. Hardly overwhelming. There is, however, one rapidly growing and potentially much more important form of traffic related to immigration. The size of immigrant communities in the US and other top destination countries, their greater wealth compared to immigrants of the past, and the panoply of communications technologies that keep them in contact with their countries of origin have all fueled a vigorous demand for regular travel back to those countries. For example, in a *USA Today* story on this topic (De Lollis 2005), Roxana Polio, a 24-year old immigrant from El Salvador living in Maryland, reported that she and other family members flew back to the Central American republic at least twice a year. Millions of other immigrants across the world are similarly inclined to travel back and forth between their former and adopted homes.

Not surprisingly, airlines have taken notice and have begun to target "home trotting" immigrants (De Lollis 2005). Pakistan International Airways (PIA), for instance, offers nonstop flights between three Pakistani cities (Karachi, Islamabad, and Lahore) and Toronto – the latter city being home to a sizeable Pakistani immigrant community. There are many more such links over shorter distances, with a particularly striking increase in the number of services among the small and medium cities across the US–Mexican border. As part of its more general internationalization (see Chapter 6), Delta Air Lines, too, has added many Mexican cities to its network since 2003. Continental Airlines, meanwhile, employs a "Latinization" formula including bilingual flight crews and airport gate agents and Spanish signage to cater to the large number of immigrant passengers on its flights to Mexico. Based in part on demand from that same segment of the flying public, Continental added services to smaller provincial Mexican cities like Morelia. It has also sought to make it easier for customers without credit cards to purchase tickets using, for instance, cash transfers via Western Union (De Lollis 2005). Lufthansa's strategy for serving immigrants includes a special website, www.weflyhome.com, that targets immigrant residents of the US with strong connections to countries of origin such as Bulgaria that are accessible through the German flag carrier's network.

Airborne mobility is one of several key technologies encouraging the emergence of "transnational communities" (Portes 1996). Extremely low-cost international phone calls, e-mail, satellite TV (carrying Spanish language soap operas, for instance), and "home-trotting" all permit immigrants to keep one foot in each country, the one left behind and the one adopted. Transnational communities have enormous economic and cultural repercussions. Economically, the connections between immigrants and those they have left behind are conduits for the flow of money, much of it taking the form of remittances sent back from rich countries such as the US to poorer ones such as Mexico. Remittances are not especially new. What is new is the ability of the senders to more carefully control how their money is used by periodically traveling back to the country of origin.

Culturally, the implications of transnationalism are troubling to some. By sustaining links to countries seemingly left behind, frequent back and forth travel may slow or at least alter assimilation in the adopted country. The novelist Gary Shteyngart recognized the new ambiguity of assimilation in his own experience as an immigrant to America:

> When my parents emigrated from the Soviet Union in 1979, they were bidding farewell to gray cement buildings, the hammer and sickle, the flora and fauna of their youth – not to mention, heartbreakingly, many of their loved ones – with a finality verging on madness. Today, Russia is just nine hours away on Delta Airlines. You wake up after a long cognac-fueled nap, look out the window, and the crumbling, sepia-toned landscape you left behind gathers itself up before you, broken facades crowned with ads for Sprite ("Don't let yourself go dry – drink Sprite!") and Samsung electronics ("The White Nights – brought to you by Samsung"). But the question remains: are we, the new Sprite drinkers – Russian-born and American-bred – ultimately Russians or Americans? Or Russian-Americans? Or something entirely different? What's going on here?
>
> (Shteyngart 2004: 287)

The role of air travel as a catalyst to this threat to the nation-state is ironic because national governments have been instrumental in the development of aviation technology and the airline industry. Today, that technology and that industry defy national boundaries, fostering new flows of people – businessmen and businesswomen, tourists, immigrants and their descendants – on an increasingly global scale. The thousands of international routes upon which they travel are like so many tiny punctures through the fabric of the nation-state, weakening its integrity as a container for everything from everyday commerce to the allegiance of those who call it home.

9 The high ways of trade

Not-so-special deliveries

In late September 2005, less than a month after Hurricane Katrina laid waste to New Orleans and a broad swath of the Gulf Coast, an unusual aircraft bearing an unusual load took off from General Mitchell International Airport in Milwaukee (Gantenbein 2005). The aircraft was a cavernous Antonov An-124 freighter, of which there are fewer than 40 in the entire world. The Soviet aircraft's capacious internal dimensions have made it a favorite for out-sized shipments; and it was just such a shipment that brought the one of big jets to Wisconsin. The payload? Nine gigantic lattice sections, each up to 13 meters in length and 32 tonnes in weight, for three boom cranes used in the oil industry. The cranes in question were not in the devastated Gulf Coast region but rather in the Caspian Sea off Azerbaijan. The disruption of oil production in the Gulf had pushed petroleum prices to near record-levels, compelling oil producers half a world away in Central Asia to rush to increase their own output. So the crane sections, which ordinarily would have spent a month making the long journey from Manitowoc, Wisconsin to Baku, Azerbaijan were hurried by air and the cranes were up and working on oil platforms in the Caspian in less than a week. Company officials for Manitowoc Crane reported that its immense products were airlifted only once every ten to twenty years.

The story of the Caspian cranes is one of countless examples of air cargo carriers acting as the firefighters of the global economy. Air cargo[1] has played this important role for most of a century. What is newer is the regular dependence of large parts of the economy upon air cargo. Not just in an emergency, not just when all else fails, but every day or second day or week.

In his article "On the Wings of Commerce" in *Harpers Monthly*, Barry Lopez (1995) tells of the payloads he encountered as an observer on board 40 747-freighter flights totaling nearly 130,000 miles (about 210,000 kilometers) in the air. The extravagant and unusual attracted his attention: Cadillac Eldorados destined for Osaka, penguins loaded in Argentina and bound for Tokyo, gold bullion from South Africa. Yet as Lopez admits, it is not the exotic but rather the ordinary that fills most freighters and bellyhold space on passenger aircraft: computers and computer components, telecommunications equipment, clothing, pharmaceuticals, fresh cut flowers, perishable fruits and vegetables, and auto parts.

Although air transportation is now standard operating procedure for many companies, the air cargo industry remains substantially smaller than its passenger counterpart,[2] but the growth of air freight has steadily outpaced that of passenger traffic for decades (see Figure 3.1). Between 1950 and 2008, global air freight tonne-kilometers grew at a scorching average annual rate of 9.3 percent compared to already hot average growth rate of 8.7 percent for passenger-kilometers (ICAO 1998; Flint 2008), and in the 1990s the ratio between the rates of growth of freight and passenger traffic was wider than in any previous decade.

Much as with air passenger traffic, the expansion of air cargo traffic has had important ramifications for life on the ground. Inexpensive passenger fares have pushed the pleasure periphery outward; inexpensive air cargo rates helped bring the fresh produce of the rest of the world into our supermarkets. The speed of air passenger services has allowed us to get very far very fast; the speed of air cargo services has allowed us to get things from very far away very fast. And much as abundant, relatively low-cost air passenger services have not only freed people to travel far but also – to some degree – forced them to travel more and farther, so too the freedom afforded by air cargo services has come with its own imperatives as businesses and their employees find that they must stretch out and move faster to keep abreast of their competitors.

In the mix: perishables, electronics, and other air freight favorites

A 1931 article by the *New York Times*' aviation correspondent assessed the future this way:

> The business of air freight is attracting more and more attention in this country and the belief is that the airways as organized at present must follow in the steps of older transportation in integrating their sources of income. The railroads obtain less than 20 percent of their income from passenger service. The percentage for the ocean lines is even less. There is a traditional maxim that has been handed down in the British merchant marine to this effect: "It is the meat carried in the holds that pays the bills."
>
> (Lyman 1931a: 122)

Today, meat (chilled or frozen) *is* carried in the bellies of airliners, but the passengers on the main deck pay the bills – at least most of them – in the airline industry. However, cargo has become much more important to the industry in the past few decades as airliner bellies and freighter main decks have been filled with an increasingly diverse assortment of goods. Several categories of freight are especially important.

Perishables

Already in the 1930s when the aforementioned *New York Times* article was published, air freight had begun to carve out a niche in the carriage of perishables like meat. The same 1931 article mentioned a daily planeload of Parisian pastries and cakes to London as well as shipments of time-sensitive Hollywood films, Dutch flowers and bulbs, and live chicks. Today, perishables are still very important, accounting for about 11 percent of worldwide air cargo by weight (McKenna 2006). As in the 1930s, the speed of air cargo extends the size of markets within which perishables can be sold fresh. Back then, the examples included a hypothetical New York baker whose cakes had to be sold fresh limiting his market to a region bounded by Philadelphia, Boston, and Albany if the treats were moved by land but a much larger region extending to Kansas City if moved by air (Lyman 1931b).

The same is true today, but the diversity of perishable products and range of places involved is much greater. Consider the flower industry. Once fragmented into thousands of local markets supplied, at high cost, by individual greenhouses, the industry has become increasingly global in scope. Today, 70 percent of flowers bought in the US traveled to the market at least partly by air, with Colombia being the top foreign supplier (Ziegler 2007: 68). Air freight allows demand for exotic varieties grown far away to be sated. Newly rich Russians, for instance, have a penchant for oversized roses with six-foot stems that are an Ecuadorian specialty, and Japanese consumers buy more than half of the tiny calla lilies that New Zealand exports (Stewart 2007).

As the flower business has gone global, speed has become increasingly important. Depending on the particular species, the value of cut flowers falls by as much as 20 to 50 percent per day after harvest (Ziegler 2007: 68). Speed is similarly crucial in rushing live tropical fish to aquariums, and even fresh-squeezed pineapple juice, which tastes better if made from fruit just harvested. Via air transportation, well-heeled Britons now enjoy air-flown juice squeezed only hours earlier in Ghana (Roberts 2003).

The growing size and scope of perishable markets has been driven by the tastes of the affluent for the exotic and the demands of consumers long divorced from the land to be able to enjoy fresh fruits, vegetables, seafood, and flowers regardless of the time of year. Having helped to make some once-seasonal produce available year-round, air cargo indirectly has fostered the expectation that all kinds of produce, no matter how exotic, will be on the shelf all the time (Roberts 2003; Van Dyne 2005). So customers used to a perennial supply of strawberries expect the same for persimmons or chicory or English cucumbers. And because they are willing to pay for their fancies, perishable supply chains have been cast far and wide.

Indeed, inexpensive air transportation – e.g., it cost just 7.5 cents per stem to ship a rose from India to Europe at the beginning of this century (Stewart 2007) – has been a crucial catalyst to the globalization and industrialization of perishables production. Of course, air transportation is only one among several enabling factors. Falling trade barriers also matter a great deal – particularly for those perishables for which high tariff and nontariff trade barriers have in the past created national markets impervious to competition. As those barriers fall, the sky is effectively cleared for increased airborne trade in fresh produce. The resulting diversification in what we eat is a less cataclysmic, but still momentous version of the Columbian Exchange that began five centuries ago.

The airline industry itself has played the role of long-distance matchmaker in this process, mating distant sources of supply and demand and profiting from the resulting traffic. In *The Sushi Economy*, Sasha Issenberg explains how a Japan Airlines (JAL) marketing executive was instrumental in sparking the global flow of fresh tuna (Issenberg 2007: 1–13). In the early 1970s, Kaheito Okazaki was tasked with finding new sources of cargo for JAL in Canada. The booming Japanese manufacturing economy meant that aircraft outbound from Japan were full but there was often too little cargo to fill freighters and bellyholds on the way back home. Okazaki identified perishables and especially tuna as a potentially lucrative commodity to fill those empty spaces. Japan's newfound wealth had fueled a huge increase in fresh seafood consumption, especially for sushi, and fishing grounds near at hand were being exhausted. JAL could bring much more distant sources closer. Okazaki's earliest efforts focused on Prince Edward Island in Canada. He discovered, via JAL's representative in Toronto, that fisherman in the Maritime Provinces regarded tuna as a nuisance, its meat being too dark and oily to suit Western tastes. After JAL developed a special refrigerated container to ferry tuna halfway around the world without compromising freshness, tuna became a lucrative catch for fisherman in Canada, and for JAL.

August 14, 1972 became the "day of the flying fish" (Issenberg 2007: 12) as the first five Canadian bluefins wowed the Tsukiji market in Tokyo with their size and freshness. They would not be the last. Today, Narita Airport effectively ranks as a Japan's top fishing harbor (Issenberg 2007: 31). From a broader perspective, the result of JAL's entrepreneurship "was a previously inconceivable placelessness, at least for those who could afford to sit in a Tokyo restaurant and eat Canadian seafood as though they were on a cliff along the Atlantic coast." (Issenberg 2007: 13). The same phenomenon has been repeated for many other perishables.

Global perishables air traffic is expected to grow robustly – about 8 percent per year, by one estimate (McKenna 2006) – in the early twenty-first century. This market segment is already vitally important in air cargo markets linking developing regions in the South with developed regions in the North. For example, perishables account for nearly 60 percent, by weight, of air cargo from Latin America to the US and Canada (Boeing Company 2006: 31). Not surprisingly, the most significant perishables gateway to the US is Miami International Airport (MIA), which handled 69 percent of all US perishable air cargo imports in 2004, including 66 percent of all inbound seafood, 55 percent of all fruits and vegetables, and a whopping 88 percent of fresh cut flowers (*Journal of Commerce Online* 2005).

In many markets, perishables have become a lucrative business prompting more airlines and airports to compete keenly for this traffic. In the past, perishables traffic has been regarded warily in many quarters of the air cargo industry because of the ease with which something can go wrong, leading to costly damage claims for spoiled produce. Now the potential gains have encouraged the construction of massive new refrigerated warehouses at hubs such as London-Heathrow. The new 69,000 square foot BA Perishables Handling Center at Heathrow reflects the same emphasis on speed that has drawn so much perishables traffic into the air. The labeling and packing of inbound perishables is done at the warehouse so that they can move, shelf-ready, directly to a supermarket chain's distribution center, cutting as much as 48 hours out of the traditional supply chain that would have entailed additional middlemen (McKenna 2006). Even before arriving at an airport like Heathrow, some particularly valuable perishables are monitored with tiny electronic sensors tucked among the produce to record any exposure to unacceptably high or low temperatures.

Electronics

Perishables are, however, not especially significant in the world's two largest air cargo markets: between North America and Asia and between Europe and Asia (Table 9.1). Overall, routes to, from, and within Asia (including the incandescent domestic Chinese market) accounted for 50.2 percent of worldwide cargo tonne-kilometers in 2005, and Boeing predicts their combined share will rise to 64.8 percent in 2025 (Boeing Company 2006). On routes involving Asian economies, electronics (broadly defined to included computers, telecommunications equipment, electronic components like semiconductors, etc.) form the mainstay of air cargo flows.

The increased importance of electronics in the air cargo mix has been based largely on four concurrent trends. First, electronic products have become much less expensive, and correspondingly their popularity has taken off. A classic example is the cellular phone. When it was introduced in 1983, the first cell phone weighed 800 grams and cost $3,995[3] (Gussow 2003). By 2008, the most popular cell phone (the Motorola RAZR V3) weighed 95 grams and could be

Table 9.1 The world's top air cargo markets

Market	2005		2025		Average annual growth rate 2005–2025 (%)
	RTKs[1] millions	Share (%)	RTKs[1] millions	Share (%)	
N. America–Asia vv[2]	38.5	21.6	151.7	26.0	7.1
Europe–Asia vv	33.7	18.9	127.8	22.0	6.9
Intra-N. America	23.7	13.3	50.5	8.7	3.9
Europe–N. America vv	17.5	9.8	50.0	8.6	5.4
Intra-Asia	17.2	9.7	74.2	12.7	8.6
Other	47.5	26.7	127.9	22.0	5.1
Total	**178.1**	**100.0**	**582.1**	**100.0**	**6.1**

Source: Boeing Company 2006.

Note
1 RTKs = revenue tonne-kilometers.
2 vv = vice versa.

purchased for less than $90.[4] Over the intervening years cell phone sales soared, with more than a billion sold in 2006 alone (*Economist* 2007a). Second, in turning ordinary products into "smart" products, the semiconductor has boosted value-per-weight ratios for many products above and beyond the threshold for air eligibility. Boeing (2006: 12) estimates that the threshold of air eligibility is approximately $16 per kilogram. Many electronics easily blow through this threshold; the Motorola RAZR was worth nearly $1,000 per kilogram in 2008, for instance. Third, the acceleration of product cycles, fostered in part by rapid advances in semiconductor technology (i.e., Moore's Law), has exacerbated the pressure to rush goods to the market.

Fourth and finally, to a greater degree than for almost any other large industry, electronics manufacturing is spatially disaggregated, meaning that the components or steps in the production process that go into a single product, such as a cell phone or laptop computer, are spread across space. Drawing together pieces from disparate production sites quickly requires what the *New York Times* columnist Thomas Friedman (2006: 518) terms a "supply chain symphony" in which air cargo carriers are often the featured performers. Friedman provides details for sixteen key components that went into his Penang, Malaysia-assembled Dell laptop. The Intel microprocessor chip, for instance, could have come from the Philippines, Costa Rica, Malaysia, or China; the memory chip from South Korea, Taiwan, Germany, or Japan; the hard disk drive from Singapore, Thailand, or the Philippines; and so on. Having been assembled in Malaysia hours after Dell received Friedman's phone order, the finished laptop was one of 25,000 dispatched on board a China Airlines 747 freighter from Penang to Nashville; but many of the intermediate components also made their way to Malaysia by air. In particular, semiconductors move mainly by air – because their value is so high in relation to their size and weight that air cargo is a minor expense, because Moore's Law usually precludes weeks at sea, and because other modes increase the risk of damage.

Today many electronics manufacturers are integrated into global supply chains that operate almost exclusively through the air. A study of electronics manufacturers (including branch plants of foreign firms) in Southeast Asia found that two factors overwhelmingly influenced the degree to which a company uses air cargo: the distance over which its production network is stretched and its cycle time – that is how fast a firm delivers a finished product after receiving a new order (Leinbach and Bowen 2004). Among the firms studied, Intel's branch plant in the Philippines had the highest measure of air cargo intensity which makes sense given that the flash memory chips manufactured there had a cycle time of just four days, the wafers from which chips were cut came from the US, and its main markets were thousands of kilometers away. Not only did Intel make heavy use of air cargo services; it was a big customer for the faster but more expensive express services of companies such as FedEx.

The importance of air cargo services to companies like Dell and Intel has two, sometimes contradictory, effects upon patterns of industrialization and development. On the one hand, by collapsing space, high-speed air transportation facilitates the growth of manufacturing in places like the Philippines that are rel-atively far from major world markets. On the other hand, unevenness in the quality and frequency of air cargo services is one factor (among many) promot-ing an "archipelago economy" (Veltz 1996, cited in Coe *et al.* 2004). In the Phil-ippines, for instance, Metro Manila is well-integrated into the global economy and has prospered partly because of that, but such islands of privilege are sur-rounded by poorer places encumbered by weak accessibility.

Above the threshold

Beyond perishables and electronics, there are many other commodities, interme-diate goods, and finished products that move by air. It is fair to say that most are extremely valuable in relation to their weight. Indeed, for US freight shipments in 2002, goods moved by air had an average value of nearly $100 per kilogram versus just $0.44 for goods moved by water (BTS 2006b) (Table 9.2). The strat-ospheric average for air freight can be interpreted as a sign that air carriers have failed to convince businesses to rely upon air freight on a more regular basis, but alternatively the same high number can be looked at as a measure of air freight's promise. If Boeing is right and goods with value-to-weight ratios over $16 per kilogram can afford air freight, then there is ample scope for the growth of this mode.

What these facts mean is that the mix of air cargo could continue to shift away from the exotic and towards the regular. The plutocrats' Bentleys and Lamborghinis (the Sultan of Brunei's family is well-known in the Southeast Asian air cargo industry for its imports of luxury automobiles), the zoo-bound leopards and aquarium-bound whalesharks, the emergency shipments of spare parts and relief supplies, and the many other special deliveries will not disappear entirely from the sky. Yet most of the increased air cargo traffic in the first decades of the new century – Boeing (2006: 6), for instance, predicted that the air cargo revenue tonne-kilometers will be three times larger in 2025 than in 2005 – will be made up of the stuff of everyday globalization.

Table 9.2 Value intensity of US freight shipments by mode, 2002

Transportation mode	Value per kilogram (dollars)
All modes	0.73
Air (including truck and air)	97.48
Parcel, USPS, or courier	41.29
Truck and rail	1.63
Truck	0.85
Water	0.44
Pipeline	0.27
Rail	0.22

Source: BTS 2006b.

Airborne supply chains

The great humming conveyor belts of trade aloft are among the moving parts in the machinery of supply chains, most of whose elements are firmly grounded on the earth's surface – containerships, 18-wheelers, delivery vans, warehouses, distribution centers, and so on. In recent years, many firms have reengineered the configuration of these elements to speed up their supply chains. Accordingly many companies have, including Dell, made air cargo a central element in their supply chain management (SCM) strategies. SCM draws together aspects of materials management and physical distribution, including demand forecasting, purchasing, inventory management, warehousing, materials handling, packaging, order processing, and transportation (Hesse and Rodrigue 2004). SCM can be thought of as the application of Taylorist managerial techniques, which emphasize the meticulous management of time use by factory workers, to the logistics networks leading in and out of the factory. Taylorism on the assembly line was integral to Ford's vaunted productivity a century ago. Now, a variant of that same approach is at work on assembly lines that stretch across the global scale.

The new importance of SCM has been driven by changes both in production and in consumption. On the production side of the equation, the manufacture of many goods is not only fragmented geographically but fragmented among multiple firms. To return to the earlier cited case of Dell, not only do components such as the microprocessor, graphics card, and LCD display come from places far from the point of final assembly; they also come from other firms (Intel, Foxconn, and one of seven companies, respectively) (Friedman 2006). This kind of "externalization" of production, or vertical disintegration, obviously makes supply chains more complex and their management more important. On the demand side, the keener emphasis on customization, market segmentation, and rapid changes in consumer product design have compelled firms to move faster. Mass markets have been replaced, in many industries, by ephemeral market slices that manufacturers and retailers must tap while they can. Doing so requires not only rapid distribution of finished goods but also accelerating the supply chains feeding the production of those goods.

Furthermore, "demand-pull" supply chains have supplanted the more traditional "supply-push" supply chains (Lasserre 2004). In the latter, a company decides well in advance what to produce based on its experience and market research and how much to produce based on its optimal level of production and then "pushes" the resulting output into the market, hoping that actual demand matches forecast demand. In a "pull" supply chain, conversely, consumers "pull" production with each individual purchase. Advances in information and communications technology, especially Internet-based systems, have facilitated the shift to "pull" supply chains. In an early form, point-of-sale (POS) data was fed backwards from retail outlets to distribution centers to assemblers and component manufacturers and so on, enabling production to be constantly adjusted based on sales. Benetton, for instance, was a pioneer in this regard, developing an integrated system intended to ensure that customers could find the desired colors and styles of its various articles of clothing across its retail network (Knox *et al.* 2003: 197). More recently, the Internet has become the backbone for systems that link a company to its suppliers and customers, transmitting real-time information far more detailed than that available just at the point of sale (Lasserre 2004).

The downside of a "pull" supply chain is its lack of predictability and its vulnerability to interruption. Dell, for instance, had to scramble to lock up chartered air freight capacity to avoid being crippled by the US West Coast dockworkers' strike in 2000. Dell protected its just-in-time system by chartering 18 747 freighters at about $500,000 per plane to ferry lower value parts (e.g., motherboards) from Asia that normally arrive in the US by sea (Holzner 2006: 101–2). More generally, "pull" supply chains, while offering the prospect of higher profit, require innovative and tightly managed logistics strategies.

Fundamentally, SCM is now more about optimizing the management of capital rather than simple transportation (Lasserre 2004), but fast and reliable transportation is critical because it makes possible higher profits by accelerating the turnover of capital and reducing capital waste represented by unsold inventory. Dell, admittedly an atypical case, credits its low inventories as the basis for its consistent, high profitability. In turning its inventory a remarkable 107 times per year (Holzner 2006: 91), Dell maximizes the productivity of its capital investment.

It is important to concede that while the greater emphasis on SCM has made air cargo services more important, most of the world's trade still moves by sea and on land. Air transportation enjoys a vast speed advantage over alternate modes, but the advantage has been narrowed by the development of containerization. In his book *The Box: How the Shipping Container Made the World Smaller and the World Economy Bigger*, Marc Levinson (2006: 267) explains that containerization has made ocean and rail freight faster by radically speeding up the loading and unloading of freight. As a specific example of the wonders of containerization, Levinson reports that a 35 ton container of coffee-makers could make the 18,000 kilometer trip from a factory in Malaysia to a warehouse in Ohio in as little as 22 days and a cost "less than a single first-class air ticket" (2006: 7). Via air, the same journey could be completed in fewer than three days but at a dramatically higher cost – something on the order of 30–40 first class tickets if the coffee-makers were sent by FedEx International Priority (IP) Freight. Furthermore, because containerization has helped make surface transportation systems more predictable, firms have been able to reduce inventories. In the US, Levinson reports, nonfarm inventories in 2004 were about one trillion dollars lower than they would have been if they had stayed at the same level, relative to sales, as in the 1980s (M. Levinson 2006: 269).

Moreover, most air freight moves much more slowly (and costs much less) than FedEx IP. Slow handling at airports, particularly customs clearance on arrival, often eats into the speed advantage of air cargo. Paperwork is a primary reason why a transpacific shipment by air typically takes six to six-and-a-half days door-to-door. Consequently, airlines have much to gain through a proposed move to a largely paperless "e-freight" initiative, which could shave the transpacific door-to-door time, for instance, to three days (Perrett 2007). If that initiative bears fruit, it could reverse the trend observed between 2000 and 2005 during which ocean container freight grew at twice the rate of air freight.

One way to gauge the significance of sea freight and air freight in the contemporary global economy is to reconsider the rankings of top US trade gateways (Table 9.3). Near the top of the list is New York's John F. Kennedy International Airport, which handled $161 billion in trade in 2007 – just behind the seaports at Los Angeles and New York/New Jersey. Six other airports rank in the top 20 gateways; and it is worth noting that the trade deficits for airport gateways were generally much smaller than for the other two modes – reflecting the greater propensity of high value American exports to move by air.

What is also evident in Table 9.3, however, is that the principal freight gateways to the US are multimodal: JFK International is only a short drive from the Port of New York/New Jersey and in Los Angeles the airport is close to two great seaports. Beyond the US, Singapore, Shanghai, Hong Kong, Dubai, and the Netherland's Randstad[5] are similarly important both in sea and air freight flows. And each of these cities also has excellent ground transportation access. In today's economy, places that draw together air, sea, and land networks are especially attractive to the growing number of businesses that have adopted multimodal SCM strategies.

Table 9.3 US trade gateways, 2007

Rank	Gateway	Mode	Exports billions of dollars	Imports billions of dollars	Total billions of dollars
1	Port of Los Angeles	Water	29.9	150.4	180.2
2	Port of New York and New Jersey	Water	40.6	124.6	165.2
3	John F. Kennedy Int'l	Air	77.0	84.2	161.2
4	Port of Long Beach	Water	26.7	120.4	147.1
5	Detroit	Land	73.3	63.3	136.6
6	Port of Houston	Water	53.4	61.2	114.6
7	Laredo, Texas	Land	47.4	63.0	110.4
8	Chicago-O'Hare Int'l	Air	33.4	53.1	86.6
9	Los Angeles Int'l	Air	41.6	38.0	79.6
10	Buffalo-Niagara Falls	Land	38.6	40.0	78.6
11	Port Huron, Michigan	Land	30.7	46.3	77.1
12	San Francisco Int'l	Air	29.7	31.9	61.6
13	Port of Charleston, South Carolina	Water	19.8	41.1	60.9
14	Port of Savannah, Georgia	Water	18.3	31.3	49.6
15	Port of Norfolk, Virginia	Water	20.7	28.8	49.5
16	El Paso, Texas	Land	20.0	29.1	49.1
17	Anchorage Int'l	Air	10.7	34.5	45.3
18	Port of Baltimore	Water	14.0	28.0	42.0
19	Dallas-Ft. Worth Int'l	Air	18.1	23.4	41.5
20	Louis Armstrong New Orleans Int'l	Air	18.2	22.9	41.1

Source: BTS 2009d.

Airlines of the Internet: the integrators

Scores of carriers compete for the world's rising volume of air cargo but four in particular are especially significant: FedEx, UPS, DHL, and TNT. These four companies are integrators, meaning they provide integrated air and ground transportation services, which is one source of their speed. Two (UPS and TNT) began as ground transport providers and only much later developed air services; the other two grew in the opposite direction, getting their start in air services and then stretching their legs upon the ground. UPS and FedEx are based in the US, although both have expanded internationally in a voracious fashion.[6] TNT and DHL meanwhile are examples of the fast and loose nature of business nationality in today's economy. The former got its start as a company with two trucks in Australia but is now owned by the Dutch post office. The latter began arranging the airborne delivery of sea freight documents between San Francisco and Honolulu but is now owned by Deutsche Post World Networks, the German post office.

Today, all four companies share in common carefully cultivated, widely recognized brand images, and a widespread point-to-point delivery presence. And they have been ideally situated to benefit from the expansion of e-commerce because they have the presence to cope with the extreme spatial fragmentation of sales on sites like eBay and Amazon.com. This is especially true of FedEx and UPS. The contribution of the Internet to the vibrant growth of FedEx in particular is somewhat surprising because only a few years ago, the digitization of letters, legal briefs, manuscripts, contracts, and proposals was seen as a threat to the company's core business (Haddad 2001). Document traffic *is* proportionately less important to the integrators than it used to be, but their fortunes have been buoyed by Internet-generated traffic.

As early as 1996, FedEx was extolled as the "Airline of the Internet" (Lappin 1996). From its inception, the company recognized the implications of advanced in information technology for the distribution and transportation industries. Famously, the germ of the company, first known as Federal Express (so named to give the impression of government backing), was a paper written by its founder, Fred Smith, while he was a student at Yale. Smith argued:

- first, that businesses purchasing labor-saving but exorbitantly expensive computer systems, such as IBM mainframes, would require urgent deliveries of spare parts when their mission-critical systems failed; and
- second, that the passenger airline networks were poorly suited to provide express cargo services.

Federal Express stepped into the breech with its overnight network based at an unused military hangar in Memphis. After a slow start, the combination of savvy marketing (including the firm's famous fast-talking "When it absolutely, positively has to be there overnight" television ad), aggressive pursuit of opportunities opened by airline deregulation, and the use of advanced information technology raised FedEx to a rarefied stature in the culture: sometime in the early 1990s, the word "FedEx" entered the English language as a verb (*Washington Post* 1994; Wetherbe 1996: 156–7). An even more important measure of FedEx's success is the degree to which the company's services and those of its competitors have been woven into the fabric of commerce. As James Gleick (1999: 85) observes in his book *Faster: The Acceleration of Just About Everything*, "In the world before FedEx, when 'it' could not absolutely, positively be there overnight, it rarely had to. Now that it can, it must." The "speed imperative" (we can move fast, therefore we must move fast) that FedEx has both fed upon and fostered is an illustration of the way in which air transportation has redefined the pace of everyday life.

FedEx was ideally situated to harness the Internet. In 1984, about a decade before the Internet came to fruition, FedEx began issuing its PowerShip system, which included a dedicated PC linked to the company's Cosmos system, to thousands of high volume customers. PowerShip enabled customers to print their own shipping labels and track their shipments (Lappin 1996; Wetherbe 1996: 79, 130–1). Later the company offered many more customers dial-up software called FedEx Ship with the same kinds of features. In providing a widely distributed digital interface between customers and FedEx, PowerShip anticipated the impact of the Internet, both in democratizing access and in using information technology to reduce costs. Even before going onto the Internet, FedEx was transacting 60 percent of its business electronically.

So it was unsurprising that FedEx was among the very first businesses to offer an interactive website as opposed to simply marketing its services brochure-like (Spector 2002: 10–11). In 1994, the FedEx site allowed customers to track their shipments online. Two years later shipping labels could be generated from the website. With its own website up and winning accolades in the Internet's infancy, FedEx turned to harness the traffic generated by other companies' websites. FedEx had the IT network and the physical network of planes and trucks to parlay the explosion of e-commerce into an engine of new traffic growth. Smith saw the symbiosis between the Internet and FedEx as something akin to the nineteenth century relationship between the telegraph and railroad: "When the telegraph came along there was a corresponding development of the rail system. The telegraph created the connections and the railroad allowed fulfillment. Well, today the Internet creates the connections, and we provide the fulfillment." (quoted in Lappin 1996).

Many early Internet ventures faltered because they could not reconcile the freedom to take orders from anywhere in cyberspace with the practical necessity of delivering the goods quickly (Lasserre 2004). What the Internet mandated was "precision logistics" (Lappin 1996) – the ability to move small shipments to thousands of businesses, large and small, and to millions of households at a speed commensurate with the Internet's proclivity for immediate gratification. FedEx and, to a lesser degree, the other integrators were better prepared than other transportation firms to satisfy this need. Likewise, the integrators had the network scope to handle the reverse logistics[7] that have grown as a corollary of e-commerce.

Even more promising to the integrators is B2B (business to business) e-commerce and the more general development of SCM. In pursuit of that business, the integrators have diversified aggressively into warehouse logistics, finance, customs brokerage, less-than-truckload (LTL) ground transportation, and heavy freight operations. UPS, for example, spent billions buying Fritz, a freight forwarder with a huge presence in the warehouse logistics business; Menlo (formerly Emery) a heavy air freight carrier; and Overnite, a leading LTL carrier; as well as dozens of other companies (Foust 2004). As these other enterprises were folded into its stable, UPS began boasting of its jack-of-all-trades product line with its advertising slogan, "What can Brown do for you?" A lot, it seems.

Moreover, UPS is not just about moving goods. Like the other integrators, it has moved into more knowledge-intensive services, including the design of new supply chain strategies. UPS, for instance, developed a streamlined supply chain for Nikon in order to speed the delivery of hot-selling digital cameras to retailers throughout the Americas (UPS Supply Chain Solutions 2005). The system the camera maker adopted feeds its Americas-bound output from factories in South Korea, China, and Indonesia into the UPS hub at Louisville, Kentucky. There, at its Supply Chain Logistics Center, UPS can "kit" the products with particular kinds of batteries or other accessories or repackage according to the specifications of individual retailers, meaning that Nikon has outsourced some of the customization characteristic of the contemporary economy to its logistics provider. The cameras are always "visible" to Nikon via the UPS information technology system, so that if some shipments are running late or if there is a change in the pattern of demand, Nikon and UPS can respond immediately. UPS does not necessarily carry the cameras every step of the way in the process. It sometimes acts as a broker for sea freight services on Nikon's behalf; but because the emphasis of this supply chain solution is speed to market, because it is being managed by UPS, and because its nerve center is the UPS hub, much of the traffic generated by Nikon is routed over UPS air services. In fact, UPS proudly states that, if necessary, cameras manufactured in Asia can be on store shelves in the Americas two days later.

Perhaps the most spectacular transformation of an integrator is that of DHL. The company's initials stand for the three American founders of the company (Adrian Dalsey, Larry Hillblom, and Robert Lynn), which is ironic because one of the weaker links in the DHL chain today is the American market. Deutsche Post, after having been privatized in 2000 and under pressure from the advent of e-mail and the Internet, acquired a controlling share of DHL in 2002 (*Economist* 2006c). It also bought Airborne, an American integrator substantially smaller than its rivals FedEx and UPS (to try to boost Deutsche Post's profile in the world's biggest domestic market). On the ground, Deutsche Post's purchases included Danzas/AEI and then Exel, the world's first and ninth ranked air freight forwarders, respectively, before their acquisition (Ott 2003). All of these and other companies, too, have been folded into the DHL brand. The goal is to make DHL "the Coca Cola brand of logistics," its bright yellow livery ubiquitous and inevitable (*Business Times* 2003). As with UPS and FedEx, the rationale for diversification is to create a kind of one-stop shop for the logistics needs of major corporate clients while still serving millions of ordinary door-to-door consumers. The results have been mixed. In 2008, DHL announced that it was withdrawing from the US domestic air and ground market (but would continue to serve higher yielding international routes to and from the US). The decision meant the loss of 9,000 jobs across the US, including more than 7,500 jobs in DHL's Wilmington, Ohio, hub (Driehaus 2008).

Finally, TNT is the smallest and most vulnerable of the four dominant international integrators. Although the company claims to be the world's leading B2B express delivery company and boasts of the biggest door-to-door air and road express delivery network in Europe, it has the smallest number of aircraft by far. And in 2006, TNT sold its logistics division in order to raise cash with which to build up its core mail and express businesses and more specifically to fund its expansion into Asia (Guha and Smith 2006).

Indeed, all four integrators are in hot pursuit of the Chinese market. FedEx got a headstart through its 1995 purchase of Evergreen International's air traffic rights there. More recently, both FedEx and UPS have rapidly expanded their Chinese services; and, as a result of favorable traffic rights decisions by the US government, Big Brown had more flights to China than any cargo or passenger US airline by 2006 (UPS 2006). Meanwhile, by 2004, FedEx's daily MD-11 flight from Shanghai to Memphis – with its payload of cell phones, digital cameras, and the like – was the company's single greatest source of revenue (Harney and Roberts 2004).

All four integrators operate complex, global networks. As noted in Chapter 5, FedEx and UPS in particular operate true hubs across the world. In its early years, FedEx's centralization was so strict that, famously, a parcel shipped from one floor of a San Francisco skyscraper to another floor of the same building would be routed via Memphis; but as the firm's traffic has grown it has developed a more complex system of tiered hubs (Figure 9.1). In the FedEx system, for instance, the Superhub at Memphis is complemented by a national hub at Indianapolis and regional hubs at Newark, Oakland, Ft. Worth, and Miami (which is primarily a hub for traffic to and from Latin America). In addition, Anchorage serves as a sorting hub between the carrier's North American and Asia-Pacific networks. Outside the US, FedEx operates what it terms Global Network Hubs at Paris, Guangzhou, Dubai and a half dozen other cities. As described in Chapter 5, FedEx established its intra-Asian hub at Subic Bay in 1995, taking advantage of extraordinary seventh freedom rights; but the weakness of the local traffic base and the airport's short runway prompted FedEx to move its intra-Asian hub to the new Guangzhou Baiyun International Airport (Lau and Ward 2005). The latter is located in the Pearl River Delta region (see Figure 10.1) where the blistering rate of economic growth ensures ample local traffic support, and, as in the Philippines a decade ago, the air services agreement between China and the US now permits American cargo carriers to establish Chinese hubs. From this system of hubs, FedEx deploys the world's largest fleet of freighter aircraft (Table 9.4).

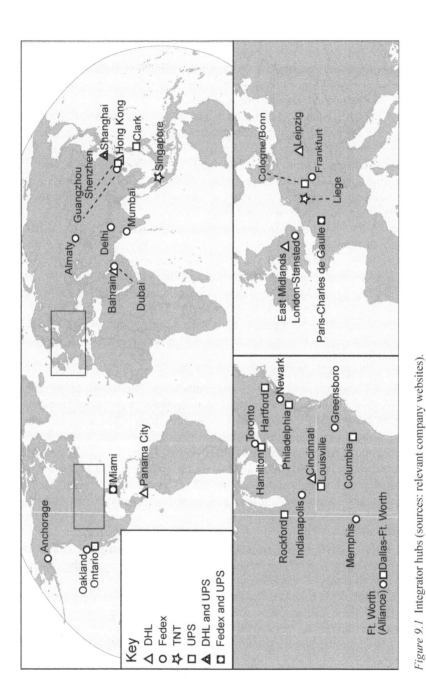

Figure 9.1 Integrator hubs (sources: relevant company websites).

In 2008, the four major integrators operated complex, global hub-and-spoke networks. The most important air hubs are shown here.

Table 9.4 Largest freighter fleets,[1] 2008

All-cargo airlines			Combination airlines		
Carrier	Nationality	Fleet	Carrier	Nationality	Fleet
FedEx	USA	351	Korean	South Korea	23
UPS	USA	230	Lufthansa	Germany	23
ABX[2]	USA	91	China Airlines	Taiwan, China	20
Astar[2]	USA	43	Cathay Pacific	Hong Kong	18
TNT	Netherlands	28	Air France/KLM	France/Netherlands	18
European Air Transport[3]	Belgium	28	EVA	Taiwan, China	16
			Singapore Air Cargo	Singapore	14
DHL	Germany	22	Japan Airlines	Japan	13
Kalitta Air	USA	18			

Source: *Air Transport World* 2008a.

Notes
1 Only jet aircraft that were operated (i.e. not in storage) by the airline are counted.
2 ABX and Astar provided airlift capacity to DHL to and from their common Wilmington, Ohio, hub and at 15 other stations across the US. The downsizing of DHL's American presence (described in the text), will adversely affect Astar and ABX.
3 European Air Transport is a subsidiary of Deutsche Post World Net and provides European airlift capacity to DHL.

Going our separate ways: the development of freighter networks

Altogether the four main integrators fly nearly half of the world's jet freighters; but there are scores of all-freight operators across the world. Some are large, very successful carriers with long histories. Cargolux, for instance, has been flying freighters since 1970, and its fleet of 16 747Fs bearing the airline's three-box logo served more than 70 airports worldwide from its Luxembourg hub in 2008 (Figure 9.2). Yet most of the all-freight carriers are fly-by-night operations in more than one sense. Dozens fly in Africa, for example, overcoming that continent's limited ground transportation infrastructure with aging DC-8, 707, and 727 freighters. The air cargo business has fairly low entry costs, partly because there is an abundant supply of old passenger jets suitable for conversion to freighters.

Surprisingly, most of the big carriers in the air cargo industry are combination airlines (they carry both passengers and cargo), many of which regarded air cargo only as a sideline until recently. Although the largest freighter fleets operated by combination carriers are much smaller than those of the big three integrators, the size of their combined passenger and freight fleets and networks permits them to move huge volumes of cargo. Air France-KLM is larger in tonne-kilometers performed than all but FedEx; and Korean Air and Lufthansa rank just behind UPS (Table 9.5). In fact, most of the twenty largest freight carriers (in terms of freight tonne-kilometers) are combination carriers. The far greater number and geographic reach of their passenger aircraft make them a formidable weapon in the air cargo industry. And among Lufthansa Cargo's

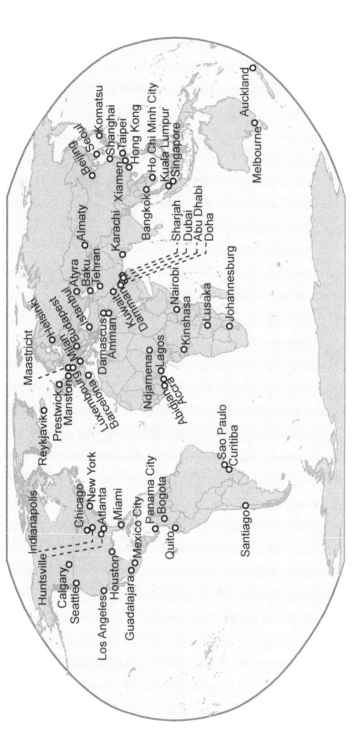

Figure 9.2 Cargolux network, 2008 (source: Cargolux 2008).

In 2008, Luxembourg-based Cargolux operated a remarkably global network, which reflected the particular importance of oil production centers (e.g. Baku, Calgary, Dammam, and N'Djamena) to the air cargo industry.

most important customers, for instance, has been DHL, which has relied on Lufthansa to provide global long-haul capacity on its freighters and passenger jets while the various airlines under the DHL umbrella provide mainly short- and medium-haul lift (*Air Cargo World* 2006).

Overall, about 60 percent of air cargo is carried on passenger aircraft; but a variety of factors suggest that the share carried in freighters – once disparaged as "virility symbols" by BA (Putzgar 1997) – will grow. First, the much-discussed ascent of the low-cost carriers (LCCs) and of regional jet (RJ) operations has slowed or even reversed the growth of belly-hold capacity in many markets (Conway 2004). The 737s and A320s operated by LCCs have very little belly capacity; and RJs have even less.[8] Second, the tonnage controlled by the biggest forwarders, the traditional intermediaries between airlines and shippers in the air cargo business, has risen rapidly and big forwarders tend to favor carriers with freighters.[9] Already in 2003, the combined market share of the 15 largest air freight forwarders was 60 percent, and further consolidation seems likely (Ott 2003; Bowen and Leinbach 2004). Finally, the trend towards time-sensitive SCM favors freighters over passenger aircraft because freighters are more easily scheduled to suit the needs of shippers (e.g., for late night departures) and because shipments are less likely to be offloaded from a freighter than from a passenger jet. On the latter, passengers and their baggage have priority and if strong headwinds on a long-haul route force a carrier to trim its load, it is the cargo that will be offloaded first.

Overall, Boeing predicts that the number of jet freighters, combining con-verted and production freighters, will rise from 1,789 jet freighters in 2005 to

Table 9.5 The world's top cargo airlines, 2007

Rank	Carrier	Nationality	Freight tonne-kilometers (millions)
1	FedEx	USA	15,985
2	Air France-KLM	France–Netherlands	11,365
3	UPS	USA	9,930
4	Korean Air	South Korea	9,678
5	Lufthansa	Germany	8,451
6	Singapore Airlines	Singapore	7,340
7	Cathay Pacific	Hong Kong, China	7,099
8	China Airlines	Taiwan, China	6,299
9	Cargolux	Luxembourg	5,512
10	Atlas Air	USA	5,387
11	Emirates	United Arab Emirates	5,084[1]
12	British Airways	United Kingdom	4,891
13	EVA Air	Taiwan, China	4,784
14	JAL Group	Japan	4,773
15	Air China	China	3,686

Source: *Air Transport World* 2008d.

Note
1 Figure is for 2006.

3,563 in 2025, with 75 percent of the increase attributable to conversions[10] (Boeing Company 2006: 1–2, 106). That sharp forecasted increase in the global freighter fleet is testament to the confidence of Boeing at least in the future of the airborne world; but the forecast also presents a daunting challenge for the hubs at which that traffic will be concentrated. The significance of these and other air cargo hubs is an ironic feature of contemporary globalization. Inexpensive air cargo services have fostered a measure of "placelessness" in the consumption of tuna, tennis shoes, and many other goods, but those same services have made some places on the ground much more important.

Moving places

Some airports, such as Los Angeles International are well-connected both in passenger and cargo networks, but one of the important trends in the air cargo industry is the divergence between the hubs and gateways through which air cargo traffic flows and those through which air passenger traffic flows (Figure 9.3). That trend is likely to become more pronounced in the years ahead and will play an important role in structuring the geography of both opportunities and burdens in the airborne world.

The divergence is only partial, of course, because so much cargo is carried by combination carriers routing their aircraft to cater primarily to passengers. Of the world's 30 busiest air passenger hubs, 18 are also on the list of the world's 30 busiest air cargo hubs, although their order is quite different (Table 9.6). More interesting, however, are the 12 airports that are not on both lists. The busiest air cargo hub, unsurprisingly, is Memphis. Another FedEx hub, Indianapolis, also ranks among the top 30 for air cargo; and, of course, UPS has powered Louisville into the top stratum of air cargo hubs.

Other airlines have operated cargo hubs at cities such as Dayton, Toledo, Fort Wayne, and Wilmington, Ohio – where, as mentioned above, DHL and its affiliates had a massive US hub until late 2008. These airports lay among a region with a particularly high concentration of significant cargo hubs (Figure 9.4). Airlines favor hubs in this region because it offers good proximity to most of the North American population (Noviello *et al.* 1996). For instance, the promoters of Rickenbacker, a former military airfield near Columbus, boast that it lies within a one-day truck drive of 50 percent of the Canadian population, 58 percent of the US population, and 61 percent of US manufacturing capacity (CRAA 2006). Moreover, the use of hubs in the interior of the country as gateways to the American market avoids some of the congestion associated with coastal gateways like JFK and LAX (Lasserre 2004).

In Europe especially, the divergence there between air cargo and air passenger traffic is likely to grow. Europe's stringent regulation of nighttime operations at major hubs and the limited scoped for capacity additions at those airports will constrain future air cargo growth (Conway 2002). Frankfurt announced that it would restrict night flights in return for a fourth runway that will open in 2012 (Turney 2006). In response, the airport's most important cargo carrier warned,

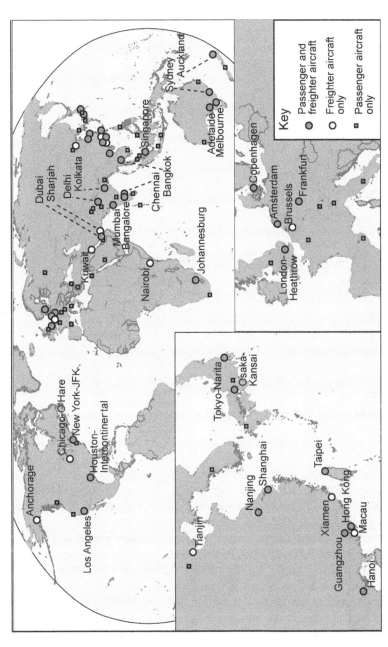

Figure 9.3 Singapore Airlines cargo network, 2008 (source: author's analysis of OAG 2008).

Like other combination carriers, SIA moves cargo via both its passenger and freighter aircraft. The airline's freighters were deployed on a network in which gateways to China were prominent.

Table 9.6 The world's top cargo hubs, 2007

Rank	Airport	Cargo (tonnes)	Average annual % growth since 2000
1	Memphis Int'l	3,840,491	6.4
2	Hong Kong Int'l	3,774,191	7.5
3	Ted Stevens Anchorage Int'l	2,825,511	6.6
4	Pudong Int'l (Shanghai)	2,559,310	18.1
5	Incheon Int'l (Seoul)	2,555,580	4.5
6	Paris Charles de Gaulle Int'l	2,297,896	5.2
7	Narita Int'l (Tokyo)	2,254,421	2.2
8	Frankfurt	2,168,915	3.5
9	Louisville Int'l-Standiford Field	2,078,947	4.6
10	Miami Int'l	1,922,985	2.3
11	Changi (Singapore)	1,918,160	1.7
12	Los Angeles Int'l	1,848,760	(1.4)
13	Dubai Int'l	1,668,505	16.2
14	Amsterdam Airport Schiphol	1,651,385	3.9
15	John F. Kennedy Int'l (New York)	1,607,731	(1.7)
16	Taipei Taoyuan Int'l	1,605,681	4.1
17	Chicago-O'Hare Int'l	1,533,503	0.6
18	Heathrow (London)	1,395,905	(0.1)
19	Suvarnabhumi (Bangkok)	1,220,001	5.0
20	Beijing Capital Int'l	1,192,553	6.4
21	Indianapolis Int'l	1,101,068	(0.8)
22	Newark Liberty Int'l	963,794	(1.6)
23	Luxembourg-Findel Int'l	856,741	8.0
24	Haneda (Tokyo)	852,952	1.5
25	Kansai Int'l (Osaka)	845,976	(2.4)
26	Brussels	747,434	1.2
27	Dallas-Fort Worth Int'l	723,022	(3.2)
28	Hartsfield-Jackson Atlanta Int'l	720,209	(3.0)
29	Cologne Bonn	710,244	7.5
30	Guangzhou Baiyun Int'l	694,923	5.3

Source: ACI 2008.

"An absolute night flight ban at Frankfurt would threaten the very existence of Lufthansa Cargo [....] Should an absolute night flight ban be unavoidable, then Lufthansa Cargo would look for alternatives within Germany, or outside Germany." (quoted in *Air Cargo World* 2006). Airlines abhor moving from key hubs, however, because airports such as Frankfurt already have the constellation of major forwarders and nearby logistics centers that generate traffic for freighter flights; and for combination carriers like Lufthansa, traffic feed from the bellies of passenger aircraft is crucial to the success of freighter operations.

Nevertheless, the shift away from Frankfurt may have begun. In 2009, DHL and Lufthansa formed a new, jointly owned cargo airline, Aero Logic, whose hub is in Leipzig – not Frankfurt. The new carrier commenced Boeing 777 freighter services on two Europe–Asia routes: Leipzig–Bahrain–Singapore–Delhi–Leipzig operated by Lufthansa and Leipzig–Tashkent–Hong Kong vv

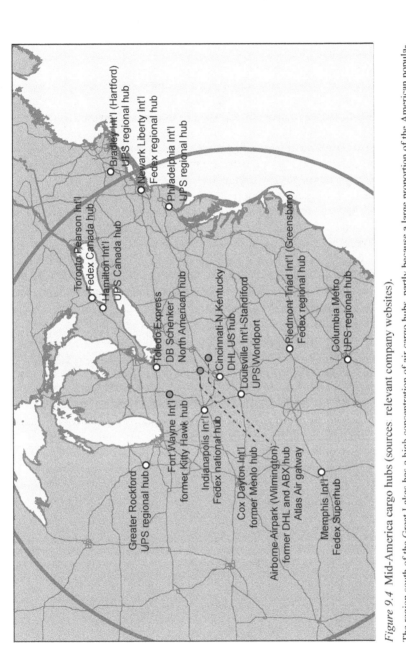

Figure 9.4 Mid-America cargo hubs (sources: relevant company websites).

The region south of the Great Lakes has a high concentration of air cargo hubs, partly because a large proportion of the American population lies within one day's trucking distance. The partially shown circle has a radius of 1,150 kilometers (an estimate of how far a trucker could travel given US working day and speed limit laws) centered on Louisville, where UPS has its principal hub.

operated by DHL (*Journal of Commerce Online* 2009). DHL had already moved its principal hub from Brussels to Leipzig primarily because the Belgian government would not approve the expansion of night flights that the carrier's planned growth required (Wastnage 2005). Leipzig has no nighttime restrictions, and its position in European market has become more central following the accession of 12 new members to the European Union since 2004.

It is not just in Europe that nighttime operations matter. In a worldwide survey of freighter operators, the single most important factor influencing a cargo airline's choice of a hub airport was the freedom to operate through the night (Gardiner *et al.* 2005). Carriers can help their cause by operating quieter aircraft, and that is one reason UPS and FedEx, in particular, have invested heavily in production (and therefore newer) freighters. The issue of airport noise is dealt with in greater detail in Chapter 10.

Finally, it is worth emphasizing that among the world's top air cargo hubs, one of the fastest recent growth rates has been recorded by Dubai (see Table 9.6). The emirate has promoted its geographic appeal in terms similar to those used in Rickenbacker but on a global scale (Flottau 2007). Eighty percent of the world's population lies within an eight-hour flight of Dubai, and the emirate is well-positioned to serve as a hub both for the well-established traffic between east and west but also the growing volume of commerce between north and south (e.g., perishables from Africa bound for Europe). To exploit that advantage, Emirates had outstanding orders for 18 new freighters in 2008 (and some of its orders for the A380 may take the form of production freighters), and on the ground, a new terminal was opened at Dubai International in 2006 and the new Al Maktoum International Airport (see Figure 10.2) has an ultimate design capacity of 12 million tonnes of cargo, far more than moved through any airport in the world in 2007 (Bowen and Cidell, forthcoming). Together, these developments point to a future in which Dubai – by dint of its geography, wealth, and ambition – *could* rival Singapore, Hong Kong, Frankfurt, and Los Angeles as one of the hinge points mediating the rising flow of airborne trade.

And it is to those places – the world's great airports – that the next chapter turns.

10 Points of departure

Airports in the airborne world

Building the gateways to the future

In May 2009, China commenced work on a new airport for the city of Turpan located in the vast northwestern region of Xinjiang (BBC News Monitoring Service 2009). The airport, to be built at an estimated cost of less than $60 million, is expected to markedly improve access to a city that was once one of the key stops along the ancient Silk Road. In fact, millennia old ruins near the airport site are likely to help fill the seats when flights begin, opening up new opportunities for the local economy. In a Xinhua news agency report on the airport, one local grape farmer said, "I will make a good fortune if many tourists come." (BBC News Monitoring Service 2009).

The Turpan Jiaohe Airport is a small part of the massive expansion of airport capacity during the past two decades. New airports have been built and existing ones expanded with new terminals and runways. Often the costs have been extraordinary (Table 10.1). The two most expensive new airports cost more than $20 billion each (after adjusting for inflation) partly because they were built atop land reclaimed from the sea. Airport "terraforming" (Fuller and Harley 2004: 105) is a particularly stark way that aviation has reshaped life on the ground.

While large air transportation infrastructure projects have been sprinkled across much of the world (though their absence in sub-Saharan Africa and Latin America is conspicuous), two regions stand out has as having especially significant clusters. China's Pearl River Delta (PRD) features five airports that opened between 1991 and 2005 located no more than 120 kilometers from one another (Figure 10.1). Reflecting the booming manufacturing economy of the region, two of the airports (Hong Kong International and Guangzhou-Baiyun International) already rank among the world's 30 busiest in cargo flows and a third (Shenzhen Bao'an International) is likely to move onto the list as the UPS intra-Asian hub there takes shape. On the other hand, the Zhuhai Airport has generally failed to attract much business and ranks as one of the airport industry's "white elephants."[1]

Six thousand kilometers due west, a more recent cluster of massive new airports is found in the Persian Gulf (Figure 10.2). The conjunction of airport expansion and airline expansion is particularly obvious here. For example, the tiny peninsular state of Qatar will open its new Doha International Airport in

Table 10.1 The world's most expensive airports

Country	Airport	Year opened	Cost[1] (billions of 2008 US dollars)
China	Hong Kong Int'l	1998	25.3
Japan	Kansai Int'l (Osaka)	1994	20.3
Saudi Arabia	King Abdul Aziz Int'l (Jeddah)	1982	9.7
Saudi Arabia	King Khalid Int'l (Riyadh)	1983	9.4
Japan	Central Japan Int'l (Nagoya)	2005	7.9
Germany	Munich-Franz Josef Strauss	1992	7.6
South Korea	Seoul Incheon Int'l	2001	7.5
USA	Denver Int'l	1995	6.6
Malaysia	Kuala Lumpur Int'l	1998	4.1
Norway	Oslo-Gardermoen	1999	3.5
Thailand	Bangkok Int'l Suvarnabhumi	2006	3.5
Japan	Kobe	2006	2.9
Japan	Narita Int'l (Tokyo)	1978	2.9
China	Guangzhou-Baiyun Int'l	2004	2.8
USA	Dallas-Ft. Worth Int'l	1974	2.5

Source: Bowen and Cidell (forthcoming).

Note

1 Costs have been adjusted for inflation using the GDP price deflator available at S. Williamson (2008). The figures include, to the extent possible, the cost of ground transport systems built specifically for each new airport.

2010 to serve as the new hub for the hugely ambitious Qatar Airways. Yet Qatar's plans seem puny by comparison with Dubai, its rival 45 minutes by plane down the shore of the Persian Gulf. Although Dubai International Airport is already just one of seven international airports in the United Arab Emirates, the emirate is building another. Construction on the Al Maktoum International Airport began in 2005, and if it reaches its planned maximum development, its extent will be staggering. It will cover an area larger than Heathrow and Los Angeles International combined, its passenger capacity will be 120 million per year, and its cargo capacity will be twice the current capacity of Memphis International (Flottau 2005b). The airport's ambitions are matched only by those of its home town carrier, Emirates.

Al Maktoum International is a signal that the new airport boom is not over. That is especially true in Asia. China is probably only beginning decades of fevered new airport construction. In 2006, the world's most populous country and its fastest growing big economy had only 196 airports certified to handle transport aircraft. By comparison, the US had 14,000 such airports and Australia 444 (Thomas 2005a). India, too, will need many new airports; but there the work had hardly gotten started by 2009.[2]

Yet new airports comprise only one part of the great build-out in air transportation capacity. Of the 39 projects globally that cost at least $500 million (and that were completed, or underway at the time of this writing and scheduled for completion by 2010) only 11 were wholly new airports (Figure 10.3). No large

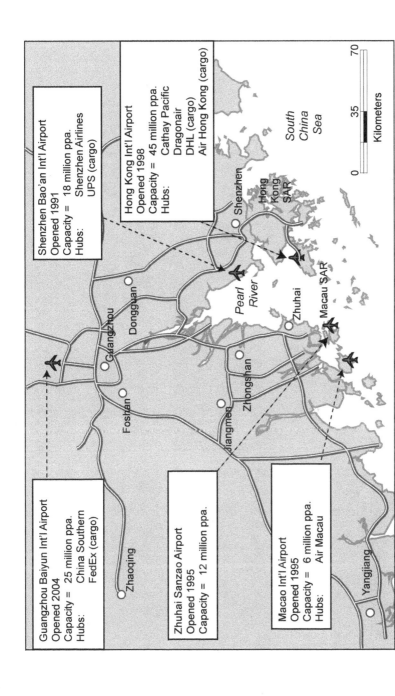

Figure 10.1 Pearl River Delta airports (sources: relevant airport and airline websites).

Southern China's Pearl River Delta is home to five new airports, most of which have at least one significant airline hubbing operation. PPA = passengers per annum.

The following text appears within the figure:

Guangzhou Baiyun Int'l Airport
Opened 2004
Capacity = 25 million ppa.
Hubs: China Southern
FedEx (cargo)

Shenzhen Bao'an Int'l Airport
Opened 1991
Capacity = 18 million ppa.
Hubs: Shenzhen Airlines
UPS (cargo)

Hong Kong Int'l Airport
Opened 1998
Capacity = 45 million ppa.
Hubs: Cathay Pacific
Dragonair
DHL (cargo)
Air Hong Kong (cargo)

Zhuhai Sanzao Airport
Opened 1995
Capacity = 12 million ppa.

Macao Int'l Airport
Opened 1995
Capacity = 6 million ppa.
Hubs: Air Macau

Zhaoqing
Foshan
Guangzhou
Dongguan
Shenzhen
Hong Kong SAR
Jiangmen
Zhongshan
Zhuhai
Macau SAR
Yangjiang
Pearl River
South China Sea

0   35   70
Kilometers

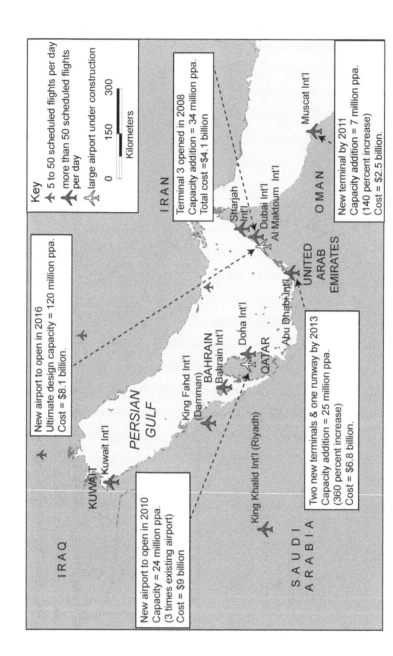

Figure 10.2 Persian Gulf airports (sources: contemporary media accounts and relevant airport websites).

In the early twenty-first century, the Persian Gulf was the setting for a massive expansion of airport capacity, fueled by a mixture of high oil prices, the bold (perhaps reckless) plans of competing governments, and the ambitions of airlines such as Emirates. PPA. = passengers per annum.

new airports were built in the US during the decade, yet there were ten large airport expansion projects from JFK to San Jose. The sums involved are often only slightly less stupefying than for a wholly new airport. The cost for a fifth runway at Atlanta's Hartsfield-Jackson International Airport? $1.3 billion (Hirschman and Grantham 2006). In fairness it was not just any runway but rather "The Most Important Runway in America" as christened by its backers.

New terminals are expensive, too. The cost for London-Heathrow's new Terminal 5 (T5) and its associated road, rail, energy, water diversion, and parking infrastructure? $8.7 billion, a cost that was greatly inflated by the nearly 20 years that passed between the beginning of the design process and the airport's opening (Bowen and Cidell forthcoming). Other passenger terminals with at least a $500 million price tag were recently finished or under way in 2009 at more than a dozen hubs including Detroit, Dallas-Ft. Worth, New York-JFK, Madrid-Barajas, Munich-Franz Strauss, Toronto-Pearson, Paris-Charles de Gaulle, Singapore-Changi, and Beijing Capital International. The new terminal in Beijing – Terminal 3 – is the world's largest and was opened a few months before Beijing hosted the 2008 Summer Olympics. The terminal was meant to impress and to judge by coverage in the world press, it did.

In Beijing and beyond, new airports and new terminals are symbols of cities, regions, and countries that have "arrived." Thus, the newest airports tend to be spectacular architectural achievements crafted by the world's most talented minds or what geographer Kris Olds (1995) calls the "global intelligence corps." Beijing's Terminal 3 for instance was designed by Norman Foster + Partners, the London-based firm whose work spans the globe.

That mere functionality is not the point of new airports is most evident where they meet the sky. At Detroit and dozens of other new and expanded airports across the globe, terminal departure halls soar upward to vast roof structures. The high ceilings within the terminal let in abundant daylight, avoiding the "horrible subterranean experience" of some older airports (quoted in Rowe 2006). And vast rooflines create a sense of grandeur and can serve as a kind of airport signature. Indeed, a terminal's exterior roofline is often its most defining feature, from the billowing white tent-like structures atop Denver International to the gentle metallic swells of Kansai to the rolling waves of Madrid-Barajas. Airports may be places where one is particularly likely to feel "placelessness" (Gottdiener 2001: 59–61), but in major hubs, airport designers and architects have sought for decades to craft memorably striking places.[3]

Yet even in remote towns such as Turpan that are far from the nerve centers of the airborne world, airports – even plain ones – are potentially important in putting places on the map in a world made richer in opportunity but also more ruthlessly competitive by globalization.

Globalization and the topography of the airborne world

The first reference to "globalization" in the *New York Times*[4] was in a 1974 article about multinational companies. The term did not reappear until 1981. For

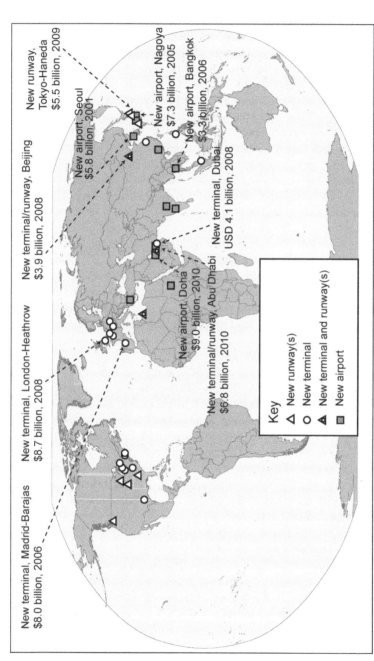

New terminal, Madrid-Barajas
$8.0 billion, 2006

New terminal, London-Heathrow
$8.7 billion, 2008

New terminal/runway, Beijing
$3.9 billion, 2008

New runway,
Tokyo-Haneda
$5.5 billion, 2009

New airport, Seoul
$5.8 billion, 2001

New airport, Nagoya
$7.3 billion, 2005

New airport, Bangkok
$3.3 billion, 2006

New terminal, Dubai
USD 4.1 billion, 2008

New airport, Doha
$9.0 billion, 2010

New terminal/runway, Abu Dhabi
$6.8 billion, 2010

Key
△ New runway(s)
○ New terminal
▲ New terminal and runway(s)
▣ New airport

Figure 10.3 Significant airport infrastructure projects, 2001–2010 (sources: contemporary media accounts).

All of the depicted projects cost at least $500 million and were either completed between 2001 and 2008 or were scheduled for completion in 2009 or 2010. The ten most expensive projects are labeled.

the whole of the 1980s, there were 155 articles mentioning globalization. The total rose to 797 in the 1990s and 1,568 between 2000 and 2005 alone. And it was in 2005 that perhaps the most celebrated account of globalization, Thomas Friedman's *The World Is Flat*, was first published. The book's title refers to the fact that a host of new technologies, such as the Internet, the personal computer, wireless communications, and work flow software have "flattened" the world so that a person or company in India (or some other part of the developing world) can compete on a level playing field with a person or company in the US or Japan or Europe. While flattening the world, these same technologies have also shrunk the world, according to Friedman, from size "large" five centuries ago to size "tiny" today (Friedman 2006: 9–11).

Oddly, transportation technologies play almost no role in Friedman's account of the flat world; yet air transportation in particular has never been more important as this book has tried to make clear. Air transportation especially is a crucial means of reconciling the apparent contradiction (Schoenberger 1994) between production systems fragmented on a global basis (e.g., in the case of a Dell laptop sold worldwide and assembled from dozens of widely sourced components) and the new urgency of time-based competition. And the global collaboration among individuals and businesses that Friedman celebrates as the signal feature of the flat world has stimulated a huge expansion in business traffic. Friedman himself doubtless piled up a lot of frequent flyer miles jetting around the world visiting the corporate chieftains whose insights and exploits are integral to *The World Is Flat*.

One reviewer (Ikenberry 2005: 167) of Friedman's book caustically quipped that the world is not flat; it just looked that way from a business class seat. At ground level, the world is much more "spiky" (Florida 2005). A relative handful of city-regions are overwhelmingly important, particularly with respect to the geography of innovation. They are the "peaks" that tower over the "valleys" of languishing areas struggling to attract and retain jobs, talent, and investment. The world may seem flatter because the dynamic hotbeds of creativity are more dispersed (with the addition of cities such as Shanghai and Mumbai) and better connected than in the past. And space has been warped in a fashion as the peaks are often better connected to one another than to nearby, less dynamic hinterlands.

So the world may have shrunk but not in an even fashion. Hubs, such as New York and Tokyo, move towards one another faster in terms of time-space than less important places. In this regard, there is an important difference between the new communications technologies Friedman highlights and the older, but still critically important, transportation technologies he largely ignores. Cell phone service, for instance, is widely available across vast swaths of the developing world that lie far from any airport, much less one that is well-connected to global airline networks.

The places that *are* well-connected tend to rank high in the hierarchy of world cities, the command and control centers from which the global economy is run. World cities are home to corporate headquarters and to specialized producer services in fields such as advertising, banking and finance, law, and accounting. Although world cities are fixed in space, their importance derives primarily from movement – that is, from their advantageous position in the networks over which flow people, goods, ideas, information, and money. Airline networks mediate those flows, and, therefore, geographers, sociologists, and other social scientists have used the flows of airline passengers (Smith and Timberlake 1995; Shin and Timberlake 2000; Smith and Timberlake 2001; Matsumoto 2004), air cargo (Matsumoto 2004), scheduled flights (Bowen 2002), and air travel times and costs (Zook and Brunn 2006) to gauge the stature of cities in the world. A handful of favored places consistently emerge near the top of the hierarchy of cities, especially London.

The results of the Zook and Brunn (2006) study are especially interesting because they demonstrate that cities with advantageous positions in airline networks enjoy enormous accessibility advantages. They are easy to get to both in terms of time and money. The two geographers used an Internet-based airline reservations system to find flights from 25 hubs to each of over 200 hundred cities across to the world. London scored well in both the average time (18 hours and 25 minutes) and average cost ($673) from the other 24 hubs. Conversely, Bissau, the capital of Guinea-Bissau suffered daunting disadvantages in both dimensions with an average time (54 hours and 30 minutes) and average cost ($5,701). The disparity in these measures attest to the unevenness of time-space (and cost-space) convergence and show that, in terms of air travel, the world is not yet flat.

Because air transportation is so important, uneven access within the world's airline networks has far-reaching implications. Friedman's Dell laptop (described in greater detail in Chapter 9) is no more a flat earth computer than the Boeing 787 is a flat earth airplane. Both companies have established global production networks whose architecture reflects the advantages of particular places across the world and among those advantages is accessibility in the airborne world.

The enduring importance of physical transportation makes the world larger than Friedman allows. And that means that inequality between places persists and may even deepen, and that the uneven topography of the air transportation accessibility helps to make it so. In Southeast Asia, for instance, Singapore's gross national product per capita was 4 times higher than that of Malaysia and 15 times higher than that of Indonesia in 1984; by 2006, the corresponding figures were 5 times and 20 times. Singapore has moved further ahead for many reasons, but among these is the superior accessibility of Changi Airport.

The world is, after all, not flat; nor is it tiny. Although we are no longer trapped within the visible horizon, most of everyday life and certainly most of the economy, which is Friedman's focus, is confined to a horizon defined by a few hours flying. It is worth noting that in 2008 more than 70 percent of jet-operated scheduled flights were domestic (author's analysis of data in OAG 2008). The persistent importance of short connections (and of localized economic activity) gives an enduring advantage to places that are in or near affluent regions and sustains the disadvantage of places that are not.

Engines of prosperity

The links from an airport – whether they are short-haul or long-haul – to the rest of the world amplify the economic impact of air transportation upon local and regional economies. More specifically, air transportation accessibility is often a catalyst for new forms of economic development in favored communities. Those catalytic effects will be discussed more fully below but first it is worth briefly reviewing three other categories of economic effects that airports have upon their environs: direct, indirect, and induced (A. Graham 2003: 204–16).

Direct effects include the thousands of workers employed at airports themselves, by airport operators, airlines and handling agents, air traffic control agencies, freight forwarders, concessionaires, and so on. In one selection of European and North American airports, the number of direct jobs was about a thousand per million passengers per annum, although the actual number varied widely. World-wide, it was estimated that nearly 3.5 million people worked at airports in 2001 (A. Graham 2003: 207, 211).

Indirect effects and induced effects are a step removed from actual airport operations. The former are generated by the expanded business with the suppliers to an airport and its tenants; in other words, indirect effects are the result of backward linkages (Hakfoort *et al.* 2001). As the FedEx hub has grown in Memphis, for instance, so has the company's local spending on everything from janitorial services to jet fuel. Induced effects, on the other hand, are produced by the spending of those who work for airports and for airport suppliers. Essentially, induced effects are the result of forward linkages from the airport. Major hubs employ tens of thousands of people – the equivalent of a small city, a city which typically has its own supermarkets, drug stores, and the like.

The balance among these three categories of jobs depends on the city studied, the size of the area studied, and the structure of the local economy beyond the airport's gates (Hakfoort *et al.* 2001). In a selection of studies from Europe, however, the multiplier relating the number of indirect and induced jobs combined to direct jobs was almost always greater than 2.0. Suffice to say that the direct, indirect, and induced employment of airports globally amounts to something on the order of ten million and that that number is growing quite rapidly.

Direct, indirect, and induced effects describe the economic impact of any enterprise, not just an airport. A steel mill, a Wal-Mart, and an ice cream shop also have these effects – though in widely varying magnitudes. What sets an airport apart is the magnitude of the catalytic effects it may engender. Airports fundamentally alter the accessibility of the places they serve, warping the fabric of space and conferring an important advantage to favored locations – an advantage that has grown more important with the globalization of economic activity. In terms of employment, catalytic effects refer to the jobs created because of the increased reach and reduced transportation costs of businesses located in an airport's hinterland.

Catalytic effects are not easy to measure. In a mid-1990s study of several air freight hubs (Memphis, Louisville, and Cincinnati), two techniques were used to measure the broader effects of expanded hub employment in order to assess the likely impact of FedEx plans for a bigger hub at Indianapolis[5] (Oster *et al.* 1997). The differences in results are important and have to do with the catalytic effects of airports, especially hub airports. The first approach, input-output modeling, found that the employment multiplier for the air transportation sector in these cities was a little more than two, meaning that for every job added in the air transportation sector (e.g., at the FedEx hub), another indirect or induced job would be created too. The second approach, econometric modeling, found much higher multipliers. In the case of Memphis, for instance, the multiplier of 3.75 meant that for every air transportation job, an estimated 2.75 additional indirect or induced jobs would be created. Why the difference? Input-output analysis is based on a static picture of a regional economy. It often fails to account for the way in which an improved transportation system alters the economic structure of a region. To take a specific example, input-output analysis essentially assumes that the relationship between employment at a community's airport and at its restaurants will hold steady over time; but as FedEx hub grew in Memphis the relationship between the hub and the city's restaurant industry changed. Along with the usual patronage of eateries by FedEx employees, a new dimension emerged as some of the city's famed barbecued ribs restaurants began shipping nationally overnight via FedEx from satellite kitchens near the airport.

The catalytic effects of airports are magnified, of course, at the airline industry's great hubs. Certainly the world's busiest airport, Atlanta Hartsfield-Jackson, has had a profound impact upon the economy of the metropolitan area that surrounds it. Once, Atlanta vied with Birmingham, Alabama, for primacy in the South (Massey 1988). In the nineteenth century, Birmingham had the advantage of abundant nearby iron ore, coal, and limestone to fuel its rise as an iron and steel powerhouse after the Civil War. It became the "Pittsburgh of the South." Atlanta had the advantage of transportation access. Antebellum Atlanta, which was larger than Birmingham, had been one of the few southern cities with rail lines extending both east-west and north-south. After the Civil War, the two cities both grew as the South slowly recovered from its defeat, but Birmingham grew faster so that its population in 1930 was only slightly smaller than that of its rival to the east. And for a time, Birmingham seemed to enjoy brighter prospects in the evolving US air transport networks. Even in the 1950s, Eastern Air Lines experimented for a time with a minihub at Birmingham to draw traffic away from Delta's dominant operation at Atlanta (Braden and Hagan 1989: 37, 126). By then, however, Atlanta's importance an air hub was secure; and that importance was high among the factors that propelled Atlanta to the first tier among southern cities – along with Dallas-Ft. Worth, Houston, and Miami, all of which are also top airline hubs and gateways. By 2000, Atlanta's metropolitan population was 4.2 million, more than four times that of metropolitan Birmingham. It is not simply Atlanta's population that has grown rapidly. The city's economy has expanded smartly, too, partly due to its airline accessibility.

Corporate headquarters comprise one dimension of the Atlanta economy that has grown with its airport. In fact, Atlanta ranks in the top ten metropolitan areas in the US in terms of Fortune 1000 headquarters (Table 10.2). Many firms based in Atlanta are homegrown, of course, like Coca Cola; but others have been drawn to Atlanta partly by its air services. Ironically, one of the enterprises to call the city home is UPS. Although Louisville is the main operational hub for the integrator, it moved its headquarters from suburban New York to Atlanta in 1991 because housing costs in its former Greenwich, Connecticut, home were repelling potential employees and because Atlanta gave the company easy access to the rest of the world.

More generally, air travel, particularly the advent of inexpensive jet travel, permitted the centralization of headquarters functions, making fewer cities bigger winners, and it is no surprise that corporate headquarters are concentrated in airline hubs (Irwin and Kasarda 1991; Ivy *et al.* 1995; Debbage 1999; Debbage and Delk 2001). Another interesting relocation example from the US concerns the paper and consumer products manufacturer Kimberly-Clark. Until

Table 10.2 Fortune 1000 headquarters and airline hubs in the US, 2006

Metropolitan area	Population (thousands)	Fortune 1000 headquarters	Airline hub, focus city, or international gateway
New York-N. New Jersey-Long Island, NY–NJ–PA	18,323	115	CO, B6, DL
Chicago–Naperville–Joliet, IL–IN–WI	9,098	59	AA, UA, WN
Houston–Sugar Land–Baytown, TX	4,715	48	CO, WN
Dallas–Fort Worth–Arlington, TX	5,162	43	AA, WN
Los Angeles–Long Beach–Santa Ana, CA	12,366	38	AA, UA, WN
Minneapolis–St. Paul–Bloomington, MN–WI	2,969	33	NW
San Jose-Sunnyvale–Santa Clara, CA	1,736	32	–
Philadelphia–Camden–Wilmington, PA–NJ–DE–MD	5,687	29	US
San Francisco–Oakland–Fremont, CA	4,124	29	UA, WN
Atlanta-Sandy Springs–Marietta, GA	4,248	27	DL, FL
Washington–Arlington–Alexandria, DC–VA–MD–WV	4,796	22	UA
St. Louis, MO–IL	2,969	21	–
Boston–Cambridge–Quincy, MA–NH	4,391	20	–
Detroit–Warren–Livonia, MI	4,453	20	NW
Cleveland–Elyria–Lorain, OH	2,148	18	CO
Bridgeport–Stamford–Norwalk, CT	883	17	–
Cincinnati–Middletown, OH–KY–IN	2,010	16	DL
Denver–Aurora, CO	2,179	16	UA, WN
Columbus, OH	1,583	15	–

Source: based in part on data available in CNN Money 2006.

Notes
AA = American Airlines, B6 = jetBlue Airways, CO = Continental Airlines, DL = Delta Air Lines, FL = AirTran, NW = Northwest Airlines, UA = United Airlines, US = US Airways, WN = Southwest Airlines

the mid-1980s, the company was based in tiny Neenah, Wisconsin. The paucity of air services in northeastern Wisconsin inspired the papermaker to set up its own airline in 1983, out of which evolved Milwaukee-based Midwest Airlines; but in 1985, Kimberly-Clark, which has no stake in the airline today, decided to move its headquarters to Irving, Texas, a Dallas suburb immediately adjacent to Dallas-Ft. Worth International Airport.

To some degree, the link between accessibility and headquarter operations boils down to a chicken-and-egg question: does the concentration of headquarters jobs in a city generate the traffic that behooves airlines to increase the number of flights there and the number of cities to which it is connected or does better air accessibility attract headquarters jobs? Of course, the relationship works in both directions; but at least one study (Ivy *et al.* 1995) found that the second direction (i.e., accessibility drawing jobs) was stronger. The success of cities such as Atlanta and Dallas in attracting headquarters from other, smaller cities substantiates that finding.

Airline accessibility is not just catalytic for the growth of headquarters functions. In his book *The Work of Nations*, economist and former US Labor Secretary Robert Reich (1991) identifies good air accessibility and a large university as catalysts for what he terms symbolic-analytic work – that is jobs that involve using sophisticated knowledge to solve problems and set strategies. Countries, regions, and cities with more jobs of this sort prosper in the contemporary global economy; and Reich (1991: 238–9) writes,

> So important are these public amenities, in particular the university and the airport, that their presence would stimulate some collective symbolic-analytic effort on parched desert or frozen tundra. A world-class university and an international airport combine the basic rudiments of global symbolic analysis – brains and quick access to the rest of the world.

Reich's contention has been corroborated by one study (Button and Taylor 2000) which found that employment in the "New Economy" (i.e., knowledge-intensive, fast growth sectors) employment grew more rapidly in US cities with better international access to Europe, specifically. The study found that an increase in the number of European destinations served by nonstop flights from an American city from three to four would result, all other things being equal, in an increase of about 1,150 New Economy jobs.

New Economy jobs are not associated solely with passenger travel, however. Cities with superior air cargo access have also benefited significantly. The concentration of domestic and international services provided by FedEx in Memphis has attracted dozens of other businesses (SRI International 2001: Chapter 5). GlaxoSmithKline and Pfizer Pharmaceutical, for instance, both operate large facilities in Memphis. The hundreds of jobs they have created are not in research and development, of course; but supply chain management – a fast-growing, knowledge-intensive activity in its own right – is very much a part of the New Economy.

The lengthening of the shipping day is a special advantage for Louisville and Memphis. In the case of FedEx, for instance, the deadline for accepting packages for next-business-day delivery is four hours later in Memphis than spoke-city Minneapolis; and if customers themselves drop of their packages at a FedEx office, the deadline is as late as midnight (Rosenbloom 2001). In order to take advantage of this late-night window of opportunity, companies like Nike and Hewlett-Packard have set up distribution centers in Memphis as have many smaller businesses including, for example, a New York City-based document printer whose Memphis operation caters to corporate clients nationwide whose own in-house copy centers shut down at 5:00 p.m. Not for nothing does the sign near Memphis International proclaim "Welcome to Memphis – America's Distribution Center" (Lappin 1996).

It is these larger effects of a hub that make capturing one so attractive to a city. Some local critics of the FedEx hub at Greensboro, North Carolina, where the express giant was to open a new national hub in 2009 or 2010, disparaged the jobs to be created as mainly modestly paid, third-shift positions. Perhaps – although it is worth noting that employment with FedEx was so highly sought after in Memphis in the 1990s that some of the company's buildings bore no corporate logos to avoid being besieged by job-seekers (Lappin 1996). FedEx will employ hundreds in Greensboro directly, but the local economic impact will far exceed the jobs in the FedEx hub itself. Many will be high-paying, daytime jobs. In a world competing on time, cities with well-connected airports are a step ahead.

Of course not all links are equal; long-haul, international flights have a greater economic impact and some cities are willing to heavily subsidize such connections. In 2009, the Port of Portland, Oregon made a one-time cash payment of $3.5 million to Delta Air Lines in order to sustain Delta's nonstop service from the city's airport to Tokyo (Millman and Esterl 2009). Pittsburgh offered a more complex set of financial inducements to get the same airline to begin nonstop services between Pittsburgh International and Paris. Incentives like these make sense for small- and mid-sized cities given the well-documented economic value of international accessibility (Button and Taylor 2000; InterVISTAS-ga2 2006). At the Port of Portland, for instance, the city estimated the daily Tokyo flight generates $61.2 million in annual local economic impacts (Millman and Esterl 2009).

Advent of the aerotropolis

The increased importance of aviation has not just fostered new development in favored cities; it has also altered the nature of urban development in many hubs, creating what sociologist John Kasarda calls an "aerotropolis." Kasarda (2000) coined the term to describe the airport-oriented commercial districts that have emerged around major hubs. It is in these districts that the direct, indirect, induced, and catalytic effects of airports are maximized. Often, these aerotropoli have sprung up along the corridors connecting central business districts to airports that were deliberately located far away to minimize the clash with neighboring land uses.

In Kasarda's conception (Kasarda 2005), an aerotropolis comprises a series of rings centered on a hub airport. The inner ring is blanketed by distribution centers, logistics complexes, and just-in-time manufacturers – all businesses feeding and fed by high-speed supply chains. The next ring has a more cerebral feel – office parks, research labs, corporate headquarters, and the like. These functions need the long-range accessibility afforded by a well-served airport, but also the space, quiet, and local accessibility permitted by a location not immediately adjacent to the airport. This second ring is also home to hotels, convention centers, and other businesses catering to the ring's office workers. The third ring is largely residential, home to those who work at and near the airport. Cutting across these rings are aerolanes – multi-lane highways and high-speed rail systems providing access to the airport's hinterland.

Kasarda (2000) described "aerotropoli" such as the 42-kilometer corridor from Dulles International Airport to Washington, DC, where such "new economy" titans as America Online have established their corporate headquarters and the region around Amsteram's Schiphol Airport where, at a least a decade ago, land near the airport was the most valuable in the metropolitan area. On the other side of the world, many of the aerotropolis elements are evident in the area surrounding Changi Airport in Singapore, though not necessarily in Kasarda's idealized ring and aerolane formation (Figure 10.4).

New aerotropoli are taking shape. Consider the case of Denver. When it opened, Denver International seemed far from Denver itself, particularly compared to the airport it replaced. DIA's distance provided room for growth and minimized the clashes with neighbors that have stymied airport projects elsewhere. Yet in placing the airport so far from the city, a corridor was created, a corridor which a decade after DIA opened was on its way to becoming a vibrant axis of development (Davidson 2006). Before the new airport opened, new development in the Denver metropolis was primarily toward burgeoning suburbs to the city's south and toward the mountains in the west. Now the roads leading to the airport in the east are lined with massive new construction projects. Developments encompassing 35,000 acres and worth $20 billion were underway in 2006, including a large airport-adjacent retail site and a master-planned community that will ultimately have 12,000 homes. The DIA Partnership, an economic development advocacy group, envisions the DIA becoming the growth engine for the "greatest airport-centered region in the world." (Davidson 2006: 20).

Denver will have a bevy of rivals for that distinction. Dubai for one. As noted in Chapters 6, 8, and 9, the aerial ambitions of Dubai and its hometown carrier Emirates are boundless, and the new Al Maktoum International Airport has been developed specifically with its future potential as an aerotropolis in mind (Lindsay 2006). Similarly, Kuala Lumpur International Airport (KLIA) was designed from the outset as one anchor of a development corridor stretching to the north through former palm oil plantations to the city of Kuala Lumpur. The region around KLIA is just one of several aerotropoli that have recently taken shape in Asia. The speed of the region's economic growth, the development

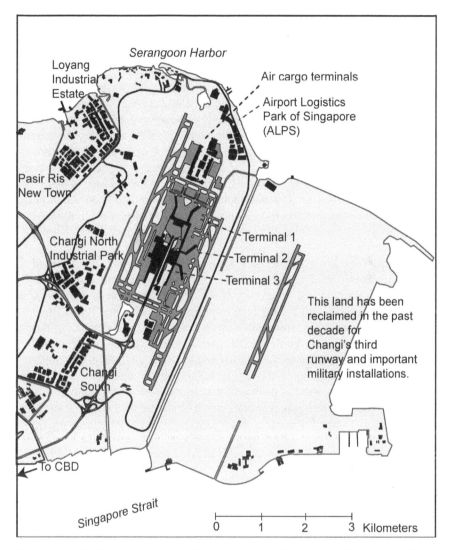

Figure 10.4 The Singapore aerotropolis (sources: based in part on information available at Streetdirectory 2008).

Development near Changi has been strongly influenced by the airport since it opened in 1980 (see *Figure 3.4*). The Airport Logistics Park of Singapore (ALPS), Changi South and Changi North contain distribution centers (DCs) operated by many of the world's leading logistics firms, including DHL, UPS, and Schenker. The Loyang area, meanwhile, contains light manufacturing and distribution operations for some high-tech, air freight-dependent firms, such as Photronics, a manufacturer of photo masks used in the semiconductor industry. Farther from the airport are some residential areas including the sprawling Pasir Ris New Town.

orientation of Asian governments, the newness of so many of its major airports, and the construction of those airports on distant, "virgin" ground have made the region fertile ground for the aerotropolis.

For existing airports, especially those close to the cities they serve, it is much more difficult for a well-coordinated aerotropolis to form. Often, several different communities with conflicting aspirations and zoning laws are involved. And existing development may confound the neat circular zones in Kasarda's aerotropolis. Still, there is abundant evidence that, however haphazardly, the aerotropolis or something like it is becoming more common. Consider the case of Dallas-Ft. Worth. As noted in Chapter 7, the distance of Dallas-Ft. Worth from Dallas was so great it created an advantage for Southwest Airlines, which served the much closer Love Field. Yet in the decades since, the distance to Dallas-Ft. Worth has been filled in with development, and communities in the airport's shadow are thriving. For example, seven Fortune 1000 firms are headquartered in nearby Irving, including ExxonMobil and the aforementioned Kimberly-Clark.

Moreover, some beleaguered older cities, including Detroit, have latched on to the aerotropolis idea as a means of rejuvenation (Lindsay 2006). It is too early to tell how easily this new urban form can be fit atop the existing palimpsest of development in such cities. And even in places like Dubai and Kuala Lumpur, the full realization of the aerotropolis vision is contingent upon a host of factors (Charles *et al.* 2007). In particular, the aerotropolis is dependent on relatively inexpensive oil. Furthermore, the centrality of aviation in the contemporary economy is subject to many threats, including airline terrorism and environmental taxes. Finally, most of the world's trade continues to move on the ground and at sea; and, to the degree that that remains true, the importance of the aerotropolis will be limited. I return to these constraints on aviation's future in the final two chapters.

The airport business

The aerotropolis is about the emergence of airports as commercial centers increasingly autonomous of the cities they serve. That transformation is often evident even before leaving the airport property. For example, Seoul's new airport (Incheon International, which like several other new Asian airports is built in part on reclaimed land) has a 12,000 square meter shopping mall, while the gateway to Kuala Lumpur has a golf course, Formula One track, cinema, and a shooting range (A. Graham 2003: 145). The abundance of retail space typified by these new Asian airports is not just an Asian phenomenon but it is new. Until World War II, retail activity in airports everywhere was largely limited to restaurants, often featuring an expansive view of the tarmac and runways (Pearman 2004: 54). The postwar development of duty-free shops diversified the range of retail activities modestly, emphasizing cigarettes and liquor – "sinful" products normally subject to heavy import duties but compact enough to be easily carried away by departing or arriving international passengers. The first airport duty-free shop was opened at Shannon in 1947 to lure passengers on refueling North Atlantic flights to spend time and money shopping at the airport (A. Graham 2003: 158).

Today, retail activity at top airports extends far beyond duty-free sales of liquor and cigarettes. In the United Kingdom, the total retail space in 2002 at the seven United Kingdom airports then owned by BAA (formerly the British Airport Authority, now simply known as BAA), including Heathrow and Gatwick, was 100,000 square meters, up from about 40,000 in 1990 (A. Graham 2003: 169). To put these figures into context, a typical American Wal-Mart Supercenter has about 17,000 square meters of retail space. A similar trend has taken hold at airports in other advanced economies, although the US lagged behind Europe in seizing upon the potential market represented by the tens of thousands of passengers and airport employees who pass through even a modest hub daily. In fact, a key spur to the 1990s expansion of retail space in American airports was BAA's development of the AirMall at Greater Pittsburgh International Airport. The mall, featuring 100 outlets and many brand name retailers, opened in 1992; and its success encouraged copycat developments elsewhere (Vinella 2007).

Retail sales comprise only one slice of the non-aeronautical activities at leading airports. The others, such as car rentals and parking, are less interesting but often generate more revenue for the airport operator. Overall, non-aeronautical activities contribute a much higher share of income than even a decade ago. BAA, for instance, generated approximately 70 percent of its revenue from non-aeronautical activities in 2000 (A. Graham 2003: 171). The increased non-aeronautical contribution is crucial because airports are under great pressure from airlines, in a more competitive deregulated industry, to hold the line on landing fees and other aeronautical charges.

The relationship between airlines and airports has grown more complex for a variety of reasons. First, deregulation has not just amplified the downward pressure on fares and concomitantly on airport charges. It has also made the airline industry more dynamic. Airports can harness that dynamism to achieve rapid traffic growth. Baltimore-Washington International Thurgood Marshall Airport nearly doubled its passenger traffic volumes in the 1990s largely as a result of the rapid build up of Southwest Airlines' presence from eight flights a day in 1993 to 168 flights a day in 2006 (Davenport 2006). But the dynamism of the industry can hurt, too, as Pittsburgh's experience shows. US Airways, which long operated its largest hub at the airport, played a leading role in the design of its billion-dollar midfield terminal which opened in 1992. At the carrier's insistence, the terminal was made much larger than originally planned (75 gates instead of 50). When US Airways sank deeper into its financial funk, however, the airline began downsizing its hub operation. By 2007, the terminal was handling fewer than 5 million passengers per year, far short of the 32 million for which it was designed (Pittsburgh International Airport, no date; Reed 2005). The very long lead time in the airport business exacerbates the risk of such misplaced investments.[6]

Second, airports compete more fiercely than in the past. New airports, upgraded airports, and decommissioned military airfields have increased the number of gateways to many regions. And deregulation, both at the domestic and international scales, has increased the flexibility of carriers – and indirectly passengers and freight shippers – to choose the airports they serve. Low-cost carriers (LCCs), by building up services at secondary airports, have increased the number of metropolitan regions served by multiple gateways and have increased the number of gateways in regions that already had more than one airport. As noted in Chapter 7, in some metropolitan regions LCCs have favored the use of smaller, more distant airports in order to avoid the high costs and congestion of more conventional gateways. And some of the airports that have attracted LCCs display the same hungry aggressiveness of the airlines that now call them home. In Belgium, for instance, Charleroi Airport, located 55 kilometers south of Brussels used a variety of inducements – including payments for each new route started – to encourage Ryanair to increase its presence there (A. Graham 2003: 191–2). The incentives worked because the LCC, having started off at Charleroi with just two daily flights to Dublin in 1997, later made the airport its first continental base. By 2008, about 160 Ryanair flights per day linked Charleroi to 26 European cities (Figure 10.5). Although the European Commission ruled in 2004 that some of the incentives Ryanair had received from Charleroi and the Wallonia regional government were illegal (C. Baker 2004), the airport's place in the "New Europe" crafted by LCCs seems reasonably secure.

The case against the Charleroi incentives was brought before the European Commission by Charleroi's competitor, the main Brussels airport in Zaventum. The relationship between the two airports could hardly have been expected to be friendly after the one in Charleroi renamed itself the Brussels South Charleroi Airport (A. Graham 2003: 192). Other airports in Europe, including the rechristened Stockholm Skavsta and Paris Beauvais Tille Airport, have also adopted *noms de guerre* to capture larger hinterlands. On the other side of the Atlantic, Stewart International Airport became New York Hudson Valley International Airport, Rockford's airport became Chicago/Rockford International, and Savannah's was renamed Savannah/Hilton Head International (De Lollis 2006). Some might be surprised to learn that none of these three "International" airports in the US had any scheduled international passenger flights as late as 2008. But they hope to, and carefully chosen names are a part of the marketing campaign to achieve that longer-term goal.

A third basic change in the airport business is the privatization of airports themselves (A. Graham 2003: 8–18). Only two decades ago, virtually all airports were publicly owned by a local, regional, or national government, by a semiautonomous public authority, or by some combination of these. Airports were a public utility operated to provide an important service – part of the commanding heights of the economy firmly in control of the state. Yet in the 1970s, as discussed in Chapter 5, attitudes towards state intervention in the economy shifted. One result has been the commercialization of airports in many cases and privatization in a smaller number of cases. Britain led the way. In 1987, the same year shares were offered in BA, the British government also privatized BAA (A. Graham 2003: 17), which at the time operated the three principal London airports and four in Scotland.[7] In the years since, airport privatization has advanced further in Britain and Australia than in other countries but it is expected to become more common in the twenty-first century.

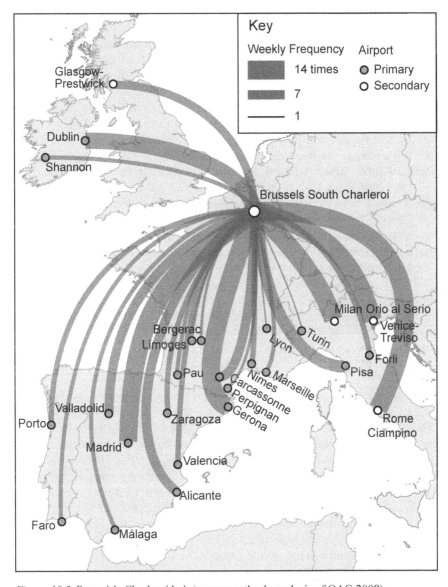

Figure 10.5 Ryanair's Charleroi hub (source: author's analysis of OAG 2008).

In 2008, Ryanair, which accounted for the great majority of passenger flights at the airport, linked Charleroi to points throughout Western Europe.

Meanwhile the airport industry has not only been partially privatized; it has also been globalized – though again to a more limited degree than is true of the airline business. For example, in 2007, Singapore-based Changi Airports International had a 50 percent share of a company called Alterra, which owned the main airports in Lima, Peru; San Jose, Costa Rica; and Curacao (CAAS 2007). Other airport operators, too, have spread their wings across the globe to bid for ownership stakes and management contracts far from their home markets.

To the degree that the privatization and globalization of the airport business spread and deepen, the relationship between airports and airlines will be further transformed from the staid practices of the past. Decades ago, airports and airlines alike tended to be state-owned enterprises relatively insulated from competition. Now, many airlines and, to a lesser extent, airports are intensely competitive, profit-oriented, international companies (A. Graham 2003: 132). Still, government remains a potent force in the airport business. The stakes are too high for the government to yield the airport business altogether to the vagaries of the market. As discussed earlier in this chapter, airports have enormous implications for urban, regional, and national economic development and governments want more than ever before to harness that power, even if it means working indirectly through privately owned companies. In the case of Britain, for instance, the national government has a strong interest in maintaining the primacy of London-Heathrow in European air transport networks regardless of the fact that the airport operator, BAA, is a private firm that was acquired by a Spanish construction company in 2006.

Further, airports remain lightning rods of controversy, and government retains an important obligation to manage the many costs of expanded air transportation. Indeed, although privatization has taken a handful of airports out of public ownership, it has not taken them out of public view – or earshot.

Noisy neighbor

No challenge for large airports is greater than the noise generated by ever more people and cargo taking wing. A report by the Airports Council International (ACI 2005: 2), observed, "Aircraft noise is the single major cause of community opposition to current operations and to airport capacity development to meet future traffic growth." More alarmingly, a 2002 *Flight International* story (Phelan 2002: 28) began, "Anger at airport noise is near boiling point." The report cited the 100 objections to the planned expansion of London-Stansted submitted per day in 2002 to British authorities (Phelan 2002). As noted in Chapter 9, opposition to aircraft noise was a key factor in the refusal of the Belgian government to meet DHL's demands for expanded night flying at its Brussels hub – a decision which led the express giant to base its European operation at Leipzig instead. Meanwhile on the other side of the Atlantic, planned airport expansions, including Boston-Logan, have inspired perennial opposition motivated primarily by concerns about noise; and more recently smaller airports too, such as Hanscom in suburban Boston, have become lightning rods for noise-inspired opposition (Andre 2004: 43–67).

The problem of aircraft noise is not new, of course. In the 1950s and 1960s, research done in a variety of fields showed that noise, despite its seemingly innocuous definition as any undesired sound, actually has serious health effects. Chronic exposure to elevated noise levels was linked, unsurprisingly, to deafness (particularly in the aged); but experiments with laboratory animals also showed effects ranging from higher cholesterol to increased susceptibility to infection (Berland 1970: 88–91). Noise could even kill: exposure to sounds greater than 150 to 160 dB was found to be fatal to some animals. For people exposed to aircraft noise, more specifically, there is weak evidence of cardiovascular effects and exacerbation of existing mental illnesses along with stronger evidence of sleep disruption and added stress and annoyance (POST 2003).

In response to the growing clamor to do something about aircraft noise in the 1960s, national governments responded with regulation. Aircraft noise has been addressed at the international level, too. Indeed, prodding the aircraft and airline industries to reduce noise has been perhaps the biggest achievement of the International Civil Aviation Organization (ICAO). ICAO rules govern the volume of acceptable noise produced on takeoff and landing by commercial aircraft. Noise is measured at three points: directly beneath an aircraft descending on approach, directly beneath an aircraft flying overhead on departure, and at a distance to the side of a departing aircraft. Although ICAO lacks the authority to enforce these standards worldwide, as a practical matter most countries and manufacturers follow its guidelines. For manufacturers, the convenience of having a single global set of standards to meet is, of course, substantial.

Spurred by ICAO and by national government regulation, airframe and aircraft engine manufacturers in conjunction with university researchers and government scientists at institutions such as the National Aeronautics and Space Administration (NASA) have made great strides (Table 10.3). The first step forward in reducing noise was the supplanting of the turbojet by the turbofan in the 1960s. The jet of hot gases expelled from a turbofan moves more slowly than that from a turbojet, producing less noise. The development of progressively higher bypass engines furthered this trend and its salutary effect. Turbofans developed in the 1990s were about 20 decibels quieter than the turbojets of the late 1950s. Because the decibel scale is logarithmic, the reduction means that a contemporary commercial jet is about one-fourth as loud as an early 707 (Garvey 2001).

Most airliners now flying meet what are called Chapter 3 noise standards, which ICAO adopted in 1978 for newly designed aircraft. As an example of these standards, a Boeing 747-400 is permitted to generate no more than 105 dB on approach to an airport. To put that number in perspective, a crying baby can pierce the air with 110 decibels. Older aircraft, like the Boeing 727-200, that were designed to meet less rigorous Chapter 2 standards continued to fly for years after the Chapter 3 standards went into effect. The US, for instance, began requiring their phase-out in 1995 but the process was only completed in 2003. In the interim, older aircraft were a leading cause of noise complaints at airports in developed economies. The Boeing 727, for instance, with its trademark triple-slotted parasol wing, is one of the noisiest commercial aircraft still flying. The

Table 10.3 Perceived noise of selected jetliners

	Aircraft	First delivery	Takeoff (EPNdB)[1]	Approach (EPNdB)
Mid-sized narrow-bodies	Boeing 737-200	1967	84–93	101–105
	Boeing 737-300	1984	84–87	100
	Airbus A320	1988	84–89	96–97
	Boeing 737-700	1997	80–87	96
Large narrow-bodies	Boeing 707-320	1959	114	120
	Boeing 757-200	1982	84–89	95–100
	Airbus A321	1993	82–90	95–98
	Boeing 737-900	2001	85–88	96
Large wide-bodies	Lockheed L-1011	1972	96–99	102–104
	Airbus A300 B4	1974	89–94	99–103
	Boeing 767-200	1982	84–93	96–102
	Airbus A330-300	1993	87–96	97–99
	Boeing 777-300	1998	88–94	99–101
Jumbos	Boeing 747-200	1972	100–110	103–108
	Boeing 747-400	1989	97–102	101–105
	A380	2007	96	101

Source: Rand Europe and Avioplan 2000.

Note
1 EPNdB = effective perceived noise decibels, a standard measure of aircraft noise.

global 727 fleet (counting only aircraft still in operation) numbered nearly 400 in 2008 (*Air Transport World* 2008c). Most were flown by cargo airlines, including more than 80 FedEx 727s fitted with the "hushkits" (*Air Transport World* 2008a).

Yet in the world's advanced economies, the overall reduction in noise achieved through the replacement of Chapter 2 by Chapter 3 aircraft has been enormous. One common way of measuring that effect is to consider the noise "footprint" on the ground. The footprint is the area contained within a noise contour line around an airport. Much like the isopleth lines that join points of common altitude on a topographical map, a contour line on a noise exposure map links all the points near an airport that are exposed to a common average daily noise level. And just as the lines on a topographical map fall away from mountain peaks towards the valleys below, the contours on a noise exposure map fall away from the airport. The contour most often highlighted in analyses of noise near airports is the one representing the 65-dB day-night level (DNL). The DNL measures the average noise exposure but it does so in a way that gives added weight to noises at night and to isolated, noisy events (GAO 1996). The significance of the 65 dB contour is that average noise levels higher than this threshold are normally considered incompatible with residential land uses, unless special soundproofing measures are taken. Improvements in aircraft engine technology have meant shrinking noise footprints, even with the overall expansion in air traffic (Figure 10.6).

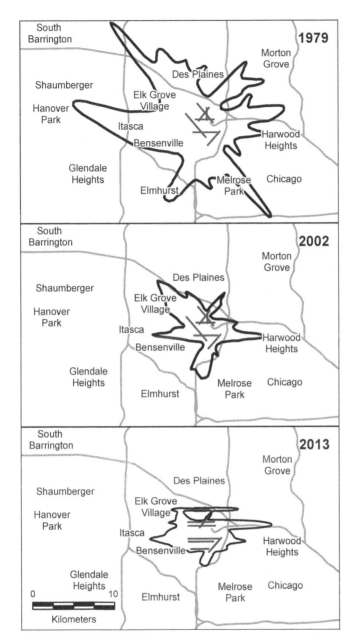

Figure 10.6 Changes in noise pollution and the runway configuration at O'Hare (sources: ONCC 2005; OMP 2006; figure drawn by David Cordner, Central Washington University).

If the O'Hare Modernization Program (OMP) is completed as planned, by 2013 the airport will have a new runway configuration organized mainly around six parallel runways. By then its noise footprint, as shown by the 65 decibel day-night level noise contour (see text for explanation) will be much smaller than a generation earlier due mainly to advances in aviation technology.

All of which begs the question: why is noise still such a contentious issue? Several factors explain its persistence (Cidell 2008). First, the improvement in noise has been gradual, making it harder to appreciate the strides made so far. Second, while the noise produced by individual arriving and departing airliners has certainly improved, there are so many more of them that the gains have been partly offset. Third, commercial air traffic has expanded robustly at many smaller airports that were once confined to general aviation. Fourth, the growth of the air cargo industry has increased nighttime operations, which are much more disruptive. Fifth, because airports are magnets of development, population in their vicinity has generally increased. Airports located specifically to be far from built-up areas in order to minimize their noise impact are increasingly surrounded by encroaching development. Sixth, increased prosperity in many countries has lifted millions into the middle- and upper-income classes that tend to be more concerned with noise pollution.[8] Seventh and finally, the issue of noise pollution is a highly technical one and the barrage of different measures, specialized terminology, and abbreviations with which the matter is discussed breed distrust and confusion. For example, one Minneapolis resident, referring to a map of noise contours for the Minneapolis-St. Paul International Airport said in a public hearing, "I saw the map, and the map is a lot of waves and things like that, which is completely beyond my understanding. All I know is that the planes fly in a straight line over my house." (quoted in Cidell 2008: 1213).

With the noise issue not subsiding, in 2001 ICAO took the next step with the approval of Chapter 4 standards. These new requirements, which went into effect in 2006 for newly designed aircraft, mandate an additional 10 dB cumulative improvement (adding together the flyover, sideline, and approach noise levels) versus the Chapter 3 standards. The A380, for instance, will easily meet these standards because the Superjumbo has a cumulative margin of nearly 20 dB under the Chapter 3 standards for an airplane of its size. In fact, the Chapter 4 standards have been criticized as being too easy to meet given the advance in aircraft engine and airframe technology.

Interestingly, turbofan engines have improved so markedly that airframes are responsible for a growing share of total aircraft noise. For example, the A340-500/600 airframe generates 2 dB more noise than the engines on approach to an airport (Phelan 2002). Slats and flaps are the primary source of noise on that airframe, while on the rival 777, flaps and the nose landing gear are the leading contributors. The airframe and especially the landing gear have been singled out in the effort to reduce the noise produced by the 787 (Laurenzo 2006). The expectations are high for the Dreamliner: it is projected, for instance, that no part of its 85-dB footprint will fall outside the perimeter of Heathrow Airport (Hawk 2005).

For its part, ICAO advocates what it calls a "balanced approach" in addressing the problem of aircraft noise. Land-use planning and management and noise abatement (e.g., soundproofing) can complement advances in airframe and aircraft engine technology. In Chicago, for instance, the city (which owns the airport) has spent hundreds of millions, raised through passenger facility charges and the federally funded Airport Improvement Program (AIP), to soundproof nearly 6,000 homes and more than 100 schools near O'Hare (ONCC 2005).

Longer-term solutions include new operational procedures. Continuous descent is particularly promising (Laurenzo 2006). In a conventional approach to landing, a jet descends in a series of steps; and while the plane is on an individual step, the pilot must apply power (i.e., generate more noise) to maintain a constant altitude. In a continuous descent approach, conversely, an airliner essentially glides from high altitude approaching the runway at a steeper angle and without any of the steady-altitude steps. The result is significantly less aircraft noise. However, continuous descent challenges the standard air traffic control operating procedure built up over decades and may not work well in the skies over the most congested airports – precisely where relief from noise is most needed.

The most dramatic solution to airport noise is to move. Concern about noise is one reason that Denver International Airport is twice the size of Manhattan; the runways are cocooned in an empty buffer zone from which no lawsuits are likely ever to emanate. And while noise was hardly the sole reason Hong Kong built its new airport on the far side of once-peaceful Lantau Island, there is no question that HKIA has radically reduced the number of people within the footprint of Hong Kong's gateway to the airborne world. Approximately 380,000 people lived within the 65-dB contour of the old Kai Tak airport, where screaming jumbo jets passed just above apartment buildings on their approach to the sole runway. Conversely, *no one* lived within the 65-dB contour of the new airport when it opened. Yet, as explained earlier in this chapter, both HKIA and DIA are nuclei for growing aerotropoli, meaning that development (e.g., the Hong Kong Disneyland Resort) and people are gravitating to these airports' immediate environs.

Keeping pace: development and delay in the airborne world

Traffic growth at places such as HKIA and DIA will augment both their positive and negative impacts upon the communities in which they are situated. Boeing, which – it should be conceded – has a stake in aiming high, predicts that over the period 2007 to 2026 air passenger and air freight traffic will grow at average annual rates of 5.0 and 6.1 percent, respectively (Boeing Company 2008a). If the company's numbers are right, then in fewer than two decades, the number people airborne at any one moment will more than double to roughly two million.[9] And, on average, about two airliners will take off and two will land somewhere in the world every second.

That this growth must be accommodated seems to be taken for granted almost everywhere, for now at least. The inevitability of air traffic is even written into US law. In her book *Take Back the Sky: Protecting Communities in the Path of Aviation Expansion*, Rae Andre notes that in the US, the Airport Noise and Capacity Act of 1990 (ANCA) provides federal funds for communities adversely affected by aircraft noise with this important proviso: *"Funds may not be used to encourage reduction in aircraft operations.*" (Andre 2004: 103, emphasis in original). Partly as a result of such pro-aviation policies in the US and elsewhere, capacity has barely kept pace with demand at many airports. One result is that on many routes across the US, for instance, travel times are substantially higher now than several decades ago (Table 10.4).

There are some relatively inexpensive information technology (IT) solutions to congestion. For instance, four-dimensional trajectories (4DT), used in the continuous descent approaches described earlier in this chapter, allow both greater predictability and flexibility in sequencing airport arrivals and departures. One benefit could be the ability to extract greater capacity from existing airport infrastructure. Specifically, 4DT could allow airports to interleave landings and take-offs on individual runways, boosting capacity by an estimated 15 percent at Heathrow for instance (Hughes 2008).

Still, IT solutions probably will not be enough to meet the need for space and time on the ground. And so we build. In a world whose most important form of freedom is mobility,[10] congestion is a kind of tyranny. Because that freedom is so highly prized, the transformation of the landscape (and airscape) continues with new airports, new terminals, new runways, and new rail lines and highways under construction worldwide. An important example is O'Hare. In 2006, more than 30 percent of flights arrived there late, easily the worst record for any of the top ten airports in the US. A key reason: all but one of O'Hare's seven runways intersected in the old configuration. So the airport is being reconfigured in one of the most expensive, complicated, and controversial airport infrastructure projects in the world. When it is finished, only three of the seven runways will intersect in the new plan, making the airport's layout more like Hartsfield-Jackson and Dallas-Ft. Worth (see Figure 10.6). Those who use the airport, especially the 60

Table 10.4 Fastest air travel times from New York, 1980 and 2008

	Travel time in hours and minutes[1]		
	1980	*2008*	*Change*
Boston	0:53	1:00	+0:07
Chicago	1:47	2:00	+0.13
Cleveland	1:13	1:25	+0:12
Dallas-Ft. Worth	2:50	3:35	+0:45
Detroit	1:17	1:50	+0:33
Los Angeles	4:45	5:50	+1:05
Miami	2:29	2:50	+0:21
Philadelphia	0:42	0:57	+0:15
San Francisco	5:00	6:00	+1:00
Washington, DC	0:47	1:02	+0:15

Source: author's analysis of OAG 1980, 2008.

Note

1 The times shown are the fastest scheduled air time for a morning departure from any New York airport to any airport in the indicated destination city.

percent of O'Hare passengers who transfer between flights there, will welcome the reductions in delays when the new runways and terminal are completed in 2013. Yet in defending the plan, its backers were at pains to point out that it will generate 200,000 *local* jobs and $18 billion in added activity to the *local* economy (OMP 2006, emphasis added) making more palatable the cost of the plan – $7 billion and the dislocation of nearly 200 businesses and 530 residences in adjacent communities (Newbart and Sweet 2005).

O'Hare is a crucial component in the machinery of the global airline industry, but it is hardly the only one to be overstressed. The US Federal Aviation Administration estimates that six large American airports will require additional capacity beyond what is currently planned by 2015 and an additional eight airports will fall short of required capacity by 2025 (Figure 10.7). Further, the FAA suggests that four metropolitan areas in the US may each need a new commercial airport by 2025: Atlanta, Chicago, Las Vegas, and San Diego (FAA 2007).

In Europe, too, the problem of delay is daunting. Eurocontrol, the European air traffic control authority, predicted that in a "business as usual" scenario, available airport capacity in 2025 would be unable to support 3.3 million forecasted instrument flight rule (IFR) movements; in other words, thousands of flights per day in Europe would not be able to take off and land when and where airlines would like (Eurocontrol 2006). The result will be some fairly substantial redrawing of airline networks in the region. Eurocontrol estimates, for instance, that London-Heathrow will fall from third place among European airports in terms of movements (behind Frankfurt and Paris-Charles de Gaulle) to sixth, as Madrid, Amsterdam, and Munich move in front.

Perhaps more than any other place, London illustrates the dilemmas surrounding the further development of air transportation. The five airports serving the metropolitan area together handle more passengers than any other city's airport system (Figure 10.8).[11] Yet the most important of the airports, Heathrow, already operates at 99 percent of the capacity afforded by its pair of runways. Accordingly, in early 2009, the British government announced that planning for a third runway could go forward, but the new runway can open only after a second runway is added at Stansted first and only if certain conditions are met. Specifically, Heathrow's third runway must not significantly increase the size of the area within the airport's 57-dB DNL noise contour, the added airside capacity must be complemented by new public transportation links on the ground to and from the airport, and the United Kingdom must be able to meet European Union air quality standards that become effective in 2010.

The runway and a new accompanying sixth terminal at Heathrow are not expected to be finished before 2015 at the earliest (DfT 2009). Meanwhile, a variety of interest groups have lobbied fiercely against the new runway and its effects upon the environment and airport-adjacent communities. Arrayed on the other side of the issue are those who emphasize the critical dependence of the British economy upon air transportation and the threat that limited air transportation capacity will undermine country's competitive advantage. Indeed, other European hubs, including Amsterdam-Schiphol and Paris-Charles de Gaulle,

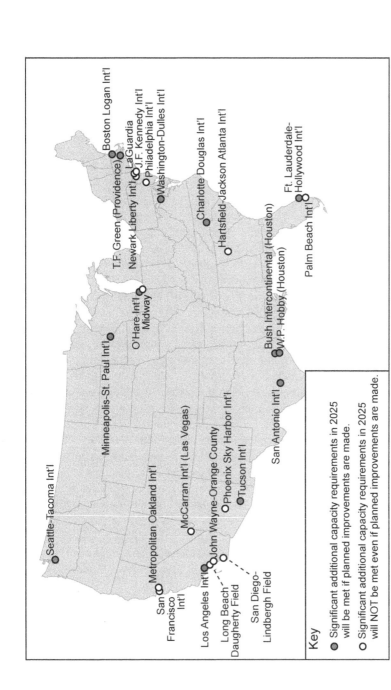

Figure 10.7 Capacity constrained US airports in 2025 (source: FAA 2007).

Twenty-seven airports will, according to Federal Aviation Administration forecasts require additional capacity in 2025, including all three of the major airports serving the New York City metropolitan area, both of Chicago's main airports, and three of the five main airports in metropolitan Los Angeles.

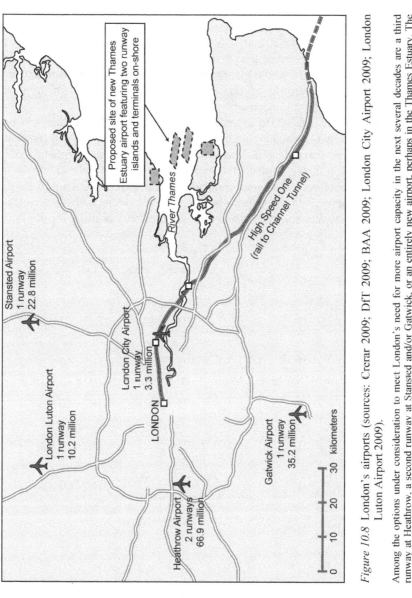

Figure 10.8 London's airports (sources: Crerar 2009; DfT 2009; BAA 2009; London City Airport 2009; London Luton Airport 2009).

Among the options under consideration to meet London's need for more airport capacity in the next several decades are a third runway at Heathrow, a second runway at Stansted and/or Gatwick, or an entirely new airport, perhaps in the Thames Estuary. The caption next to each airport indicates the number of primary runways in use and the number of passengers handled in 2008.

have begun to encroach upon Heathrow's own turf. In 2008, nonstop passenger service was available from Heathrow to just 9 British cities versus 15 (not including London) from Charles de Gaulle and 17 from Schiphol (OAG 2008).

If the third runway at Heathrow is not built, the government may instead authorize the construction of a second runway at Gatwick. For his part, the mayor of London, Boris Johnson, proposed building an entirely new airport east of the capital in the Thames Estuary (Crerar 2009). The concept has been judged less technologically demanding than the land reclamation done for several Asian airports (e.g., Kansai) and would place much of the airport's noise footprint over water. The site would also be beyond the main built-up area of the metropolis and on the "right" side of London with regard to air traffic flow.[12]

Deciding where, if at all, to expand London's airport infrastructure will be complicated and time-consuming. In the decades ahead, other cities will confront similar challenges. Particularly as liberalization spreads, as new airlines take off, and as incomes rise, the demand for more airport capacity will climb. In a growing number of countries, democratically elected governments are likely to deliberately choose *not* to keep pace. The blessings of airborne mobility are great but so are its costs, and the "predict and provide" mentality is losing favor.[13]

11 Dangers hidden in the air

The broader costs of the commercial aviation

The burdens of airborne freedom

Freedom has been a recurrent theme through this book and in the rhetoric of air transportation. For instance, the tagline in much of Southwest Airlines' advertising – "You are now free to move about the country." – plays upon the familiar announcement shortly after takeoff to evoke the possibilities opened up by low-cost air travel. Of course the freedom of the sky is not really free. The last few chapters have pointed to some of the costs that are not incorporated – or at least not fully incorporated – into airfares and cargo rates, especially low fares and rates.

In this penultimate chapter, we consider several kinds of costs not previously dealt with in the book: the security and health risks posed by the easier movement of people in an airborne world and the potential role of aviation in global climate change. Coping with these challenges will be a formidable challenge in aviation's second century and could reverse some of the changes in the speed and scope of everyday life brought by the first century.

Open skies vs. clean skies?

Aviation is a significant source of so-called greenhouse gases and therefore shoulders part of the blame for predicted climate change. In 1992, aviation accounted for an estimated 2 percent of anthropogenic carbon dioxide (CO_2) emissions; by comparison, road traffic contributes an estimated 18 percent. But CO_2 is only part of the story. Other greenhouse gases produced through the burning of aviation fuel (kerosene) include ozone and water vapor. The effects of all these gases are amplified by the fact that they are released at high altitude[1] (DfT 2003: 40). Overall, air transport was estimated to account for 3.5 percent of the greenhouse effect worldwide in 1992, but its contribution may quadruple by 2050 (IPCC 1999; Meikle 1999).

The forecasted increase in aviation's contribution is premised on rapid traffic growth. Certainly, recent expansion has raised the profile of air transportation as a factor in global climate change. The European Commission, for instance, asserts that carbon dioxide emissions from aviation in Europe grew 70 percent between 1990 and 2002 – a period of significant airline liberalization in that region. During the same 12-year span, total European carbon dioxide emissions fell, meaning that aviation became a larger factor in the production of this particular greenhouse gas (Paylor 2005).

In Europe and beyond, air pollution is beginning to rival noise as the top environmental issue related to commercial aviation (Paylor 2005). Fortunately, there are a variety of means via which the emissions of air transportation could be mitigated. To be sure technology is part of the answer. More fuel-efficient aircraft are also less air polluting aircraft. The long-term trend in aircraft technology has been towards greater fuel efficiency, but trimming fuel costs has been an especially important objective in the past decade or so. As noted in Chapter 4, the Airbus A380 and the Boeing 787 are both marvels of fuel efficiency by comparison with older airliners. The Superjumbo promises a 15 percent improvement in fuel efficiency over the 747-400; and a design criterion for the Dreamliner was a 20 percent fuel efficiency improvement over similar-sized aircraft.

The problem, of course, is that to the degree that airlines simply pass on their cost savings to passengers and shippers, the new aircraft will encourage further air traffic, which will offset at least partially the emissions improvement for individual aircraft (*Independent* 2005). Moreover, engine efficiency gains have begun to flatten out. A report in the industry trade journal *Aviation Week & Space Technology* (Wall and Barrie 2006) noted that recent engine efficiency improvements averaged about 1.5 percent per year but that traffic growth was about 5 percent per year.

There are other, partial technological fixes to the problem of emissions. One idea is to develop a hybrid jetliner, possibly by 2020 (*Economist* 2006a). Like a hybrid car, a hybrid aircraft would rely upon a mixture of engine technologies. Specifically, the auxiliary power unit (APU), a small gas-turbine engine that generates electricity for an airliner's lighting, air conditioning, pressurization, and other on-board electrical systems would be replaced by a fuel cell. The fuel cell, which generates electricity by combining fuel and oxygen, would be more efficient and produce substantially less pollution than a kerosene-burning APU. There is, however, no plan to replace an airliner's main engines with fuel cells. For the foreseeable future, the extremely concentrated, relatively easily tapped energy of refined petroleum products will power economically viable airliners.[2] This is a basic difference between air transportation and highway transportation. Both are significant polluters, but the latter is much more amenable to alternative, more environmentally friendly energy sources.

A promising "soft" technology to lighten aviation's burden is continuous descent (Harvey 2006). Changing the way that airliners approach airports, as described in Chapter 10, would not only mitigate aircraft noise and perhaps congestion; it would also reduce emissions. Continuous descent is only one way, however, in which air traffic control improvements could trim emissions. A new, more direct route linking China and Europe, for instance, saves 30 minutes per flight and 84,000 tonnes of CO_2 per year on the route (IATA 2007). The director-general and chief executive officer of the International Air Transport Association

(IATA), Giovanni Bisignani, has asserted that saving one minute per flight worldwide would save four million tonnes of CO_2 annually (or somewhat less than 5 percent of aviation's total CO_2 contribution) (Paylor 2005). Not coincidentally, saving one minute per flight would also save the airlines billions of dollars in fuel, labor, and other expenses.

So the airline industry has tried to leverage fear of global warming to win support for expanded airport infrastructure. Certainly, aircraft idling on taxiways or circling overhead awaiting runway landing slots account for significant "wastage." However, significant additions to infrastructure are likely to be slow, particularly in the most congested parts of the world.

While new technology and new infrastructure may be the airline industry's preferred avenues to achieve greenhouse gas reductions, the airline industry's regulators have focused on taxes, fees, and emissions trading schemes as means to the same objective. The basic idea is to use financial inducements to "make the polluter pay." The premise of such initiatives is that passengers and shippers do not now pay the full costs, particularly the environmental externalities, associated with air transportation; but how much more airlines and their customers should have to pay is hotly debated. Environmentalists point out that aviation fuel for international flights, in keeping with a decades-old agreement, is not taxed. In contrast, gasoline and diesel fuel are taxed, often heavily, in almost every country (Milner 2005). Is this disparity a subsidy for aviation? Not in the eyes of the industry trade journal *Airline Business*, which described air transport as "the world's favourite tax cow" (O'Toole 2005a). Taxes on a $200 roundtrip fare in the US already amounted to 26 percent in 2005, up from about 7 percent in 1972. The same article contended that taxes on aviation in the US already exceed "sin taxes" on cigarettes and hard liquor. Additionally, US carriers have been saddled with new security fees since the September 11, 2001 attacks. And in a number of other countries such as France and Brazil, aviation has been taxed (e.g., €1 per passenger in France) to raise development aid for poor countries (Butterworth-Hayes 2006a). Feeling besieged, air carriers are loathe to bear any new taxes.

Moreover, if the purpose of the tax were to discourage "unnecessary" travel, a percentage tax might have little effect. Growth in the industry is now led by the LCCs whose efficiency, including their efficiency in fuel use, enables them to offer fares so low that an additional 5 or 10 or 15 percent tax would still leave the fares low enough to draw millions of new travelers into the sky. Yet it is the LCCs that have been singled out for special criticism in discussions about the airline industry's environmental impact. LCCs account for a disproportionate share of growth in the airline industry (and therefore of its mounting environmental impact) and serve mainly short-haul routes where most of the journey is spent in fuel-thirsty ascent and descent and little at cruising altitude. For such journeys, rail – where available – is a far less polluting alternative.[3] The environmental lobby group Friends of the Earth, for instance, claimed in 2005 that a typical London to Edinburgh one-way trip by rail would generate 11.9 kilograms of CO_2 per passenger versus 96.4 kilograms by air (Garrahan 2005).

A flat per-passenger or per-kilogram fee might be better in that it would affect short-haul passengers and the LCCs more heavily. For precisely this reason, the LCCs argue that flat fees are unfair (Garrahan 2005). EasyJet, for instance, contends that it is wrong to levy a £5 duty on one of its passengers paying £10 for a flight and the same duty on someone paying £600 for a British Airways (BA) flight; but it is entirely possible, depending on the kind of aircraft involved and the characteristics of their respective journeys, that the air (and noise) pollution created by the easyJet passenger is greater than that of the BA passenger.

Ultimately, both flat fees and fuel taxes are blunt instruments with which to redress the environmental costs of air transportation. An emissions trading scheme (ETS) is a more precise and potentially more effective approach. The EU set up an ETS for CO_2 in several industries in 2005 as part of its commitment to the 1997 Kyoto Protocol on atmospheric emissions. In 2008, the Council of the European Union adopted a directive extending the ETS to aviation beginning in 2012 (Council of the European Union 2008). Specifically, overall emissions for European aviation will be capped at 95 percent[4] of the average for 2004–6. Emissions allowances will be parceled out by European national governments to carriers in two ways: the first 85 percent of the emissions allowance will be freely given based on historical patterns (e.g., carriers that were large in 2004–6 will given larger allowances), and the remaining 15 percent will be auctioned. Extra allowances will be made available in special circumstances, such as for new entrants in the industry. And of course carriers that need additional allowances to accommodate strong capacity growth will be permitted to trade with other, slower-growing carriers.

Not everyone is happy about the ETS plan. Some of the carriers in Europe's LCC sector see it as a constraint on their growth potential. Michael O'Leary of Ryanair dismissed the ETS enthusiasm of BA and other members of a sustainable aviation group formed in 2005. In *The Guardian*, O'Leary scoffed, "A lot of members of the sustainable aviation group won't be around in 10 years' time. That'll be their main contribution to sustainable aviation." (quoted in Clark 2005). The LCCs especially object to proposals to simply "grandfather" the existing distribution of flights among carriers, arguing instead that the emission allowances should be auctioned from the beginning (*Economist* 2006b). The LCCs' complaint in this regard is similar to their grievances over the distribution of takeoff and landing slots at congested airports. Across the Atlantic, meanwhile, the US, which has not ratified the Kyoto agreement, is opposed to the imposition of ETS on American carriers serving Europe, adding a another potential grievance to the already troubled EU-US aviation relationship.

Whether the airlines are made to pay for their environmental consequences via taxes, fees, an ETS, or some combination, the effect will be to reverse the gains of liberalization, and the industry has not been shy about pointing this out. An IATA spokesman asked plaintively, "Are we saying we are going to try and stop people from visiting their grandmothers?" (quoted in Garrahan 2005). The industry is also quick to call attention to aviation's massive and growing economic significance, arguing that restraining already hobbled carriers might do more harm than good. After all, to the degree that air transportation has become one of the primary conduits of the global economy, airlines are not only big polluters but also catalysts for the wealth necessary to pay for the solutions to the world's environmental woes, including those not strongly related to aviation. As geographers Andrew Goetz and Brian Graham observe (2004: 271), the idea of sustainability, so central to discussions about the environment, is itself fraught with tensions because "it embraces the often-conflicting goals of environmental protection, long-term economic development, and social inclusion." There is no easy way to reconcile these goals in general, and with respect to air transportation in particular.

Consider, for instance, the ire of some environmentalists at the growing airborne trade in food. They charge that the upward climb in the number of air miles traveled by peas and fish, chilled meat and fresh squeezed pineapple juice is unsustainable and that prudent shoppers should buy local. There are a variety of reasons to buy local but the contribution of air-flown food to global climate change is small: according to one British government report, air freight accounts for just 1 percent of food tonne-kilometers and 11 percent of food transport-related CO_2 emissions[5] (DEFRA 2005). Further, the cost of discouraging airborne food shipments could be slower development in the places in which those peas and fish are harvested, the meat chilled and the pineapple juice squeezed. How much is saving "food miles" worth?

Bringing danger nearer: aviation, terrorism, and infectious disease

The airliner, having helped to change the scale of production linkages and family ties, having allowed the retreat of the pleasure periphery and the source of one's dinner farther over the horizon, has also facilitated the emergence of new threats on a global scale. Two threats in particular have attracted significant attention recently: terrorism[6] and the spread of infectious disease. Both dangers preceded the advent of aviation but both are made more difficult to stop by the speed and pervasiveness of the contemporary air transportation system.

Air transportation and the greater reach of political terror

As explained in Chapter 3, the airline industry has been one of the foremost arenas for terrorism since the 1960s. The lethality of air terrorism has changed, however, and the events of 2001 were the culmination of a decades-long trend toward a more vicious form of violence, in which those seizing airliners are fully prepared to kill massive numbers of innocents as well as themselves. More people died as a result of the September 11 attacks than in all previous bombings and fatal hijackings on commercial aircraft (including those incidents that were merely criminal rather than clear-cut instances of terrorism) combined. Of course, almost all of those killed were on the ground because the World Trade

Center towers, the Pentagon, and (apparently) the White House or US Capitol were the objects of the attacks, rather than the airliners themselves – in contrast to almost all previous incidents of air terrorism. The attacks were also unprecedented in that they took place on American soil. Although many earlier instances of air terrorism involved US carriers, particularly the traditional American flag carriers of Pan Am and TWA, almost none had occurred in the US itself before 9/11. Instead, jets were hijacked and blown apart in European and Middle Eastern skies (Figure 11.1).

The reaction to the attacks of 2001 was stunning. Shortly after the second tower was hit at 9:02 a.m., controllers began advising pilots across the country, "Every airplane listening to this frequency needs to contract your company." Airlines instructed their pilots to refuse all access to the cockpit and to land as soon as possible. At 9:25 a.m., it became official when Federal Aviation Administration (FAA) chief Jane Garvey ordered an unprecedented unscheduled "ground-stop" forbidding any further takeoffs and requiring any flight still in the air to land as soon as possible (Donnelly 2001).[7] Inbound foreign airliners were turned back and began to fill airports in Canada. US skies, meanwhile, were essentially drained of commercial traffic, with the intent of exposing what authorities initially feared might be as many as a dozen hijacked airliners.

The skies remained eerily clear of traffic for two days; and even after air traffic was permitted to resume, passenger volumes were unsurprisingly light. In October 2001, Alex Chadwick, a commentator on National Public Radio, gave an account of what it was like to travel by air again after the attacks. He ended his short piece with this observation,

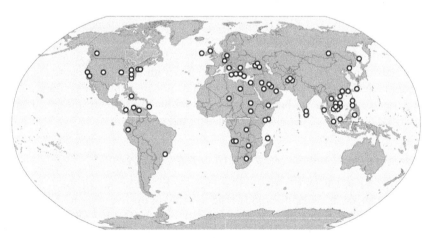

Figure 11.1 Sites of violence-related fatal air crashes (source: author's analysis of data at Airdisaster.com 2009).

Between 1955 and 2007, there were nearly 80 fatal incidents of violence against civilian airliners. Some of the incidents were attributable to isolated cases of suicide or homicide or apolitical hijackings gone awry. However, most of the incidents were politically motivated, helping to explain the concentration of events in the Middle East and Southeast Asia.

What you do not see in airports now – the particular set of passengers I've flown with for years, for as long as I can remember, but which are absent now – in airports and on airplanes, there are no longer any children.

(Morning Edition 2001)

It took until 2003 for global air passenger traffic and 2004 for US passenger traffic to reach to the highs set in 2000.

So the fall-off in passenger traffic was temporary. Yet other responses to the attacks were more durable. As in the case of the 1985–90 flare of violence against civil aviation (Wallis 2003: 1–2, 28), the responses after September 11, 2001 generally fell into two categories: better equipment and better procedures. In the US, the initial new equipment included billions of dollars worth of computer-aided tomography scanners and trace detection systems intended to look for explosives and their residue in passenger baggage for use in all 429 primary airports (more than 10,000 enplaning passengers annually) (Gilden 2002). The massive expenditure was to meet a government mandate that all luggage in the US be screened for explosives by December 31, 2002, one of the requirements laid down by the Aviation and Transportation Security Act (ATSA) passed two months after the attacks.

ASTA also required more intense experimentation with biometric identification systems that use iris, hand geometry, or facial matching for airport employees and for "trusted travelers." One of the most advanced efforts in this regard is in Singapore. There, Changi Airport and hometown carrier SIA introduced the Fully Automated Seamless Travel (FAST) system in November 2004 (Croft 2005). Each of 9,000 participants from SIA's frequent flyer program was issued a FAST card encoded with the person's fingerprint, facial details, and photograph. Instead of stopping three times to have his identity checked, receive a boarding pass, and clear immigration, a participant swipes the FAST card and then stares into a camera while placing his finger upon a scanner. After his details are verified, a boarding pass is printed and a special door automatically opens to the departure gates beyond. The FAST system is a compromise between the need for speed in the air transportation system and escalating security concerns.

In the sky, too, there was new equipment after the September 11 attack. Cockpit doors were reinforced across the US airliner fleet, and some airlines – notably jetBlue – installed cabin cameras to better monitor the passenger area of the airplane (Wilson 2004). There was also renewed interest in bomb-proofing airliners, but doing so would almost certainly increase an airplane's weight and reduce its revenue-generating potential. So carriers are not enthusiastic (Wallis 2003: 128–9).

More important in many ways than the new and improved surveillance and security hardware are the new procedures adopted by airports and airlines. The most obvious change to Americans after September 11, 2001 was the added time necessary to get through airport security checks. Air travelers in the US were advised to arrive at the airport as many as two hours early, making American airports more like those in Israel where rigorous security standards had been the norm for decades. Yet the geography of airline services to and from an airport like Indianapolis International, which handles about the same number of passengers annually as Tel Aviv Ben Gurion International, creates tremendous pressure to speed up security procedures in the US. From Tel Aviv in 2008, 60 percent of passenger flights were at least four hours in duration versus just 5 percent of flights from Indianapolis. Similarly, 95 percent of flights from the Israeli gateway were international versus just 1 percent from Indianapolis (author's analysis of data in OAG 2008). Passengers on longer, international flights are much more tolerant of time-consuming security procedures. The different geographies of air services as well as the different threat levels – even allowing for the newly acute sense of vulnerability after the 2001 attacks – are among the factors that mandate different security procedures at different airports.

Most of the new American security procedures remained beyond the view of passengers, by design. These included more armed air marshals on more flights and better Advanced Passenger Information (API) systems to electronically screen passengers who might pose a threat. Nor was cargo neglected. Indeed, by 2003 there was a rising chorus that all the attention to improve airline security had neglected the industry's "soft underbelly." At the end of 2003 fewer than 10 percent of the millions of tonnes of cargo shipped on passenger flights were inspected (*USA Today* 2003). There was some interest in preventing *any* air cargo from being loaded on passenger aircraft, a move that would have been financially crippling to many combination carriers. That prospect was averted but instead the US government imposed various measures to "push the borders back" by exercising better security over the places where imports originate (*CFO* 2003; Stundza 2005). Details about international shipments bound for the US must be electronically transmitted to US Customs four hours before departure; initially, the requirement was to have been eight hours but the ferocious protests from the industry resulted in the lower standard (Conway 2003).

Together, the changes at airports and on airplanes since 2001, inspired by fear, have further upset romantic, even quaint conceptions of aviation. Since its early days, air travel has been depicted as the route to a smaller, friendlier world. The jetliner would slice through the divisions of the past, drawing together the distant and the distrustful. That way of thinking persists. As geographers Martin Dodge and Rob Kitchin put it:

> Implicit in the rhetorical messages of aviation is the deeply utopianist logic that "making the world a smaller place", will "make the world a better place". Air travel is presented as a benevolent force that is inherently good for commerce and can bring greater understanding between people. The airline industry strives to portray an image that transcends the geopolitics of the terrestrial world and offers an uncomplicated world without frontiers.
>
> (Dodge and Kitchin 2004: 207)

The terrorist attacks upon the airline industry and the responses of airlines across the world have belied such simple imagery. Especially since 2001, the frontiers have been sharpened and division, of those deemed safe from those deemed dangerous, has been a preoccupation of airlines and airports (Adey *et al.* 2007).

Ultimately, security experts concede that it will be impossible to render the airline industry completely immune from terrorism attacks and too expensive to try. There are literally thousands of entry points into the air transport system. Further, the money spent on aviation security is money that cannot be spent on other kinds of security and, as the train and bus bombings in Madrid (2004), London (2005), and Mumbai (2006) made clear, the airline industry is hardly the only element of the world's circulatory system threatened by terrorist attacks. So a balance must be struck between aviation security and its costs, including its opportunity costs.

Will there be another terrorist attack like that of September 11, 2001? Certainly, there have been a number of attempts made since then to bring down airliners. In December 2001, with the US still reeling from the September attacks, "shoe bomber" Richard Reid attempted to set off an improvised explosive device in his shoe on a flight from Paris to Miami; but the effort fizzled, literally, and the cabin crew and other passengers subdued the Al-Qaeda-linked soloist. In August 2006, after discovering an alleged plan to blow up as many as ten transatlantic jetliners, Britain raised its terror threat level to "critical," indicating that an attack was judged imminent (*Economist* 2006d). The plot, purportedly involving British-born, Pakistani, and Afghani Muslims and liquid explosives (concealed perhaps in baby bottles), was foiled. Yet, from a broader perspective, the plot was bad news for the airborne world in general because it showed that the airline industry remained at the center of the terrorist's bull's-eye.

Secret travelers: air travel and the diffusion of infectious disease

While terrorism has bedeviled the airline industry for decades, disease is a newer source of alarm and a potentially much more serious problem. The US National Intelligence Council (2004: 34) in *Mapping the Global Future* identified a global pandemic as the single greatest threat to the global economy. Certainly disease is a crucial threat to the airline industry.

There are two ways in which the air transportation system can serve as a mechanism for the spread of disease. The first is person-to-person transmission aboard airliners. For example, air travel apparently played a mediating role in the first mumps epidemic in the US in 20 years (Alexander 2006). Public health authorities studying the Iowa-centered outbreak concluded that two infected airline passengers, one of whom probably contracted the disease in the Dominican Republic, unwittingly spread mumps to six other states in the Midwest. Yet it is important to note that the air circulation system on commercial jets is designed to make such transmission unlikely.[8]

However, aircraft cabin air flow and filtration systems have little effect on second dimension of the air travel-infectious disease conundrum: the acceleration of disease diffusion via airline passengers. Before air travel, it took days or even weeks to cross the Pacific, Atlantic, or Indian Oceans or to traverse the breadth of continents, affording a degree of protection against pandemics. Often a disease would run its course on board a ship with its victims either dead or no longer infectious by the time of arrival. Conversely, because air travel makes it possible to easily reach almost anywhere in the world within 36 hours, an infected person might not yet even be symptomatic upon arrival. The speed of air travel therefore makes it much more difficult to contain an infectious disease, particularly one that is easily transmissible and that originates in or spreads to areas well-connected to the global airline grid.

SARS (Severe Acute Respiratory Syndrome) certainly had the second of these properties. The disease smoldered for several months within southeastern China but spread much more rapidly after it reached Hong Kong. The index, or first, case of the disease is believed to have begun in Guangdong Province in the autumn of 2002. The disease remained more or less confined to that province until late February 2003 when a nephrologist who had treated victims of the mysterious disease in Zhongshan, one of the booming manufacturing centers in the province's Pearl River Delta, traveled by bus to Hong Kong (Greenfeld 2006: 151–2). There, the doctor stayed at the Metropole Hotel just one night before checking into a nearby hospital, but it was long enough for him to unwittingly infect at least a dozen other people. Among them were two off-duty stewardesses from Singapore and an elderly Chinese immigrant couple from Toronto.

Unaware of their illness, the couple and the stewardesses flew out of Hong Kong helping the SARS virus leap across the Pacific Ocean and the South China Sea, respectively. They were not alone. Having been contained to the People's Republic of China (PRC) for months, in the last week of February, SARS spread to seven new countries (including Canada and Singapore) and Taiwan (Figure 11.2). Air travel was the means via which SARS traveled to almost all of these places. The significance of air transportation is readily apparent in the highly uneven manner in which the disease spread over space. SARS reached Canada before Mongolia, Australia before India, and France before Russia – even though China neighbors Mongolia, India, and Russia. SARS affected 10 European countries and both the US and Canada, but only one country in Africa (South Africa) and none in Latin America. Overall, the correlation between the strength of a country's airborne connections to China, especially Hong Kong, and the speed with which SARS arrived was very strong (Bowen and LaRoe 2006).

Much as September 11 inspired an unprecedented response, the certain knowledge by March 2003 that SARS was spreading from country to country primarily via air travel also provoked an unprecedented response. On March 15, March 27, and April 2, the World Health Organization (WHO) issued a series of progressively more severe travel advisories (Bowen and LaRoe 2006). On April 2, the WHO issued what it described as the "most stringent travel advisory issued

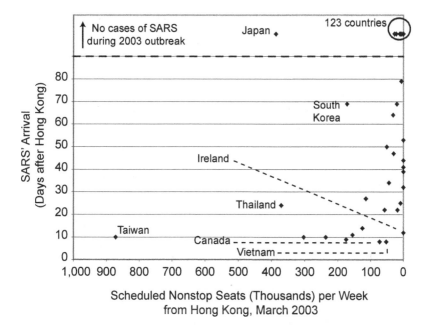

Figure 11.2 Air transportation and the diffusion of SARS (sources: Bowen and LaRoe 2006; author's analysis of data in OAG 2003).

The pattern of diffusion of Severe Acute Respiratory Syndrome (SARS) in 2003 was shaped by air transportation accessibility. The horizontal axis shows the number of seats per week in March 2003 on scheduled nonstop flights to the 150 most populous countries (not including China, the origin of the outbreak) and Taiwan. The vertical axis shows how many days elapsed between the arrival of SARS in Hong Kong on February 15, 2003 and its arrival in a particular country. Overall, the "closer" a country was to Hong Kong in terms of air accessibility, the faster SARS arrived there. Bowen and LaRoe (2006) offer a more thorough analysis of the same phenomenon.

in its 55-year history," urging that all but emergency travel in areas of local transmission be postponed. Individual countries adopted their own measures to impede the spread of the disease. In Singapore, where perhaps the most concerted effort was marshaled, all arriving passengers from SARS-affected areas were subjected to physical screening for the symptoms of the disease after March 31. Three weeks later, Changi Airport implemented a comprehensive system of thermal infrared screening to check all arriving and departing passengers for fevers.

As with the "War on Terror," then, airports became a frontline in the "war" against SARS. And as with the War on Terror, the focus on airports has been criticized. Although air transportation was the primary means via which the virus traveled from country to country, many more people contracted SARS in health care settings than in airliners and airports. In Canada, where new infections in hospitals were particularly important, of the nearly 800,000 people scanned at the two key gateway airports, only 191 were referred for further checks and none was found to be infected (St. John *et al.* 2005). More broadly, the panicked response to SARS, including the months-long virtual collapse of air travel to, from, and within East Asia has been criticized as incommensurate with the scale of the SARS threat (McKercher and Chon 2004). Fewer than 8,100 people were infected by SARS, the great majority of them in the PRC and its immediate neighbors to the south and east. And on a global scale, SARS was not a significant killer at all; AIDS claimed more victims every three hours in 2003 than the 774 people killed by SARS during its eight-month outbreak.

It is perhaps easy to criticize the overreaction to SARS in retrospect; but at the time, little was known about the disease apart from the fact that it was spreading quickly via air travel. As it turned out, SARS was not a very easy disease to get. The virus spread via large droplets requiring close contact, and individuals with the disease were only infectious when they were also symptomatic. These characteristics led two public health care experts to opine, "SARS might almost be classified as 'easy' to manage." (Weiss and McLean 2004: 1138).

SARS seems to have receded into history, but as this book was being finished, a new infectious disease threat was making headlines around the world and once again air travel was strongly implicated in the disease's diffusion. In early 2009, a new influenza A virus called H1N1 spread from Mexico to countries across much of the world. Once again, the density of air connections to the country that was home to the index case (in this instance Mexico) strongly predicted the speed with which the virus would infect people elsewhere (Khan *et al.* 2009). Compared to SARS, H1N1 appeared to be easier to get but less lethal, though it may be too early in the outbreak to draw such conclusions.

The threat of aviation-spread infectious disease – like the threat of terrorism – has been met by new procedures and new equipment. New surveillance systems (including, for instance, experimental detect-to-protect systems that can detect and identify a threatening biological agent in an airport within minutes), new agreements to share information among governments, and better databases to track the movement of passengers all share the same goal: speed. We could be caught on a treadmill, however, trying to outrun diseases whose own speed has been accelerated by an air transportation system that ranks as one of humanity's greatest technological achievements.

Part IV
Beyond the horizon

12 Coming back down to earth?

The cloudy future of air transportation

The view from Victorville

In early 2009, the number of commercial aircraft in storage reached nearly 2,300 or about 10 percent of the world's total fleet (Ascend 2009). The grounded airliners were stored mainly in deserts of the American Southwest and Central Asia. At one important site, the Southern California Logistics Airport (formerly George Air Force Base) in Victorville, California, scores of aircraft were lined up in neat rows in mid-2009 forming a multibillion dollar parking lot on the edge of the Mojave. Some of the jets were old, Douglas DC-8s and Boeing 747-100s for instance; but some were much newer, including Boeing 747-400s and Airbus A320s forced from the sky by one of the worse downturns in the airline industry's history. Singapore Airlines, for instance, which is famous for its youthful fleet, had 18 aircraft in storage in early 2009 including at least one freighter in Victorville (Wong 2009). Many of the grounded airliners will see revenue service again. Indeed, the whole point of desert storage is to minimize corrosion during what is expected to be temporary storage. But this time may be different, with many fewer grounded planes returning to work.

Indeed, in an industry prone to crisis, this crisis seems different and may more strongly shape the future trajectory of air transportation, and it is that future trajectory that is the subject of this final chapter. In the near term, it is easy enough to predict further consolidation especially in the most liberalized markets, a high fatality rate among fragile neophyte low-cost carriers, and a slowdown in the pace of sales and rate of innovation by the world's plane-makers. Boeing and Airbus, for instance, have put off the introduction of replacements for the 737 and A320 and have instead opted for major mid-career revamps of each narrow-body workhorse (Kingsley-Jones and Ostrower 2009). Airbus, specifically, has said that no A320 replacement will be introduced before 2020.

What then? What will happen after 2020 as we move even deeper into the second century of air transportation? Prognosis in so dynamic a part of the economy is a hazardous affair, but in this final chapter I sketch two basic scenarios. In the first, technological change, so important to the historical development of aviation, perpetuates its expansion. In the second, the decades-long growth of air transportation at the expense of alternate modes is reversed; fewer people and fewer goods move by air; and everyday life slows down and becomes less spa-tially attenuated. The chapter ends with my speculation about which scenario is more likely to come to fruition.

Higher still? New technologies and the future of flight

Interestingly, this book was written at a time of a great global conflict, the so-called War on Terror. During the past century, conflict was usually associated with great leaps in aviation technology. In particular, the practical jet engine was, as described in Chapter 2, a byproduct of World War II. World War I and the Cold War also delivered important gains in the realm of civil aviation. Yet there is no indication that the present conflict will be a catalyst for a new burst of growth in commercial aviation. On the contrary, it has clouded the skies with fear. Still, civil aviation technology and military aviation technology are not completely divorced from one another, and it is possible that technologies crucial to airliners a century hence will have debuted in military applications. One might imagine, for instance, much larger versions of the tiny pilotless drones (unmanned aerial vehicles[1]) used over the Middle East in recent years being dra-matically scaled up to make more mundane cargo flights.

A pilotless commercial airliner might fit into the longer-term labor-saving trends within air transportation (e.g., the supplanting of three-person flight crews by just a pilot and copilot), but safety concerns alone make such a prospect extremely remote. Here we focus on two possible directions of technological change in aviation that build more directly on the trends of the past and seem more realistic.

Go faster

From the Wright Brothers' first flight to the early 1970s, commercial aircraft moved faster and faster, but then the world's airlines reached a speed plateau, and a subsonic one at that. Only the miniscule Concorde fleet of 14 aircraft flew faster than the speed of sound (specifically the Concorde cruised at just over Mach 2.0), and concerns about noise pollution and exorbitant fares so limited the aircraft's scope of operation that it rarely flew beyond a few key transatlantic spans (Figure 12.1). Since 2003, even those supersonic links have now been silenced, marking "a rare example of time/space divergence through the discard-ing of uncommercial transport technology" (Knowles 2006: 412).

Is there any prospect of a return to supersonic flight? The will to go faster, the "fever of speed," seems irrepressible in human nature (Gleick 1999); and, in fact, new supersonic jets are being developed along two separate tracks (*Econo-mist* 2005b). NASA and a consortium of large aerospace firms are behind a venture to develop a business jet whose sonic boom would be so mild that the plane could fly at supersonic speeds over both land and sea. The other track is less technologically innovative but could yield a product that would come to market sooner. The company leading this track, Reno-based Aerion, aims to

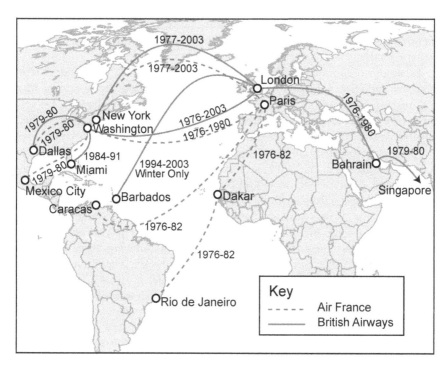

Figure 12.1 Former Concorde services, 1976–2003 (source: *Aviation News* 2003).

Although the Concorde was initially deployed to a dozen cities, for most of its nearly 30 year reign as the world's fastest airliner, it was flown among just four: London, Paris, New York, and Washington.

produce[2] an eight- to twelve-seat business jet that, like the Concorde, would fly at supersonic speeds primarily over water. Aerion's plane, scheduled for introduction around 2015, would not be quite as fast as the Concorde (Mach 1.6 versus Mach 2.0), but it would be much more efficient that the Concorde at subsonic speed. It would also be much quieter on takeoff and landing so that the airplane could meet ICAO Chapter 4 noise standards (Collogan 2008). The net result is broadly similar to that of the more ambitious plans of those in the first track: a supersonic jet that could operate profitably over many more routes than could the Concorde.

Nevertheless, it seems a fair bet that if and when supersonic business jets debut they will do so on the same transoceanic routes that have attracted all-business class airlines using conventional airliners. Even if a new supersonic jet could fly above Mach 1 without generating a sonic boom, transoceanic routes – including across the Pacific, whose breadth the Concorde could not span – will still make the most supersonic sense because it is on the longest routes that the jet's speed advantage will be most fully realized. One might imagine then that any supersonic network would begin with spans linking the three dominant world cities (New York, London, and Tokyo) with aviation superstars Singapore and Dubai in the mix as well. A sparse network of supersonic business services among world-cities would be a logical extension of the deepening airborne caste system discussed in Chapter 8.

What about supersonic travel for the rest of us? That is a much longer-term prospect, although a Japanese-French venture is exploring the feasibility of a 300-seat jet that would fly at supersonic speeds over water. Perhaps by the sesquicentennial of the Wright Brothers' flight at Kitty Hawk, the budget travelers' supersonic airliner will have arrived.

In the very long-term, one might imagine not just supersonic (Mach 1–5) but hypersonic (greater than Mach 5) air travel. In 2002, a group of Australian scientists became the first in the world to successfully fire a scramjet engine in the air. After being dropped from an airplane high over the Outback, the scramjet flew at a Mach 7.6 for six seconds, smashing the previous speed record and sparking visions of two-hour flights from New York to Tokyo (Kyriacou 2006). A scramjet, or supersonic combustion ramjet, works by drawing oxygen from the atmosphere rather than carrying it on board as in a rocket. The result could be a much lighter, extremely fast aircraft. Yet the scramjet is a very long way from having any commercial relevance, as suggested by the six-second duration of the 2002 test (the craft traveled fewer than 20 kilometers); though it is worth noting that NASA has plans to conduct up to five-minute long tests of its scramjet-powered X-51 Waverider (Warwick 2008). China and Russia are also working on scramjet technology. So progress is being made and this new technology, whose early applications are expected to be mainly military, might one day find commercial use.

If affordable, practical supersonic or hypersonic technology does make its way to the airborne world and push subsonic airliners from the skies, the speed advantage of aviation versus alternative modes would be enlarged. The same thing happened a half century ago when jets replaced piston-engine airplanes, and, like then, its wider speed margin would perpetuate the long-term growth of aviation at the expense of other modes.

Go smaller

Alternatively, it may not be the subsonic airliner that will be relegated to history's dustbin but rather the 300-seat airliner. As noted earlier in this book, one of most prominent recent trends in the airline industry has been the move towards smaller aircraft as wide-body twinjets have replaced the 747 in intercontinental markets and regional jets have found wide use in medium-haul sectors. What if the trend towards smaller planes were taken further? In his book *Free Flight: From Airline Hell to a New Age of Travel* James Fallows (2001) advocates a widespread air-taxi system in which thousands of very light jets (VLJs) such as those developed by companies such as Albuquerque-based Eclipse, Duluth-based Cirrus, and Honda would ferry handfuls of passengers and small consignments of cargo directly from origin to destination over fairly short distances. Such a system could liberate many passengers from the "airline hell" of crowded airport access roads, crowded planes, crowded and delay-prone hubs, circuitous routings, inconvenient schedules, and punishing fares imposed on those flying last-minute or to small cities. By diverting much of the traffic now funneled through O'Hare, Los Angeles International, Heathrow and other hubs, an effective air-taxi system would remove some of the most important shackles on the growth of air travel and air freight. Fallows (2001: 227) notes that twenty US hub airports were already at the saturation point by the end of the 1990s but there were four thousand other airports where capacity was, on average, ten times actual demand.

For the reasons explored in Chapter 10, expanding existing hubs is usually a very expensive, lengthy process. So making better use of the untapped capacity in the US airport system and in that of other countries may prove important to sustaining the growth of the airborne world. And an air-taxi system could be fast. By avoiding crowded hubs most of the time and by flying directly from an airport near a passenger's origin to one near her destination, an air-taxi could dramatically reduce overall travel time. Moreover, NASA officials have noted that 98 percent of Americans live within a 30-minute drive of a public airport; so the ground time for airborne trips could be shortened, too.

Fallow's vision seemed to come nearer to fruition in 2007, when one Florida-based air taxi company called DayJet began flying a large fleet of Eclipse VLJs in just such a fashion in the American Southeast. Fares, which were continuously set in real-time by the company's sophisticated computer system linked to an Internet portal, varied widely depending on the passenger's flexibility because greater flexibility enabled the carrier to more easily combine multiple passenger journeys on a single three-passenger jet.

DayJet was like many LCCs in exploiting new information technologies, but its network was unlike that of any LCC or network carrier in that it had no fixed links. Rather, passengers had to begin or end a journey at one of the company's so-called "DayPort" (about a dozen medium-sized airports including, for example, Jacksonville International) and could choose a "DayStop" (several dozen, mainly small airports such North Palm Beach County General Aviation Airport) as the other endpoint. Even more than LCCs, DayJet assiduously avoided major hubs; so although its operations were concentrated in Florida and Georgia, it flew to neither Miami International nor Hartsfield-Jackson Atlanta International.

It may have seemed like a good idea, but DayJet no longer exists. It was an early victim of the US credit crunch and the more general economic downturn that has filled the airplane parking lots in Victorville (Larson 2008). Eclipse, the manufacturer of DayJet's fleet, also declared bankruptcy in 2008. In the longer term, however, a ubiquitous air-taxi system might serve as an intermediate stop on the way to the aviation futurist's Holy Grail: the Personal Transport System (PTS). The PTS would offer the freedom in the sky that the passenger car has long afforded on the ground. As Fallows observes,

> For more than a generation, the money, effort, and innovation in civil aviation have gone towards planes that carry one hundred passengers or more between Atlanta and Chicago, New York and Los Angeles, or any other "hub pair", at over 400 miles an hour, with ever-higher reliability and ever low-cost per mile. While Boeing and Airbus have fought for this market, airplane makers like Gulfstream, Lear, Challenger, Raytheon, and Cessna have poured out ever faster and sleeker jets that can take corporate officials or individual millionaires wherever they want to go whenever they want to go there. In the history of transportation, the result is like a land-travel system consisting of long distance rail lines for most passengers and private limousines for a tiny elite. A transportation system, that is to say, like one without the ordinary automobile.
>
> (Fallows 2001: 11–12)

In aviation's second century, that missing piece of the puzzle may be put in place. Boeing and NASA, among others, are researching the technologies necessary for individuals to travel in miniature airplanes (*Engineer* 2006); but the hurdles to be surmounted are many. At close to a million dollars a copy, even an Eclipse jet was vastly more expensive than virtually any car on the planet, though economies of scale would help lower the cost. Then, there is the practical matter of training conceivably millions of would-be pilots to operate a vehicle in three dimensions (Hugill 1993: 250).

In making it possible for an ordinary person to fly on his own, however, a PTS would further the long-term trend towards expanded convenience and mobility. Specifically, NASA officials have argued that a PTS could broaden the typical American's daily activity space from a radius of 50 kilometers to 500 kilometers (Fallows 2001: 77). Boeing's design guidelines for the PTS provide for a range as high as 900 kilometers (*Engineer* 2006).

One can imagine the PTS and the hypersonic transport discussed above coming together a century or two from now to form an integrated system offering far greater freedom than today's transportation system. Travelers might fly in their own personal aircraft or in air-taxis over short and medium routes but move in supersonic or hypersonic commercial transports between continents. Then, the world truly will have been shrunk to a size "tiny."

Grounded? Energy, environment, and transportation choices

Perhaps, however, the airborne world has already reached its maximum extent. Two constraints upon the future growth of aviation are particularly important: oil prices and environmental policy.

Oil prices and the competition among transportation modes

In 2009, Canadian economist Jeff Rubin published a book[3] arguing that high oil prices will spell the end of globalization. A little more than a year earlier, Rubin had attracted worldwide attention with a prediction that the price of oil would reach

$225 by 2012 (Hamilton 2009). That prediction later looked silly as the price of oil tumbled from $147 a barrel in July 2008 to less than $35 near the end of the year. Still, Rubin has proven right in the past. In 2000, he predicted oil prices would top $100 later in the decade. He was right then. What if he is right this time?

The experience of 2008 gives us a taste of the bitter travails that would await the airline industry in a world of extremely high-cost oil. In 2002, when petroleum prices averaged about $25 per barrel, jet fuel costs amounted to just 16 percent of the total operating costs of the members of the International Air Transport Association (Doganis 2006: 11). By the middle of 2008 petroleum prices had risen to nearly $150 per barrel and fuel accounted for about 40 percent of IATA members' costs and as much as 50 percent for some carriers (IATA 2009). In a startling analysis conducted for *The Wall Street Journal*, a consultancy found that for a selection of US transcontinental flights, fuel costs accounted for between 54 and 73 percent of the average ticket price near the mid-2008 oil price peak (McCartney 2008). Higher fuel costs affected US airlines worse than those in most other markets due to the concurrent weakness in the US dollar, but few carriers elsewhere in the world escaped the brunt of the new oil shock. An analysis by Credit Suisse, for instance, suggested that no European airline could be profitable (without fuel hedging) if oil prices exceeded $120 per barrel (Anselmo 2008b).

Many airlines, including a disproportionate number of LCCs, failed in 2008. Most of the survivors were forced to slash capacity. To take one example, Continental Airlines announced in June 2008 that it would reduce its fleet from 375 to 344 aircraft (with the reduction accounted for entirely by less fuel efficient Boeing 737-300 and -500 airplanes) and its staffing by 3,000 by the end of 2009 (Continental Airlines 2008). The carrier's domestic capacity would be cut by 11 percent in the fourth quarter of 2008 versus the same quarter in the previous year and further reductions of 3–5 percent were planned for 2009. Interestingly, Continental's planned reductions on international routes were, in keeping with the discussion of network carrier globalization in Chapter 6, much more modest.

By mid-2009, oil prices had stabilized at half the mid-2008 peak. Oil prices have yo-yoed over the past six decades (Figure 12.2) and are sure to fluctuate in the future, but Jeff Rubin is not alone in expecting higher prices to be a reality in the twenty-first century. Here it is important to reiterate that because an airplane needs a highly concentrated form of energy to maximize the available payload (i.e., passengers and cargo) at takeoff, it is far more difficult to find substitutes for oil-based fuels for a jetliner than for a passenger car (Charles *et al.* 2007). Should the dire forecasts of sustained prices of more than $200 per barrel oil be borne out, the result could be a return to a more elite passenger airline industry and an air cargo industry once again relied upon primarily as a last resort. Other modes could capture back some of the traffic they have lost to the air.

Which modes could divert traffic from the airlines? The answer is fairly obvious: rail and to a lesser extent the passenger car for passenger traffic and sea, rail, and truck for cargo. Even at more modest oil prices, the airline industry at the beginning of its second century is under threat from surface transportation.

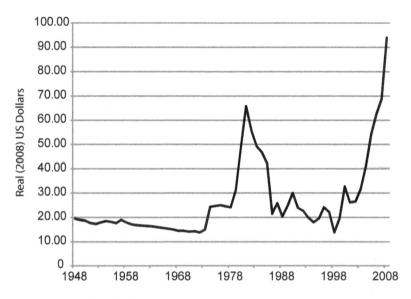

Figure 12.2 Crude oil prices, 1948–2008 (sources: US Energy Information Agency 2009; S. Williamson 2008).

The graph shows the average annual domestic first crude purchase price adjusted for inflation using a gross domestic product deflator.

Rail most poses a challenge to passenger airlines in Western Europe. Rail lines in the region claim that they account for more than 60 percent of leisure trips of fewer than six hours traveling time and a similar share of business trips of fewer than four hours (*Economist* 2007c). From Naples to Milan, from Seville to Barcelona, from Amsterdam to Marseille, from London to Stuttgart, it is possible to travel across Europe at speeds in excess of 250 kilometers per hour (Figure 12.3). Europe is pouring money into high speed rail (HSR) as part of a broader effort to tie the European Union together at ground-level. By 2020, Warsaw, Lisbon, and Bordeaux are among the cities that will be added to the region's HSR network.

In Japan, meanwhile, the *shinkansen* has captured a significant share of intercity travel for decades. One result, for instance, is that from Nagoya, in the middle of the Tokaido Megalopolis, there are scheduled flights neither to Haneda Airport, the primary domestic gateway to Tokyo (261 kilometers away), nor to Osaka (147 kilometers away). In 2004, the first two lines of South Korea's bullet train opened and air travel on the affected routes has fallen. In 2003, Korean Air and Asiana together provided more than 10,000 seats per day each way between Seoul and Busan, which are 353 kilometers apart; by 2008, daily air capacity was about 5,600 seats each way (author's analysis of data in OAG 2003 and OAG 2008). China, too, has made a commitment to building an HSR system of its own (Pierson 2007).

Rail has a number of advantages over air travel, apart from being more fuel-efficient and environmentally friendly. Especially in the wake of the 9/11 attacks,

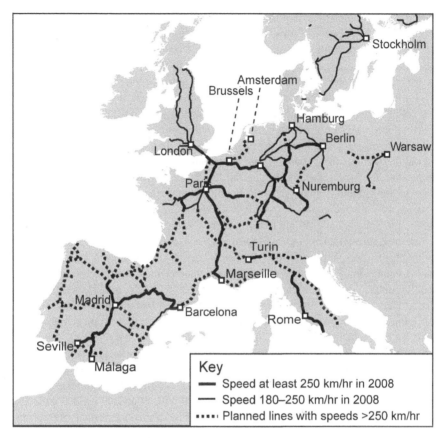

Figure 12.3 Europe's high-speed rail network (source: based on information at UIC 2008).

Europe's airlines face significant competition from the region's high-speed rail network.

going by air means travel via long lines, repeated security screenings, and an atmosphere taut with apprehension. By comparison rail travel is relaxed. Once in motion, rail typically offers more room to stretch one's legs, more freedom to get up and move, and few or no restrictions on the use of cell phones and other electronic devices. Rail travel delivers its passengers directly to downtown stations instead of distant suburban airports – to say nothing of the faraway gateways sometimes employed by LCCs.

However, rail is a more expensive and slower alternative for most itineraries, especially where LCCs are present. In 2006, a reporter tested the relative merits of rail and air travel between his home in south London and downtown Amsterdam and found that travel by easyJet took four hours and cost $147.52, including the time and cost of ground transportation – even though the journey had been via London's remote Luton Airport. By rail, the journey took 7 hours and 33 minutes and cost $322.14 (Soriano 2006). The reporter's rail journey took nearly twice as long despite the fact that most of its length was on high-speed rail lines with speeds in excess of 250 kilometers per hour. Over routes where high speed rail is not yet available, the time advantage of air travel is enormous. Between Warsaw and Budapest, for instance, Wizz Air offered a one-way fare of $18 for a one-hour flight versus $116 and 14 hours by rail in 2006 (Soriano 2006).

Further, rail is still beset by national divisions that, even in Europe, make it difficult to travel between countries without changing trains en route (Knowles 2006). Furthermore, rail has not been liberalized to the same degree as air transportation, and partly because of this difference, rail lines are less sophisticated than airlines in matters such as yield management (*Economist* 2007c) – which makes rail more expensive for most travelers. Nor is rail free from the terror threat, as the bombings in Madrid and London showed. Finally, the fact that rail terminals are downtown is less advantageous than it might seem since so many people and so much economic activity have shifted to the suburbs, even in Europe.

Beyond Western Europe and Northeast Asia, there are few places where rail is much of a long-term threat to passenger airlines,[4] at least not yet. In the US, rail accounts for about 1 percent of long-distance (more than 50 miles or about 80 kilometers) passenger trips in the US (BTS 2006a). The obstacles to substantially increasing that proportion are formidable and include the high cost of building the infrastructure for HSR. Conventional passenger trains can share the rails with freight train, although they do so at the cost of being shunted aside to clear the way for higher priority goods traffic; but HSR generally needs its own rails upon which to ride. Building such a network in North America could be fantastically expensive (D. Levinson *et al.* 1997), a cost that would be especially hard to recoup in the large sections of America with relatively light population density. Here then is still another advantage of air transportation: its flexibility. An airline can profitably serve communities far from the corridors to which an economically efficient HSR system is limited. Nor are the costs of HSR just measured in dollars and cents. The noise of passing trains is bothersome to those who live nearby and so the proposal to build new lines is met with a NIMBY[5] response not unlike that which airports have provoked.

Still, the political and perhaps financial merits of rail are likely to grow as the twenty-first century progresses, further bolstering the vitality of a mode once seemingly vanquished by the airlines. Interestingly, HSR featured prominently in the infrastructure-led stimulus packages adopted by a number of countries during the global recession that began in 2007. In the US, for instance, the Obama Administration's stimulus package of early 2009 included $8 billion as a down payment on what the government envisioned as ultimately ten HSR corridors spread throughout the country (Knowlton 2009).

In terms of cargo, meanwhile, containerships, rail, and truck transport could reverse some of the spectacular gains recorded by the airline industry. Indeed, in the arena of long-distance cargo transportation, aviation faces and will continue to face much more serious competition from alternate modes. Ocean container freight has grown at a faster rate than air cargo for a decade (Boeing Company

2006). And over short- and medium-haul distances, air freight has yielded back some of its traffic to trucking. In the US domestic market, for instance, air cargo carriers lost about 8 percent of the expedited shipment market to ground parcel services in the first few years of this century (Scherck 2005). Approximately 85 percent of second-day domestic air shipments in the US are delivered within 2,000 kilometers of their origin, a range over which ground services can offer guaranteed delivery within three days (Scherck 2005).

Of course, the balance between modes is not just about competition. In both passenger and freight movements, multiple modes are increasingly integrated to provide more seamless services. For instance, more than 1,000 city-pairs in North America were served by "truck flights" in 2006 (Boeing Company 2006: 24). Truck flights are ground-based services that feed into and are fed by longer-haul air services. In 2008, for instance, British Airways (or its contractors) operated nearly 1,000 truck flights from the carrier's American air gateways such as Phoenix and Baltimore to US cities too small to warrant air services such as Richmond and El Paso (author's analysis of OAG 2008).[6] Companies like FedEx and UPS, as discussed in Chapter 9, are premised on just such intermodal integration.

Meanwhile in passenger transportation, there is a similar move towards intermodal services. Much of the cost of the Hong Kong International Airport (see Table 10.1) was spent well beyond the airport itself on a new expressway, bridge, and tunnel to link the airport to the city center 34 kilometers away. The bridge alone ranks as one of the greatest engineering marvels of the twentieth century. When it was finished in 1997, it was the second longest suspension bridge in the world and featured two decks – the one on top for automobiles and trucks, the one on the bottom for trains. The incorporation of rail-based mass transit in the plan for the airport is in keeping with a more general pattern across much of the world (Table 12.1). Shanghai's Pudong Airport, for instance, is served by the world's only operating magnetic levitation train. The 30-kilometer line from the airport to Shanghai's new central business district takes just eight minutes with the train traveling up to 430 kilometers per hour.[7]

Recall, too, that one of the conditions for the addition of a third runway at Heathrow is further improvement in the rail connections between the airport and the rest of the metropolis so that the added air pollution of arriving and departing jetliners would be at least partially offset by fewer cars stuck on congestion-choked airport access highways. That condition points to what may prove the most important factor shaping the future of the airborne world: public policy. And one central goal of policy in a growing number of places in the world is a more environmentally sustainable transportation system. That goal shows up in Britain's policy towards London's airports. How else might it shape the future trajectory of aviation?

Go greener

As described in the previous chapter, there are number of near- and medium-term options, from continuous descent to emissions trading schemes, to make

Table 12.1 Passenger rail access at large airports

Airport	Distance to CBD (km)	Rail access
Hartsfield-Jackson Atlanta Int'l	14.5	Metro
Chicago-O'Hare Int'l	29.0	Metro
Heathrow (London)	24.1	Metro, commuter rail, HSR[1]
Haneda (Tokyo)	17.7	Metro
Los Angeles Int'l	27.4	Light rail via bus
Paris-Charles de Gaulle Int'l	23.0	Metro
Dallas-Ft. Worth Int'l	27.4	Commuter rail via bus
Frankfurt	35.0	Metro, HSR
Beijing Capital Int'l	28.0	Metro
Madrid-Barajas Int'l	16.0	Metro
Denver Int'l	37.0	None
Amsterdam Airport Schiphol	19.0	Metro, HSR
John F. Kennedy Int'l (New York)	24.0	Commuter rail, metro via rail link
Hong Kong Int'l	32.2	Metro, HSR
Las Vegas McCarran Int'l	11.3	None[2]
George Bush Intercontinental (Houston)	32.2	None
Phoenix-Sky Harbor Int'l	4.8	None
Suvarnabhumi (Bangkok)	28.9	HSR to start in late 2009
Changi (Singapore)	17.7	Metro
Orlando Int'l	9.7	None

Sources: relevant airport websites.

Notes
1 HSR = high speed rail.
2 There are plans to extend the city's monorail to the airport.

aviation more environmentally friendly. There are also interesting possibilities for the technology of the airliner itself. Very large aircraft like the A380 tend to be fuel-efficient, and, at least before the Superjumbo proved not to be such a super-seller, there was some discussion in aviation circles of a 1,000 seat airplane over the horizon.

An important, similarly environmentally friendly alternative to very large aircraft is slower aircraft. In particular, government policies that mandate sharp reductions in aviation's environmental costs might augur well for turboprops, which travel more slowly than jets but are more fuel efficient. In the 70-seat size category, for instance, turboprops use 60 percent less fuel than jets and concomitantly produce about 60 percent fewer emissions (Sparaco 2008). Furthermore the speed advantage of jets[8] is less daunting when total journey time is taken into consideration; on a short-haul route, travel by turboprop might mean arriving at the destination gate about 20 minutes later. Still, turboprops suffer by comparison with jets in their perceived comfort and the sight of whirring propellers makes turboprops seem antiquated to many travelers, despite the fact that the two main turboprop manufacturers[9] – the French-Italian consortium Avion de Transport Regional (ATR) and Canada's Bombardier – have incorporated a variety of new technologies, such as composite materials, in their newest models.

Ultimately, more than 40 years of "jetmania" (Sparaco 2008) may help to explain why in mid-2008, the number of jets on order by the world's airlines outnumbered turboprops by 18 to 1 (*Air Transport World* 2008c). Nevertheless, the return of very high fuel prices or more stringent environmental policies would could foster a golden age for turboprops more than 50 years after they were overtaken by jetliners.

In the medium-term, engine technologies more innovative than the conventional turbofans and turboprops might help the airline industry to clean up its act in a sense. One promising alternative is the open rotor jet engine, also called the propfan (Norris 2008). In a propfan, the jet engine's rotor rotates around the outside of the nacelle instead of inside it, creating a fuel-efficient, ultra-high bypass engine. Noise, however, has impeded the introduction of the propfan. The same nacelle that dampens the fuel efficiency of a conventional jet engine also dampens its noise footprint. So much work remains to be done by General Electric, Rolls-Royce, Pratt & Whitney, and the other companies (and research institutes such as Cambridge University's Whittle Laboratories) involved in the development of this technology (Norris 2008).

Still, the turboprop and even the propfan are relatively old technologies. The world seems overdue for something radically new. After all, if the nineteenth century gave us railroads and steamships and the twentieth century automobiles and airplanes, is it inconceivable that the twenty-first century will offer its own new forms of transportation? Maybe that new way will be some as-yet-unknown means of getting from place to faraway place very fast and doing so in an environmentally friendly way.

Or maybe we'll stay home.

Controlled flight

Aviation's second century will be about choices. For most of its first century, the airborne world strained at the bit, taking as much as technology, the market, and the political shackles thrown over the airline industry would allow. When it became possible to cruise profitably at 800 kilometers per hour, or to ferry 400 people in a single airplane, or to fly nonstop from New York to London, airlines did so. The airborne world was on a kind of autopilot, growing and (less frequently) pulling back in response to the vagaries of the forces acting upon it; its destination was simply up, to expand wherever possible and to draw more traffic into the sky.

This century will be different. We are likely to more often stop short of what is possible and to exercise more direct control over the trajectory of the airborne world. One can see this already in, for instance, Britain's decision not to add a new runway at Heathrow before 2015 at the earliest, despite the fact that airlines could readily use additional capacity now. One can see it, too, in the restrictions on night flights at Frankfurt and in panoply of security measures provoked by terrorist attacks and scares. For now, the willingness to countenance restraints upon aviation is greatest in Europe. In many other parts of the world, especially in poorer countries, aviation is just spreading its wings. Sooner or later, though, the same tough decisions about how to balance the benefits of air transportation against its costs will arise.

Some have called for reregulation, including Robert Crandall, the same former head of American Airlines who proved so adept at taking advantage of opportunities in a liberalized market (see Chapter 5). Specifically, Crandall has advocated regulating the US air transportation system as a public utility (Velocci 2008). In his vision, that would mean greater government control over prices, service frequencies, and aircraft size as well as changes in US bankruptcy law (to limit the "revolving door" phenomenon discussed in Chapter 6) and efforts to move airlines towards labor cost parity. Crandall's remarkable proposal, made around the same time the desert parking lots in places like Victorville were beginning to fill, lends credence to the view that this crisis is different.

Will economic reregulation of aviation return in the way Crandall suggests? Perhaps. Much depends on the depth and duration of the airline's current financial calamity. What seems more certain is not new economic regulation, but new environmental regulation. The overall effects might be the same, however, in curtailing the future growth of the airborne world. And that probably means that a Jetson-like personal air transportation system and hypersonic air travel will remain distant prospects indeed. Almost certainly, a hundred people each flying in their own jets or a hundred people travelling together in a hypersonic craft would use far more fuel (and create far more air pollution and probably noise pollution) than the same five score traveling aboard a single, subsonic narrow-body jetliner.

Fundamentally, we must decide: what is air transportation for? Mobility is good, but some have begun to worry about "hypermobility" – mobility beyond rationality (Adams 1999). And, as this book has sought to make clear, the costs of air transportation are many. We can bring the faraway near but that means bringing faraway dangers – including disease and the threat of terror – closer, too. We can reach distant sun-bleached beaches, high altitude ski resorts, and pristine national parks in a few hours but en route we leave a trail of pollutants. We are linked as never before to people on the other side of the planet – to farmers and factory-workers, collaborators and competitors – but the more our everyday connections are spread thin the more weakly we are bound to the people at home – to family members we see too infrequently, to neighbors who remain strangers, and to fellow citizens with whom we share fewer common interests. Technology can reduce some of the problems that have grown up with the airborne world. Thermal scanners. Iris scanners. Palm scanners. Bomb-proof jetliners. Noise dampening airframes. Ultra high efficiency engines. But technology cannot fix everything.

So we will face tough choices in the years ahead about new technologies, new and expanded airports, and new ways of managing air transportation and its costs. Ultimately, much as powered flight is a balance between thrust and drag and between lift and gravity, the airborne world in its second century must strike its own balance between the forces that would produce still more traffic aloft and those that would hold us more firmly upon the earth.

Notes

1 Introduction

1 Figures based on Annual Review of Civil Aviation published in the *ICAO Journal* by the International Civil Aviation Organization and in IATA (2009). Unless otherwise stated, all money figures in this book are reported in current US dollars.
2 The estimate of about 540,000 aloft at any given moment in 2003 is based on the total number of passengers for the year (1.691 billion), the average distance traveled (1,828 kilometers), and the average schedule speed of commercial air traffic (650 kilometers per hour). These figures in turn were derived from ICAO (2004) and the author's analysis of data in OAG (2003).
3 Pacific Southwest Airlines (PSA) introduced low intrastate fares in California before Southwest Airlines did so in Texas but the effect of the latter airline upon the industry has been vastly greater.
4 "Flyover country" is a phrase either applied in a chauvinistic fashion by coastal elites towards the mid-section of the US or in an almost self-congratulatory fashion by people living in that mid-section.
5 In the early 1990s, charges levied on airliners passing nonstop through its airspace, typically en route between Bangkok and Hong Kong, comprised one of the largest sources of foreign exchange earnings for Laos (Kamm 1990).

2 Jetting toward a smaller world: early commercial aviation

1 The 787 is available in several versions. The dimensions cited are for the most popular, the 787-8. The 787-9 is larger.
2 Here and throughout the remainder of the book, year 2008 US dollar equivalents of certain historical dollar values are reported in the endnotes. All conversions are based on the relevant gross domestic product deflator available from S. Williamson (2008).
3 TWA later became Trans World Airlines, reflecting the vastly enlarged scope of its operations.
4 The movie industry, another new industry based in the American West, gave the nascent business of air travel an important nod of approval in 1935 (Hudson 1972: 61). Until then, Hollywood film idols had been contractually forbidden to fly because it was considered too dangerous to risk such valuable resources on so hazardous a mode of transport.
5 The stressed metal skin of the wing, which employed technology that German designers had been working on for more than a decade, carried part of the load and so permitted lighter-weight supporting structures within the wing.
6 United Air Lines (later United Airlines) and Boeing were parts of the same company at the time.

7 The long journey was completed in luxury commensurate with the $1,438 roundtrip fare ($18,400 in 2008 dollars).

8 Delta was also drawn to Atlanta by the greater ease with which finance capital could be raised there than in its corporate headquarters at Monroe, Louisiana (Braden and Hagan 1989: 106).

9 Adjusted for inflation, these costs are $5,900 (1946); $4,700 (first class in 1955); and $3,400 (tourist class in 1955) in year 2008 dollars.

10 Though airlines have long since overtaken the once-dominant ocean liners, the extent to which air travel grew up in the shadow of the great ocean lines is evident in the language of aviation. Air carriers refer to their chief pilots as "captains" and dress them accordingly. Flight attendants are "stewards" and "stewardesses" and lavatories are located in the "forward" and "aft" sections of the cabin (Gandt 1995: 19).

11 $1.1 billion in 2008 dollars.

12 Jetliners typically cruise above the weather in the less turbulent stratosphere while piston-engine aircraft cruise in the troposphere.

13 The westbound flight had to refuel at Gander, Newfoundland.

14 $1.8 billion in 2008 dollars.

15 Aircraft noise is commonly measured in decibels with certain frequencies to which the human ear is more sensitive given added weight. This measure is abbreviated dB(A).

3 Far and wide: wide-body jetliners and the growth of the global airline industry

1 To put the figures in this paragraph into perspective, $1 billion in 1970 was equal to about $4.4 billion in 2008. See endnote 2 for Chapter 2 for information on adjustments for inflation made in this book.

2 The battle between Airbus and Boeing, discussed in this chapter and the next, is more fully told in John Newhouse's (2007) more recent book, *Boeing versus Airbus: The Inside Story of the Greatest International Competition in Business*.

3 Interestingly, in the years since then, new aircraft like the Airbus A320 and Boeing 777 have been designed from the outset so that the fuselage can be easily stretched or shortened because adjusting the length of the fuselage is a much less expensive alternative to developing an entirely new aircraft.

4 $100 million in 2008 dollars.

5 $1.1 billion in 2008 dollars.

6 In fact, the scale of the overall project was so great that the Johnson Administration feared that spending on the plane by Boeing and its suppliers would further overheat an already inflationary economy (Rodgers 1996: 250).

7 Developing an engine powerful enough for the 747's debut forced Pratt & Whitney to make compromises, and as a result the engines prove unreliable during the 747's initial year of service. A further problem was that there simply were not enough working engines ready for Boeing to meet its delivery schedule, saddling the planemaker with an outsized parking lot of "hangar queens" (Serling 1992: 310) – aircraft that could not be put into revenue service because cement blocks hung from their wings instead of JT9Ds.

8 One month after Kennedy's assassination, the New York International Airport at Idlewild was renamed for the dead president.

9 In 1975, Lockheed became the central target of a Senate investigation into American corporate malfeasance abroad (Boulton 1978: 261–71). The investigation uncovered massive bribes paid to various parties in Japan in order to win sales of the L-1011 to Japan Airlines and All Nippon Airways.

10 Both jetliners were hobbled by problems common to other airliners. Like the 747, the L-1011 was delayed and its costs inflated by problems with its engine choice. Specifically, problems with the highly innovative Rolls-Royce RB.211 nearly led to the

bankruptcy of both Lockheed and Rolls-Royce (Heppenheimer 1995: 253). As for the DC-10, like the de Havilland Comet a generation earlier, the McDonnell Douglas trijet was severely affected by several high profile crashes shortly after its debut. In particular, poorly designed cargo doors caused the crash of a THY Turkish DC-10 near Paris in 1974, killing all on board (see Table 3.3).

11 $30 million in 1975 was equal to about $97 million in 2008 dollars.

12 $2.6 billion in 1992, when the US Congressional Research Service released its estimate of launch aid given to Airbus, was equal to about $3.7 billion in 2008 dollars.

13 The lower figure $220 is equal to about $1,030 in 2008 dollars.

14 Recent capacity expansion at both Narita International Airport and the Tokyo International Airport (Haneda) permitted Japan Airlines and ANA to become the launch customers for the Boeing 787, which is a wide-body jet but one substantially smaller than the 747 that long served as the workhorse of each carrier's fleet.

15 Even the collision on Tenerife was indirectly related to terrorism because the airport to which the two jets were to have operated, Las Palmas, was closed due to a bomb threat, and the resulting congestion of aircraft diverted to nearby Tenerife contributed to the disaster (Gero 2000: 189–92).

16 The first bombing of an American airliner was a United Airlines DC-6 brought down by a bomb over Colorado. The bomb had been placed in a woman's luggage by her son as part of a scheme to collect her life insurance.

17 Three flights were successfully hijacked on September 6, 1970: Swissair 100 from Zurich to New York, TWA 74 from Frankfurt to New York, and Pan Am 93 from Amsterdam to New York. An attempted hijacking of El Al 219 from Amsterdam to New York failed when the pilot threw the flight into a sudden dive that gave the crew and passengers an opening to subdue the PFLP team. On September 9, BOAC 775 from Bahrain to London was hijacked. All of the hijacked flights were diverted to the Middle East – the three smaller jets (a 707, a DC-8, and a Vickers VC-10) to a Jordanian airfield and the Pan Am 747 to Cairo – and were blown up.

4 Space-makers and pace-setters: Boeing and Airbus

1 In addition, Boeing offered the 737-700ER with a typical two-class seating for 76 passengers and a range of 10,200 kilometers. The jet, which was launched with an order for two from ANA, is aimed at the business-class only market.

2 Fly-by-wire (FBW) had been used in military aircraft before the A320 and in a limited capacity on some civilian airliners, including the Concorde. The A320 was the first full FBW jetliner, helping to make it, in the words of one aviation enthusiast, the "the most innovative civil airplane since the Wright Flyer" (Langewiesche 2009: 90). FBW is also used on some Boeing aircraft including the 777 and 787.

3 The new 747 is called the 747-8 in the freighter version and the 747 Intercontinental in the passenger version. The latter offers a standard three-class seating of 467 versus 416 in the 747-400. Sales of the new jet have been weak.

4 In the dark humor common in the airline industry, ETOPS is sometimes translated as "engines turn or passengers swim," but in actual practice, the safety of twinjets on over-water routes has been outstanding.

5 By comparison, in 1928, one of every hundred commercial airplane passengers in the United States was killed (A. Gordon 2004).

6 Many industry observers expect that ultimately GE will offer an engine for the A350 but through mid-2009 the plane-builder and the engine manufacturer had been unable to reach agreement on the matter.

7 Motivated primarily by the threat posed by outsourcing in general and specifically the fear that lucrative assembly jobs could go to subcontractors, Boeing's machinists went on strike in 2009. The two month strike ended with Boeing granting 15 percent pay

increases over four years and agreeing to limit the amount of outsourced work done in the company's plants (Maynard 2008b).

8 The Seattle area's advantages include a climate free of temperature extremes, access to a nearby 24-hour seaport, a runway capable of handling the modified 747 freighters used in ferrying 787 components, superior railway and highway access, favorable environmental regulations, and, of course, a pool of very highly trained workers employed by Boeing and its many nearby suppliers.

9 Several derivatives of existing aircraft (e.g., the McDonnell Douglas MD-11, a much improved version of the DC-10) were launched during the 1980s. Boeing launched important new aircraft just before (i.e., the 757 and 767) and just after (the 777) the 1980s.

10 The Wichita operations are now operated by Spirit Aero Systems, a subsidiary of a Canadian company to which Boeing sold the facility.

11 At the time of this writing (July 2009), the World Trade Organization had still not ruled on the competing claims by the US and the EU despite having promised to rule on the cases before the end of 2008. In June 2009, several European governments promised $4.9 billion of reimbursable aid toward the estimated $15.4 billion cost of developing the A350XWB (*Economist* 2009).

12 Conversely, through the end of 2008, the A380 had failed to win a single order from a US-based passenger airline. Both FedEx and UPS ordered freighter versions for use on trunk routes linking their globally dispersed hubs, but the two carriers later canceled their orders, partly due to frustrations with Airbus delays.

13 Greater wingspans typically translate into greater fuel efficiency (Morrison 1984).

14 AVIC 1 is the China Aviation Industrial Corporation, a state-owned aerospace enterprise.

15 Thomas (2000) identified Cathay Pacific as the other airline playing the role of gold standard, but now, nearly a decade later, it might be fairer to say that Stamford, Connecticut-based General Electric Capital Aviation Services (GECAS) and Los Angeles-based International Lease Finance Corporation (ILFC) are more influential in affecting new airliner development. At the end of 2008, GECAS had 1,845 aircraft in its fleet and ILFC had 955 aircraft in its fleet (GECAS 2009; ILFC 2009). Both leasing companies are critically important customers for new airliners. ILFC, whose clients range from the smallest new low-cost carriers to the airline industry's giants, had outstanding orders for 168 new Boeing and Airbus aircraft at the end of 2008, including 20 copies of the A350-XWB, an airplane whose design, as noted earlier in this chapter, ILFC strongly affected.

5 Letting go: the liberalization of the airline industry

1 The 787 purchase may also have been motivated by China's quest for a prominent place in the Dreamliner's supply chain.

2 It is worth noting, however, that in 2007, AirAsia formed a long-haul subsidiary called AirAsia X. See Figure 7.3.

3 Capacity here is measured in scheduled seats per week based on schedules published by OAG.

4 The demise of Southern Winds began with the discovery of 65 kilograms of cocaine in suitcases aboard one of the carrier's flights to Madrid in 2005. In response, the Argentine government withdrew subsidies it had given Southern Winds for operating unprofitable domestic routes and the airline collapsed (Rohter 2005; Knibb 2006)

5 FedEx opened its new hub at Guangzhou Baiyun International Airport in 2009; UPS will open a comparable facility at Shenzhen Bao'an International Airport in 2010.

6 As in the case of the US, European government involvement in aviation continues via subsidized air services to small communities. In the Europe such subsidies are paid to

carriers fulfilling what are termed Public Service Obligations (Williams and Pagliari 2004).

7 These mergers are discussed in more detail in Chapter 6.

8 Despite the small size of its fleet, Burma Airways had four fatal crashes between 1987 and 1989, prompting the US government to warn American visitors not to fly on the carrier (Erlanger 1989).

9 In 2007 Myanmar Airways International, the successor to Burma Airways reassured potential passengers visiting its website with the news that "Our pilots and engineers are all expatriates who bring with them a premium level of skill and experience from the world's leading airlines." (MAI 2007). The carrier was still state-owned but very much part of the global economy.

10 Kenya Airways was attractive to foreign investors including KLM partly because its services had been rationalized based on advice received from a British Airways aviation consulting subsidiary (Morrell 2007: 140).

11 In addition to KLM's 26 percent stake, another 52 percent of the airline was floated on the Nairobi and international stock exchanges (*Flight International* 2006b

12 In 2008, Branson tried to sell his stake in Virgin Nigeria after accusing the Nigerian government of "Mafioso style" tactics during a dispute over which terminal at the Mohamed Murtala International Airport in Lagos the carrier could use for its domestic flights (Flottau 2008).

13 Interestingly, the proliferation of competitors and the more general liberalization of aviation have effectively neutered IATA's fare-setting powers. It still acts as a clearinghouse to settle accounts between airlines for interlining cargo and passengers and plays important roles in promoting new technologies in aviation (e.g., electronic ticketing), training, schedule coordination, and data-gathering; but its once mighty power to determine the price of flight has been severely eroded. Of the 265 airlines that were members in 2005, only 100 participated in tariff coordination. A measure of the waning importance of IATA is the number of articles referring to the organization in the *New York Times*: in 1972, 43; in 1982, 19; in 1992, 11; and in 2002, just 2.

6 Survival of the fittest: network carriers in the global airline industry

1 These figures do not include the network of Northwest Airlines. As described later in this chapter, Delta and Northwest merged their operations effective October 29, 2008.

2 Hubbing also permits a carrier to lower the total number of flights in its network given a certain number of network points and frequency of service. Imagine an airline serving ten cities. There are 90 possible city-pairs among the ten cities. To offer five-times daily point-to-point nonstop service between each of the city-pairs would necessitate 450 flights per day; but if one of the cities is made a hub, the number of necessary flights is only 90.

3 Yield refers to the amount of revenue per passenger-kilometer.

4 PEOPLExpress bought its own expensive yield management system, but the system did not go live until the day Texas Air acquired the financially desperate start-up (Petzinger 1995).

5 Viton (1986) found that given certain reasonable assumptions, marginal cost pricing, to which carriers would be pushed by unfettered competitive forces, would never be sufficient to cover average costs on US domestic trunk routes.

6 In addition, some carriers have reduced the concentration of activity in hubs – both temporally and spatially. In 2002, American Airline introduced a "rolling hub" concept at Chicago-O'Hare and Dallas-Ft. Worth via which the carrier spread arrivals and departures more evenly through the day, reducing the number of aircraft, gates, and staff required to accommodate a particular volume of traffic (Pinkham 2003). And

some network carriers have begun to bypass their hubs altogether, adopting more of the point-to-point service associated with LCCs (Maynard 2005). In the Delta Air Lines system, for instance, hub-bypass routes were spun from places such as Tampa (e.g., to Greensboro, North Carolina), Columbus, Ft. Lauderdale, Indianapolis, and Washington-National (Abbey 2005).

7 The case of Pittsburgh is discussed in fuller detail in Chapter 10.

8 In 2008, the ten poorest countries measured by per capita gross domestic product were Burundi, the Democratic Republic of Congo, Liberia, Guinea-Bissau, Eritrea, Malawi, Ethiopia, Sierra Leone, Niger, and Afghanistan. The ten richest were Luxembourg, Norway, Qatar, Switzerland, Denmark, Ireland, Iceland, the United Arab Emirates, Sweden, and the Netherlands.

9 On an interline route that is not served by an alliance, each carrier has an incentive to set fares that maximize its own profit, the result being a combined fare that is too high, discourages travel, and reduces the overall profit of the carriers on the route. When two carriers work in tandem under antitrust immunity, they set fares that maximize their combined profit, the result generally being lower fares than in the uncooperative alternative (Brueckner 2003).

10 The eight carriers are AeroMéxico Cargo, Air France Cargo, Delta Air Logistics, Korean Air Cargo, CSA Cargo, Alitalia Cargo, KLM Cargo, and Northwest Airlines Cargo.

11 It is important to note however that in order to win approval from the European Commission, Lufthansa and Swiss had to surrender some airport takeoff and landing slots at Frankfurt, Zurich, and six other European cities (Flottau 2005a).

12 Brussels Airlines is essentially what is left of the former Belgian state carrier SABENA, which collapsed in 2001.

13 Author's analysis of data in OAG (2008). Following the example of Burghouwt and Hakfoort (2001), intercontinental flights from Europe are defined as nonstop scheduled flights between Europe and the rest of the world, where Europe is defined as Austria, Belgium, Denmark, Finland, France, Gibraltar, Germany, Greece, Ireland, Italy, Luxembourg, Monaco, the Netherlands, Norway, Portugal, Spain, Sweden, Switzerland, and the United Kingdom.

14 There is a similar fleet difference between the two carriers: more than three-quarters of American's jets are narrow-bodies versus fewer than half for BA (*Air Transport World* 2008a).

15 As noted earlier in this chapter, the record on mergers is mixed. The recent merger between US Airways and America West, for instance, has been hobbled by significant problems melding the two carriers' unionized pilots. Delta and Northwest learned from that experience and worked out arrangements with their pilots first before consummating the merger (Palmeri 2008).

16 The regional rank of US carriers here is measured by scheduled seats per week.

17 In April 2003, the Pension Benefit Guarantee Corporation (PBGC), an entity established by the US federal government, took over the responsibility for pensions owed to US Airways' pilots. In a press release at the time, the PBGC noted that four of the ten largest pension takeovers by the agency had been in the airline industry and that the airline industry accounted for 17 percent of PBGC claims but only 2 percent of participants in pension plans insured by the corporation (PBGC 2003).

18 The southern emphasis of American Airlines' network (see Figure 2.2) served the carrier well during the decades-long Sunbelt shift in US population and economic activity.

7 A world taking wing: low-cost carriers and the ascent of the many

1 Although Southwest successfully thwarted efforts to force the carrier to move to Dallas-Ft. Worth, a 1979 law known as the Wright Amendment prohibited nonstop flights

from Love Field to any state other than Texas, New Mexico, Oklahoma, Arkansas, and Louisiana. The law was relaxed somewhat in 2006 to permit nonstop services to additional nearby states and in 2014 all geographic restrictions on operations from Love Field will be lifted.

2 Airbus has captured a larger proportion of recent LCC orders, however, with its A318, A319, A320, and A321 product line.

3 In June 2009, Southwest commenced services to LaGuardia Airport, its first foray to one of the three main airports serving the New York City area.

4 Neeleman had set up a Salt Lake City-based budget carrier called Morris Air that Southwest acquired in 1994, and he helped to establish another LCC, WestJet, in Calgary in the mid-1990s. More recently, Neeleman, who has Brazilian and American citizenship, established Brazilian LCC Azul Linhas Aéreas Brasileiras (J. Bailey 2008)

5 In 2005, the passengers aboard one of jetBlue's A320 were able to watch live television coverage of their jet after it was discovered that its nose landing gear had become stuck in a sideways position. One passenger on the plane, which made a successful emergency landing in Los Angeles, told CNN, "We couldn't believe the irony that we were watching our own demise on TV – it was all too post-post-modern." (quoted in Elsworth 2005).

6 Other LCCs that are subsidiaries of network carriers include Air India Express (Air India), Mango (South African Airways), Snowflake (SAS), Tiger Airways (whose parent company is 49 percent owned by SIA), and Transavia (Air France-KLM).

7 There were some fifth freedom carriers on the route such as Japan Airlines.

8 Interestingly, Lion Air, an Indonesian LCC, became the launch airline for the 737-900ER, the largest version of the Baby Boeing family.

9 In 2007, Jet Airways merged with fellow full-service carrier Sahara Airlines (based in India despite its name), Kingfisher acquired a controlling stake in LCC operator Air Deccan, and the two state-owned carriers – Air India and Indian Airlines – merged (Krishnamoorthy and Choudhury 2007)

10 A recent study also demonstrated the significant downward pressure on network carrier fares exerted by the threat of market entry by Southwest (Goolsbee and Syverson 2008).

11 In early 2009, the crash of a regional jet near Buffalo indirectly raised the issue of pilot salaries. The crash of Continental Connection flight 3407 from LaGuardia to Buffalo, which killed all 49 on board and one person on the ground, was blamed on pilot error. The copilot of the flight, who earned less than $25,000 per year, lived with her parents in Washington State apparently because she could not afford to live in the major metropolitan areas in which the carrier's operations were concentrated. It was suggested in Congressional hearings after the crash that the exhaustion engendered by very long distance commuting may have contributed to the disaster (Halbfinger *et al.* 2009).

8 People on the move at 1,000 kilometers per hour

1 First class on British Airways' 747s has a seat pitch of 78 inches at the time of writing.

2 Between 2005 and 2008, several new carriers entered the transatlantic market offering purely all-business class (ABC) services. They included MAXjet and eos airlines from the United States, Silverjet from the UK, and L'Avion from France. None survived the market downturn in 2008, though British Airways bought L'Avion and used its resources and the new freedoms granted by the 2007 US-EU air services agreement to commence ABC services between Paris and New York and later between Amsterdam and New York under the brand name Open Skies (Wall 2008b).

3 As described further in Chapter 10, many corporations have moved their headquarters specifically to improve their air transportation accessibility.

4 Although deep vein thrombosis, which may lead to a stroke or heart attack, can strike people in a variety of circumstances, it is strongly associated with air travel, especially travel on very long flights. An average of one person per month on Tokyo-bound flights succumbed to DVT according to a 2001 account (Anonymous and Thomas 2001: 90–2).

5 Boeing hopes that the 787 will reduce jet lag through a combination of larger windows, better lighting, higher humidity, and higher air pressure at cruising altitude.

6 Amid a weak economy in both the US and Japan, Hawaiian tourist arrivals fell in both 2007 and 2008, tumbling to 6.7 million in the latter year (State of Hawaii 2009).

7 As indicated in Table 8.10, although the United Arab Emirates has enjoyed rapid growth of inbound tourism, its 2005 total was less than half the emir's goal for 2010.

8 It is worth noting, however, that inbound tourism to Bhutan has grown sharply in recent years. The total of 21,000 for 2007 was up from just 9,000 in 2004.

9 If one assumes that all Mexican and Canadian migrants arrive by means other than flying and that all other immigrants fly, then in 2005 about 84 percent of legal immigrants to the US arrived by air. In practice, it is likely that many migrants from Mexico and Canada do arrive by air too inasmuch as the air routes from America's two neighbors are more heavily traveled than from any of the other countries to which the US is linked except the United Kingdom (BTS 2002: 16).

10 More spectacular, and too often tragic, are the cases of stowaways aboard commercial airliners. Remarkably, the Federal Aviation Administration (FAA) reported that ten people stowed away in wheel wells on US airliners between 1947 and 1996 and that five lived to tell about it (A. Baker 2001).

9 The high ways of trade

1 The term cargo refers to both freight and mail. In contrast to the early days of aviation, mail is of relatively little consequence to the airline industry today. In 2005, passengers, freight, and mail accounted for 55, 44, and 1 percent, respectively, of the traffic of the global airline industry measured in terms of tonne-kilometers (*ICAO Journal* 2006).

2 Passenger revenue for the world's airlines was seven times greater than cargo revenue in 2007 (Flint 2008).

3 $7,500 in year 2008 dollars.

4 Of course, the actual cost of the phone was hidden in the cost of a multiyear cell phone service contract.

5 The Randstad (a ring of cities in the Netherlands) contains Amsterdam Airport Schiphol and the Port of Rotterdam.

6 In 1988, FedEx purchased Flying Tigers, which had a widespread international network, partly due to its own acquisition of Seaboard Airlines earlier in the decade.

7 Reverse logistics refers to the return of damaged, faulty, or unwanted merchandise.

8 Some LCCs refuse cargo altogether because it slows down airport turnaround times and requires investment in expensive equipment and marketing.

9 Freighters more easily accommodate the large pallets upon which big forwarders consolidate cargo.

10 Both new production freighters and conversions have their advantages and disadvantages. The latter are much less expensive to acquire, even including the cost of conversion. For instance, in 2007 a converted 767 started at $10–15 million but a new 767F listed for about $155 million (Jackman 2007; Boeing Company 2007c). Newer freighters, on the other hand, typically have better fuel efficiency, lower maintenance costs, and better reliability – the latter being a key concern in an era of tight supply chains.

10 Points of departure: airports in the airborne world

1 Perhaps the most spectacular "white elephant" is Montreal's Mirabel Airport. Opened in 1975 as Montreal's answer to the jumbo jet, the airport was expected to handle 60 million passengers by 2010, but annual traffic never exceeded 3 million (*Toronto Star* 2004), partly because the older Dorval Airport continued to serve most domestic routes to and from Montreal while Mirabel was the city's international gateway. The division of routes made it difficult for either airport to function as an effective hub. Mirabel was closed to scheduled air traffic in 2004.

2 Interestingly, the two newest large airports in India (both opened in 2008) serve Bangalore and Hyderabad, the cities most associated with India's recent high-tech boom.

3 The use of airports to craft a favorable image is evident, too, in their naming. In 2001, for instance, New Orleans International Airport was renamed Louis Armstrong New Orleans International Airport, and Liverpool's gateway was renamed Liverpool John Lennon Airport in 2002.

4 In the headline, lead paragraphs, or citation.

5 Those plans were realized in that Indianapolis did become the second most important hub for FedEx in the US.

6 Mineta San Jose International Airport in California is somewhat similar to Pittsburgh International in that a massive expansion has lost much of its economic rationale. The new billion dollar terminal project was conceived at a time when San Jose's local economy (it is the hub of Silicon Valley) was thriving and the airport was important in the network of American Airlines. When the terminal is finished in 2010, it is unlikely that either will be true. As a sign of flagging demand at the airport, in 2009, American Airlines suspended its nonstop "Nerd Bird" flight that had linked San Jose and Austin, another center of high tech innovation.

7 In 2008, BAA put Gatwick Airport up for sale and in 2009, the United Kingdom's Competition Commission (CC) ordered the company to sell Stansted Airport and either Ediburgh or Glasgow Airport. At the time this book was written (July 2009) BAA was appealing the order (Competition Commission 2009).

8 It is worth noting here that one study found that Hispanics living in the Phoenix area bore a disproportionate share of the noise impact associated with Phoenix Sky Harbor International Airport (Sobotta *et al.* 2007).

9 The estimate of 2 million is based on Boeing's prediction that the number of passengers globally for the year will be 6.8 billion (up from 2.1 billion in 2006) and that the average distance traveled will be 1,670 kilometers. The estimate further assumes that the average schedule speed of commercial aircraft will remain about 650 kilometers per hour (see note 2 in Chapter 1).

10 In his research on the meaning of freedom, Harvard sociologist Orlando Patterson found that the freedom Americans prized most was not in the familiar 1st Amendment trinity of freedom of religion, speech, and assembly nor anywhere else in the US Constitution but rather mobility, the freedom to move (*On Point* 2005).

11 Heathrow, Gatwick, Stansted, London Luton, and London City handled 138 million passengers in 2008, far ahead of the 108 million who moved through New York's metropolitan airports (John F. Kennedy International, Newark Liberty International, LaGuardia, Stewart International, Westchester County, and Long Island Islip MacArthur) and the 100 million that passed through Tokyo's Narita and Haneda (based on information at relevant airport authority websites).

12 In 2008, 70 percent of the international passenger flights to Heathrow came from countries lying east of the airport (author's analysis of OAG 2008).

13 The record of airport traffic forecasting is not encouraging (Feldman and Milch 1982, Chapter 3). There has been a tendency for forecasters to tell their clients (typically the sponsors of new airport infrastructure) what they want to hear – and that has generally meant unabated growth. Further, the assumptions that underlie traffic forecasts are

often unrealistic (e.g., steady, robust economic growth) and little consideration is given to alternatives to new infrastructure, such as the maximal use of existing runways and terminals through congestion pricing.

11 Dangers hidden in the air: the broader costs of commercial aviation

1 There is some evidence that night flights and wintertime flights are significantly more important in their potential global warming impact than flights during the day or other seasons (Stuber *et al.* 2006).
2 Both Boeing and Airbus have experimented with synthetic fuels aimed at reducing the industry's dependence on oil and mitigating its environmental record. Airbus has pursued natural gas-to-liquid fuel technology while Boeing has worked on biomass-to-liquid fuel (Wall 2008a). The latter alternative is a promising long-term alternative but to avoid diverting biomass from the food supply (e.g., with corn-based fuels), Boeing and IATA have suggested harvesting algae from an area of sea the size of Belgium would be sufficient to meet the industry's current fuel requirements (Ott 2008).
3 Nor is flying necessarily more environmentally sustainable than travel by car. A Dutch study found that for a short-haul (i.e., 500 kilometers) trip, going by air produced three times more CO_2 emissions than a conventional gasoline-powered automobile (*Economist* 2006b).
4 The cap will be set at 97 percent of historical emissions for 2012.
5 Truck transport by comparison accounted for 65 percent of UK food transport-related CO_2 emissions.
6 Broadly defined, terrorism is an organized system of intimidation to achieve political aims.
7 The only previous occasions when all commercial airliners in the US and Canada were grounded occurred in the early 1960s when on three separate days civilian air traffic was suspended for as many as 12 hours so that the military could test its early warning systems (Mola 2002).
8 Aircraft cabin air circulates fast enough to completely change the air 15–20 times per hour, faster than in a typical office building. Further, air enters the cabin at the top and exits at the bottom of the same row, compartmentalizing air flow, and most airliners, especially large ones are equipped with high efficiency particulate (HEPA) filters (Gendreau 2005).

12 Coming back down to earth? The cloudy future of air transportation

1 The most famous drone, the Predator, is manufactured by Northrop Grumman, but Boeing and Airbus have also gotten into the business. Boeing bought a company called Insitu, whose workforce, which is sprinkled among 15 sites along the Columbia River gorge in Washington State, grew dramatically from fewer than a dozen people in 2002 to more than 600 in 2009 (Bernton 2009).
2 Aerion is designing the jet but will rely upon an as-yet-unnamed partner to manufacture the plane (Collogan 2008).
3 The book's title, *Why Your World Is about to Get a Whole Lot Smaller: Oil and the End of Globalization*, uses the notion of a "smaller" world in exactly the opposite way as it is used in Friedman's book *The World Is Flat: A Brief History of the Twenty-first Century* and in this book.
4 Of course, rail remains more important than air travel in many developing countries, such as India, but the trend in such markets has been away from travel by train.

5 The acronym NIMBY means "not in my backyard" and refers to opposition to the development of an undesirable land use near one's home.

6 BA can rely upon its oneworld partners to reach the passenger market in places such as El Paso but as noted in Chapter 6, alliances are almost completely absent in the cargo business.

7 The money-losing Maglev has less to do with efficiency than the same image-making that has inspired the architecturally stunning new airports built in China and elsewhere in recent decades.

8 For example, the 70-seat Bombardier Q400 cruises at about 670 kilometers per hour versus 875 kilometers per hour for the similar-sized CRJ 700, also built by Bombardier (Bombardier 2009b).

9 Perhaps not coincidentally, each of the main airliner markets is a duopoly at the beginning of the twenty-first century: Airbus and Boeing in large commercial aircraft, Bombardier and Embraer for regional jets, and ATR and Bombardier for turboprops.

References

Abbey, D. (2005) "Small is beautiful," *Airline Business*, February: 59.

ACI [Airports Council International] (2005) *Aircraft Noise Rating Index*, Geneva: March 9.

—— (2008) "Passenger traffic 2007 final," online, available at: www.airports.org (accessed June 4, 2009).

ACSI [American Consumer Satisfaction Index] (2009) "Scores by industry: Airlines," online, available at: www.acsi.org/index (accessed August 6, 2009).

Adams, J. (1999) "The social implications of hypermobility," in *The Economic and Social Implications of Sustainable Transportation*, proceedings from the Ottawa Workshop, Project on Environmentally Sustainable Transport, Organization for Economic Cooperation and Development, October 1998.

Adey, P., Budd, L., and Hubbard, P. (2007) "Flying lessons: Exploring the social and cultural geographies of global air travel," *Progress in Human Geography*, 31(6): 773–91.

Air Berlin (2009) "Air Berlin flight timetable," online, available at: www.airberlin.com (accessed July 30, 2009).

Air Cargo World (2006) "Frankfurt blackout," May 6: 41.

Air Transport World (1998a) "Best of times, worst of times," July: 56–63.

—— (1998b) "The world's top 25 airlines in 1997," July: 63.

—— (2008a) "Individual airline fleets," July: 111–26.

—— (2008b) "World airline financial results 2007," July: 41–6.

—— (2008c) "World commercial turbine fleet," July: 110.

—— (2008d) "The world's top 25 airlines 2007," July: 39.

Airbus (2007) *Global Market Forecast 2007–2026*, online, available at: www.airbus.com/en/corporate/gmf (accessed May 6, 2009).

—— (2009a) "Aircraft families," online, available at: www.airbus.com/en/ aircraft-families (accessed July 13, 2009).

—— (2009b) "Historical orders and deliveries," online, available at: www.airbus.com/en/corporate/orders_and_deliveries (accessed May 15, 2009).

Airdisaster.com (2009) "Accident database," online, available at: www.airdisaster.com (accessed July 31, 2009).

Airline Business (1995) "Airline ownership survey," December: 52–4.

—— (2005) "KLM kicks off all-business class service," October.

—— (2009) "Low-cost traffic ranking," May: 74–5.

Airline Pilot Central (2007) "Hourly pay rates for various airlines," online, available at: www.airlinepilotcentral.com (accessed November 15, 2007).

Airliners.net (2008) "Aircraft data," online, available at: www.airliners.net/aircraft-data (accessed June 1, 2008).

Alexander, K.L. (2006) "Air of caution at CDC after mumps outbreak," *The Washington Post*, April 18: D1.

Allen, O.E. (1981) *The Airline Builders*, Alexandria, Virginia: Time-Life Books.

American Experience (2007) *Hijacked!* [Television program produced by Ilan Ziv.] Aired March 19.

Anderson, J.D. (2002) *The Airplane: A History of Its Technology*, Reston, Virginia: American Institute of Aeronautics and Astronautics.

Andre, R. (2004) *Take Back the Sky: Protecting Communities in the Path of Aviation Expansion*, San Francisco: Sierra Club Books.

Anonymous and Thomas, A.R. (2001) *Air Rage: Crisis in the Skies*, Amherst, New York: Prometheus Books.

Anselmo, J.C. (2008a) "Inside the 787 meltdown," *Aviation Week & Space Technology*, April 21: 41.

—— (2008b) "Crude thinking," *Aviation Week & Space Technology*, May 26: 55.

Apter, D.E. and Sawa, N. (1984) *Against the State: Politics and Social Protest in Japan*, Cambridge, Massachusetts: Harvard University Press.

Arnott, S. (2009) "EU competition probe could hit BA's American dream," *The Independent* (London), April 21: 38.

Ascend (2009) "Aviation 2020 webcast – Dealing with the downturn," online, available at: ascendworldwide.com/content/Ascend-Aviation2020-webcast-23-04-09.pdf (accessed July 2, 2009).

Asian Aviation (1989) "Bangkok Airways planning new routes and fleet growth," October: 56.

Aviation News (2003) "Concorde chronology," November 2003, online, available at: www.aviation-news.co.uk/concordeChronology.html (accessed February 21, 2008).

Aviation Week & Space Technology (1976) "British Airways Mideast traffic surges," April 12: 27.

—— (1981) "New terminal opens at Orlando," October 5: 49.

—— (1988) "Air France, British Airways plan April start-up with first A320s," April 4: 64.

—— (2005a) "Healthy climate," June 20: 15.

—— (2005b) "High spirits," July 18: 51–2.

BAA (2009) "Facts and figures," online, available at: www.baa.com (accessed August 1, 2009).

Bailey, E.E., Graham D.R., and Kaplan, D.P. (1985) *Deregulating the Airlines*, Cambridge, Massachusetts: MIT Press.

Bailey, J. (2008) "Founder of jetBlue is planning a startup airline for Brazil," *New York Times*, March 28: C3.

Baker, A. (2001) "Stowaway fell from jet near airport, police say," *New York Times*, August 8: B1.

Baker, C. (2003) "Aer Lingus reacts to low-cost threat," *Airline Business*, March: 9.

—— (2004) "Playing by the rules," *Airline Business*, March: 30.

Baldanza, B. and Field, D. (2006) "Lifting the spirit," *Airline Business*, April: 32–6.

Balfour, F. (2004) "Will Asia's low-cost airlines fly high?," *Business Week*, June 21: 28.

Barrie, D. (2005) "Cash crunch," *Aviation Week & Space Technology*, May 23: 28.

Barnes, W (2004) "Nok Air puts faith in budget market growth," *The Financial Times*, July 23: 29.

BBC News Monitoring Service – Asia Pacific (2009) "China starts building airport near 2,200-year-old ancient city in Xinjiang," May 6.

Bedingfield, R.E. (1971) "Airline's 747 fleet cuts costs 23%," *New York Times*, May 5: 65.

Belobaba, P.R. (1987) "Airline yield management: An overview of seat inventory control," *Transportation Science*, 21(2): 63–73.

Berkvist, R. (1961) "A shrinking globe: Jets transform oceans into ponds, travelers into demons for speed," *New York Times*, April 16: 3.

Berland, T. (1970) *The Fight for Quiet*, Englewood Cliffs, New Jersey: Prentice Hall.

Bernton, H. (2009) "Soaring success: Drones lift Gorge economy," *The Seattle Times*, July 26: C1, C6.

Biddle, W. (1991) *Barons of the Sky: From Early Flight to Strategic Warfare, The Story of the American Aerospace Industry*, New York: Simon & Schuster.

Bieger, T. and Wittmer, A. (2006) "Air transport and tourism – Perspectives and challenges for destinations, airlines, and governments," *Journal of Air Transport Management*, 12: 40–6.

Bisignani, G. (2006) "Think again: Airlines," *Foreign Policy*, January/February: 22–8.

Bleach, S. (2007) "The superjumbo is a go!," *Sunday Times* (London), October 28: Travel, 20.

BLS [US Bureau of Labor Statistics] (2007) "Occupational employment and wages," May 2006, online, available at: www.bls.gov (accessed June 24, 2007).

—— (2009) "Occupational employment and wages," May 2008, online, available at: www.bls.gov (accessed August 7, 2009).

Blue Air (2009) "Flights schedule," online, available at: www.blueair-web.com (accessed July 15, 2009).

BOAC [British Overseas Airways Corporation] (1962) *BOAC Timetable October 1st, 1962*, online, available at: www.timetableimages.com (accessed March 25, 2009).

Boeing Company (2006) *World Air Cargo Forecast 2006/2007*, online, available at: www.boeing.com/commercial/cargo/index.html (accessed August 5, 2007).

—— (2007a) "787 Dreamliner," online, available at: www.boeing.com/commercial/787family/background.html (accessed May 25, 2007).

—— (2007b) "787 Dreamliner: International development team," online, available at: www.boeing.com/commercial/787family/dev_team.html (accessed May 25, 2007).

—— (2007c) "Commercial aircraft – jet prices," online, available at: www.boeing.com/commercial/prices/index.html (accessed July 15, 2007).

—— (2008a) *Current Market Outlook*, onlinea available at: www.boeing.com/commercial/cmo/index.html (accessed June 2, 2008).

—— (2008b) "Out-of-production models," online, available at: www.boeing.com/commercial/out_of_production.html (accessed May 31, 2008).

—— (2009a) "Commercial airplanes," online, available at: www.boeing.com/commercial/products.html (accessed June 13, 2009).

—— (2009b) "Orders & deliveries," online, available at: active.boeing.com/commercial/orders/index.cfm (accessed May 23, 2009).

Boles, T. (2008) "Indian Kingfisher takes flight to London's Heathrow," *Sunday Express* (London), August 31: (Finance) 1.

Bombardier (2009a) "Program status reports," April 30, 2009, online, available at: www.bombardier.com/en/aerospace/media-centre/program-status-reports (accessed May 15, 2009).

Bombardier (2009b) "Q Series turboprofits," online, available at: www.bombardier.com/en/aerospace/products/commercial-aircraft/q-series (accessed July 4, 2009).

Bond, D. (2002) "Lufthansa sees BBJ limits, but looks for opportunities," *Aviation Week & Space Technology*, May 27: 44.

—— (2004) "Opening door in China," *Aviation Week & Space Technology*, September 13: 53.

—— (2005) "Bankruptcy's revolving door," *Aviation Week & Space Technology*, September 19: 34–5.

—— and Wall, R. (2007) "First steps," *Aviation Week & Space Technology*, April 2: 60–1.

Borders, W. (1977) "Tourism boom ending isolation of the Maldives," *New York Times*, December 26: 7.

Boston Globe, The (2005) "No-frills flying," June 4: 14.

Boulton, D. (1978) *The Grease Machine*, New York: Harper & Row.

Bowe, C. (2002) "Change of scenery pays off for Boeing," *Financial Times*, January 3: 22.

Bowen, J.T. (1991) "Airline competitive adaptations and congestion in major hubs: The case of Delta Air Lines," unpublished thesis, University of Kentucky.

—— (1993) "The global airline industry and economic development in Singapore," unpublished dissertation, University of Kentucky.

—— (2002) "Network change, deregulation, and access in the global airline industry," *Economic Geography*, 78(4): 425–39.

—— (2007) "Global production networks, the developmental state, and the articulation of Asia Pacific economies in the commercial aircraft industry," *Asia Pacific Viewpoint*, 48(3): 312–29.

—— and Cidell, J.L. (forthcoming) "Mega-airports: The political, economic, and environmental implications of the world's expanding air transportation gateways," in S. Brunn and A. Wood (eds.) *Engineering Earth: The Impacts of Megaengineering Projects*, Dordrecht, Netherlands: Kluwer Academic Publishers.

—— and LaRoe, C.L. (2006) "Airline networks and the international diffusion of Severe Acute Respiratory Syndrome (SARS)," *Geographical Journal*, 17(2): 130–44.

—— and Leinbach, T.R. (1995) "The state and liberalization: The airline industry in the East Asian NICs," *Annals of the Association of American Geographers*, 85(3): 468–93.

—————— (2004) "Market concentration in the air freight forwarding industry," *Tijdschift voor Economische en Sociale Geografie*, 95(2): 174–88.

—————— and Mabazza, D. (2002) "Air cargo services, the state, and industrialization strategies in the Philippines: The redevelopment of Subic Bay," *Regional Studies*, 36(5): 451–67.

Bowermaster, D. (2005) "Boeing, Japan say aerospace deals now official," *The Seattle Times*, May 27: D1.

Bowie, B. (2005) "Building the A380," *New Scientist*, June 11: 34–41.

Braden, B. and Hagen, P. (1989) *A Dream Takes Flight: Hartsfield Atlanta International Airport and Aviation in Atlanta*, Athens: The University of Georgia Press.

Brimelow, P. (1995) *Alien Nation: Common Sense about America's Immigration Disaster*, New York: HarperPerennial.

Brown, A.E. (1987) *The Politics of Airline Deregulation*, Knoxville: University of Tennessee Press.

Brueckner, J.K. (2003) "International airfares in the age of alliances: The effects of code-sharing and antitrust immunity," *The Review of Economics and Statistics*, 85(1): 105–18.

Brunn, S., Cutter, S., and Harrington, J. (eds.) (2004) *Geography and Technology* Dordrecht, Netherlands: Kluwer Academic Publishers.

BTS [US Bureau of Transportation Statistics] (2002) *U.S. International Travel and Transportation Trends*, Washington, DC.

—— (2003) *America on the Go: U.S. Business Travel*, online, available at: www.bts.gov/ publications/america_on_the_go/us_business_travel (accessed November 13, 2005).

—— (2006a) *America on the Go: Long Distance Transportation Patterns: Mode Choice*, online, available at: www.bts.gov/publications/america_on_the_go/ long_distance_ transportation_patterns (accessed April 14, 2007).

—— (2006b) *Freight in America*, online, available at: www.bts.gov/publications/freight_ in_america (accessed June 23, 2007).

—— (2007) *National Transportation Statistics 2007*, online, available at: www.bts.gov/ publications/national_transportation_statistics/2007/index.html (accessed May 27, 2008).

—— (2009a) "Air carrier statistics. Form 41 traffic," online, available at: www. transtats. bts.gov (accessed May 26, 2009).

—— (2009b) "Historical air traffic data," online, available at: www.bts.gov/programs/ airline_information/air_carrier_traffic_statistics (accessed August 9, 2009).

—— (2009c) "Number of employees – Certificated carriers 2008 year end data," online, available at: www.bts.gov/programs/airline_information/number_of_employees/ certif- icated_carriers (accessed May 10, 2009).

—— (2009d) *Pocket Guide to Transportation 2009*, online, available at: www.bts.gov/ publications/pocket_guide_to_transportation (accessed May 17, 2009).

Bukhari, S. (2002) "Haj by the numbers," *Saudi Aramco World*, May/June: 27.

Burghouwt, G. and Hakfoort, J. (2001) "The evolution of the European aviation network," *Journal of Air Transport Management*, 7: 311–18.

Business Times, The (Singapore) (2003) "DHL brand unites merger of DHL, Danzas, Deutsche Post," April 2: 16.

Business Travel News (2007) "Heathrow 2.0; pact shakes airport," 24(11), June 11: 4.

Butler, R. (1997) "Transportation innovations and island tourism," in D.J. Lockhart and D. Drakakis-Smith (eds.) *Island Tourism: Trends & Prospects*, London: Pinter, 36–56.

Butterworth-Hayes, P. (2006a) "Europe looks set to cap air transport growth," *Aerospace America*, May: 4.

—— (2006b) "Airbus moves give rise to new questions," *Aerospace America*, June: 4.

Button, K. and Taylor, S. (2000) "International air transportation and economic develop- ment," *Journal of Air Transport Management*, 6: 209–22.

CAAS [Civil Aviation Authority of Singapore] (2007) "International ventures," online, available at: www.caas.gov.sg/caas/en/About_CAAS/International_Ventures.html (accessed August 6, 2007).

Calder, S. (2009) "Now Ryanair wants to charge you a pound to spend a penny," *The Independent* (London), February 28: 4.

Capell, K. (2006) "A closer continent: How the explosion in bargain Euro-fares is break- ing down borders and creating a new class of commuters," *Business Week*, May 8: 44.

Cargolux (2008) "Network and offices," online, available at: www.cargolux.com/ Cus- tomers/NetworkOffices (accessed October 12, 2008).

Carvajal, D. (2006) "Tourist businesses offer comfort to soccer widows," *New York Times*, June 2: E2.

Castles, S. and Miller, M.J. (1999) *The Age of Migration: International Population Move- ments in the Modern World*, New York: Guilford Press.

Cazeneuve, B., Habib, D.G., Menez, G., Syken, B., Woo, A., and Schecter, B.J. (2004) "Teams on the move," *Sports Illustrated*, December 27: 110–12.

CFO (2003) "Containing terrorism: federal antiterrorism programs have spurred a sea change in supply-chain security," September: 87.

Charles, M.B., Barnes, P., Ryan, N., and Clayton, J. (2007) "Airport future: Towards a critique of the aerotropolis model," *Futures*, 39(9): 1009–28.

Cheng, B. (1962) *The Law of International Air Transport*, New York: Oceania.

Chin K.-L. (1999) *Smuggled Chinese: Clandestine Immigration to the United States*, Philadelphia: Temple University Press.

Chiu, A. (2005) "Airlines target migrant workers in spring rush," *South China Morning Post*, January 12: 1.

Cidell, J. (2008) "Challenging the contours: Critical cartography, local knowledge, and the public," *Environment and Planning A*, 40: 1202–18.

Clark, A. (2005) "Worried about air pollution? Sell your car, says Ryanair boss," *The Guardian*, June 22: 2.

CNN (2006) "Typo takes tourist 13,000 km out," January 13, online, available at: www.cnn.com (accessed March 12, 2006).

CNN Money (2006) "Fortune 500 2006," from the April 17, 2006 issue, online, available at: www.money.cnn.com/magazines/fortune/fortune500/full_list (accessed September 13, 2007).

Coe, N., Hesse, M., Yeung, H.W.-C., Dicken, P., and Henderson, J. (2004) "'Globalizing' regional development: A global production networks perspective," *Transactions of the Institute of British Geographers*, 29: 468–84.

Collogan, D. (2008) "Aerion test results promising, but OEM partner needed soon," *The Weekly of Business Aviation*, October 13: 172.

Compart, A. (2008) "U.S. DOT finalizes approval for Skyteam immunity," *Aviation Daily*, May 23: 3.

Competition Commission (2009) "BAA ordered to sell three airports," press release dated March 19.

Condom, P. (2007) "The next challenge," *Interavia*, Summer: 3.

Connelly, M. (2005) "Faster overseas flights for summer," *New York Times*, May 22: E2.

Continental Airlines (2008) "Continental Airlines to reduce capacity, fleet, staffing," press release dated June 5.

Conway, P. (2002) "Awaiting the call," *Airline Business*, November: 53

—— (2003) "In safe hands?," *Airline Business*, November: 57.

—— (2004) "Diverging paths," *Airline Business*, November: 46.

—— (2008) "New era for Lufthansa – DHL," *Airline Business*, March: 25.

Coppinger, R. (2004) "Asian boom forces Boeing rethink," *Flight International*, July 27: 27.

Council of the European Union (2008) "Council gives green light to the inclusion of aviation in the EU Emissions Trading System," press release dated October 24.

CRAA [Columbus Regional Airport Authority] (2006) "About Rickenbacker," online, available at: www.rickenbacker.org/about (accessed August 13, 2007).

Creaton, S. (2004) *Ryanair: How a Small Irish Airline Conquered Europe*, London: Aurum.

Crerar, P. (2009) "Estuary airport? Easy," *Evening Standard* (London), January 26: 6.

Croft, J. (2005) "Almost ready for prime time," *Air Transport World*, April: 56–8.

CRS [US Congressional Research Service] (1992) *Airbus Industrie: An Economic and Trade Perspective*, 102nd Congress, Serial K. Washington: US Government Printing Office.

Cunningham, J.F. (1960) "The travel trade leads the way to Hawaii," *New York Times*, November 6: 43.

Cuthbert, G. (1987) *Flying to the Sun: A Quarter Century of Britannia Airways, Europe's Leading Leisure Airline*, London: Hodder and Stoughton.

Davenport, C. (2006) "At burgeoning BWI, a chance to lighten up," *The Washington Post*, January 12: T12.

Davidson, K. (2006) "Prairie potential; DIA corridor will create an "aeropolitan" of new growth and industry over next 30 years," *Colorado Construction*, 9(8) April: 18–23.

Davies, R.E.G. (1964) *A History of the World's Airlines*, London: Oxford University Press.

—— (1972) *Airlines of the United States since 1914*, London: Putnam.

—— (1992) *Aeroflot: An Airline and Its Aircraft*, Rockville, Maryland: Paladwr Press.

Debbage, Keith G. (1999) "Air transportation and urban-economic restructuring: competitive advantage in the US Carolinas," *Journal of Air Transport Management*, 5: 211–221.

—— and Delk, D. (2001) "The geography of air passenger volume and local employment patterns by US metropolitan core area: 1973–1996," *Journal of Air Transport Management*, 7: 159–67.

DEFRA [United Kingdom Department of Environment, Food, and Rural Affairs] (2005) *The Validity of Food Miles as an Indicator of Sustainable Development*, Report ED50254, online, available at: www.defra.gov.uk (accessed June 2, 2009).

De Lollis, B. (2005) "Airlines see potential in travel by immigrants," *USA Today*, December 27: B1.

—— (2006) "Airport play the name game to attract new business," *USA Today*, February 23: B1.

Denstadli, J.M. (2004) "Impacts of videoconferencing on business travel: The Norwegian experience," *Journal of Air Transport Management*, 10: 371–6.

DfT [United Kingdom Department for Transport] (2003) *The Future of Transport*, online, available at: www.dft.gov.uk/about/strategy/whitepapers/previous/fot (accessed August 19, 2007).

—— (2009) *Adding Capacity at Heathrow: Decisions Following Consultation*, online, available at: www.dft.gov.uk/pgr/aviation/heathrowconsultations (accessed August 4, 2009).

Dick, R. and Patterson, D. (2003) *Aviation Century: The Early Years*, Erin, Ontario: Boston Mills Press.

Dobruszkes, F. (2006) "An analysis of Europe's low-cost airlines and their networks," *Journal of Transport Geography*, 14: 249–64.

Dodge, M. and Kitchin, R. (2004) "Flying through code/space: the real virtuality of air travel," *Environment and Planning A*: 36: 195–211.

Doganis, R. (1991) *Flying Off Course: The Economics of International Airlines*, 2nd edn, London: HarperCollins Academic.

—— (2006) *The Airline Business*, 2nd edn, New York: Routledge.

Done, K. (2000) "The long flight to integration ends in a smooth landing' *Financial Times*, June 23: 19.

—— (2006) "Superjet crisis to cost EADS over pounds 3 billion," *Financial Times*, October 4: 1.

—— (2007) "Singapore takes delivery of first Airbus A380," *Financial Times*, October 16: 30.

Donnelly, S. (2001) "The day the FAA stopped the world' *Time*, September 14, online, available at: www.time.com (accessed August 3, 2007).

Dorman, C. (2006) "Virgin Blue scorns low-cost model," *The Age* (Melbourne), September 2: 2.

DOS [US Department of State] (2008) "Open Skies partners," November 25, online, available at: www.state.gov/e/eeb/rls/othr/ata/114805.htm (accessed July 24, 2009).

DOT [US Department of Transportation] (2009) "What is essential air service (EAS)?," online, available at: ostpxweb.dot.gov/aviation/rural/easwhat.pdf (accessed July 16, 2009).

Driehaus, B. (2008) "DHL to cut 9,500 jobs in the U.S. and an Ohio town takes the brunt," *New York Times*, November 11: B3.

Duval, D.T. (2005) "Public/stakeholder perceptions of airline alliances: The New Zealand experience," *Journal of Air Transport Management*, 11: 448–54.

Duvall, M. and Bartholomew, D. (2007) "The promise and peril of PLM," *Baseline*, 1(69): February.

Earth Policy Institute (2007) "Gross world product, 1950–2006," online, available at: staging.earth-policy.org/datacenter/xls/indicator2_2006_1.xls (accessed July 13, 2009).

Economist, The (1994) "Banking on a big bird," March 12: 73.

—— (1998a) "Flying visits," Travel and tourism survey, January 10: 5–7.

—— (1998b) "Home and away," Travel and tourism survey, January 10: 1–5.

—— (2004) "Turbulent skies – low-cost airlines," July 10: 59–61.

—— (2005a) "Nose to nose," June 25: 67–9.

—— (2005b) "Breaking the sound barrier – again," Technology Quarterly, December 10: 3–4.

—— (2006a) "Flight of fancy?," Technology Quarterly, March 11: 15.

—— (2006b) "The sky's the limit," June 10: 67–9.

—— (2006c) "Chain reactions," June 17, A Survey of Logistics: 14–18.

—— (2006d) "Fear of flying – After Britain's terror alert," August 19: 20–1.

—— (2006e) "The Italian exception," October 14: 71.

—— (2006f) "Set Airbus free to soar," November 11: 16–18.

—— (2007a) "A world of connections," April 28, A special report on telecoms: 3–4.

—— (2007b) "Odd couple," May 5: 79–82.

—— (2007c) "A high-speed revolution," July 7: 61–2.

—— (2008) "Flying in formation; British Airways and Iberia," August 2: 67.

—— (2009) "Hard pounding; Airbus and Boeing resume their feud," June 20: 69.

Elsworth, C. (2005) "Air passengers watch their jet in crisis live on inflight TV," *The Daily Telegraph* (London), September 23: 19.

Embraer (2008) *2008 Annual Report*, online, available at: www.embraer.com/english/content/home (accessed May 15, 2009).

Engineer, The (2006) "Interview: Letting fly," January 16: 29.

Erlanger, S. (1989) "Closely observed in Burma," *New York Times*, April 2, Section 5: 8.

Eurocontrol (2006) *Eurocontrol Long-Term Forecast: IFR Flight Movements, 2006–2025*, online, available at: www.eurocontrol.int (accessed July 19, 2007).

European Commission (2008) "Common aviation with the neighbouring countries by 2010 – progress report," January 2008, online, available at: ec.europa.eu/transport/ air/international_aviation/external_aviation_policy/neighbourhood_en.htm (accessed June 24, 2009).

Evans-Pritchard, A. (2007) "Berlin demands to take Airbus wings from UK," *The Daily Telegraph* (London), February 24: 31.

FAA [US Federal Aviation Administration] (1967) *FAA Statistical Handbook of Aviation 1967*, Washington.

—— (2007) *Capacity Needs in the National Airspace System, 2007–2025*, Washington.

Fallows, J. (2001) *Free Flight: From Airline Hell to a New Age of Travel*, New York: Public Affairs.

Feldman, E.J. and Milch, J. (1982) *Technocracy versus Democracy: The Comparative Politics of International Airports*, Boston, Massachusetts: Auburn House Publishing.

Field, D. (2008) "Continental dumps Skyteam," *Airline Business*, August: 12.

Fingleton, E. (2005) "Boeing, Boeing, gone: Outsourced to death," *American Conservative*, January 24.

Flight International (1984) "World airline directory," March 31: 807–98.

—— (2002) "Opening the skies," November 12: 3.

—— (2003) "The 60-year itch," April 1: 3.

—— (2006a) "World airline directory – Part one," April 4: 35–55, 58–91.

—— (2006b) "World airline directory – Part two," April 11: 35–54, 56–9, 62–98.

—— (2006c) "World airline directory – Part three," April 18: 33–102.

—— (2009) "Russia delivers, barely," February 3: 26.

Flint, P. (2008) "A world turned upside down – World airline report," *Air Transport World*, July: 26–36.

Florida, R. (2005) "The world is spiky," *Atlantic Monthly*, October: 48–51.

Flottau, J. (2005a) "Lufthansa gets the nod," *Aviation Week & Space Technology*, July 11: 41.

—— (2005b) "Grand central," *Aviation Week & Space Technology*, December 5: 51.

—— (2006) "Oneworld carriers reach deal with London Heathrow," *Aviation Daily*, March 14: 2.

—— (2007) "How Emirates grows," *Aviation Week & Space Technology*, May 21: 50–1.

—— (2008) "Virgin to withdraw from Virgin Nigeria venture," *Aviation Daily*, August 22: 5.

—— (2009) "Open questions," *Aviation Week & Space Technology*, January 19: 40.

Folsom, M. (1961) "Aloha means "We love you, please come back"," *New York Times*, June 4: 54.

Foust, D. (2004) "Big Brown's new bag," *Business Week*, July 19: 54.

Francillon, R.J. (1979) *McDonnell Douglas Aircraft since 1920*, London: Putnam.

Francis, G., Dennis, N., Ison, S., and Humphreys, I. (2007) "The transferability of the low-cost model to long-haul airline operations," *Tourism Management*, 28: 391–8.

Freiberg, K. and Freiberg, J. (1996) *NUTS! Southwest Airlines' Crazy Recipe for Business and Personal Success*, Austin: Bard Press.

Friedlander, P.J.C. (1958) "Economy air fares; Austerity service to be introduced on Atlantic flights on April 1," *New York Times*, February 2: 1.

Friedman, T. (2006) *The World Is Flat: A Brief History of the Twenty-First Century*, Updated and expanded edition, New York: Farrar, Straus and Giroux.

Fuller, G. and Harley, R. (2004) *Aviopolis: A Book about Airports*, London: Black Dog Publishing.

Gandt, R. (1995) *Skygods: The Fall of Pan Am*, New York: William and Morrow Company.

Gantenbein, B. (2005) "Next day delivery," *Western Builder*, November 3: 4.

GAO [United States General Accounting Office] (1996) "Aircraft noise at Memphis International Airport," RCED-97-37R.

Gardiner, J., Ison, S., and Humphreys, I. (2005) "Factors influencing cargo airlines choice of airport: An international survey," *Journal of Air Transport Management*, 11: 393–9.

Garrahan, M. (2005) "Balancing act on fuel emissions," *Financial Times*, June 13: Business Travel: 1.

Garvey, J.F. (2001) "Complex noise issues calls for environmentally and economically responsible solution," *ICAO Journal*, 57(4): 20–21; 33–34.

Gates, D. (2003) "Digital methods to speed widebody's final assembly," *The Seattle Times*, July 15: C1.

—— (2005) "Parts from around world will be swiftly integrated; Boeing 787," *The Seattle Times*, July 15: C1.

GE Aviation (2009) "Commercial engines," online, available at: www.geae.com/ engines/ commercial (accessed July 20, 2007).

GECAS [General Electric Capital Aviation Services] (2009) "Global fact sheet," online, available at: www.gecas.com/News/GECAS_Fact_Sheet.pdf (accessed July 21, 2009).

Gendreau, M.A. (2005) "Transmission of infectious diseases during commercial air travel," Testimony before the Committee on Transportation and Infrastructure Subcommittee on Aviation, United States House of Representatives, April 6.

Gero, David (2000) *Aviation Disasters: The World's Major Civil Airliner Crashes Since 1950*, 3rd edn, Sparkford, England: Patrick Stephens Limited.

Gessing, P.J. (2005) "Re-deregulate the airlines," *National Review*, August 15, online, available at: www.nationalreview.com (accessed August 2, 2007).

Gilden, J. (2002) "The world of travel keeps on changing," *Los Angeles Times*, May 12: L3.

Gittell, J.H. (2003) *The Southwest Airlines Way: Using the Power of Relationships to Achieve High Performance*, New York: McGraw Hill.

Gleick, J. (1999) *Faster: The Acceleration of Just about Everything*, New York: Pantheon Books.

GlobalSecurity.org (2006a) "AA 11 crashes into WTC North Tower," online, available at: www.globalsecurity.org/security (accessed July 23, 2007).

—— (2006b) "UA 175 crashes into WTC South Tower," online, available at: www.globalsecurity.org/security (accessed July 23, 2007).

Globe and Mail (2005) "Disney's world," April 30: T6.

Goetz, A.R. and Graham, B. (2004) "Air transport globalization, liberalization, and sustainability: Post-2001 policy dynamics in the United States and Europe," *Journal of Transport Geography*, 12: 265–76.

Goetz, A.R. and Sutton, C.J. (1997) "The geography of deregulation in the U.S. airline industry,' *Annals of the Association of American Geographers*, 87(2): 228–63.

Goolsbee, A. and Syverson, C. (2008) "How do incumbents respond to the threat of entry? Evidence from the major airlines," *Quarterly Journal of Economics*, 123(4): 1611–33.

Gordon, A. (2004) *Naked Airport: A Cultural History of the World's Most Revolutionary Structure*, New York: Metropolitan Books.

Gordon, R.J. (2004) "Network hubs vs. point-to-point: Is there a problem?," paper presented at Embry-Riddle Aeronautical University Airline Economics Seminar, Washington, DC, April 2004.

Gottdiener, M. (2001) *Life in the Air: Surviving the New Culture of Air Travel*, Lanham, Maryland: Rowman & Littlefield.

Graham, A. (2003) *Managing Airports: An International Perspective*, Burlington, Massachusetts: Butterworth-Heinemann.

—— (2006) Have the major forces driving leisure airline traffic changed? *Journal of Air Transport Management*, 12: 14–20.

Graham, B. (1995) *Geography and Air Transport*, New York: John Wiley.

Greenberg, P. (2001) *The Travel Detective: How to Get the Best Service and Best Deals from Airlines, Hotels, Cruise Ships, and Car Rental Agencies*, New York: Villard.

Greenfeld, K.T. (2006) *China Syndrome: The True Story of the 21st Century's First Great Epidemic*, New York: HarperCollins.

Grimes, P. (1980) "The case for business class," *New York Times*, April 13: 25.

Guha, M. and Smith, S. (2006) "TNT sells contract logistics business to Apollo," *Financial Times*, August 24: 23.

Gussow, D. (2003) "20 years later, it's the manners that bug cell phone pioneer," *St. Petersburg Times* (Florida), March 24: 1E.

Haddad, C. (2001) "Ground wars," *Business Week*, May 21: 64.

Hakfoort, J., Poot, T., and Rietveld, P. (2001) "The regional economic impact of an airport: The case of Amsterdam Schiphol Airport," *Regional Studies*, 35(7): 595–604.

Halbfinger, D.M., Wald, M.L., and Drew, C. (2009) "A commuter pilot's life; exhausted, hungry, and poorly paid," *New York Times*, May 17: A1.

Hamilton, T. (2009) "A maverick's message on oil," *Toronto Star*, May 16: B1.

Hammond, A.L. (2001) "Digitally empowered development," *Foreign Affairs*, March/April: 96–106.

Hanlon, P. (1996) *Global Airlines: Competition in a Transnational Industry*, Oxford: Butterworth-Heinemann.

Harney, A. and Roberts, D. (2004) "Midnight in Memphis, new dawn in China," *Financial Times*, August 9: 15.

Harvey, F. (2006) "An entire sector shows it can see green," *Financial Times*, July 17: 5.

Hawk, J. (2005) "The Boeing 787 Dreamliner: More than an airplane," paper presented at the AIAA/AAAF Aircraft Noise and Emissions Reduction Symposium, Monterey, California, May 2005.

Henly, S.G. (2007) "On top of the world," *The Sun Herald* (Sydney, Australia): July 8: Travel: 20.

Heppenheimer, T.A. (1995) *Turbulent Skies: The History of Commercial Aviation*, New York: John Wiley & Sons.

Hesse, M. and Rodrigue, J.-P. (2004) "The transport geography of logistics and freight distribution," *Journal of Transport Geography*, 12: 171–84.

Hirschman, D. and Grantham, R. (2006) "Fifth runway opens, but use will be gradual," *The Atlanta Journal-Constitution*, May 28: 1D.

Holmes, S. (2005) "A plastic dream machine," *Business Week*, June 20: 32–5.

Holzner, S. (2006) *How Dell Does It*, New York: McGraw-Hill.

Hooper, P. (1997) "Liberalising competition in domestic airline markets in Asia – The problematic interface between domestic and international policies," *Transportation Research E: Logistics and transportation Review*, 33(3): 197–209.

—— (1998) "Airline competition and deregulation in developed and developing country contexts – Australia and India," *Journal of Transport Geography*, 6(2): 105–16.

—— (2005) "The environment for Southeast Asia's new and evolving airlines," *Journal of Air Transport Management*, 11: 335–47.

Howard, C. (1996) "Go I-20 west to Birmingham for great deals," *The Atlanta Journal-Constitution*, July 21: 1K.

Hudson, K. (1972) *Air Travel: A Social History*, Totowa, New Jersey: Rowman and Littlefield.

Hughes, D. (2008) "2020 ATM today; reduction in fuel burn, emissions, and noise add up," *Aviation Week & Space Technology*, April 28: 53.

Hugill, P.J. (1993) *World Trade since 1431: Geography, Technology, and Capitalism*, Baltimore: Johns Hopkins University Press.

IATA [International Air Transport Association] (2007) "UK press briefing – Remarks by Giovanni Bisignani," press release dated January 18.

—— (2009) *World Air Transport Statistics*, 53rd edn, Montreal.

Iatrou, K. and Alamdari, F. (2005) "The empirical analysis of the impact of alliances on airline operations," *Journal of Air Transport Management*, 11: 127–34.

ICAO [International Civil Aviation Organization] (1963) *Airport Traffic*, Series AT, No. 2, Montreal.

—— (1998) "1997 Airline finances amongst best in past 50 years," press release dated June 16.

—— (2007) "Buoyancy in airline traffic continues in 2007," press release dated December 21.

—— (2008) "Economic woes impact traffic growth in 2008; ICAO medium term forecast points to recovery in 2010," press release dated December 18.

ICAO Journal (1986) "Traffic by non-scheduled carriers increased modestly last year," 41(6), June: 29–30.

—— (2004) "Annual review of civil aviation 2003," 59(5), September/October: 4–38.

—— (2006) "Annual review of civil aviation 2005," 61(5), September/October: 6–34.

Ikenberry, G.J. (2005) "Review of Thomas Friedman's *The Earth Is Flat: A Brief History of the Twenty-First Century*," *Foreign Affairs*, September/October, 84(5): 167–70.

ILFC [International Lease Finance Corporation] (2009) "Form 10-K Annual report' dated March 25, 2009, online, available at: www.ilfc.com/investor.htm (accessed July 21, 2009).

Independent, The (2005) "The hidden costs of cheap flights," May 28: 34.

InterVISTAS-ga2 (2006) *The Economic Impact of Air Service Liberalization*, Consultancy study sponsored by Airports Council International, Air Transport Action Group, Boeing, European-American Business Council, General Electric, International Air Transport Association, Pacific Air Travel Association, Pratt & Whitney, US-Asean Business Council, US Chamber of Commerce, and the World Travel & Tourism Council.

Ionides, N. (2004) "Growth in sight?' *Airline Business*, April: 50.

—— (2005a) "Asian tigers," *Airline Business*, April: 64–6.

—— (2005b) "Second time lucky," *Airline Business*, May: 67, 69.

IPCC [Intergovernmental Panel on Climate Change] (1999) *Aviation and the Global Atmosphere*, Cambridge: Cambridge University Press.

Irving, C. (1993) *Wide-body: The Triumph of the 747*. New York: William Morrow and Company.

Irwin, M.D. and Kasarda, J.D. (1991) Air passenger linkages and employment growth in U.S. metropolitan areas. *American Sociological Review* 56: 524–37.

Issenberg, S. (2007) *The Sushi Economy: Globalization and the Making of a Modern Delicacy*, New York: Gotham Books.

Ivy, R.L., Fik, T.J., and Malecki, E.J. (1995) "Changes in air service connectivity and employment," *Environment and Planning A*, 27: 165–79.

Iyer, P. (1995) "Where worlds collide: In Los Angeles International Airport, the future touches down," *Harper's Magazine*, August: 50–7.

Jakle, J.A. (1985) *The Tourist: Travel in Twentieth-Century North America*, Lincoln: University of Nebraska Press.

Jackman, F. (2007) "Cultivating conversions," *Aviation Week & Space Technology*, May 7: 58.

Journal of Commerce Online (2005) "Miami leading ex-im air hub; shakes off lackluster past showing," May 26, online, available at: www.joc.com (accessed June 12, 2006).

—— (2009) "Lufthansa, DHL launch joint cargo airline June 19," online, available at: www.joc.com (accessed June 1, 2009).

Kaminski-Morrow, D. (2009) "SAS embarks on major overhaul," *Airline Business*, March: 23.

Kamm, H. (1990) "Communist Laos mixes strict political dogma with capitalist economics," *New York Times*, January 27: 21.

Kasarda, J.D. (2000) "New logistics technologies and infrastructure for the digitized economy," paper presented at the 4th International Conference on Technology Policy and Innovation, Curitiba, Brazil, August 2000.

—— (2005) "Gateway airports, speed, and the rise of the aerotropolis," in D.V. Gibson, M.V. Heitor, A. Ibarro-Yunez (eds.), *Learning and Knowledge for the Network Society*, West Lafayette, Indiana: Purdue University Press, 99–108.

—— Green, J., and Sullivan, D. (2004) *Air Cargo: Engine of Economic Development*, online, available at: www.kenan-flagler.unc.edu (accessed June 23, 2006).

Kasper, D. (1988) *Deregulation and Globalization: Liberalizing International Trade in Air Services*, Cambridge, Massachusetts: Ballinger Publications.

Khan, K., Arino, J., Hu, W., Raposo, P., Sears, J., Calderon, F., Heidebrecht, C., McDonald, M., Liaw, J., Chan, A., and Gardam, M. (2009) "Spread of a novel influenza A virus via global air transportation," *New England Journal of Medicine*, 361: 212–14.

Kingsley-Jones, M. and Ostower, J. (2009) "Narrowbody revamps edge closer," *Flight International*, January 13–19: 11.

Kirsner, S. (2005) "Embracing bicoastal life," *The Boston Globe*, July 18: E1.

Knibb, D. (2002) "Change," *Airline Business*, February: 60.

—— (2005) "Growing pains," *Airline Business*, June: 36–8, 41.

—— (2006) "Latins reluctant to relinquish state role," *Airline Business*. April: 16.

Knowles, R.D. (2006) "Transport shaping space: differential collapse in time-space," *Journal of Transport Geography*, 14(6): 407–25.

Knowlton, B. (2009) "Obama seeks high-speed rail system across U.S." *New York Times*, April 17: 16A.

Knox, P., Agnew, J., and McCarthy, L. (2003) *The Geography of the World Economy*, 4th edn, New York: Arnold.

Krishnamoorthy, A. and Choudhury, S. (2007) "Buyouts quell Indian air wars," *International Herald Tribune*, July 12: 13.

Krotz, L. (1996) *Tourists*, Boston: Faber and Faber.

Kua, J. and Baum, T. (2004) "Perspectives on the development of low-cost airlines in South-East Asia," *Current Issues in Tourism*, 7(3): 262–76.

Kyriacou, K. (2006) "Roger, scramjet is all systems go," *Sunday Mail* (South Australia), April 23: 24.

Langewiesche, W. (2009) "Anatomy of a miracle," *Vanity Fair*, June: 82–91.

Lappin, T. (1996) "The airline of the Internet," *Wired*, 4(12), online, available at: www.wired.com (accessed June 24, 2006).

Larson, G. (2008) "Dusk for DayJet," *Aviation Week & Space Technology*, September 29: 28.

Lasserre, F. (2004) "Logistics and the Internet: Transportation and location issues are crucial in the logistics chain," *Journal of Transport Geography*, 12(1): 73–84.

Lau, J. and Ward, A. (2005) "FedEx to build $150m hub in China," *Financial Times*, July 14: 30.

Laurenzo, R. (2006) "Hushing the roar of air traffic growth," *Aerospace America*, June: 38.

Lawton, T.C. and Solomko, S. (2005) "When being the lowest-cost is not enough: Building a successful low-fare model in Asia," *Journal of Air Transport Management*, 11(6): 355–62.

Leinbach, T.R. and Bowen, J.T. (2004) "Air cargo services and the electronics industry in Southeast Asia," *Journal of Economic Geography* 4(2): 1–24.

Levinson, D., Mathieu, J.M., Gillen, D., and Kanafani, A. (1997) "The full cost of high-speed rail: An engineering approach," *Annals of Regional Science*, 31(2): 189–215.

Levinson, M. (2006) *The Box: How the Shipping Container Made the World Smaller and the World Economy Bigger*, Princeton, New Jersey: Princeton University Press.

Lindsay, G. (2006) "Rise of the aerotropolis," *Fast Company*, July/August: 76–85.

Lindsey, R. (1969) "Move viewed as tactical," *New York Times*, September 20: 58.

—— (1970) "Like Radio City with Wings," *New York Times*, January 25: 151.

—— (1971) "Europeans flock to U.S., lured by low air fares," *New York Times*, March 28: 1.

London City Airport (2009) "Facts and figures," online, available at: www. londoncityairport.com (accessed August 1, 2009).

London Luton Airport (2009) "Key facts," online, available at: www.london-luton.co.uk (accessed August 1, 2009).

Lopez, B. (1995) "On the wings of commerce," *Harper's Magazine*, October: 39–55.

Lufthansa (2009) *Annual Report 2008*, online, available at: reports.lufthansa.com/ 2008/ ar (accessed July 19, 2009).

Lyman, L.D. (1931a) "Plans for air express to Far East maturing," *New York Times*, January 11: 122.

—— (1931b) "Air freight means new markets," *New York Times*, July 26: 7.

Lynn, M. (1997) *Birds of Prey: Boeing vs. Airbus*, New York: Four Walls Eight Windows.

McCartney, S. (2008) "Flying skinks, especially for the airlines," *The Wall Street Journal*, June 10: D1.

McIntyre, I. (1992) *Dogfight: The Transatlantic Battle over Airbus*, Westport, Connecticut: Praeger.

McKenna, E. (2006) "Race against time and temperature," *Air Cargo World*, February 6: 28.

McKercher, B. and Bauer, T.G. (2003) "Conceptual framework of the nexus between tourism, romance, and sex," in T.G. Bauer and B. McKercher (eds.), *Sex and Tourism: Journeys of Romance, Love and Lust*, Binghampton, New York: Halworth Hospitality Press, 3–18.

—— and Chon, K. (2004) "The over-reaction to SARS and the collapse of Asian tourism," *Annals of Tourism Research*, 31(3): 716–19.

McMillin, M. (2003) "World assembly required?," *The Wichita Eagle*, March 2: 1.

Mahtani, D. (2005) "Air travel in West Africa prepares for take-off," *Financial Times*, June 28: 15.

MAI [Myanmar Airways International] (2007) "Our crew," online, available at: www. maiair.com (accessed May 31, 2007).

Marshall, I. (1997) *Passage East*, Charlottesville, Virginia: Howell Press.

Mason, K.J. (2000) "The propensity of business travelers to use low cost airlines," *Journal of Transport Geography*, 8(2): 107–19.

—— (2001) Marketing low-cost airline services to business travelers. *Journal of Air Transport Management*, 7(2): 103–9.

Massey, D.K. (1988) "Airports spin the wheel of fortune," *American Demographics*, February: 42–5, 60–1.

Mathews, N. (2005) "The gold rush," *Aviation Week & Space Technology*, July 18: 46–9.

Matsumoto, H. (2004) "International urban systems and air passenger and cargo flows: Some calculations," *Journal of Air Transport Management*, 10(4): 241–9.

Maynard, M. (2005) "In airline shift, more nonstop flights make schedule," *New York Times*, May 4: A1.

—— (2008a) "At jetBlue, growing up is hard to do," *New York Times*, October 5: B1.

—— (2008b) "Boeing deal includes 15% raise over 4 years," *New York Times*, October 29: B2.

Mecham, M. (1995) "Year's biggest order goes to Boeing 777," *Aviation Week & Space Technology*, November 20: 28.

—— (2004) "Natural selection," *Aviation Week & Space Technology*, November 15: 48–50.

—— (2005a) "Small view," *Aviation Week & Space Technology*, June 13: 52–3.

—— (2005b) "Range wars," *Aviation Week & Space Technology*, June 13: 64–6.

—— (2006) "The flat-earth airplane," *Aviation Week & Space Technology*, July 3: 43–6.

—— (2009) "Starts and fits," *Aviation Week & Space Technology*, June 29: 24.

Meikle, J. (1999) "Scientists call for higher air fares to cut pollution," *The Guardian*, June 5: 17.

Meyer, D. (2005) "Corporate travel 100 spending back above $8B," *Business Travel News*, 22(12): 3–54.

Michaels, D., Kranhold, K., and Lunsford, J.L. (2005) "Rolls-Royce takes fight to GE," *The Wall Street Journal*, March 11: B2.

Miller, R. and Sawers D. (1970) *The Technical Development of Modern Aviation*, New York: Praeger Publishers.

Millman, J. and Esterl, M. (2009) "Air hubs pay to keep their spokes," *The Wall Street Journal*, July 10: A3.

Mills, J. (2006) "How airlines can put you to sleep," *Financial Times*, May 15: 11.

Milner, M. (2005) "Air travel: The real cost of a £50 ticket from London to Edinburgh," *The Guardian*, July 7: 2.

Miyagi, M. (1969) "Impact of jet aircraft to the airline network of the United States," unpublished dissertation, The Ohio State University.

Mola, R. (2002) "This is only a test; in the early 1960s Cold War games thrice grounded the airlines," *Air & Space Smithsonian*, February/March: 50–5.

Mondey, D. (1983) *Airliners of the World*, New York: Crescent Books.

Morning Edition [Radio program produced by National Public Radio] (2001) "Chadwick flies again," radio essay by Alex Chadwick, aired October 26.

Morrell, P.S. (2007) *Airline Finance*, 3rd edn, Burlington, Vermont: Ashgate.

Morrison, S.A. (1984) "An economic analysis of aircraft design," *Journal of Transport Economics and Policy*, 18(2): 123–43.

—— (2001) "Actual, adjacent, and potential competition: Estimating the full effect of Southwest Airlines," *Journal of Transport Economics and Policy*, 35(2): 239–56.

Nativi, A. (2009) "Alitalia shows signs of recovery but fears trains, Linate competition," *Aviation Daily*, June 5: 5.

Nelkin, D. (1974) *Jetport: The Boston Airport Controversy*, New Brunswick, New Jersey: Transaction Books.

New York Times, The (1929) "$650 for India air flight," February 19: 18.

—— (1939) "Yankee Clipper reaches England," July 10: 5.

—— (1962) "Philadelphia airport busier," July 27: 48.

—— (1972) "Isolated Maldive Islands now letting the world in," April 9: 2.

Newbart, D. and Sweet, L. (2005) "FAA OKs O'Hare expansion – and then court grounds it' *Chicago Sun-Times*, October 1: 5.

Newhouse, J. (1982) *The Sporty Game*, New York: Alfred A. Knopf.

—— (2007) *Boeing versus Airbus: The Inside Story of the Greatest International Competition in Business*, New York: Alfred A. Knopf.

Nisse, J. and Discover, H.T. (2001) "The lowdown: It's beaten Boeing but Airbus can't takeoff," *Independent on Sunday* (London), June 17: 5.

Norris, G. (2003) "Sonic cruiser is dead – long live Super Efficient?," *Aviation Week & Space Technology*, January 7: 16.

—— (2008) "Push or pull?," *Aviation Week & Space Technology*, November 24: 43.

—— Kingsley-Jones, M., Learmont, D., and Phelan, M. (2003) "Working life: Preparations for introducing the A380 are providing a major challenge for airlines, airports, and maintenance companies," *Flight International*, May 20: 26.

Noviello, K., Cromley, R.G., and Cromley, E.K. (1996) "A comparison of the air passenger and air cargo industries with respect to hub locations," *The Great Lakes Geographer*, 3(2): 75–85.

OAG [Official Airline Guide] (1972a) *Official Airline Guide Quick Reference North American Edition*. October 1.

—— (1972b) *Official Airline Guide Quick Reference Worldwide Edition*. October 1.

—— (1975) *Official Airline Guide Quick Reference North American Edition*. January 1.

—— (1980) *Official Airline Guide Quick Reference Worldwide Edition*. October 1.

—— (1984a) *Official Airline Guide Quick Reference North American Edition*. October 1.

—— (1984b) *Official Airline Guide Quick Reference Worldwide Edition*. October 1.

—— (1998) OAG Max database for April 1998. The data database is a compilation of airline schedules for virtually every airline in the world (CD-ROM).

—— (2003) OAG Max database for March 2003. The database is a compilation of airline schedules for virtually every airline in the world (CD-ROM).

—— (2008) OAG Max database for April 2008. The database is a compilation of airline schedules for virtually every airline in the world (CD-ROM).

Olds, K. (1995) "Globalization and the production of new urban spaces: Pacific Rim megaprojects in the late 20th century," *Environment and Planning A*, 27: 1713–43.

OMP [O'Hare Modernization Program] (2006) "Learn about OMP," online, available at: egov.cityofchicago.org (accessed July 11, 2006).

On Point (2005) "What freedom means," interview with Orlando Patterson, radio program produced by WBUR, aired January 26.

ONCC [O'Hare Noise Compatibility Commission] (2005) *2005 Annual Report*, online, available at: www.oharenoise.org (accessed August 12, 2006).

Oneworld (2009) "Member airlines," online, available at: www.oneworld.com/ow/member-airlines (accessed June 15, 2009).

Oster, C.V., Rubin, B.M., and Strong, J.S. (1997) "Economic effects of transportation investments: The case of Federal Express," *Transportation Journal*, 37(2), Winter: 34–44.

O'Toole, K. (2005a) "Taxing times," *Airline Business*, March: 9.

—— (2005b) "Coming together," *Airline Business*, April: 37–9.

Ott, J. (2003) "Air transport cargo redux," *Aviation Week & Space Technology*, March 31: 46.

—— (2008) "Algae advances," *Aviation Week & Space Technology*, March 17: 66.

—— Lott, S., Wall, R., and Taverna, M.A. (2006) "Lessor gods," *Aviation Week & Space Technology*, April 3: 22.

Pae, P. (2005) "A plane as big as the globe," *Los Angeles Times*, January 17: C1.

—— (2006) "Singapore Air will tuck you into bed – for $10,000," *Los Angeles Times*, October 30: C1.

—— (2007) "Floating luxury, super-sized," *Los Angeles Times*, November 3: C1.

Palmeri, C. (2008) "A cautionary tale for airline mergers," *Business Week*, March 17: 66.

Parris, M. (2003) "The day the future flew into the past," *The Times* (London), Home News, October 25: 1.

Paulson, M. (1999) "Seattle leads nation in export trade," *Seattle Post-Intelligencer*, November 10: A1.

Paylor, A. (2005) "The greening of aviation," *Air Transport World*, June: 24–8.

PBGC [US Pension Benefit Guarantee Corporation] (2003) "PBGC becomes trustee of US Airways' pension plan for pilots," press release dated April 1.

Pearman, H. (2004) *Airports: A Century of Architecture*, New York: Harry N. Abrams.

Pearson, A. (1997) "Shifting sands," *Airline Business*, August: 46.

Perrett, B. (2007) "Paper chase," *Aviation Week & Space Technology*, May 7: 68.

Peterson, B.S. and Glab, J. (1994) *Rapid Descent: Deregulation and the Shakeout in the Airlines*, New York: Simon & Schuster.

Petzinger, T. (1995) *Hard Landing: The Epic Contest for Power and Profits that Plunged the Airlines into Chaos*, New York: Times Books.

Phelan, M. (2002) "Sound thinking," *Flight International*, December 17: 28.

Pierson, D. (2007) "The pursuit of harmony; now at speeds of 125 mph," *Los Angeles Times*, May 6: A14.

Pilling, M. (2005) "Protect and survive," *Airline Business*, October: 7.

Pinkham, R. (2003) "Capped hubs," *Airline Business*, June: 57.

Pittsburgh International Airport (no date) "Summary of airline traffic, December 2007," online, available at: www.pitairport.com (accessed June 13, 2008).

Poon, J. (1997) "The cosmopolitanization of trade regions: global trends and implications, 1965–1990," *Economic Geography*, 73: 390–404.

Portes, A. (1996) "Global villagers: The rise of transnational communities," *The American Prospect*, March/April: 74.

POST [UK Parliamentary Office of Science and Technology] (2003) "Aircraft noise," POSTNOTE, number 197, June.

Pratt and Whitney (2009) "Commercial engines," online, available at: www.pw.utc.com/Products/Commercial (accessed July 20, 2007).

Pritchard, D. and MacPherson, A. (2004) "Outsourcing US commercial aircraft technology and innovation: Implications for the industry's long term design and build capability," Canada-US Trade Center Occasional Paper Number 29, July.

—— (2005) "Boeing's diffusion of commercial aircraft design and manufacturing technology to Japan: Surrendering the US aircraft industry for foreign financial support," Canada-US Trade Center Occasional Paper Number 30, March.

Putzgar, I. (1997) "Atlas Air's on top of the world," *Journal of Commerce*, January 27: 7.

Raab, D. (2007) *Terror in Black September: The First Eyewitness Account of the Infamous 1970 Hijackings*, New York: Palgrave Macmillan.

Raguraman, K. (1997) "Airlines as instruments for national building and national identity: Case study of Malaysia and Singapore," *Journal of Transport Geography*, 5(4): 239–56.

Ramesh, R. (2005) "Indian airspace buzzes with first-time flyers as budget airlines stage a revolution," September 30: 21.

Rand Europe and Avioplan (2000) *Future Acoustic Characteristics of Aircraft in Civil Aviation*, Report for Onderzoek Nederlandse Luchtvaart, a program of the Dutch Civil Aviation Authority, online, available at: www.rand.org/pubs/rand_europe/ 2005/ RE2000.9.pdf (accessed July 15, 2006).

Ranson, L. (2005) "Five companies take 35% stake in GEnx engine," *Aviation Daily*, January 25: 6.

Reed, D. (2005) "Airports gamble on building fancy – and costly – terminals," *USA Today*, July 18: 1B.

Reich, R.B. (1991) *The Work of Nations*, New York: Alfred A. Knopf.

Reisner, M. (1986) *Cadillac Desert: The American West and Its Disappearing Water*, New York: Viking.

Renton, A. (2005) "Learning the Thai sex trade," *Prospect*, April 21: 56–62.

Reynolds-Feighan, A. (2001) "Traffic distribution in low-cost and full-service carrier networks in the US air transportation network," *Journal of Air Transport Management*, 7(5): 265–75.

Roberts, D. (2003) "Par avion," *Financial Times*, Weekend Magazine: 18.

Robyn, D. (2003) "The benefits of open skies," *Airline Business*, March: 82.

Rodgers, E. (1996) *Flying High: The Story of Boeing and the Rise of the Jetliner Industry*, New York: Atlantic Monthly Press.

Rohter, L. (2005) "Cocaine inquiry raises concerns about traffic through Argentina," *International Herald Tribune*, March 16: 7.

Rolls-Royce (2009) "Large aircraft engines," online, available at: www.rolls-royce.com/civil/products/largeaircraft (accessed July 20, 2007).

Rosenbloom, J. (2001) "Midnight express," *Inc.*, July: 76.

Rowe, M. (2006) "Ready to land; BAA's Terminal 5," *Independent on Sunday* (London), April 23: 19.

Ruane, M. and Gugliotta, G. (2003) "With first flight, a "Great line had been crossed"," *The Washington Post*, December 18: A3.

Rubin, J. (2009) *Why Your World Is about to Get a Whole Lot Smaller: Oil and the End of Globalization*, New York: Random House.

St. John, R.K., King, A., de Jong, A., Bodie-Collins, M., Squires, S.G., and Tam, T.W.S. (2005) "Border screening for SARS," *Emerging Infectious Diseases*, 11(1): 6–10.

Sampson, A. (1984) *Empires of the Sky: The Politics, Contests, and Cartels of the World Airlines*, New York: Random House.

Sanchanta, M. (2007) "ANA all business about Mumbai," *Financial Times*, February 7: 10.

Sanger, D.E. (2003) "Wright Brothers celebration lacks a key element: flight," *New York Times*, December 18: 36.

Sapte, B. (no date) "Southwest Airlines: Route development since 1971," online, available at: www.erau.edu/research/BA590/chapters/ch2.htm (accessed March 20, 2008).

Scandinavian Airlines (2009) "SAS Group launches Core SAS," press release dated February 3.

Scherck, T. (2005) "Clearing the skies for airfreight," *Journal of Commerce*, January 10: 47.

Schlangenstein, M. (2007) "Southwest slows its growth plan," *The Seattle Times*, June 28: E1.

Schoenberger, E. (1994) "Competition, time, and space in industrial change," in G. Gereffi and M. Korzeniewicz (eds.), *Commodity Chains and Global Capitalism*, Westport, Connecticut: Greenwood Press, 51–66.

Sealy, K.R. (1966) *The Geography of Air Transport*, London: Hutchinson University Library.

Searles, R.A. (2009) "Revisiting alternative engine concepts," *Business & Commercial Aviation*, 104(1): 56.

Seattle Times, The (2006) "Forecast dimmer for profit on A380," October 20: D3.

Segal, D. (1995) "Boeing's latest jet is no Plane Jane," *The Washington Post*, June 8: B11.

Serling, R.J. (1982) *The Jet Age*, Alexandria, Virginia: Time-Life Books.

—— (1992) *Legend and Legacy: The Story of Boeing and its People*. New York: St. Martin's Press.

Shaw, G. and Williams, A.M. (1994) *Critical Issues in Tourism: A Geographical Perspective*, Oxford: Blackwell.

Shaw, S. and Thomas, C. (2006) "Social and cultural dimensions of air travel demand: Hyper-mobility in the UK?," *Journal of Sustainable Tourism*, 14(2): 209–15.

Shaw, S.-L., Lu, F., Chen, J., and Zhou, C. (2009) "China's airline consolidation and its effects on domestic airline networks and competition," *Journal of Transport Geography*, 17(4): 276–84.

Shifrin, C.A. (2005) "Comfort zone," *Airline Business*, February: 60.

Shin, K.H., and Timberlake, M. (2000) "World cities in Asia: Cliques, centrality, and connectedness," *Urban Studies*, 37(12): 2257–85.

Shteyngart, G. (2004) "The new two-way street," in T. Jacoby (ed.), *Reinventing the Melting Pot: The New Immigrants and What It Means to Be Americans*, New York: Basic Books, 285–92.

Skyteam (2009) "Our Skyteam carriers," online, available at: www.skyteam.com/about/carriers/index.html (accessed June 15, 2009).

Skytrax (2009) "Airline seat pitch guide," online, available at: www.airlinequality.com/Product/seats_global.htm (accessed August 6, 2009).

Smith, D.A., and Timberlake, M. (1995) "Conceptualizing and mapping the structure of the world-system's city system," *Urban Studies* 32(2): 287–302.

———— (2001) "World city networks and hierarchies, 1977–1997: An empirical analysis of global air travel links," *American Behavioral Scientist* 44: 1656–78.

Sobotta, R.R., Cambell, H.E., and Owens, B.J. (2007) "Aviation noise and environmental justice: The barrio barrier," *Journal of Regional Science*, 47(1): 125–54.

Solberg, C. (1979) *Conquest of the Skies: A History of Commercial Aviation in America*, Boston: Little, Brown & Company.

Sorenson, N. (1991) "The impact of geographic scale and traffic density on airline production costs: The decline of the no-frills airlines," *Economic Geography*, 67(3): 333–45.

Soriano, C. (2006) "Travelers are winging it in Europe," *USA Today*, May 19: 4D.

Southwest Airlines (2009) "Southwest Airlines cities," online, available at: www.southwest.com/travel_center/routemap.html (accessed July 15, 2009).

Sparaco, P. (2004) "Franco-Dutch leader," *Aviation Week & Space Technology*, May 10: 42.

—— (2008) "Give turboprops their due," *Aviation Week & Space Technology*, December 15: 41.

Spector, R. (2002) *Anytime, Anywhere: How the Best Bricks-and-Clicks Businesses Deliver Seamless Service to Their Customers*, Cambridge, Massachusetts: Perseus Books.

SRI International (2001) *Global Impacts of FedEx in the New Economy*, online, available at: www.sri.com/policy/csted/reports/economics/fedex (accessed June 19, 2009).

Star Alliance (2009) "Star Alliance member airlines," online, available at: www.staralliance.com/en/meta/airlines/index.html (accessed June 15, 2009).

State of Hawaii (2009) "Monthly visitor statistics," online, available at: hawaii.gov/dbedt/info/visitor-stats/tourism (accessed June 18, 2009).

Stewart, A. (2007) *Flower Confidential*, Chapel Hill: Algonquin Books.

Stoller, G. (2006) "Frequent business travellers pack guilt," *USA Today*, June 22: 1A.

Streetdirectory (2008) "Singapore map," online, available at: www.streetdirectory.com (accessed November 12, 2008).

Stuber, N., Forster, P., Radel, G., and Shine, K. (2006) "The importance of the diurnal and annual cycle of air travel for contrail radiative forcing," *Nature*, 441(7095): 864–7.

Stundza, T. (2005) "Supply headaches," *Purchasing*, March 3: 24–5.

Taaffe, E.J., Gauthier, H.L., and O'Kelly, M.E. (1996) *Geography of Transportation*, 2nd edn, Upper Saddle River, New Jersey: Prentice Hall.

Talbot, D. (2003) "Boeing's flight for survival," *Technology Review*, September: 35–44.

Taylor, M. and Kissling, C. (1983) "Resource dependence, power networks, and the airline system of the South Pacific," *Regional Studies*, 17(4): 237–50.

Thomas, G. (2000) "The gold standard," *Air Transport World*, November: 32.

—— (2005a) "China's runway challenge," *Air Transport World*, February: 32–5.

—— (2005b) "Has the low-fare moment passed?," *Air Transport World*, August: 20–2.

Thompson, W.N. (1999) "Casinos in Las Vegas: Where impacts are not the issue," in C.H.C. Hsu (ed.), *Legalized Casino Gaming in the United States*, New York: Halworth Press, 93–112.

Thornton, D.W. (1995) *Airbus Industrie: The Politics of an International Industrial Collaboration*, New York: St. Martin's Press.

Timmons, H. and Bajaj, V. (2009) "Despite India's health, airlines fight to survive," *New York Times*, June 19: B1.

Toronto Star, The (2004) "Mirabel runways clear," November 1: A19.

Tosches, N. (2006) "Dubai's the limit," *Vanity Fair*, June 2006: 150–70.

Tretheway, M.W. (2004) "Distortions of airline revenues: Why the network airline business model is broken," *Journal of Air Transport Management*, 10(1): 3–14.

—— and Mak, D. (2006) "Emerging tourism markets: Ageing and developing economies," *Journal of Air Transport Management*, 12(1): 21–7.

—— and Oum, T.H. (1992) *Airline Economics: Foundation for Strategy and Policy*, The Centre for Transportation Studies, University of British Columbia.

Trubshaw, B. (2000) *Concorde: The Inside Story*, Stroud, England: Sutton.

Turner, C. (1959) "Hawaii hails Thanksgiving – and statehood," *New York Times*, November 1: 35.

Turner, L. and Ash, J. (1976) *The Golden Horde: International Tourism and the Pleasure Periphery*, New York: St. Martin's Press.

Turney, R. (2006) "Frankfurt's nights," *Air Cargo World*, November 6: 18.

Tyson, L.D. (1992) *Who's Bashing Whom? Trade Conflict in High Technology Industries*, Washington, DC: Institute for International Economics.

UIC [International Union of Railways] (2008) "European HS Network," image updated February 22, 2008, online, available at: www.uic.org (accessed February 2, 2009).

UNCTAD [United Nations Conference on Trade and Development] (2008) *World Investment Report 2008: Transnational Corporations and the Infrastructure Challenge*, New York: United Nations.

UNWTO World Tourism Barometer (2008) "Regions," 6(2), June: 20–38.

—— (2009) "International tourism challenged by deteriorating global economy," 7(1), January: 1, 5.

UPS (2006) "UPS expands air network in China," press release dated April 6.

UPS Supply Chain Solutions (2005) "Nikon focuses on supply chain innovation – and makes new product distribution a snap," online, available at: www.ups-scs.com/ solutions/case_studies/cs_nikon.pdf (accessed June 28, 2009).

USA Today (2003) "While guards search purses and shoes, cargo gets a pass," October 7: 22A.

US Energy Information Agency (2009) "U.S. crude oil wellhead acquisition price by first purchasers (dollars per barrel)," online, available at: tonto.eia.doe.gov/dnav/ pet/pet_pri_dfp1_k_a.htm (accessed August 15, 2009).

US National Intelligence Council (2004) *Mapping the Global Future: Report of the National Intelligence Council's 2020 Project*, NIC 2004-13. Washington: GPO.

Van Dyne, L. (2005) "Guess what's coming for dinner," *Washingtonian*, 40(8), May: 62–7, 93–100.

Vance, J.E. (1986) *Capturing the Horizon: The Historical Geography of the Transportation since the Transportation Revolution of the Sixteenth Century*, New York: Harper & Row.

Vecchi, A. and Wickham, J. (2006) "Clusters and pipelines, commuters and nomads: Business travel in the Irish software industry," GaWC [Globalization and World Cities] Research Bulletin 212, online, available at: www.lboro.ac.uk/gawc (accessed July 3, 2007).

Velocci, A. (2008) "Crandall calls for reregulation, changes to pricing, bankruptcy, labor rules," *Aviation Daily*, June 11: 1.

Veltz, P. (1996) *Mondialisation, Villes et Territoires: L'Economie Archipel*, Paris: PUF.

Vencat, E.F. and Caryl, C. (2006) "A Boeing of Asia?," *Newsweek International*, May 15: 42–4.

Veseth, M. (2005) *Globaloney: Unraveling the Myths of Globalization*, Lanham, Maryland: Rowman & Littlefield.

Vinella, S. (2007) "Pittsburgh's Airmall is model for Hopkins' plan," *Plain Dealer* (Cleveland), May 14: A1.

Viton, P.A. (1986) "Air deregulation revisited: Choice of aircraft, load factors, and marginal cost fares for domestic air travel," *Transportation Research A*, 20A(5): 361–71.

Vowles, T.M. (2001) "The "Southwest Effect" in multi-airport regions," *Journal of Air Transport Management*, 7(4): 251–8.

Wall, R. (2008a) "Advocating alternatives," *Aviation Week & Space Technology*, May 26: 67.

—— (2008b) "It's just business," *Aviation Week & Space Technology*, July 7: 44–5.

—— and Barrie, D. (2006) "Dishing the dirt: Aviation industry's green record," *Aviation Week & Space Technology*, July 17: 128.

Wallis, R. (2003) *How Safe Are Our Skies? Assessing the Airlines' Response to Terrorism*, Westport, Connecticut: Praeger.

Warwick, G. (2008) "Hyper reality," *Aviation Week & Space Technology*, November 3: 62.

Washington Post, The (1994) "FedEx, from lexicon to logo," June 24: F2.

—— (2005) "Gambian fans are caught offside in Peru," September 22: E2.

Wastnage, J. (2005) "Cargo carriers applaud Europe's new noise rules," *Flight International*, January 25: 8.

Watters, B. (1979) *The Illustrated History of Air Travel*, New York: Crescent Books.

Weiss R.A. and McLean, A.R. (2004) "What have we learnt from SARS?," *Philosophical Transactions of the Royal Society of London B*, 359: 1137–40.

Westlake, M. (1990) "The mating planes," *Far Eastern Economic Review*, February 15: 37–8.

Wetherbe, J.C. (1996) *The World on Time: The 11 Management Principles That Made FedEx an Overnight Sensation*, Santa Monica, California: Knowledge Exchange.

Whittaker, S. (2006) "Doing it all – and travelling, too," *The Gazette* (Montreal), April 8: G1.

Whymant, R. (1986) "No more leaning on the Rising Sun flag: What privatisation will mean to Japan Airlines," *The Guardian* (London), July 16.

Williams, G. and Pagliari, R. (2004) "A comparative analysis of the application and use of public service obligations in air transport within the EU," *Transport Policy*, 11(1): 55–66.

Williamson, H. (2005) "Low-cost flights expected to keep football fans on the move," *Financial Times*, December 10: 4.

Williamson, S.H. (2008) "Six ways to compute the relative value of a U.S. dollar amount, 1774 to present," online, available at: www.measuringworth.com/ uscompare (accessed July 4, 2009).

Wilson, J.R. (2004) "Smile, you're on cabin camera," *Air Transport World*, February: 54, 57.

Windle, R.J. (1991) "The world's airlines: A cost and productivity comparison," *Journal of Transport Economics and Policy*, 25(1): 31–49.

Witkin, R. (1970) "Substitute 747 off for London," *New York Times*, January 22: 1.

Wong, M.L. (2009) "Looking for SIA's grounded planes? Try the desert," *The Straits Times* (Singapore), March 15: 1, 15.

World Almanac and Book of Facts, The (2005) New York: World Almanac Books.

Wynbrandt, J. (2004) *Flying High: How JetBlue Founder and CEO David Neeleman Beats the Competition Even in the World's Most Turbulent Industry*, Hoboken, New Jersey: John Wiley & Sons.

Yergin, D. and Stanislaw, J. (1998) *The Commanding Heights: The Battle Between Government and the Marketplace That Is Remaking the Modern World*, New York: Simon & Schuster.

Yu, R. (2005) "Chinese airlines order 42 Boeing 787 Dreamliners," *USA Today*, August 9: 4b.

Zanger, S. (2006) "Aerospace expansion challenges Chinese to meet training goals," *Aviation Week & Space Technology*, January 16: 349–50.

Ziegler, C. (2007) *Favored Flowers: Culture and Economy in a Global System*, Durham, North Carolina: Duke University Press.

Zook, M.A. and Brunn, S.D. (2006) "From podes to antipodes: Positionalities and global airline geographies," *Annals of the Association of American Geographers*, 96(3): 471–90.

Index

Note: Page numbers in *italics* denote tables, those in **bold** denote figures.